OXFORD WORLD'S CLASSICS

THE OXFORD SHAKESPEARE

General Editor · Stanley Wells

The Oxford Shakespeare offers new and authoritative editions of Shakespeare's plays in which the early printings have been scrupulously re-examined and interpreted. An introductory essay provides all relevant background information together with an appraisal of critical views and of the play's effects in performance. The detailed commentaries pay particular attention to language and staging. Reprints of sources, music for songs, genealogical tables, maps, etc. are included where necessary; many of the volumes are illustrated, and all contain an index.

A. R. BRAUNMULLER, the editor of *King John* in the Oxford Shakespeare, is Professor of English and Comparative Literature at the University of California, Los Angeles. His previous publications include *George Peele* and *A Seventeenth-Century Letter-Book*, and an edition of the anonymous *The Captive Lady* for the Malone Society. He is co-editor of the *Cambridge Companion to English Renaissance Drama* (1990) and has recently published *Natural Fictions: George Chapman's Major Tragedies*.

THE OXFORD SHAKESPEARE

Currently available in paperback

The rest of the plays and poems are forthcoming

OXFORD WORLD'S CLASSICS

WILLIAM SHAKESPEARE

The Life and Death of King John

Edited by
A. R. BRAUNMULLER

OXFORD
UNIVERSITY PRESS

OXFORD
UNIVERSITY PRESS

Great Clarendon Street, Oxford OX2 6DP

Oxford University Press is a department of the University of Oxford.
It furthers the University's objective of excellence in research, scholarship,
and education by publishing worldwide in

Oxford New York

Auckland Bangkok Buenos Aires Cape Town Chennai
Dar es Salaam Delhi Hong Kong Istanbul Karachi Kolkata
Kuala Lumpur Madrid Melbourne Mexico City Mumbai Nairobi
São Paulo Shanghai Singapore Taipei Tokyo Toronto

with an associated company in Berlin

Oxford is a registered trade mark of Oxford University Press
in the UK and in certain other countries

Published in the United States
by Oxford University Press Inc., New York

First published by the Clarendon Press 1989
First published as a World's Classics paperback 1994
Reissued as an Oxford World's Classics paperback 1998

British Library Cataloguing in Publication Data

Data available

Library of Congress Cataloging in Publication Data

Shakespeare, William, 1564–1616.
The life and death of King John.
(Oxford world's classics)
1. John, King of England, 1167?–1216—Drama.
I. Braunmuller, A.R., 1945–   . II. Title.
III. Series: Shakespeare, William, 1564–1616.
Works. 1988.
PR2818.A2B7   1989   822.3'3   88–1437

ISBN 0–19–812930–0 (hbk.)
ISBN 0–19–283607–2 (pbk.)

3 5 7 9 10 8 6 4 2

Printed in Spain by
Book Print S.L., Barcelona

PREFACE

ANY editor soon comes to recognize the 'play of the text', the instability and mutability of even those texts that survive, as *King John* does, in a single, supposedly 'authoritative' version. Although anonymous and named editors over the centuries have laboured to produce an 'accurate' or 'true' text, their efforts plainly testify that there is no such thing, that texts exist in productions and readings, in actors and readers and editors, rather than marble, and I have benefited from their attempts in making my own. Ernst Honigmann's Arden edition and Robert Smallwood's New Penguin edition have been especially helpful in answering my questions or prompting me to ask different ones, and Professor Honigmann has generously shared with me his continuing interest in the play. Stanley Wells and John Jowett have both offered help, information, and provocative disagreement.

Although A. A. Milne assured us that 'King John was not a good man, | And no good friends had he', this edition has many friends. For assistance with the play's stage history and reputation, I thank Martin Battestin, Roland Mushat Frye, Thomas Lockwood, Stephen Parks, Gail Kern Paster, Arthur H. Scouten, and George Winchester Stone, Jr., and for help with textual matters, G. R. Proudfoot and Thomas L. Berger, both of whom gracefully improved early versions of the textual introduction. Throughout my work, the 'Tivoli Research Group'—Lee Bliss, Roger Dahood, Anne and Bertrand Goldgar, Joanna Udall—listened to and criticized various fantastic theories, and I received most salutary help from Judith Anderson, Richard Ashcraft, Janet Cowen, Talbot Donaldson, Elizabeth Story Donno, Daniel Donno, G. R. Elton, Charles Gullans, Richard Hosley, R. S. Kinsman, William McGovern, Emily Paster, Alan Roper, Scot Waugh, Paul Werstine, and Stephen Yenser. Robert Dent, R. A. Foakes, F. J. Levy, and David Stuart Rodes were kind enough to criticize various portions of the introduction and commentary. Niky Rathbone of the Birmingham Shakespeare Library and the staffs of my university's Research Library, of the North Library and Students' Room of the British Library, and of the Huntington Library repeatedly did more than duty, or even dedication, required. Christine Buckley proved an incisive and helpful reader as the manuscript approached publication. In the final stages, Frances Whistler improved the text immeasurably.

Over several years the Center for Medieval and Renaissance Studies at my university provided me with the help of diversely learned research assistants: in chronological order, Messrs. Mark Infusino, Peter Wright, Clay Stalls, and Stephen Wight. My research was also generously assisted by grants from the Research Committee of my university's Academic Senate and from the Institute of the College of Letters and Science, and by a fellowship from the American Council of Learned Societies under a programme funded by the National Endowment for the Humanities.

A. R. BRAUNMULLER

Los Angeles and London
1982–7

CONTENTS

Contents

LIST OF ILLUSTRATIONS

The illustrations on pp. 272–3 and 284 are from the Ashburnham copy of the 1623 Folio, by permission of the Shakespeare Centre Library.

INTRODUCTION

A CONVENTIONALLY ordered introduction to a Shakespearian text separates fact from opinion and places the former before the latter. Introductions thus begin, like this one, by studying the text in relation to the time and circumstances of its original composition, including any documentary evidence; continue with a study of the accidentally, mechanically, or unauthoritatively introduced matter in, or shape of, the text as a physical set of marks on paper; and conclude, again like this one, with extended critical comment and a review of the play in the theatre. Alas, by placing first factual, documentary, and bibliographical analysis, often quite minute and sometimes tedious, this order (falsely) implies a hierarchy of value and (regrettably) defers until the end the very reasons why most people wish to read such an edition—interest in the play as a structure of thought and feeling, interpretation and performance.

There is nothing sacred about this introductory convention, and I would willingly avoid it here but for the intricate and disputed (or 'obscure and elusive') relation between *King John* and the anonymous *Troublesome Reign of King John*.[1] Determining the relation between them bears little on what I personally find most interesting and rewarding about Shakespeare's *King John*. Issues of priority and originality, source and borrowing, have, however, deeply influenced critical discussion of the play,[2] and many readers will wish to consider the question for themselves before turning to a critical study necessarily limited in scope and inevitably selective. Once started in the usual manner, it seemed best to continue so; the section devoted to the play's text slenderly anticipates the subsequent critical analysis because bibliographical techniques alone will not solve, or even fully elucidate, the play's main textual oddity, the division of Acts 2 and 3. After a critical introduction that considers various ways *King*

---

[1] The quoted phrase is from E. A. J. Honigmann, ed., *King John*, Arden Shakespeare, rev. 4th edn. (1954), p. lviii.

[2] Honigmann, ibid., p. lix, formulates a common critical anxiety: 'To praise the contrivance of a play which deviates very little from its "source-play" would be dangerous.' Praise-for-contrivance need not be the end-all of critical response.

John may be thought a political document and a theatre-text 'about' politics, I conclude with a review of the play's varied stage history, a happy contrast, at least until the twentieth century, with its more staid critical fortunes.

Date and Sources

Date. Given the complexities of *King John*'s date and sources, separating the two is necessarily arbitrary. No records of a pre-Restoration performance of *King John* have been found, nor, more curiously, any record of who owned the rights to its printing.[1] Since the play apparently uses information from the second edition of Holinshed's *Chronicles*, it must post-date 1587.[2] For more than two hundred years, it has been assumed that *King John*'s composition and, presumptively, performance occurred sometime before Francis Meres listed it among Shakespeare's 'tragedies' in *Palladis Tamia* (1598).[3] That assumption conforms to other arguments about the play's date, but more precise dating depends upon one's belief about *King John*'s relation to immediate Elizabethan political events and concerns, to an anonymous two-part play, *The Troublesome Reign of King John* (1591), and to other Shakespearian and non-Shakespearian

[1] See below, pp. 19–20.

[2] A thorough treatment of *King John*'s historical sources appears in Honigmann's edn., pp. xi–xviii; for Holinshed, see especially pp. xii–xiii. See also John R. Elliott, 'Shakespeare and the Double Image of King John', *Shakespeare Studies*, 1 (1965), 64–84; pp. 65–72.

[3] Meres probably did not leave university until 1593; he is known to have resided in London in 1597 and 1598, and by 1602 he was 'rector and schoolmaster at Wing, Rutland' (E. K. Chambers, *William Shakespeare: Facts and Problems*, 2 vols. (Oxford, 1930), i. 208 and ii. 193). Chambers speculated that Shakespeare's *Henry VI* plays do not appear in Meres's list because they 'may not have been played in London between his arrival and the compilation of his list' (i. 208). The same argument would hold that *King John* was performed in London during Meres's residence there. E. A. J. Honigmann finds that Meres 'betrays imperfect sympathies with popular dramatists' and thinks the evidence 'suggests that Meres was not up-to-date in theatre affairs in 1598' (*Shakespeare's Impact on his Contemporaries* (1982), p. 76). Since many of Meres's comparisons and opinions come from other English writers and from standard Latin quotation-books, his knowledge of, or involvement in, 'theatre affairs' may be second-hand and unreliable, at least as negative evidence; see D. C. Allen, *Francis Meres's Treatise 'Poetrie': A Critical Edition*, University of Illinois Studies in Language and Literature, 16, nos. 3–4 (1933). Meres was, however, sufficiently *au courant* to mention '*the Author of Skialethia*', Edward Guilpin, whose book was entered in the Stationers' Register on 15 September 1598, one week after Meres's own.

texts that contain lines 'paralleling' passages and phrases in *King John*.

While Shakespeare's play could evoke a myriad of personal or communal associations with Tudor history, efforts to date *King John* by linking actions or presumed attitudes in the play with specific years and episodes in Elizabeth's reign suffer from an embarrassment of riches: the French might temporarily be friends, as they were during the stormy alliance with Henri IV, but they were more often, and for much longer, foes; attempts on Elizabeth's life and government, some by poison, some by promoting a rising of disaffected and/or recusant aristocrats, were common, as were assassinations of foreign monarchs; attitudes toward native Roman Catholics, toward the Papacy, and toward foreign or native priests attempting to reconvert the nation were necessarily very mixed; the party actively supporting Mary Queen of Scots might be small, but there was a wider, if mixed, sympathy for her as an exiled queen, or as a claimant to the throne (like Arthur in *King John*), or simply as the victim of politics. And so on.[1]

Besides topical allusions, the other principal form of 'internal' evidence is stylistic. Studies of vocabulary and of metrical habits typically attempt to attribute anonymous plays or to arrange Shakespeare's plays in order of composition. *King John* has figured in the most persuasive of these studies, and in each the play has been seen as closely related to *Richard II* (1595) and *The Merchant of Venice* (1596–8), plays with which *King John* has also been associated by critical and dramatic arguments. Karl Wentersdorf developed a series of 'metrical indices' based upon syllabic and pause variation, and through appeal to the idea of a 'lyric phase' or 'lyric mood' in Shakespeare's writing, he placed *King John* in the theatrical season 1595–6, after *Richard II* and before *1 Henry IV* among the histories.[2] Extending Alfred Hart's vocabulary studies, MacD. P. Jackson constructed tests that 'group' Shakespeare's plays in their treatment of 'rare' words and then compared the compositional sequence those tests implied with Wentersdorf's differently derived sequence. *King John* appears as

[1] For claims about *King John*'s topical references, see below, pp. 59–61.

[2] Karl Wentersdorf, 'Shakespearean Chronology and the Metrical Tests', in Walther Fischer and Karl Wentersdorf, eds., *Shakespeare-Studien: Festschrift für Heinrich Mutschmann* (Marburg, 1951), pp. 161–93; pp. 187–8.

the thirteenth of Shakespeare's plays in both sequences of composition, although the vocabulary tests associate it most closely with *The Taming of the Shrew* and *1 Henry IV*.[1]

The relation between *King John* and *The Troublesome Reign of King John* has proved a sufficiently controversial question to win the latter play a nickname, 'The Troublesome Play of King John'. Originally published in 1591 without attribution, *The Troublesome Reign* was reprinted as 'Written by W. Sh.' in 1611 and as 'Written by W. Shakespeare' in 1622. If *King John* preceded *The Troublesome Reign*, Shakespeare's play must pre-date 1591; if *King John* followed *The Troublesome Reign*, then it must be regarded as Shakespeare's most important source. *The Troublesome Reign* is therefore relevant to both *King John*'s date and its sources.

King John and *The Troublesome Reign* share the following identical or near-identical lines and phrases:[2]

the Kingdom of *England*, with the Lordship of *Ireland*, *Poiters*, *Aniow*, *Torain*, *Maine* . . . That *England*, *Ireland*, *Poiters*, *Aniow*, *Torain*, *Main*,
(*TR* 1.32–4, 36)

To *Ireland*, *Poyctiers*, *Aniowe*, *Torayne*, *Maine*,	(TLN 16)
Next them a Bastard of the Kings deceast.	(*TR* 1.490)
With them a Bastard of the Kings deceast,	(TLN 359)
Then I demaund *Volquesson*, *Torain*, *Main*, *Poiters* and *Aniou*, these fiue Prouinces,	(*TR* 1.827–8)
Then do I giue *Volquessen*, *Toraine*, *Maine*, *Poyctiers*, and *Aniow*, these fiue Prouinces	(TLN 847–8)

---

[1] MacDonald P. Jackson, *Studies in Attribution: Middleton and Shakespeare*, Jacobean Drama Series, 79 (Salzburg, 1979), pp. 148–58 and 212.

[2] Unless otherwise noted, I cite in modernized form the two parts of *The Troublesome Reign* ('*TR*') from the text in Geoffrey Bullough, *Narrative and Dramatic Sources of Shakespeare*, vol. 4 (1962); parenthetical citations give first the part, then the line number(s). For comparison, both *TR* and *King John* are here cited in the original spelling and italicization; 'TLN' refers to the T[hrough] L[ine] N[umbers] in the Norton facsimile of the Folio prepared by Charlton Hinman (New York, 1968). All but the fourth of these parallels, slightly corrected here, appeared in Appleton Morgan, comp., *The Life and Death of King John*, The Bankside Shakespeare, 30 (?) vols., vol. 18 (New York, 1892), pp. viii–ix; Honigmann, *Impact*, p. 81, added the parallel concerning Dover Castle. Morgan also draws attention to the close parallels between *TR* 1.968–76 and TLN 1063–73, Pandulph's first speech. Shortened references are given in full below, 'Abbreviations and References'.

> all places yeeld:
> The Land is theirs, and not a foote holds out
> But *Dover* Castle   (*TR* 2.644–6)
>
> All Kent hath yeelded: nothing there holds out
> But Douer Castle   (TLN 2198–9)
>
> For that my Grandsire was an Englishman.   (*TR* 2.748)
> (For that my Grandsire was an Englishman)   (TLN 2503)

The two plays also share some shorter phrases, and similar or identical words appear at analogous moments in the respective actions.[1]

More striking than verbal similarities, the selection and compression of historical material and the sequence of events are sometimes extremely close between *The Troublesome Reign* and *King John*. Geoffrey Bullough and J. L. Simmons have provided the most elaborate comparisons, and my summary depends upon theirs.[2] *The Troublesome Reign* purports to be a two-part play (perhaps a publisher's commercially motivated imitation of *Tamburlaine*), with the first part comprising 1,840 lines and the second, which opens with the scene of Arthur's death, comprising only 1,196 lines. If we use this division as a measure, Shakespeare's play devotes proportionately more of its lines (1,987) to the matter of the 'first part' and fewer (728) to that of the 'second part'. With minor variations between events dramatized and narrated, and with some significant differences in emphasis, the actions of *The Troublesome Reign* and *King John* are closely parallel up to the end of *King John*, Act 3 (i.e., Constance's lament for Arthur's capture and Pandulph's counsel of military action to force John into submission).

Thereafter, the two plays diverge more and more. Comparing

---

[1] See Chambers, i. 367, 'in some 150 places a few words from *The Raigne* are picked up and used, by no means always in the same context'; John Dover Wilson, ed., *King John*, The New Shakespeare (Cambridge, 1936), pp. xxiv–xxxi, and his notes contain a very full but sometimes unpersuasive list of verbal parallels. John W. Sider reviews the arguments about the relation between *King John* and *The Troublesome Reign* in his edn. of the latter (New York, 1979), pp. xxii–xliii.

[2] Bullough, iv. 5–22; J. L. Simmons, 'Shakespeare's *King John* and its Source: Coherence, Pattern, and Vision', *Tulane Studies in English*, 17 (1969), 53–72. A compact and still useful comparison by Edward Rose, 'Shakespeare as Adapter', appeared in *Macmillan's Magazine*, 39 (November, 1878), 69–77, was reprinted in Charles Praetorius' facsimile of the 1591 quarto of *The Troublesome Reign* (1888), and is fully summarized and developed in G. C. Moore Smith's edn. of *K. John* (1900).

an episode in this latter part of the two plays illustrates both their differences and the critical issues raised by their similarity. I choose this episode, the two plays' handling of Peter of Pomfret, because it has been offered as evidence that *The Troublesome Reign* post-dates *King John*; it is, writes William Matchett, one of the 'many scenes in which *TR* muddles issues, or reproduces the outline of an action [in *King John*] while missing the thematic point'.[1] I think this view is mistaken, at least so far as it claims priority for *King John*.

After the moment in the action represented by the end of Act 3 of *King John*, both plays return to England and the promised destruction of Arthur, but *The Troublesome Reign* first dramatizes the Bastard's ransacking of a monastery, shows him discovering clerical lust as well as clerical avarice, and ends with his arrest of 'Peter, a Prophet' (1.1287.1). Both plays then dramatize the attempt to blind Arthur, although Hubert's responses and emotions are slightly different and more tersely expressed in *The Troublesome Reign*. The next episode comprehends the same events in both plays, but the sequence is different, as is, again, the balance between representation and narration. In *The Troublesome Reign*, the scene analogous to *King John* Act 4, Scene 2 opens with John boasting about his military and other successes and ordering his nobles to prepare a new coronation ceremony; while they do so, the Bastard reports his deeds and the arrest of Peter of Pomfret; John delays seeing Peter, is recrowned, and grants the nobles' 'boon', the release of Arthur. Five moons suddenly appear, and John orders the Bastard to fetch the 'wizard', Peter, 'to descant of this show' (1.1596–7). Peter offers a political allegory that seems to please John, but then predicts that 'ere Ascension Day', John will give up his 'crown, estate, and royal dignity' (1.1637, 1639). Enraged, John orders Peter's imprisonment. (*The Troublesome Reign* does not provide an exit for the Bastard, but it seems likely that he here escorts Peter off-stage.) The King then revokes his earlier promise:

> The brat shall die that terrifies me thus.
> Pembroke and Essex, I recall my grant.
>
> (1.1654–5)

---

[1] William Matchett, ed., *King John*, the Signet Shakespeare (New York, 1966), p. 154; Matchett considers six other examples.

Hubert enters and (falsely, of course) reports Arthur's death; the nobles briefly harangue John and leave. The King threatens the departing nobles, 'Proud rebels . . . | Saucy, uncivil, checkers of my will', and then soliloquizes on his uncomfortable position— by killing one enemy, he has purchased 'ten times ten thousand foes' (1.1680–1, 1690). John now attacks Hubert, who first shows the royal 'hand and seal' (1.1715) for the murder and then reveals that Arthur is still alive. Part 1 of *The Troublesome Reign* ends with John dispatching Hubert to recall the nobles.

King John does not dramatize the Bastard's attack on the monasteries and, following the attempt to blind Arthur (Act 4, Scene 1), begins the next scene with John and his nobles returning from 'this double coronation' (4.2.40). As in *The Troublesome Reign*, the nobles request Arthur's release, and Hubert enters after John agrees, 'Let it be so'.[1] While the King speaks inaudibly with Hubert, the nobles speculate that Arthur has been killed, and when John announces the boy's death, they leave with angry words. John does not threaten them, but rather repents his order. A messenger arrives with news of the French invasion-force and of the deaths of Constance and Eleanor, and the Bastard immediately enters with Peter of Pomfret and reports his prophecy. John orders Hubert off with Peter and commands the prophet's death 'on that day at noon whereon he says | I shall yield up my crown' (4.2.156–7). He sends the Bastard after the rebellious nobles, claiming 'I have a way to win their loves again; | Bring them before me' (4.2.168–9), and then orders the messenger to follow the Bastard, 'for he perhaps shall need | Some messenger betwixt me and the peers' (4.2.178–9). Alone on stage for the only time in the play, John repeats 'My mother dead!' (4.2.181) and turns to meet Hubert, who describes the five moons and the people's fearful whisperings about the 'many thousand warlike French | . . . in Kent' and 'Arthur's death' (4.2.199–200, 202). John then castigates Hubert for murdering Arthur, learns that Arthur has not been killed, and sends Hubert after the 'angry lords' with this news.

Of the two plays' different handling of this episode, Matchett writes,

[1] The sequence of John's reply and Hubert's entrance are debatable; see 4.2.68n.

The Bastard comes onstage [in *The Troublesome Reign*], bringing Peter of Pomfret to John, *before*—and remains onstage during—John's decision, openly announced to the nobles, to kill Arthur, which announcement itself precedes Hubert's entry with the (mis)information that Arthur is dead. The Bastard is still onstage when Hubert tells John that Arthur is in fact alive. This removes from the Bastard any necessity of making up his mind about either John or Hubert and thus drains most of its meaning from the scene in which he is tested by the finding of Arthur's body.[1]

This summary of events in *Troublesome Reign* is misleading and may arise from an over-hasty study of the text; it also assumes, without argument, that *The Troublesome Reign* would be like *King John* if it could. When John orders Peter to be imprisoned (1.1645–7: 'Hence with the Witch . . . Lock him up sure . . .'), there is no stage direction, but some character must escort him off; since John and the nobles remain on stage and Hubert soon enters, it seems likely that the Bastard, who captured Peter originally and brought him to John, also takes him to prison. The Bastard, therefore, need not hear John order Arthur's death or know that Hubert believes Arthur still to be alive. Furthermore, the scene (2.1–109) in *Troublesome Reign* analogous to Act 4, Scene 3 of *King John* does not include the Bastard; so far as I can deduce from a quarto lacking many essential stage directions, the Bastard in *The Troublesome Reign* is never on stage with Arthur's body. There is consequently no scene where the Bastard 'is tested by the finding of Arthur's body', no scene to be drained 'of its meaning'. In fact, the Bastard decides (in the King's presence) to remain with John without obvious soul-searching and then tamely agrees when John asks him to

> post to Saint Edmundsbury,
> Dissemble with the nobles, know their drifts;
> Confound their devilish plots and damned devices.
> Though John be faulty, yet let subjects bear;
> He will amend and right the people's wrongs. . . .
> Then Philip show thy fealty to thy King,
> And amongst the nobles plead thou for the King.
> (2.242–6, 251–2)

When the nobles complain of Arthur's death, the Bastard briefly defends the King, 'For Arthur's death, King John was innocent, |

[1] Matchett's edn., p. 155.

He [i.e., Arthur] desperate was the deathsman to himself'
(2.456–7), and then calls their complaints 'petty wrongs' (2.462).
We may wonder how the Bastard knows of Arthur's suicide, we
may here accuse the dramatist of sloppy craftsmanship, but we
cannot assume that he sought (and failed) to create a Bastard
like Shakespeare's character in *King John*.

Different conceptions of John may also partly explain the two
plays' very different ordering of the incidents concerning Peter
of Pomfret. In *The Troublesome Reign*, John is more plainly
indecisive and confused, ordering, regretting, raging, and repent-
ing by turns. In *King John* the rather clumsy dramaturgy—
Hubert's re-entrance after escorting Peter to prison is not motivated at all, for instance—emphasizes the King's isolation. The
weight of the scene falls on John's (and others') *reactions* to events
rather than the events themselves: thus, the five moons do not
need to be displayed and Peter can be more summarily dismissed,
never to return, while in *The Troublesome Reign* he is brought
back before his execution on Ascension Day as a prelude to John's
submission to Pandulph.[1] The narrative organization of *The
Troublesome Reign* is arguably clearer, certainly simpler, than in
King John, and Shakespeare's Bastard and John are also very
different and probably more interesting. By reducing Peter of
Pomfret's presence (like the five moons, the prophet would be
equally effective if he were only spoken of, not seen) and
accepting the slight awkwardness of John's treble dispatch
of intermediaries—Bastard, anonymous messenger, Hubert—
Shakespeare makes possible the effective sequence of revelation
and accusation in Act 4, Scene 3. The writer of *The Troublesome
Reign* was not trying to prepare for that scene, or at least he did
not write one like it. My own opinion is that *King John*'s more
complicated (and slightly more awkward) sequence might have
developed out of that in *The Troublesome Reign* rather than the
reverse, but the two plays are sufficiently different and their
choices have enough internal consistency to be independent
reactions to the historical sources.

Economy of hypothesis suggests that *The Troublesome Reign* and
King John can be related in a finite number of ways. In the following

---

[1] The acting versions of Garrick and Kemble take Shakespeare's method a step
further and delete Peter entirely, thereby making Hubert's role in the scene more
logical and, in my view, more effective.

summary, I use the phrase 'in some form' to acknowledge the possibility of a sequence of revised texts, written or performed, of texts incorporating theatrically derived changes, of 'drafts', of texts either author knew in manuscript or performance, etc.

1. *The Troublesome Reign* in some form was written and perhaps performed before *King John*, and *King John* was written with a close knowledge of *The Troublesome Reign*. This 'knowledge' principally influenced the sequence of events in the first three acts of *King John* and to a much smaller extent its language.[1]

2. *King John* in some form was written and perhaps performed before *The Troublesome Reign*, and *The Troublesome Reign* was written with a close knowledge of *King John*. This 'knowledge' principally influenced the sequence of events in *The Troublesome Reign* and to a much smaller extent its language.[2]

3. Some unknown text, probably a complete play, but possibly a scenario or 'plot', was written and perhaps performed before either *The Troublesome Reign* in some form or *King John* in some form was written, and the two surviving plays were written by authors aware of this hypothetical text.[3]

In short, the parallels (mostly of sequence, slightly of language) between *The Troublesome Reign* and *King John* may have arisen in one of three ways: *The Troublesome Reign* → *King John*; *King John* → *The Troublesome Reign*; X → *The Troublesome Reign* and X → *King John*. (Hypothetically, X could be multiplied into a series of drafts, states, or performances so that X → *The Troublesome Reign* and X′ → *King John* or vice versa.)

---

[1] This majority view is ably expounded in Robert Smallwood, ed., *King John*, The New Penguin Shakespeare (Harmondsworth, 1974), pp. 365–74; it may embrace the possibility of Shakespeare's hand in *The Troublesome Reign*, as Alexander Pope for one believed. W. J. Courthope argued, in *A History of English Poetry*, 6 vols. (1895–1910), that 'Shakespeare alone was the author' of *The Troublesome Reign* (iv. 55, and see iv. 463–6).

[2] Among recent writers, Ernst Honigmann has most fully developed this view in his edn. and in *Impact*; for earlier scholars' agreement, see Honigmann's edn., p. xviii n. 2.

[3] See, for example, E. M. W. Tillyard, *Shakespeare's History Plays* (1944), p. 217: '*The Troublesome Reign* [may] turn out to be a bad quarto (though perhaps in a different way bad) not of *King John* as we have it but of an early play by Shakespeare on the same theme. This play would then be the original both of *The Troublesome Reign* and of *King John* . . .'. Suzanne Tumblin Gary argues that *TR* is a 'plot-based adaptation' of *King John*, i.e., it derives from an outline of the action of Shakespeare's play; see 'The Relationship between *The Troublesome Reign* and Shakespeare's *King John*' (unpublished Ph.D. dissertation, University of Arizona, 1971).

Finally, any of the three relations might include the following possibility:

4. Non-authorial collation of *The Troublesome Reign* in some form with *King John* in some form produced the surviving evidence. Collation between printed quartos of Shakespeare's plays and other hypothetical witnesses has been virtually demonstrated to lie behind texts in the Folio, although *King John* would be the only instance of collation between a Shakespearian witness and a (probably) non-Shakespearian quarto.[1] Collation of a manuscript of *King John* with *The Troublesome Reign* might account for the similarity of some of the stage directions in the two plays and, less plausibly, for the presence of Essex and the sheriff in *King John*, Act I.[2]

Most of the verbal links between *The Troublesome Reign* and *King John* have proved to be 'reversible', or at least debatable; appealing to hypothetical plays, scenarios, or plots is playing tennis without a net; since the authors of both known plays resorted to historical sources independently, the presence or absence in one play of historical detail absent or present in the other cannot indicate the chronology of composition.[3] On the available evidence, the ordering of the plays finally turns upon two points: those who believe that *The Troublesome Reign* preceded *King John* emphasize the absence (or near-absence) of any of Shakespeare's vivid and powerful language;[4] those who believe that *King John* preceded *The Troublesome Reign* emphasize what Tillyard called 'the masterly construction' of *The Troublesome Reign* and imply or state that it must derive from Shakespeare,

[1] Honigmann, *Impact*, p. 62, applies this point to *King John*; more generally, see Fredson Bowers, 'Authority, Copy, and Transmission in Shakespeare's Texts', in *Shakespeare Study Today*, ed. Georgianna Ziegler (New York, 1986), pp. 7–36; pp. 10–16.

[2] See Sidney Thomas, ' "*Enter a Sheriffe*": Shakespeare's *King John* and *The Troublesome Raigne*', *Shakespeare Quarterly*, 37 (1986), 98–100 and the subsequent exchange among Thomas, Ernst Honigmann, and Paul Werstine, vol. 38 (1987), 124–30.

[3] Bullough, iv. 5–6, and Sider, pp. xliii–xlvii, discuss the sources of *The Troublesome Reign*.

[4] Honigmann has responded that this view 'assumes that hack writers would naturally aim to produce bad quartos at a date when bad quartos were entirely unknown' (*Impact*, p. 57). On the contrary, the view need only assume that 'hack writers' (*a*) would take the easy way and imitate pre-existing dialogue, and/or (*b*) could not escape the influence of Shakespeare's language so completely as the author of *The Troublesome Reign* seems to have done.

although his acknowledged play is itself 'badly proportioned'.[1] The debate conceals a germ of Bardolatry: Shakespeare was a master of both plotting and dramatic language; he did not need and would not use, even as a guide, another writer's arrangement of an action; any author who seems his peer or superior must some way owe that quality to Shakespeare.

My own view is that there were several playwrights in the late 1580s and 1590s who could work up a plot from Holinshed and the other chroniclers with at least as much skill as Shakespeare shows in the first tetralogy, while there were few or none who could equal (with whatever difference) the quality of Shakespeare's dramatic verse. Thus, for example, Marlowe's compression and rearrangement of chronicle material in *Edward II* is, perhaps unexpectedly, first-rate, and Peele's handling of the strictly historical sources for *Edward I* not far behind. It does not seem impossible that other writers had this ability, or enough of it to plot *The Troublesome Reign* from Holinshed's *Chronicles*. On the other hand, the author of *The Troublesome Reign* had a rather ordinary command of English dramatic verse, as did many of his named and anonymous contemporaries.

Parallel passages in Shakespearian and non-Shakespearian texts notoriously invite perilous speculation; moreover, many of the texts to which *King John* may be related are themselves of uncertain date. Even the one unequivocal reference poses problems: *King John* 1.1.244 names a character from, and alludes to an incident in, *Soliman and Perseda* (attributed to Thomas Kyd, entered for printing in 1592), but there is no certain date for that play's composition or performance, although the most persuasive case so far presented argues for 1591–2 and specifically claims that it post-dates *The Troublesome Reign*.[2]

King John shares many verbal and stylistic traits with *Edward III*, an anonymous play entered for printing in late 1595, printed in 1596, and attributed to Shakespeare in a catalogue appended to Thomas Goffe's *The Careless Shepherdess* (1656).[3] Shakespeare

---

[1] Tillyard, pp. 217–18.

[2] Arthur Freeman, 'Shakespeare and *Solyman and Perseda*', *Modern Language Review*, 58 (1963), 481–7; p. 485.

[3] See, e.g., the notes to 1.1.0.2 (Chatillon), 1.1.37, 2.1.103, 5.1.57–9, and 5.7.35 below and Fred Lapides, ed., *The Raigne of King Edward the Third* (New York, 1980), pp. 7–31, especially pp. 19–21, summarizing the extensive work of Alfred Hart, *Shakespeare and the Homilies* (Melbourne, 1934), pp. 219–41, and of

probably knew *Edward III* even if he had no hand in writing it, for an episode in Act 4 of *Edward III* best explains the Bastard's mysterious reference to the French who 'thrill and shake | Even at the crying of your nation's crow' (*King John* 5.2.143–4). Describing the scene before the battle of Crécy in 1346, Holinshed, here following Froissart's earlier account (which the author of *Edward III* apparently knew), wrote: 'there fell a great rain and an eclipse with a terrible thunder, and before the rain, there came flying over both armies a great number of crows, for fear of the tempest coming'.[1] Omens and portents litter Holinshed's pages, but Brinsley Nicholson pointed out that the author of *Edward III* might have developed this reference into an elaborate prophecy of French defeat at the battle of Poitiers (in 1356): 'flint stones' will rise against the French and 'feathered fowl' (*Edward III* 4.3.69, 68)—called 'ravens' (4.5.28, 42) and later 'crows' (4.6.5, 12)—will terrify hardy soldiers.[2] The prophecy is fulfilled, and the English comment, 'the amazed French | Are quite distract with gazing on the crows . . . What need we fight . . . | When railing crows out-scold our adversaries' (*Edward III* 4.6.4–5, 11–12). It seems probable that the Bastard alludes anachronistically to the fictitious episode in *Edward III*. Unfortunately, the dates of *Edward III*'s composition and performance are unknown; it post-dates the Armada (1588), and 'the period 1589–1592' embraces the scholarly consensus.[3]

Among the many parallel passages that have been used to locate *King John* in relation to other Elizabethan plays, one in Act 2 has occasioned extensive debate. Promising to 'smoke your skin-coat an I catch you right', the Bastard tells Austria,

---

Karl P. Wentersdorf in his unpublished Ph.D. dissertation, University of Cincinnati, 1960. Hart makes several telling comparisons between the vocabulary of *Edward III* and *King John*; see especially p. 222 on the plays' very similar (and high) proportions of vocabulary size to number of lines. I cite *Edward III* in modernized spelling from the text in C. F. Tucker Brooke, ed., *The Shakespeare Apocrypha* (Oxford, 1908).

[1] Raphael Holinshed, *The Third Volume of Chronicles, beginning at Duke William the Norman* . . . (1587), 372a; Mm4ᵛ. (Reference to Holinshed's third volume is by page and column (a or b) and by signature.)

[2] *Notes & Queries*, 35 (1867), 251.

[3] Lapides, ed., *Edward III*, p. 37; see also MacD. P. Jackson, *N. & Q.*, 210 (1965), 329–31, p. 331 ('hardly . . . later than 1592'; 'about 1590'), and Karl P. Wentersdorf, 'The Date of *Edward III*', *SQ*, 16 (1965), 227–31; p. 231 ('about 1589–90').

> You are the hare of whom the proverb goes,
> Whose valour plucks dead lions by the beard.
> (2.1.139, 137–8)

Blanche joins the ridicule by praising Richard Coeur-de-Lion, whose lion-skin Austria now wears:

> O, well did he become that lion's robe
> That did disrobe the lion of that robe.
> (2.1.141–2)

The 'proverb' has been found in English as early as 1580,[1] but was evidently given currency by Kyd's very popular *The Spanish Tragedy*, which also has a parallel to Blanche's remark:

> He hunted well that was a lion's death,
> Not he that in a garment wore his skin:
> So hares may pluck dead lions by the beard.[2]

In 1592, Thomas Nashe quoted the last line (substituting 'pull' for 'pluck') and acknowledged, '*Memorandum*: I borrowed this sentence out of a play', and at the turn of the century Nashe's version was quoted in *The Return from Parnassus, Part 1*.[3] The 'proverb' does not appear in *The Troublesome Reign*, but the Bastard responds to Lymoges's claim that 'your betters are in place' with 'Not you, Sir Doughty, with your lion's case', and Blanche exclaims, 'Ah, joy betide his soul to whom that spoil belonged' (1.551–2). John Dover Wilson thought *The Spanish Tragedy* (usually dated *c*.1587) here imitated *King John* and must therefore post-date Shakespeare's play.[4] In view of the proverb's currency, however, it seems probable that both plays employ a common stock and that *The Spanish Tragedy* pre-dates *King John*,

[1] The proverb is H165 in Morris Palmer Tilley, *A Dictionary of the Proverbs in England in the Sixteenth and Seventeenth Centuries* (Ann Arbor, Michigan, 1950); other instances appear in *The Oxford Dictionary of English Proverbs*, 3rd edn., rev. F. P. Wilson (Oxford, 1970), and in R. W. Dent, *Proverbial Language in English Drama, 1475–1616* (Los Angeles and Berkeley, 1984). Citations of the proverb in Freeman, 'Shakespeare and *Solyman and Perseda*' and the same author's *Thomas Kyd: Facts and Problems* (Oxford, 1967), p. 74, mix examples of this proverb with examples of two others which appear at *King John* 2.1.144 (see note).

[2] *The Spanish Tragedy*, ed. Philip Edwards, The Revels Plays (1959), 1.2.170–2.

[3] See, respectively, *Strange News* in R. B. McKerrow, ed., *The Works of Thomas Nashe*, revised by F. P. Wilson, 5 vols. (Oxford, 1958), i. 271 and *1 Return from Parnassus*, ll. 1452–3 in *The Parnassus Plays*, ed. J. B. Leishman (1949).

[4] See Wilson's edn., pp. liii–liv and, for agreement, W. W. Greg, *The Shakespeare First Folio* (Oxford, 1955), pp. 254–5.

as Philip Edwards and Arthur Freeman claim.[1] That Shakespeare's passage matches Kyd's 'pluck' does, it is true, faintly suggest a borrowing.[2] Negative evidence—*The Troublesome Reign* does not use the proverb in a ready-made context that Shakespeare seized—implies that the author of *The Troublesome Reign*, 'an unknown writer with a memory-box filled with scraps from other men's plays', did not know *The Spanish Tragedy*, perhaps because it post-dates *The Troublesome Reign*.[3]

The evidence considered here proves some of the following points and strongly suggests the remainder: *King John* post-dates the second edition of Holinshed's *Chronicles*; *The Troublesome Reign* post-dates *The Spanish Tragedy* and *Soliman and Perseda*; *King John* post-dates *The Spanish Tragedy*, *Soliman and Perseda*, *The Troublesome Reign*, and *Edward III*; *King John* was performed before 1598. Further, metrical, stylistic, and critical observations suggest that in Shakespeare's career *King John* follows such works as *Lucrece* and *Richard III*, and belongs to the period of *Romeo and Juliet* and, among the histories, *Richard II*, with which it shares an exclusive or almost exclusive use of verse and the absence of a subordinate action that parallels the royal political action. In the absence of further evidence and argument, I believe *King John* was composed and performed in the mid-1590s, most probably 1595–6.

Sources. Along with his fellow countrymen, literate and illiterate alike, Shakespeare could hardly escape a general knowledge of John's reign and of the 'official', positive Tudor interpretation of it, and he may have known the negative views of John inspired by the succession debate (see pp. 58–60). He read Holinshed's detailed account of the period, and he may have read several less accessible accounts, perhaps through pursuing Holinshed's marginal citations.[4] Most of the early histories

---

[1] Edwards, ed., *The Spanish Tragedy*, 1.2.170–2n and Freeman, 'Shakespeare and *Solyman and Perseda*', p. 485. Edwards proposes the sequence *The Troublesome Reign*, *The Spanish Tragedy*, *King John*.

[2] Note, however, that Shakespeare never uses 'pull' in connection with 'beard', only 'pluck(s)' (four times) and 'tug' (once).

[3] Honigmann, *Impact*, p. 79; he supplies numerous examples on pp. 79–82.

[4] The second edn. of Holinshed was heavily censored, and among the cancelled pages was Thomas Thynne's history of the Archbishops of Canterbury, containing a lengthy account of Stephen Langton's conflict with John. On other historical

were written by chroniclers hostile to John, as Tudor writers noted:

Consider the story of King John, where I doubt not but they [the Roman Catholic chroniclers] have put the best and fairest for themselves and the worst of King John, for I suppose they make the chronicles themselves.

Verily, whosoever shall consider the course of the history written of this prince, he shall find that he hath been little beholden to the writers of that time in which he lived, for scarcely can they afford him a good word, except when the truth enforceth them to come out with it as it were against their wills. The occasion whereof (as some think) was for that he was no great friend to the clergy.[1]

Sixteenth-century English texts generally treat King John as a proto-Protestant martyr to Catholic hostility and ambition and, often, as a forerunner of both Henry VIII and Elizabeth. Bishop John Bale's play *King Johan* (probably performed before Cranmer in 1539, but not printed until 1838) links John with Moses and Henry VIII with Joshua, as men who led their people out of bondage and into the promised land.[2] William Tyndale's *The Obedience of a Christian Man* (1528 and many later editions) 'sets forth the essential features of his [John's] character and reign as they were understood by Bale and later sixteenth-century reformers'.[3] John also appeared in an immensely popular work

sources Shakespeare may have examined—Matthew of Paris, *Historia Maior*, and the Latin manuscript texts of Ralph of Coggeshall and the *Wakefield Chronicle*—see Honigmann's edn., pp. xvii–xviii and 163–7 and the refutation in Kenneth Muir, *The Sources of Shakespeare's Plays* (1977), pp. 80–3. Although the *Wakefield Chronicle* appears to be the only source for the information that Eleanor 'The first of April died' (4.2.120), Holinshed mentions her death and that date (but specifically in connection with a portentous meteor) on the same page (Muir, p. 82, citing W. G. Boswell-Stone).

[1] William Tyndale, *The Obedience of a Christian Man* (1528), fols. 157–157ᵛ and Holinshed, 196; R6ᵛ, respectively. W. L. Warren, *King John*, 2nd edn. (1978), pp. 3–16, scrutinizes the contemporary and near-contemporary historical sources, emphasizing their limitations and bias.

[2] See Barry Adams, ed., *John Bale's 'King Johan'* (San Marino, California, 1969), pp. 1, 20–4, and (for the parallels among John, Henry, Moses, and Joshua), *King Johan*, ll. 1107–13. 'Most students of the Elizabethan drama agree that *King Johan* exerted no direct influence on either the *Troublesome Raigne* or Shakespeare's *King John*' (Adams, p. 15).

[3] Ibid., p. 25; Tyndale's main discussion of John occurs in the summary conclusion of *Obedience*, fols. 157–157ᵛ. For another early positive treatment of John, see the anonymous, but pro-Tyndale, tract of *c*.1530, *A Proper Dialogue*

by Bale's younger contemporary and friend, John Foxe, *The Acts and Monuments* (1563 and later editions),[1] and in the official government *Homily Against Disobedience and Wilful Rebellion* (1571), appointed to be read aloud annually in church.[2] The sixth part of the *Homily*, considering rebellions 'stirred up by the . . . Bishops of Rome' (i.e., the Popes), discusses John's reign and then moves immediately to 'King Henry the Eighth his days, and King Edward the Sixth, and . . . our gracious Sovereign's days that now is', mentioning the rebellions of 1536, of 1549, of the mid-1560s in Ireland, and 'yet more lately . . . the ministry of his [the Pope's] disguised chaplains'.[3]

Holinshed's *Chronicles* served as the main printed source for *The Troublesome Reign*, and Shakespeare's *King John* draws its nominally factual matter—its who, what, when—directly or indirectly from Holinshed. If we suppose, as I do, that *The Troublesome Reign* is the earlier play and further suppose that Shakespeare had some knowledge of it, then he found already accomplished the major labour of shaping drama from Holinshed's chronological narrative. That shape compresses events early in John's reign—for instance, the betrothal of Blanche and Louis (1200), or the historical Battle of Mirabeau (1202) which both plays rename 'Angiers', a city John actually besieged and captured in 1206—with much later events—John's submission to the Pope (1213) and Louis's invasion of England (1216). Along with the rearrangement of chronology, there naturally went revision of

Between a Gentleman and a Husbandman in Francis Fry, comp., *A Proper Dyaloge . . .* (1863), B1ᵛ, cited by F. P. Wilson, *Shakespearian and Other Studies*, ed. Helen Gardner (Oxford, 1969), p. 32 n. 1.

[1] Honigmann's edn., pp. xiv–xv and 5.4.42–3n, convincingly shows Foxe as a source, although Shakespeare's error of 'Swinstead' (5.3.8, 16) for 'Swineshead' need not derive from *The Act and Monuments* as Honigmann claims (p. xx), since the error also appears in *The Troublesome Reign*, John Rastell, *Pastime of People: The Chronicles of Divers Realms* (?1530), B3ᵛ, and John Stowe, *Chronicles of England* (1580), p. 251.

[2] See Lily Bess Campbell, *Shakespeare's Histories: Mirrors of Elizabethan Policy* (San Marino, California, 1947), pp. 142–3; Hart discusses their use in worship (pp. 22–3) and their probable influence upon Shakespeare's plays, including *King John* (pp. 29–76; especially pp. 36–9). Campbell surveys a number of other Tudor texts, many of them polemical ones on, respectively, the Protestant and Roman Catholic sides, that discuss John's reign, and see R. M. Frye, *Shakespeare and Christian Doctrine* (Princeton, NJ, 1963), p. 289 n. 9, for further uses of John's reign by Tyndale, Cranmer, and Jewel.

[3] John Griffiths, ed., *The Two Books of Homilies* (Oxford, 1859), pp. 593–4 (John) and pp. 594–6 (Tudor monarchs).

motive, purpose, and accomplishment. Thus, both plays place the conflict between Pope and King over Stephen Langton (consecrated Archbishop in 1207) before Arthur's death (1203); both plays treat the nobles' journey to St. Edmundsbury (1214) as prompted by and immediately following the Dauphin Louis's invasion (1216); both playwrights saw the value of combining the French marine defeats at Damme and in the Channel off the Thames estuary (respectively 1213 and 1218) and making them coincide with the English losses in the Wash (1216; attributed to John in *The Troublesome Reign*, to the Bastard in *King John*).

As these remarks show, the existence of *The Troublesome Reign* makes nearly impossible any direct and sustained analysis of how Shakespeare handled his main historical source, Holinshed's *Chronicles*, since that 'source' may have largely and already been dramatized for him. Although Shakespeare has details from Holinshed not in *The Troublesome Reign*, his treatment of Holinshed generally parallels that in the anonymous play, and Shakespeare's 'handling of his source' then becomes one dramatist's reworking of another's play rather than a dramatist's reworking of a chronicle history. Shakespeare's play, it is true, elaborates certain emotional moments—especially Constance's grief in Act 3, Scene 4 and the dialogue between Arthur and Hubert in Act 4, Scene 1—much more than does *The Troublesome Reign*, and as I have already observed, Shakespeare typically has his characters allude to or narrate events (for example, the second coronation and the multiple moons of Act 4, Scene 2) that are dramatized in *The Troublesome Reign*. Shakespeare handles two historical points very differently from the author of *The Troublesome Reign*: the motivations for and explanations of Arthur's death; the military–political situation at the very end of the play and the Bastard's place in that situation.[1] *The Troublesome Reign* represents John as first unequivocally ordering that Hubert blind Arthur and then later just as unequivocally deciding that Arthur should die, and it introduces the Dauphin suing for peace only after the Bastard has rallied the English forces and we have seen Pandulph leave to compose an Anglo-French peace. Always excepting the ahistorical Bastard, Shakespeare uses more of what Holinshed

---

[1] See pp. 77–8 for a critical account of the latter episode.

asserts as fact in these two matters than does the author of *The Troublesome Reign*, although Shakespeare's interpretation of these 'facts' diverges significantly from Holinshed's.[1]

The Text

Early Records. On 8 November 1623, Edward Blount and Isaac Jaggard, leading members of the syndicate that would soon publish the Folio, paid to enter the titles of sixteen Shakespeare plays 'as are not formerly entered to other men' in the Stationers' Register; these sixteen had not previously appeared in print, but neither *The Taming of the Shrew* nor *King John* is among them. Following E. K. Chambers in an argument from silence, W. W. Greg asserted that the existence in print of two non- or quasi-Shakespearian quartos with similar titles—*The Taming of a Shrew* and *The Troublesome Reign of King John*—led the Stationers' Company, the publishers, and the King's Men to treat, for the purposes of registration, the texts they intended to publish in the Folio as identical with the previously published quartos.[2] Although Greg cautioned against supposing the two cases to be similar in other respects, his assumption led E. A. J. Honigmann to the hypothesis that the two pairs of plays might share further resemblances in their origin and in their treatment by the compilers of the Folio.[3] It is certainly remarkable that these two plays should have been omitted from the 1623 entry for the Folio and also be antedated (in print) by plays having such similar

[1] I examine Shakespeare's use of Holinshed here in '*King John* and Historiography', *ELH*, 55 (1988), 309–32.

[2] See Chambers, i. 365 and Greg, *Folio*, p. 50 where he makes the assertion flatly, but later qualifies 'at least this seems to be the only explanation of the absence of these two plays from the new entrance' (p. 60). H. J. Oliver's edn. of *The Taming of the Shrew* (Oxford, 1982), p. 14, offers some slight evidence that *The Taming of the Shrew* and *The Taming of a Shrew* were regarded as identical by people professionally concerned with rights to the publication of the play.

[3] *Impact*, p. 84. While continuing to believe that the absence of an entry for *The Taming of the Shrew* and *King John* makes it a 'fact' that they were treated as identical with *The Taming of a Shrew* and *The Troublesome Reign of King John*, Greg adds a vague cautionary note: 'before using it [the 'fact'] as evidence of what the relationship [between the two pairs of plays] is, we should want to know whether Blount and Jaggard would, from the point of view of copyright, have treated Shakespeare's *Richard III* and *King Lear* as identical with *The True Tragedy of Richard III* (1594) and *King Leir* (1605) had not the Shakespearian versions been previously published—when they were in fact entered as distinct plays' (*Folio*, p. 60 n. 2). That is, to test Greg's assumption requires clairvoyance.

names. It needs equally to be remarked that the two cases are dissimilar in two or three factual ways:

1. *The Taming of a Shrew* was entered in the SR (2 May 1594), and three quartos appeared (in 1594, 1596, and 1607) before the Folio. Rights to the play were regularly transferred from one publisher to another on 22 January 1607 and 19 November 1607.[1] None of the quartos mentioned Shakespeare's name.

2. *The Troublesome Reign* does not appear in the SR, and there are no recorded transfers of rights to the title despite the publication of three quartos (in 1591, 1611, 1622). Shakespeare's initials are attached to the second quarto and his name to the third.

3. According to their title-pages, the quartos do not represent titles publicly played by the same company (the Queen's Men for *The Troublesome Reign of King John* in 1591 and 1611; Pembroke's Men for all three quartos of *The Taming of a Shrew*).[2] Nor were the plays published, or with one exception (Valentine Simmes for *The Taming of a Shrew* in 1607, for *The Troublesome Reign of King John* in 1611), printed by the same persons.

4. Republication of *The Taming of a Shrew* might be explained by its popularity as an entertainment; republication of *The Troublesome Reign* was probably stimulated by its political topicality.[3]

In sum, then, hypothetical comparisons between the inferential textual histories of the two 'Shrew' plays and the two 'John' plays are not justified by the silence of the 1623 entry in the SR. Coincidence, perhaps more, perhaps no less, links the two pairs of plays. More evidence is needed to decide which.

Copy for 'King John' in the Folio. A manuscript play might take several forms—'foul papers', 'fair copy', prompt-book, 'private transcript' and so on; in theory any one of these manuscripts, or a combination of them, could serve as printer's copy. W. W. Greg records, but doubts, Alice Walker's suggestion that the manuscript copy before the compositors of *King John* was 'composite', partly 'foul papers' (i.e., holograph late draft) and partly

---

[1] Oliver, ed., *The Taming of the Shrew*, pp. 13–14.

[2] Title-pages are not necessarily reliable witnesses, and it is possible that the Queen's Men and Pembroke's Men were in fact united about 1593; see G. M. Pinciss, 'Shakespeare, Her Majesty's Players, and Pembroke's Men', *Shakespeare Survey 27* (Cambridge, 1974), pp. 129–36.

[3] See Oliver, ed., *The Taming of the Shrew*, p. 34 and below, 'Copy'.

prompt-book (i.e., a script that had been prepared for, or used in, producing the play).[1] Greg himself thought foul papers served as copy for *King John*, but subsequent research has eroded many of the criteria once confidently applied to determine such questions.[2] The nature of the manuscript copy for *King John* is an unsettled case, but spelling evidence strongly suggests that it was 'composite' at least in the sense that two scribes wrote the manuscript from which the compositors set the Folio. These two scribes had varying spelling preferences (most notably, the vocative and exclamatory 'O' and 'Oh'), and the two compositors in Jaggard's printing-house sometimes followed those different preferences.[3] Copy for Folio *King John* also varied in its expurgation of profanity: one scribe was more careful than the other in replacing 'God' with 'heaven' as the 1606 'Act to Restrain Abuses of Players' required for a spoken 'stage play, interlude, show, May game, or pageant'.[4] This variation coincides with the apparent variation in spelling.

Differences in spelling and expurgation roughly divide the play into two sections, TLN 1–1893 (= 4.2.171) and TLN 1941 (= 4.2.216) to the end. (The intervening lines lack evidence that would permit their hypothetical attribution to one or the other scribe.) Unlike the second portion, the first contains variant speech-prefixes (for Queen Eleanor in modern Act 2, the Folio's 'Scaena Secunda', and for the Bastard at 3.1.131 and 133), inconsistency between stage direction and speech-prefixes in Act 2 (see Appendix A2), slightly confusing entry directions (e.g.,

[1] W. W. Greg, *The Editorial Problem in Shakespeare*, 3rd edn. (Oxford, 1954), p. 143 n. 1.

[2] Bowers, *passim*.

[3] Gary Taylor and John Jowett, 'With New Additions: Theatrical Interpolation in *Measure for Measure*', Appendix 1 in their *Shakespeare Reshaped 1606–1623* (forthcoming). On compositors' tendency to reproduce, rather than normalize, 'O' and 'Oh', see Jackson, pp. 214–15 and 219–20.

[4] Gary Taylor, 'Zounds' in Gary Taylor and John Jowett, *Shakespeare Reshaped 1606–1623* (forthcoming). Variations in spelling and expurgation could have existed earlier in the chain of transmission; the evidence would theoretically be the same if the Folio's copy had been produced by a single perfect transmitter working from an exemplar which itself showed these consistent variations. Whence the expurgation derives is, of course, uncertain; some or all of the changes (albeit in two consistently different degrees of thoroughness) need not derive from the scribes: in Caroline times, the book-holder or 'prompter' apparently pre-censored a play text before submitting it to the Master of the Revels for licensing (see, e.g., G. E. Bentley, *The Profession of Player in Shakespeare's Time, 1590–1642* (Princeton, NJ, 1984), p. 84).

'Lewis' and 'Daulphin' treated as two characters at 2.1.0.2 and 'Philip' used for the Bastard at 3.1.74.4), clumsy dramaturgy (Louis is given only a single, short speech between 2.1.18 and 2.1.497, and Arthur none between 3.1.42 and 3.3.5), indefinite directions in the dialogue and a puzzling re-entry for Constance at TLN 999 (= 3.1.74.4), and dialogue that names the Bastard as 'Philip' (3.2.4 and 5), the original name he lost when knighted as 'Sir Richard and Plantagenet' at 1.1.162. This first section also contains a clear confusion between *c* and *t* ('Ace' for 'Ate' at 2.1.63), an easy enough confusion in secretary hand, but perhaps especially easy in Shakespeare's hand;[1] it also has one putative 'Shakespearian' spelling ('moth' for 'mote' at 4.1.91) and shows a strong preference for the spelling 'O', which may have been Shakespeare's preferred spelling. These features faintly urge the possibility that the scribe was here copying Shakespeare's manuscript, 'foul papers' or otherwise.

Although the Folio's text would not be difficult to perform (again, see especially Appendix A2), neither part of the Folio's text shows unequivocal signs of deriving from a script used in the theatre (Appendix C, for example, describes its deficient sound-cues). The Folio is typically indifferent to specifying characters who are theatrically important as members of a category rather than as individuals—'and others' accompany the royal party at 2.1.83.2, 'their powers' enter with the two Kings at 2.1.333.1–4, 'Attendants' appear at 3.4.0.2 and 5.1.0.2, 'Soldiers' at 5.2.0.3, and 'his train' enters with Louis at 5.5.0.1–2. The treatment of King John's English 'Lords' in stage directions is notably vague: Pembroke, Essex, and Salisbury are named at 1.1.0.1–2 and John addresses Pembroke (1.1.30), but only Essex speaks in the first scene, and thereafter he disappears from directions and dialogue; at 2.1.83.2, 'Pembroke and others' enter, but no English lord

---

[1] See Frank Kermode, ed., *The Tempest*, Arden Shakespeare, 6th edn. (1962), Additional Notes, p. 166, on J. C. Maxwell's conjectural emendation of 'the peace of the presence' (*The Tempest* 1.1.22): the Folio's *present* was perhaps misread from manuscript *presenc*. Hand D, which may be Shakespeare's, has clearly written *present* at *Sir Thomas More*, Addition II, l. 71 (*pace* Kermode), but there are several examples of suffixal *-enc*: e.g., *obedyenc* (45); *insolenc* (90); *obedienc* (105), at least one of which might be misread in the suggested way, although Alexander Dyce (the first modern transcriber of the manuscript of *Sir Thomas More*) never mistook *c* for *t*. At 2.1.122 in the Folio, Eleanor rebukes Constance with 'Out insolent', although 'insolenc(e)' in this construction would be Shakespearian, and that word may have appeared in his manuscript.

speaks in the scene; at 3.3.0.1–3, the English party enters, but the direction mentions only 'Lords' and the handling of this undifferentiated group could have great theatrical significance (see 3.3.0.3n); at 4.2.0.1–2, John enters with 'Pembroke, Salisbury, and other Lords', and the two named lords appear in speech-prefixes, but when the nobles leave as a group, the Bastard specifically identifies only 'Lord Bigot and Lord Salisbury' (4.2.162) as being among them. Bigot, Salisbury, and Pembroke are all named at 4.3.10.1–2, and all three speak in the scene. Subsequent stage directions (5.2.0.1–3, 5.4.0.1–2, 5.7.0.1–2 and 5.7.5.1) consistently identify the group of English lords as Salisbury, Pembroke, and Bigot, although Bigot remains mute for the rest of the play and editors have had to provide him with an exit at 5.7.10. Again, these directions would probably cause even less confusion for professional producers than they do for the reader. Like the play's dialogue, however, this evidence suggests that the English lords are theatrically important as a group (of three, probably) rather than as individuals modelled on historical personages. That is, their names are just names, and their function is to represent English unity (up to 4.2), then English dissension, and finally, renewed loyalty.[1]

It is possible to speculate on why the text of *King John* shows comparatively little evidence of theatre use and on why two scribes may have been needed to prepare the copy for the Folio. The makers of the Folio seem to have been concerned that the first .play in each section (Comedies, Histories, Tragedies) be particularly well presented; *The Tempest*, especially, and *Coriolanus* show more care in their presentation than other plays in their respective sections. Chronology required that *King John* begin the section of Histories that followed the Comedies in the Folio, but Charlton Hinman has conclusively shown that *King John* was printed before *Twelfth Night* and *The Winter's Tale*.[2] That is, some

[1] This evidence militates, as does other evidence, against Emrys Jones's suggestion that the play's 'Hubert' was meant to be perceived as the historical Hubert de Burgh, justiciar of England (see Appendix A, p. 277 n. 2).

[2] I have simplified the actual sequence: printing of part of *Richard II* intervened between *Twelfth Night* and *The Winter's Tale*; see Charlton Hinman, *Printing and Proof-Reading of the Shakespeare First Folio*, 2 vols. (Oxford, 1963), i. 351. Hinman summarizes the printing of *King John* (ii. 515), and Trevor Howard-Hill, 'The Compositors of Shakespeare's Folio Comedies', *Studies in Bibliography*, 26 (1973), 61–106, studies kinds of evidence different from Hinman's and confirms his

hitch occurred in the provision of copy for *Twelfth Night*, and it may be that copy for *King John* was needed sooner than the preparers of the Folio had supposed.[1] A rushed transcription might, therefore, have demanded two copyists rather than one. This hypothesis supposes that the King's Men did not have a text of *King John* suitable for Jaggard's use (e.g., a legible manuscript), or did not have one they were prepared to release, perhaps because the play was not then in the current repertory, perhaps, indeed, because it had not been performed for many years.[2] The publication history of *The Troublesome Reign* (quartos in 1591, 1611, 1622) and the post-Restoration stage history of *King John* suggest, however, that the events of John's rule interested the London book-buying and, later, its theatre-going public during times of English conflict with, or fear of, Catholic Europe. Thus, *The Troublesome Reign* is published in the aftermath of the Armada and of a friar's assassination of Henri III of France, republished after the assassination of Henri IV of France, and published yet again when James's son-in-law, the Elector Palatine, was under attack on the Continent and there was intense speculation concerning an Anglo-Hispanic alliance.[3] At least the two later periods might have revived the King's Men's interest in *King John*, perhaps to the point of preparing a copy of the play, and the last period would have coincided conveniently with preparations for the printing of the Folio.

The several sources of variation that apparently lie behind the Folio make it impossible to determine unequivocally the origin of the Folio's copy. Two scribes copying a text that may itself have

assignment of compositors in the Folio and determines that Compositor B rather than C composed the forme containing a3 and a4ᵛ.

[1] As Hinman suggests (ii. 521).

[2] It is possible, too, that the script of an unpopular play now (in 1622 or so) more than twenty years old might have gone astray, forcing the Folio preparers back on documents that pre-dated any marking up for theatre use—hence the paucity of evidence that the Folio's copy derives from the theatre. The Folio's stage direction '*Iohn brought in*' (5.7.27.1) may indicate that the Folio's copy was written for, or was revised to serve in, a theatre building where such an entry was more convenient than a 'discovery' (in which case the direction might have been '[*Enter*] *Iohn discovered*'); see 5.3.16n, 5.7.27.1n, and C. J. Sisson's comparison of the quarto and Folio staging of *King Lear* 4.7 in *New Readings in Shakespeare*, 2 vols. (Cambridge, 1955), ii. 242.

[3] The economics of publishing as well as of propaganda need to be considered: the 1622 quarto of *The Troublesome Reign* may have been issued in anticipation of the Folio's publication, as the 1622 quarto of *Othello* seems to have been.

multiple origins plus two compositors composing the manuscript in type introduce too many variables for confident statement. It seems certain, however, that Compositors B and C were setting from copy that was prepared or revised after 1606, with at least the faint sense that the play might be spoken from the stage; it is probable, however, that the compositors' copy (and perhaps the text(s) underlying their copy) had not been used in the theatre.

Act and Scene Division. It is generally agreed that act (or in many cases, act and scene) divisions were retrospectively imposed upon many plays printed in the Folio. The vast majority of public theatre plays published in quarto between 1591 and 1616 had no numbered divisions whatsoever.[1] Indeed, none of Shakespeare's plays published before *Othello* (Q 1622) has any numbered divisions. Except for *King Lear*, *Troilus and Cressida*, *Othello*, and *Pericles*, the plays that appeared in quarto before the Folio (1623) were written prior to *c*.1600/1601; the plays Shakespeare wrote or shared in writing after his company assumed control of a private theatre (the Blackfriars, in the late summer of 1608), where act division seems to have been formally observed in performance, may have been conceived with that practice in mind.[2] Equally, some earlier plays still in the current repertory may have been reshaped to the changed performance circumstances.

---

[1] For a summary, see W. T. Jewkes, *Act Division in Elizabethan and Jacobean Plays 1591–1616* (Hamden, Conn., 1958), *passim* and especially p. 39; George Heuser, *Die aktlose Dramaturgie William Shakespeares* (Marburg, 1956), p. 92, suggests that publishing fashion, specifically the fully-divided plays in the 1616 Jonson folio, encouraged division of plays in the Folio.

[2] A suggestion first made by Dover Wilson, 'Act and Scene Division in Shakespeare', *Review of English Studies*, 3 (1927), 389 and supported by Jewkes's data comparing printed texts of public and private theatre plays (pp. 61–95). G. K. Hunter notes, however, that as soon as we suppose that a Folio editor, or some (other?) non-theatrical source, imposed act division in 'some cases, there is no logical reason for denying it in any case. The form of the plays in the Folio can be cut completely adrift from any assumptions about the theatrical habits of the age'; see 'Were There Act-Pauses on Shakespeare's Stage?' in Standish Henning *et al.*, eds., *English Renaissance Drama* (Carbondale, Illinois, 1976), p. 22. The apparent congruity between private theatre practice and printed (and divided) private theatre plays, however, makes Hunter's claim here as hard to accept as his subsequent inference that since 'A printer not feeling that act-division was an essential part of his copy was . . . at liberty to ignore the marginal material' (p. 23), virtually all the printers of all the public theatre texts published between 1591 and 1616 uniformly took this liberty and left no traces of the 'ignored' material.

Inept or inappropriate divisions in Folio plays naturally imply that they were divided *post facto*. Such divisions are especially easy to detect when a quarto exists for comparison.[1] *King John* appears to be a text originally organized only into a series of scenic units (i.e., units of continuous action without temporal discontinuities, concluding when the stage is cleared of actors).[2] Although act divisions have been imposed on this original structure, the scene divisions (and the related act divisions) in the play's second half (Acts 3–5) are largely conventional and unexceptional, generally coinciding with a cleared stage, time-breaks, changes in location, and shifts from one group of characters to another.[3] Act 5, Scene 1 was mistakenly headed 'Actus Quartus, Scaena prima', the heading that also, and correctly, heads Act 4, Scene 1. The Folio's compositors made this kind of mistake only one other time: *Love's Labour's Lost* has two acts each headed 'Actus Quartus'. In both *Love's Labour's Lost* and *King John*, the duplicate divisions were set by different compositors and were consequently less likely to be noticed. A misread or misremembered numeral might account for the errors, but they would be easier to make if the compositors misread or misremembered a Latin abbreviation: $Q^{nt\mathfrak{O}}$ or $q^{nt\mathfrak{O}}$ (= Quintus, quintus) misread as $Q^{rt\mathfrak{O}}$ or $q^{rt\mathfrak{O}}$ (= Quartus, quartus).[4] Few compositors were Latinists, as 'Actus Secunda' (*LLL*, L3^v), 'Actus Tertia' (*The Taming of the Shrew*, T1^v), and 'Actus Secunda' (*Titus Andronicus*, cc3) testify, and the abbreviations may therefore

[1] See, e.g., Greg, *Folio*, p. 205 and n. 7, comparing Quarto and Folio *Titus Andronicus*. Some Folio-only plays, like *The Comedy of Errors* and *Measure for Measure*, contain exits and re-entrances that serve only to clear the stage—the commonest method of scenic division and the plainest signal that one unit of dramatic activity and theatrical experience has ended and its successor begun. See Greg's discussion (*Folio*, pp. 210 and 356) of the Folio's direction 'Enter Antipholus and Dromio again' in *The Comedy of Errors*, Act 5, and of the Folio's marking of a new scene in *Measure for Measure*, Act 1, when the Provost enters with Claudio.

[2] Compression of time and slight shifts in location to follow characters' movements do occur within scenes, of course; in *The Structure of Shakespearean Scenes* (New Haven, Conn., 1981), James Hirsh offers (e.g., on p. 211) a complicated version of this definition.

[3] The Folio does not divide the battle in Act 3 into 3.2 and 3.3, as many editors do; see the headnote to 3.3.

[4] There is slight evidence that numerals were sometimes used: see below, p. 28 n. 3; manuscript plays from the period often mix words and numerals and Latin and English in their act and scene designations. Markings in the Folio are unlikely to have been consistent.

have been comparatively unfamiliar. Finally, the error could be authorial; in Heywood's holograph foul papers for *The Captives*, he misnumbered and then corrected the heading for Act 1, Scene 2: '*Actus* [*deleted*: 2 s], 1 *scena* 2ᵃ'.[1]

The divisions in the play's first half present more complicated puzzles. In reading order, with their line equivalents in this and most modern editions, the first four headings and divisions are:

Actus Primus, Scaena prima. [1.1.1–276]

Scaena Secunda. [2.1.1–599]

Actus Secundus [3.1.1–74]

Actus Tertius, Scaena prima. [3.1.75–347]

Observing that 'Something has gone wrong,' W. W. Greg explained, 'The division is typographically suspicious. The heading "Actus Secundus" lacks its customary "Scaena prima"—it has not even a stop after it—and there is no "Exeunt" at the end. The headings to III.i and ii want the usual rules below them.'[2] Understanding what may have gone wrong requires both bibliographical and literary-critical speculation. We must briefly consider how the Folio generally marks act- and scene-divisions and then examine the compositors' experience and their practice in setting these divisions, especially the specific features—punctuation, 'Scaena prima', rules—that Greg identifies. Finally, we will need to consider the order in which the compositors encountered the divisions in their copy.

Charlton Hinman found that six sets of standing type were successively used to head texts in the Folio—five settings of 'Actus Primus, Scaena prima' and one setting of 'Actus Primus'.[3] The uses of these formulae may be summarized thus:

---

[1] Among late 'Shakespearian' quartos, successive scenes in *The Two Noble Kinsmen*, Act 2 are numbered '3', '4', '4', '6'; see G. R. Proudfoot's edn. (Lincoln, Nebr., 1970), p. xxvi. Gary Taylor's '*King Lear*: The Date and Authorship of the Folio Version' lists some other misnumberings of scenes in the Folio and in non-Shakespearian plays (in G. Taylor and Michael Warren, eds., *The Division of the Kingdoms: Shakespeare's Two Versions of 'King Lear'* (Oxford, 1983), pp. 351–451; see p. 417).   [2] Greg, *Ed. Prob.*, p. 142 and n. 1.

[3] Hinman, i. 178–9. In the following discussion, I use 'Actus Primus, Scaena Prima' to represent all such headings, although the spelling, capitalization, and spacing differ in unimportant ways among the five settings. Similarly, I have normalized the Folio's several slightly varying forms to 'Scaena'; I have omitted the full stop that ends all but one of the headings I discuss, and I do not reproduce the Folio's italic for headings.

1. Six plays are undivided, but begin with the 'Actus Primus, Scaena Prima' formula and have no further divisions.

2. Eleven plays are divided into acts only: eight begin with 'Actus Primus, Scaena Prima', three with 'Actus Primus'; none has a full act and scene heading for Act 2.[1]

3. Nineteen plays are divided into acts and scenes; all begin with the customary full formula, and all but two—*King John* and the very irregular *Hamlet*—have 'Actus Secundus, Scaena Prima'.[2]

From this summary, we may conclude that the initial formula gives us—and a compositor who glanced over a marked manuscript or quarto from which he was about to set—no help in predicting the form of subsequent divisions in the play. Still, *King John* is unique in being divided, perhaps inaccurately, into acts and scenes while also printing 'Actus Secundus' rather than 'Actus Secundus, Scaena Prima'.

By the time they set *King John*, Compositors B and C were well experienced with the Folio's conventions. Both men had set several act-headings without 'Scaena Prima' in plays divided into acts only, but Compositor B—unnecessarily and against the Folio's general practice—had set 'Scaena prima' three times (*The Comedy of Errors*, H4ᵛ, H6ᵛ; *The Taming of the Shrew*, T4) in the headings for acts-only plays. Compositor C set only 'Actus' plus numerical designations in acts-only plays, although he was responsible for two failures of concord in *Love's Labour's Lost* and *The Taming of the Shrew*.[3] The absence of a full stop after an act- or scene-heading is unprecedented in the scores of headings composed before 'Actus Secundus' in *King John*, nor do any later headings in the Folio lack a full stop.[4] The third 'suspicious' feature Greg noted, the absence of a rule after the first two headings in Act 3, is less unusual: these occasions are the only

---

[1] *The Comedy of Errors* has 'Scaena Prima' after all the act-headings except that for Act 2, and *The Taming of the Shrew* does not mark Act 2 in any way.

[2] Like *King John*, *Hamlet* has 'Actus Secundus', but its divisions end at 2.2. For details, see Greg, *Folio*, p. 329.

[3] Since these are acts-only plays, the grammatical error may suggest that copy had been marked with numerals rather than full words or abbreviations of words. There are also grammatical errors in the 'Finis' lines for Acts 1, 2, and 4 of *Twelfth Night* in the Folio.

[4] Of course, the stop may have been *set*; the type could have broken or failed to print for some other reason.

times in the Folio that Compositor C omits the rule, but Compositor B omitted one or both rules three times, the first on the very first page of *The Tempest*.[1] The compositors probably omitted rules to save space, a goal that could be, and in the plays following *King John* was, achieved through compressing the box around act- and scene-headings rather than by omitting one or both of its boundaries.[2]

The first gathering of *King John* was composed in the 'usual' order, that is, from the forme containing a3ᵛ and a4 'outward' to the forme containing a1 and a6ᵛ. If we consider the sequence in which the relevant headings were composed, we find the following:

1. Compositor B set no headings in forme a3ᵛ:a4.

2. Compositor B set no headings in a3 and, setting a4ᵛ, saw what he set as 'Actus Secundus' without a full stop and with rules above and below. The page is not crowded: column b is three text lines shorter than column a; the catchword is 'Actus'.

3. Compositor C set no headings in a2ᵛ and, setting a5, saw what he set as 'Actus Tertius, Scaena prima' without a following rule; the page is very crowded.

4. Compositor C, setting a2, saw what he set as 'Scaena Secunda' with a following rule and set no headings in a5ᵛ.

5. At this point in the printing, there was a short interruption before Compositor C completed the gathering.

That is, after setting three pages without any act- or scene-headings, Compositor B encountered some marking (besides the entry stage directions) at the point most modern editions call 3.1.1; that marking evidently contained letters or a numeral suggesting 'Secundus'. When Compositor C set the next two formes, he placed 'Actus Tertius, Scaena prima' where it properly corresponds to Compositor B's catchword and in the next forme set 'Scaena Secunda' at a point where literary, and perhaps theatrical, considerations have led editors to mark the beginning

---

[1] The three times: *The Tempest*, A1; *The Merry Wives of Windsor*, E1; *Measure for Measure*, G3ᵛ. Oddly, these three and the two in *King John* appear to be the only examples in the Folio.

[2] Saving space will not explain, however, why Compositor C omitted the rule after 'Scaena Secunda' on *King John*, a6; that page is not crowded: column b is two text lines shorter than column a and could easily be three shorter were 'Exeunt' set in the margin opposite text rather than on a line of its own.

of Act 2. Having already set a full heading for Act 3, Compositor C would be predisposed to accept a scene-only heading since (as we have seen) his earlier experience had taught him that plays with full headings at the start of any act but the first were overwhelmingly likely to include individual scene-headings as well.[1] If the break was marked with a numeral or an abbreviation for a number, adding 'Scaena' would be an easy assumption; alternatively, Compositor C may have misread or misunderstood markings for 'Actus'.

Since the headings were set in the reverse of reading order and since two compositors were involved, an economical pattern of one individual's misunderstanding and erroneous self-correction will not explain the confusion, as the traditional account holds:

It seems fairly clear that F's '*Scaena Secunda*' is a mistake for *Actus Secundus*, the printer presumably mistaking a '2' or a 'II' in his copy for a scene division rather than an act division. At the next division he would thus have no alternative but to print '*Actus Secundus*' regardless of what was marked in his copy.[2]

If we assume, as this account does, that printer's copy was 'correctly' marked (i.e., it conformed with modern editions on where Act 2 begins), we have to believe that Compositors B and C co-ordinated their mistakes, Compositor B setting 'Actus Secundus' when he read and should have set 'Scaena Secunda' and Compositor C setting 'Scaena Secunda' when he read and should have set 'Actus Secundus' (or, more probably, 'Actus Secundus, Scaena prima'). Remarkably enough, Compositor B did once set 'Scena' (the catchword at *Henry VIII*, x1^v) for 'Actus' (the first word of 'Actus Quintus, Scena Prima', the heading of x2), but to hypothesize such a mistake here and then to

---

[1] The same argument would hold for Compositor B (who knew enough about Act 3 to set the catchword) and makes his 'Actus Secundus' even more anomalous, with the limited qualifications of his unusual treatment of two headings in *The Comedy of Errors* and one in *The Taming of the Shrew* (see p. 28 above).

[2] Smallwood's edn., p. 355. This view is a variant of Greg's, which is open to the same objections: 'All we need suppose is that in the manuscript handed to the printer the second act was accidentally headed "Scaena Secunda" instead of "Actus Secundus". The printer would naturally reproduce this incorrect heading, and would next find himself confronted with "Actus Tertius". All he could do would be to convert this into "Actus Secundus", and then alter III.ii into III.i and so on' (*Folio*, p. 250). While agreeing that Greg's explanation is unsatisfactory, Gary Taylor offers a more complex explanation for the Scaena Secunda/Actus Secundus confusion (see 'Zounds').

hypothesize a complementary mistake ('Scaena' for 'Actus') in Compositor C's next-but-one forme strains credulity. The alternative assumption is that copy was not clearly and/or not 'correctly' marked. The traditional account seems correct in proposing that some mark(s) indicating 'two' (in numerals or letters, Latin or English) appeared at two places in the copy: Compositor B surprisingly interpreted the marks he saw as 'Actus Secundus'; Compositor C, less surprisingly, interpreted the marks he saw as 'Scaena Secunda'. Further, we have the testimony of both compositors that Act 3, Scene 1 was quite clearly marked in the Folio's copy, at a point modern editions regard as seventy-four lines late.

So far, we have found tentative explanations for several 'suspicious' typographical features in the first half of *King John*. Other anomalies remain: the absence of a stage direction at the end of 'Actus Secundus'; the curiously uneven columns on this page (a4^v) of the Folio; the fact that Constance is directed to enter in successive scenes ('Actus Secundus' and 'Actus Tertius, Scaena prima'). These problems are, of course, interlinked; their solution requires more than bibliographical speculation, and a wider focus than the Folio's page a4^v.

The first significant break in the play's action occurs after 1.1.276. This first scene (or act) has a wasp-waisted structure: on a crowded stage, we hear of the political dispute between England and France and see the bastardy of Philip Faulconbridge debated and resolved; the stage empties and the Bastard solilo-quizes on what has occurred; two new characters enter to him, and the scene ends with their dialogue. Here the Folio marks a break ('Scaena Secunda'), and it is a substantial one: the action moves geographically (to France) and temporally (the period of an 'expedient' Channel-crossing). A long but continuous action then concludes with an agreement that marriage should resolve political differences: 'at Saint Mary's Chapel presently | The rites of marriage shall be solemnized' (2.1.539–40). King Philip wonders where Constance is (ll. 541–4; she left the stage, presumably, in the general exeunt before the battle, 2.1.299.1), and we learn that 'She is sad and passionate at your highness' tent' (l. 545). Her sadness is logically premature but theatrically apt: Philip has just sacrificed her interests to 'our own vantage', although she has, realistically, no way of knowing the fact. 'Some speedy messenger' is ordered to summon Constance 'To our solemnity' (ll. 555–6; the Folio has no direction for the messenger), and the newly reconciled Kings depart for St. Mary's Chapel. The Folio's '*Exeunt*' is followed by a speech-prefix, '*Bast.*', and one of the play's most famous speeches, beginning 'Mad world, mad kings, mad composition!' The Folio then directs '*Exit*' and prints 'Actus Secundus | Enter Constance, Arthur, and Salisbury'. Constance has learned (from Salisbury, we suppose) of the impending ceremony; she laments. Salisbury requests that she go with him 'to the Kings' (3.1.66); she refuses and declares, 'Here I and sorrows sit. | Here is my throne; bid kings come bow to it' (3.1.73–4). This speech closes near the bottom of the second column on a4ᵛ. Beneath Constance's last line appears a blank equal to three lines of text, ended by the catchword '*Actus*', placed a line above the direction-line and level with the last line of text in the first column. Thus far, the ordering of speakers and action has paralleled that of the first act: a crowded stage gives way to the Bastard in soliloquy followed by a brief exchange among two men and a woman.

At the head of the next page, following 'Actus Tertius, Scaena prima', we read 'Enter King Iohn, France, Dolphin, Blanch, Elianor, Philip, Austria, Constance'. King Philip enters conversing with Blanche; the party has returned from the wedding, and after only eight lines, Constance interrupts to curse the day and accuse Philip of treachery.[1]

From the moment John and Philip decide to settle their political dispute through marrying Blanche to Louis, the stage action has been curiously undefined. Since Shakespeare never dramatizes sacraments, we would expect the wedding to take place off-stage, as it does here between the '*Exeunt*' at 2.1.561 and the '*Enter*' at 3.1.74.3; similarly, Shakespeare's usual practice would then insert a short scene with different characters—what Marco Mincoff named a 'wedge' scene[2]—to separate the 'before' and 'after' scenes and clarify the fictional timetable. At a pinch, the Bastard's soliloquy might serve this function, but if 'Philip' at

---

[1] Shakespeare often uses the 'enter, conversing' device to convey the passage of time: later in *King John*, we will hear only the final three lines of a conversation that accounts for a period in which a fleet is lost (3.4.1–3).

[2] Marco Mincoff, 'Plot Construction in Shakespeare', *Annuaire de l'Université de Sofia: Faculté historico-philologique*, 37 (1940–1), 1–51.

3.1.74.3–4 is the Bastard (and there is little doubt of it), then his immediate re-entrance from St. Mary's Chapel simply reinstates the difficulty. Of course, the Constance–Arthur–Salisbury scene would 'wedge' apart the end of 2.1 and the beginning of 'Actus Tertius', and the dialogue prepares us to imagine this situation topographically—a messenger must be sent from the Kings to request Constance to join them (off-stage) at St. Mary's Chapel. Again, however, this explanation founders—precisely as the first did—on the direction for a character, Constance, to (re-)enter at 3.1.74.3–4. Closely linked to this problem is the absence of a direction for Arthur to exit; he makes his next appearance, speaking a single line, and, it seems, a recently captured prisoner, in what this edition treats as Act 3, Scene 3. His silent presence throughout Act 3, Scene 1, might underscore how peripheral his interests have become (or have always been), but it would provide a difficult task for actor and director.

Clearly, the Folio's text and, presumably, its copy are here indeterminate and 'unfinished' in two principal ways: dialogue and stage directions are mutually contradictory (either Constance refuses to attend the wedding or Constance is summoned to the wedding and enters with the group returning from it); a virtual constant of Shakespeare's stagecraft, the 'wedge' scene, is intimated once, perhaps twice, and not unequivocally carried through.[1]

Three possible sources of confusion, operating singly or in combination, need to be considered: accidental or deliberate omission of text; inept editorial interference from a non-authorial, perhaps non-theatrical, source (e.g., the imposer of act divisions); incomplete or misunderstood revision. Lewis Theobald first conjectured that a scene might have been lost from 'Actus Secundus', and several twentieth-century scholars have urged the possibility.[2] It is, however, difficult to imagine a scene that does not repeat the problem it was invented to solve—characters exiting and re-entering immediately. By 1729, Theobald had decided that nothing was missing and that the fault lay in 'Scaena Secunda'

[1] Even if we suppose Shakespeare has varied his usual practice and omitted a wedge scene, there remain the bibliographical and, inferentially, the dramatic oddities of Constance's re-entry and the strangely uneven columns on a4^v.

[2] See, respectively, Theobald, *Shakespeare Restored* (1726), p. 159; Chambers, i. 365; Wilson's edn., pp. xlviii–xlix; Heuser, pp. 157–8.

33

(which he took to be an error for 'Actus Secundus') and in the next two headings.[1] He thereby founded the dominant editorial tradition that treats the Folio's 'Actus Secundus' as the start of Act 3 and deletes the Folio's heading for 'Actus Tertius, Scaena prima'.[2] In short, Theobald turned from the first possible source of confusion to the second.

As we have seen, act breaks imposed upon an originally continuous action could explain how Constance's name comes to appear in the entry direction for 'Actus Tertius'; ordinarily, however, an earlier 'exit' would have been inserted as well. The blank at the end of a4^v (where such an exit could appear) is doubly 'suspicious': producing equal columns with the catch-word on a line of its own would have required little effort, and Compositor B had already twice composed equal columns in identical situations.[3] The Folio's copy may simply have been illegible at this point, or it may have lacked the exit direction, or Compositor B ignored an exit because the dialogue so strongly stipulates that Constance should remain on stage.

Unequal columns could also result from an error in casting off copy. The Folio's compositors strenuously avoided ending a column with an act- or scene-heading.[4] That effort eventually made page a5 very crowded and deprived the 'Actus Tertius' heading of its customary rule. Confusing copy, in particular heavily revised or interpolated material (the third possibility I mentioned), makes casting off more than usually difficult. If, for example, either the Bastard's soliloquy or the Constance–Arthur–

[1] See Theobald's letter to Warburton, 18 March 1729, Folger MS W.b. 74, fols. 69–70 and W.b. 75, fol. 93, reprinted in John Nichols, *Illustrations of the Literary History of the Eighteenth Century*, 2 vols. (1817), ii. 206–7, and repeated virtually verbatim as the second half of the long note to 3.1.74 in Theobald's edn. of 1733.

[2] The principal dissenters from this tradition are Grant White and Fleay in the nineteenth century and Honigmann in the twentieth.

[3] See *The Tempest*, A6^v and *As You Like It*, Q6^v. The mathematics of odd and even mean that Folio columns need be unequal by at most one line if the catchword and (on some rectos) the signature remain in the direction line; if, as on *King John*, a4^v, the compositor were willing to move a catchword from the direction line, equal columns could always be produced. One regrets that Compositor B did not fill the space with a 'finis Actus' phrase, as Compositor C evidently chose to do at *Love's Labour's Lost*, L3; see Greg, *Folio*, pp. 217, 223, and 296.

[4] The closest they came in plays printed before *King John* was at *The Taming of the Shrew*, T4: a heading plus the entry stage direction end column a; columns a and b are equal.

Salisbury scene had been added marginally or, more probable, on a separate sheet, then the mistaken casting off and even the omission of a stage direction at the end of the Constance–Arthur–Salisbury scene would all be plausible consequences, and the unequal columns might then testify to the compositor's confusion or misjudgement. The dramatic and theatrical value of the scene is patent: it shows Constance moving from an aggressive role (balancing Queen Eleanor's) toward the political irrelevance and maternal lament of Act 3, Scene 4; it advances the pathos of Arthur's role toward its climax in Act 4, Scene 1; it satisfactorily 'wedges' apart the Kings' departure for, and their return from, St. Mary's Chapel. However powerful, the Bastard's reflective commentary is the more likely to be Shakespeare's after- or second thought: the soliloquy ranges neatly with the earlier speech on 'worshipful society' and further establishes the Bastard's 'in-but-not-of' status, yet it is less essential to the play's momentum and quite unnecessary to its theatrical economy. If, and the 'if' is very large, either the soliloquy or the scene was interpolated, it might have carried an indication of its proper place in the text—a note that it was to end 'Actus Secundus' (or just a numeral) or perhaps—at the conclusion of the soliloquy—'finis Actus Secundus'. Such a direction, misunderstood and perhaps mispositioned, could have ended up as the curious act-heading Compositor B printed.[1] Further, if the interpolation were combined with, or marked to be inserted at, a point where scene-, or act- and scene-, division had also been marked, the chance that the interpolated material might be inserted one line (and hence one scene) too early or too late would be high.[2] Although

[1] This last speculation is less far-fetched than it may appear: the compositors sometimes set stage directions and other material—for example, 'SENNET' at 1 *Henry VI*, l5^v or 'The Order of the Coronation' at *Henry VIII*, v6^v—in type almost as large as that used in scene heads.

[2] Scenic divisions and numberings that originate in the theatre appear to have been marked in the margin, usually the left margin, of the manuscript: see, e.g., *Edmond Ironside* and *Woodstock* (in the MSR editions) and William B. Long, 'Stage-Directions: A Misinterpreted Factor in Determining Textual Provenance', *TEXT*, 2 (1985), 121–37; p. 126; authorial manuscripts, by contrast, often have the scenic divisions centred, perhaps in imitation of printed plays: see, e.g., the MSR editions of Munday's *John a Kent* (where one omitted heading has been added in the left margin, but the others are centred), Heywood's *The Captives* (mentioned above), and Massinger's *Believe as you List* (where some theatrical hand has deleted the holograph, centred divisions and replaced them with act divisions in the left margin).

a hypothetical revision or interpolation can be made to explain the Folio as printed, either one seems to me improbable, certainly unprovable. The traditional explanation, however, does not persuasively explain 'Scaena Secunda', 'Actus Secundus', and Constance's presence in the entry direction of 'Actus Tertius, Scaena prima'. On balance, the likeliest combination of elements would be: incompletely or confusingly marked act- and scene-headings—'Actus Secundus' did not properly become 'Actus Secundus, Scaena Prima'; 'Scaena Secunda' was misunderstood somehow, perhaps as 'Actus Secundus'; 'Actus Tertius, Scaena prima' was either misplaced or the usual revision of exits and entrances was only partially carried through. Honigmann adopts a conservative and defensible treatment of the Folio: 'Scaena Secunda' becomes Act 2; 'Actus Secundus' becomes Scaena Secunda (i.e., Act 2, Scene 2); 'Actus Tertius, Scaena prima' is unchanged (i.e., Act 3, Scene 1 begins where it does in the Folio).[1] I have not adopted this arrangement for three reasons: the traditional, Theobald-derived division permits easy cross-reference; since either arrangement requires an important distortion of the Folio as printed (an invented stage direction at the end of the Constance–Arthur–Salisbury scene), the choices are equal in this matter; traditional as it is, the division I have adopted paradoxically accepts less of what is demonstrably wrong, confused, or uncertain in the Folio—in a word, it remains more 'open'.

Revision. A hypothetical revision or interpolation might have caused the confusion we have just examined; stonger evidence of revision or interpolation appears in Act 3. When Constance enters at 3.4.16.1, King Philip notes her changed appearance ('A grave unto a soul') and even before she speaks, he asks, 'I prithee, lady, go away with me' (3.4.20). Mad, or nearly mad,

---

[1] There are several ways of reaching this view of the matter; Honigmann's various arguments, particularly where they coincide with the more traditional explanation quoted above, are not all equally persuasive. I agree with Honigmann and Gary Taylor that Act 3, Scene 1 was distinctly marked in the Folio's copy and accurately transmitted by the compositors, but in Taylor's words, 'we could not expect him [Shakespeare] to mark the beginning of a new structural unit in the middle of a continuous scene . . . We would hardly expect Shakespeare, a literary scribe, or a Folio editor to have placed an Act division where Folio *King John* puts it' ('Zounds').

with grief at Arthur's capture, she apparently ignores Philip, as she ignores his and Pandulph's later attempts to calm her (ll. 22, 36, 43), laments her loss, and tears her hair. Exclaiming 'Bind up those tresses', Philip offers a little allegory of love and calamity 'In the fair multitude of those her hairs' (ll. 61–7). Constance then says, 'To England, if you will' and Philip repeats 'Bind up your hairs' (l. 68). W. A. Wright suggested that 'To England, if you will' replies to Philip's much earlier request, 'I prithee, lady, go away with me', and that the intervening lines were a subsequent addition.[1] On this hypothesis, the speeches amplifying Constance's grief were inserted one or more lines too early; the repetition of Philip's request that Constance bind up her hair (ll. 61, 68) may also be evidence for the interpolation since either one might satisfactorily evoke Constance's 'Yes, that I will' (l. 69).

Finally, a Messenger's information and words to John,

> Be of good comfort, for the great supply
> That was expected by the Dauphin here
> Are wrecked three nights ago on Goodwin Sands.
> (5.3.9–11)

are clumsily repeated barely seventy-eight lines later in another Messenger's speech to Louis,

> And your supply, which you have wished so long,
> Are cast away and sunk on Goodwin Sands.
> (5.5.12–13)

The repetition might be defended as a way of emphasizing the similar situations of John, who is mortally ill, and the Dauphin, who has lost his English allies as well as his expected reinforcements, but it may also indicate hasty composition or incomplete revision.

---

[1] *King John*, Clarendon Press Series (Oxford, 1886), 3.4.68n; many subsequent editors (Wilson, Honigmann, Smallwood) have accepted Wright's hypothesis to varying degrees. As Smallwood argues (his edn., p. 351), there is no way of determining when—during the play's initial composition, or later—the hypothetical revision took place, although Wilson thought it 'more probable that such revision took place at a subsequent revival' (his edn., p. 1).

'King John': A Critical Introduction

Everyone knows two things about King John: he was Robin Hood's arch-enemy, and he granted Magna Carta, an early guarantee of Anglo-Saxon liberties that began to achieve its modern fame through being misinterpreted in the earlier decades of the seventeenth century.[1] Neither the rural outlaw nor the legal document appears in Shakespeare's *King John*. Elizabethan theatre audiences apparently enjoyed Robin Hood's evergreen political opposition,[2] and their Stuart successors learned and disputed with their lives the political significance of Magna Carta, but the absence of both, along with the chronological isolation of John's reign among Shakespeare's histories, may partly account for the play's uneven reputation with critics and producers.[3] What everyone knows about John's reign is at least subliminally 'political' knowledge, knowledge about dissent and rebellion, authority and subversion, for example. Although it lacks Robin Hood and Magna Carta, Shakespeare's play is also and variously political. By representing the contentious, mystified passage of property, power, and legitimacy from generation to generation, *King John* dramatizes—and thus both demystifies *and* makes unfamiliar—some of the most intensely serious cultural assumptions in late Tudor England.

Even as it represents the 'machinery of politics, the way its agreements and misfortunes come about' in the early thirteenth century, then, *King John* also responds—sometimes in undramatized ways, often in unconscious ways—to Elizabethan politics and

---

[1] See Faith Thompson, *Magna Carta: Its Role in the Making of the English Constitution 1300–1629* (Minneapolis, Minnesota, 1948); Herbert Butterfield, *Magna Carta in the Historiography of the Sixteenth and Seventeenth Centuries*, The Stenton Lecture, 1968 (Reading, 1969); Maurice Ashley, *Magna Carta in the Seventeenth Century* (Charlottesville, Virginia, 1965).

[2] For Tudor Robin Hood plays, see Malcolm A. Nelson, *The Robin Hood Tradition in the English Renaissance* (Salzburg, 1973), Chapters 3 and 4; Nelson finds that Robin Hood's only dramatic appearance between *c.*1600 and the Restoration comes in Jonson's fragmentary *The Sad Shepherd* (printed 1641). Magna Carta is discussed and virtually quoted in Robert Davenport's *King John and Matilda* (printed 1655, but acted *c.*1628–34).

[3] For the play's long and controversial stage history, see below, pp. 84–93; for its rather different critical fortunes, see the summaries by Harold Jenkins, 'Shakespeare's History Plays: 1900–1951', *Shakespeare Survey 6* (Cambridge, 1953), pp. 1–15, and by Dennis H. Burden, 'Shakespeare's History Plays: 1952–83', *Shakespeare Survey 38* (Cambridge, 1985), pp. 1–18.

social conditions.[1] More readily than most others, plays on
historical topics enter a covert, political dialogue with their
own present; offering a shape for the past and a method for
understanding historical process, a history play implicitly asks a
contemporary audience to consider the shape of its present and
how that present may be understood. Finally, this 'dialogue' may
well endanger the dramatist and his company in a period—like
the end of Elizabeth's reign—when censorship of mass art is
intermittently scrupulous and always punitive. To present these
aspects of *King John* fully is no task for an introduction, but the
four sections that follow explore some of the ways *King John* may
be called 'a political play'.

The first and last sections address literary and theatrical aspects
of the play, respectively dramatic language and the arrangement
of the action. Shakespeare uses the play's language to dramatize
'the machinery of politics' in ways the characters understand
(stating and negotiating their differences, for instance), and
through using iterated images and situations he writes a political
play in ways they do not recognize. In the second and third
sections of the introduction, I consider aspects of *King John* that
had or could have had political valences for an Elizabethan author
and audience, specifically the play's representation of inheritance
and of the family, and I try to suggest how these putative links
between the play and wider Elizabethan cultural and social
matters might have affected its content and procedures. In every
case, however, these neat distinctions break down, and the topics
in each section link with and qualify those in every other.

Political Language and the Language of 'King John'. The most
decisive, unmediated political speech in *King John* is the first line:
'Now say, Chatillon, what would France with us?'[2] This directness
continues through the next twenty-nine lines of question ('What

[1] The quoted phrase is from Friedrich Dürrenmatt, 'Principles of Adaptation',
in *Writings on Theatre & Drama*, trans. H. M. Waidson (1976), pp. 148–9. Ruby
Cohn discusses Dürrenmatt's German-language adaptation of *King John* (1968)
in *Modern Shakespeare Offshoots* (Princeton, NJ, 1976), pp. 29–34.

[2] 'Like *Richard II*, this play also opens with a piece of expressive sound. . . . It
is an admirable beginning, and Shakespeare used it again . . . to open the third
act of *Cymbeline*, where the same situation occurs, though this time the omission
of the ambassador's name makes Cymbeline's "Now say, what would Augustus
Caesar with us?" appreciably less abrupt . . .' (Martin Holmes, *Shakespeare and
Burbage* (1978), p. 141).

follows if we disallow of this?'), answering threat ('The proud control of fierce and bloody war'), and threatening answer ('Here have we war for war and blood for blood, | Controlment for controlment. So answer France'). John's dismissal of the French ambassador achieves defiance without bravado:

> Be thou as lightning in the eyes of France,
> For ere thou canst report, I will be there;
> The thunder of my cannon shall be heard.
> So hence. Be thou the trumpet of our wrath
> And sullen presage of your own decay.—
> An honourable conduct let him have.
> Pembroke, look to't.—Farewell, Chatillon.
>
> (1.1.24–30)

Never again are the political differences between France and England so clear-cut; never again do political speeches sound as if they were being delivered to a single audience embracing speaker, allies, and enemies. Rather, the play's later political speeches and dialogues increasingly obscure or confuse the combatants' legal and ethical positions. From the first line of Act 2, political debate is represented as speech in which some linguistic features point in one direction (sharp distinction among speakers) and others point in the opposite direction (identity of supposedly distinguished speakers).[1] In the second act, an illustrative selection includes: King Philip's astonishing first speech when he ceremoniously introduces Arthur to the Duke of Austria, murderer of his uncle and now his new ally (2.1.1.–5); the matched, boastful defiances of John's and Philip's first speeches to (and at) each other (2.1.84–109); the 'Billingsgate' argument between Queen Eleanor and Constance paralleling the Kings' speeches (2.1.121 ff.); the obsequious but recalcitrant speeches from the walls of Angers (2.1.267 ff.).[2] Almost in an ascending

[1] The dialogue is not truly separate from the political and ethical confusions, which exist only *in* that dialogue and the actions it specifies. Sigurd Burckhardt examines other uses of language in *King John* and reaches the related conclusion that Shakespeare's sceptical treatment of 'order' in Acts 1–3 'demonstrates the simultaneous disintegration of order and speech and truth'; see *Shakespearean Meanings* (Princeton, NJ, 1968), p. 138.

[2] On Constance and Eleanor's speeches, see 2.1.120n, and Wolfgang Clemen on the 'challenge' as a 'type of set speech' in *English Tragedy before Shakespeare*, trans. T. S. Dorsch (1961; repr. 1967), pp. 16, 49, 53. A similar sequence of 'public' defiances between male rulers and 'private', raucous flytings between their consorts appears in Marlowe's influential *Tamburlaine, Part One*, 3.3 (in J. S.

sequence, these examples represent the play's commonest version of the language of politics: language so used that it stipulates polarized values while it also obscures polarity.

There are two climactic examples of language understood this way: Pandulph's speeches persuading Philip to place his religious obligation before his oath of peace (especially 3.1.263 ff.) and Pembroke's plea that John release Arthur (4.2.47 ff.). The first precipitates the final breach between John and Philip; the second immediately precedes the equally disastrous break between John and his nobles. Pandulph's arguments have occasioned much commentary, ingenious, frustrated, and sometimes dismissive.[1] It is easier to study political language in Pembroke's speech, partly because (unlike Pandulph's) it does not involve religious dogma and Elizabethan religious prejudice.

Hoping to placate the English lords, John plays upon two meanings of 'well' before transforming the sound into 'willingly' and 'will':

> but ask
> What you would have reformed that is not well,
> And well shall you perceive how willingly
> I will both hear and grant you your requests.
>
> (4.2.43–6)

Pembroke portrays himself as the mere, almost the involuntary, instrument of a carefully vague 'these', and his inverted syntax places justification before request, delaying the specific (and, he suspects, unwelcome) answer for five lines:

> Then I, as one that am the tongue of these
> To sound the purposes of all their hearts,
> Both for myself and them, but chief of all
> Your safety, for the which myself and them
> Bend their best studies, heartily request
> Th'enfranchisement of Arthur, whose restraint

Cunningham's Revels edn. (Manchester, 1981)). The political element in Act 2's final episode, the marrying of Blanche to Louis, is discussed below, pp. 70–1.

[1] See the seven and a half pages of (condensed) commentary in Horace Howard Furness, Jr., ed., *King John*, A New Variorum Edition (Philadelphia, 1919); Gerald M. Greenewald, OM, devotes Chapter 5 of *Shakespeare's Attitude towards the Catholic Church in 'King John'* (Washington, DC, 1938) to Pandulph's speech at 3.1.268 ff. and finds it 'perfectly in keeping with the doctrine of oaths enunciated by the Catholic Church'.

> Doth move the murmuring lips of discontent
> To break into this dangerous argument.
>
> $(4.2.47-54)^1$

By omitting the *for* logically needed to complete the syntax of 'both for myself . . . but chief of all | [for] Your safety . . .' and using *for* to introduce another construction depending upon 'Bend' in the following line, Pembroke replaces antagonism (one party claiming redress, the other granting or denying it) with unity (one party wishing the other's good). Although John plainly expects to be asked to reform something 'that is not well', what the nobles 'heartily request' becomes John's 'safety' as much as Arthur's 'enfranchisement'. When the long-delayed reply does come, its metaphor conceals a threat: Pembroke is a respectful, loyal 'tongue', but the 'lips of discontent'—apparently belonging to no one, certainly to no lord here present—have already been moved to murmur an unspecified 'dangerous argument'.

This argument is now stated, couched as the view of an anonymous 'they' and introduced by an elegantly deceitful hypothesis that John dare not deny,

> If what in rest you have in right you hold,
> Why then your fears, which—as they say—attend
> The steps of wrong, should move you to mew up
> Your tender kinsman and to choke his days
> With barbarous ignorance, and deny his youth
> The rich advantage of good exercise.
>
> $(4.2.55-60)$

Since John believes, or must appear to believe, or cannot publicly deny, that he holds what he holds (also left unstated) 'in right', the momentum of 'If . . . | Why then' commits him to one of two courses: admitting that his 'fears' control him, or releasing Arthur. To distance himself as far as possible from this dangerous argument, Pembroke now reiterates its source—'the time's enemies', not John's enemies, not Arthur's friends, not the nobles for whom Pembroke speaks—and neatly makes the final move that smooths conflict into superficial, verbal unanimity:

> That the time's enemies may not have this
> To grace occasions, let it be our suit

---

[1] For verbal details here and throughout this speech, see the relevant commentary, below.

> That you have bid us ask his liberty,
> Which for our goods we do no further ask,
> Than, whereupon our weal on you depending
> Counts it your weal, he have his liberty.
>
> (4.2.61–6)

Just as the nobles' 'request' had been made to seem John's safety, their 'suit' is now that John 'bid' them 'ask' for his own 'weal', which is also Arthur's 'liberty.'

John's initial demand, 'ask | What you would have reformed', acknowledges the political problem that divides him from his nobles. Pembroke's response is a masterly example of political language, stating the grounds of dispute, stating the price of its resolution, threatening rebellion if the dispute is not resolved, but phrased not as conflict but as agreement, not coercion, but request. This is the predominant 'political language' of *King John*. We are asked to attribute this language, *mutatis mutandis*, to the characterization of the play's speakers; we are invited to imagine they more or less consciously manipulate language to achieve these effects.

King John also uses language in ways that are, or become, 'political' in a second sense: language that implicitly and without dramatized consciousness addresses the historical moment of the play's production. This language may be seen in the play's metaphors of vision and possession. They develop from the classical doctrine that the physical manifests the metaphysical, that the beautiful is good, the ugly, evil, or as Spenser writes, 'all that faire is, is by nature good' ('An Hymne in Honour of Beautie', line 139). For example, Constance assumes a positive connection between appearance and worth when she tries to understand her son's ill fortune:

> If thou [Arthur] that bidd'st me be content wert grim,
> Ugly and sland'rous to thy mother's womb,
> Full of unpleasing blots and sightless stains,
> Lame, foolish, crookèd, swart, prodigious,
> Patched with foul moles and eye-offending marks,
> I would not care; I then would be content,
> For then I should not love thee. No, nor thou
> Become thy great birth, nor deserve a crown.
> But thou art fair, and at thy birth, dear boy,
> Nature and Fortune joined to make thee great.

43

> Of Nature's gifts thou mayst with lilies boast
> And with the half-blown rose.
>
> (3.1.43–54)

Constance concludes that 'Fortune . . . is corrupted' and never doubts the assumption that underpins her lament. That principle has, however, already been supported, then questioned, then denied. Eleanor guesses Philip Faulconbridge's descent because his 'face' and 'accent' resemble Richard Coeur-de-Lion's (1.1.85–90), but the Bastard soon decides to imitate courtly 'dialogue of compliment', 'habit and device, | Exterior form, outward accoutrement' (1.1.201, 210–11) and asserts the distance between this behaviour and 'the inward motion':

> though I will not practise to deceive,
> Yet to avoid deceit I mean to learn,
> For it shall strew the footsteps of my rising.
>
> (1.1.214–16)

The undermining of Constance's proposition is completed when Arthur's resemblance to his father, Geoffrey, fails to establish his right to the throne of England (2.1.99–109).

A play that everywhere else proposes principles of action and dogmas of experience only to deny or subvert them naturally treats the equation of appearance and worth in the same confusing way. Premise and contradiction are dynamic, not static, for the principle issues in *action* only through sight and seeing. Hoping to end the battle for Angers by marrying his niece Blanche to the Dauphin, King John invites Louis to look at 'this book of beauty' and 'read, "I love" '. Simultaneously, he promises a 'dowry . . . equal with a queen' (2.1.486–7). Louis looks with his father's politic sight and sees himself in Blanche's eye; ritual manipulations of 'son', 'sun', and 'shadow' signify his cynical, or thoughtless, agreement to the exchange:

> in her eye I find
> A wonder, or a wondrous miracle,
> The shadow of my self formed in her eye,
> Which being but the shadow of your son,
> Becomes a sun and makes your son a shadow.
> I do protest I never loved my self
> Till now infixèd I beheld myself,
> Drawn in the flattering table of her eye.
>
> (2.1.497–504)

Only two characters protest. The Bastard makes an ethical objection in linguistic terms, coarsely attacking Louis's shabby, sonneteering double-talk in an elegant stanza (2.1.505–10). More quietly, Blanche states the patriarchal and political imperatives:

> My uncle's will in this respect is mine.
> If he see aught in you [Louis] that makes him like,
> That anything he sees which moves his liking,
> I can with ease translate it to my will.
> Or if you will, to speak more properly,
> I will enforce it eas'ly to my love.
> Further I will not flatter you, my lord,
> That all I see in you is worthy love
> Than this, that nothing do I see in you,
> Though churlish thoughts themselves should be your judge,
> That I can find should merit any hate.
>
> (2.1.511–21)

When the Kings disagree once more, Blanche's vain protests (3.1.300–9, 326–36) demonstrate how completely she and her dowry are submerged in Louis. In the bitter comedy of her betrothal, seeing activates the principle that appearance—the 'book of beauty' and 'all I see in you'—manifests inner worth. The Bastard's final soliloquy identifies what has gone wrong: 'Commodity' has been 'Clapped on the outward eye of fickle France' and

> Hath drawn him from his own determined aid,
> From a resolved and honourable war,
> To a most base and vile-concluded peace.
>
> (2.1.584–7)

Such conventional propositions about value and perception shape our experience of a central event in the play, Arthur's death. Holinshed and other historical sources mention various threats to Arthur: murder, blinding, castration.[1] At the end of

---

[1] Holinshed mentions both the murder and the blinding of Arthur at John's and his counsellors' instigation among the many rumours about Arthur's imprisonment and death (165b; P3). Ralph of Coggeshall reports that certain counsellors suggested Arthur be blinded and castrated (*Chronicum Anglicanum*, ed. Joseph Stevenson (1875), p. 139). Edward Coke explains why 'cutting out of tongues, and putting out of eyes' were made felonies in Henry IV's reign: 'the misdoers, to the end that the party grieved might not be able to accuse them, did cut out their tongues or put out their eyes' (*The Third Institute of the Laws of England* (1644), p. 63). So mutilated, Arthur would cease to threaten John's rule.

1. James Northcote's illustration of *King John*, Act 4, Scene 1, painted for the Boydell Gallery of Shakespearian themes and subjects; the brazier and the 'warrant' are important props, and the painting reflects post-1700 stagings of the scene.

Act 3, Scene 3, Hubert speaks what John can ostensibly only hint, that Arthur should be murdered. When we next see Hubert, however, he has elaborately planned not to kill Arthur, but to burn out his eyes, and he shows the boy some writing—a royal warrant, it seems (4.1.6, 4.2.70)—to that effect. This inconsistency and Arthur's later unexplained decision to disguise himself as a ship-boy have been regarded as evidence of incomplete revision or slipshod craftsmanship. Whatever its origin, the threat of Act 4, Scene 1 and the way John and others react to Hubert in Act 4, Scene 2 complement Shakespeare's earlier treatment of the responses and judgements beauty (Arthur's and Blanche's) evokes.

After Hubert relents and spares Arthur, he none the less spreads 'false reports' because 'Your uncle must not know but you are dead' (4.1.128, 127). Even without such reports, Pembroke looks at Hubert and judges, 'The image of a wicked heinous fault |

46

Lives in his eye'; he assumes that Hubert's 'close aspect' reveals his 'much troubled breast' (4.2.71–3), reveals that he has murdered Arthur. Believing the same thing, King John claims that sight measures worth and determines action: 'How oft the sight of means to do ill deeds | Makes deeds ill done!' (4.2.219–20). Not John, not Hubert, but Hubert's appearance instigated Arthur's murder. Seeing the servant's ugly face, the master expressed his ugly motive and destroyed the handsome boy:

> Hadst not thou been by,
> A fellow by the hand of Nature marked,
> Quoted, and signed to do a deed of shame,
> This murder had not come into my mind.
> But taking note of thy abhorred aspect,
> Finding thee fit for bloody villainy,
> Apt, liable to be employed in danger,
> I faintly broke with thee of Arthur's death.
> And thou, to be endearèd to a king,
> Made it no conscience to destroy a prince.
>
> (4.2.220–9)

According to John, Hubert's wordless resistance—the shake of the head, 'a pause', but especially his turning 'an eye of doubt upon my face'—would have 'made me break off' (4.2.231–3, 235), and the King would have abandoned 'my signs', the allusive, never quite explicit hints that Hubert should murder his prisoner. Yet the very 'sight' that identifies Hubert as a fit murderer and the 'eye' that might have prevented it are the means through which the murder is agreed: 'thou didst understand me by my signs | And didst in signs again parley with sin' (4.2.237–8). For Dr Johnson, this episode exemplified a general truth: 'nothing is more certain, than that bad men use all the arts of fallacy upon themselves, palliate their actions to their own minds by gentle terms, and hide themselves from their own detection in ambiguities and subterfuges.'[1] King John makes a rather different claim. In the moment of false hope when he learns Hubert has not killed Arthur, the King analyses the complicated interchange between seeing and what is seen:

> Forgive the comment that my passion made

[1] From Johnson's comment on *King John* 4.2.231–5 in his edn.; see Arthur Sherbo, ed., *Johnson on Shakespeare*, the Yale Edition of the Works of Samuel Johnson, vols. 7 and 8 (New Haven and London, 1968), vii. 425.

> Upon thy feature, for my rage was blind,
> And foul imaginary eyes of blood
> Presented thee more hideous than thou art.
>   (4.2.263–6)

Enraged and therefore incapable of seeing properly, John sees the blood he imagines has been spilt and imagines a shedder of blood, the ugly murderer he would be himself and assumes Hubert is.

Scrambling to obey his father and win a large part of France, Louis conventionally invoked the conceit of sight-as-exchange, of seeing himself reflected in Blanche's eye, of becoming her through seeing her. Similarly, Pembroke supposes he can see Hubert's crime reflected in the murderer's eye. When John accuses Hubert, the platitude produces a terrible moral identity: 'Out of my sight and never see me more!' (4.2.242). Like Pembroke, John sees a crime in Hubert's eye, but it is the king's and not the servant's crime, the king's horrible imagining and not the servant's horrible deed. Hubert's gaze is now an accusation, as it might once have been a warning. John wants never again to see Hubert and hopes never again to see himself in Hubert's eye.[1]

These passages all involve the displacement of what the eye would ordinarily 'see' by some other vision, the shadow of beauty or a father's image, the image of a crime or a blinding rage that distorts what the eye sees. Another group of speeches, also largely concentrated in the scene immediately following the attempt to blind Arthur, develops the idea of displacement or substitution in closely related figurative language.

John's nobles bluntly denounce his second coronation, even after they have failed to dissuade him from it. They regard the coronation as 'superfluous', a sign that John somehow feels his 'high royalty' has been 'plucked off' (4.2.4, 5), or worse, a reason for others to think John doubts his right to rule:

> In this the antique and well-noted face
> Of plain old form is much disfigurèd,
> And like a shifted wind unto a sail,
> It makes the course of thoughts to fetch about,
> Startles and frights consideration,

---

[1] John is intensely conscious of how he appears to others, and this characterization becomes insistent right after Arthur has begged to keep his sight. John uses the synecdoche of 'eye' for person repeatedly (4.2.2, 106, 192, 233), as do Salisbury (4.3.49) and the Bastard (5.1.47, 50).

2. A largely formulaic miniature of the coronation of King John (see Act 4, Scene 2) from a late thirteenth- or early fourteenth-century manuscript of Matthew of Westminster's *Flores historiarum*.

> Makes sound opinion sick and truth suspected,
> For putting on so new a fashioned robe.
>
> (4.2.21–7)

Although they also make an economic complaint—the second coronation is 'wasteful and ridiculous excess' (4.2.16)—the nobles have deeper fears: new garb will disfigure old form, the second coronation will undo rather than reinforce John's acknowledged royalty, shadow will prove substance in an unwelcome way.[1] Salisbury's circumlocution for 'recoronation' initially seems no more than a legal metaphor: John has been 'possessed with double pomp' (4.2.9);[2] the word rankles, and John flings it back:

> Some reasons of this double coronation
> I have possessed you with, and think them strong.
>
> (4.2.40–1)

[1] 'John feels the need to prop up his title, now bereft of its foundation in faith, by sheer iteration' (Burckhardt, p. 136).

[2] For the grammar of this phrase, see 4.2.9n, below.

The deliberately awkward syntax exploits the verb's active and passive meanings: 'reasons' may possess the nobles rather than the reverse. We can now see how Salisbury, especially when he introduces the metaphor of disfigurement, may also mean that 'double pomp' has possessed John.

This more sinister sense of 'possession' is soon linked with the visionary substitution John expresses in 'foul imaginary eyes of blood'. When the Bastard arrives, his account of the countryside seems to bear out the nobles' anxieties:

> But as I travelled hither through the land,
> I find the people strangely fantasied,
> Possessed with rumours, full of idle dreams,
> Not knowing what they fear, but full of fear.
>
> (4.2.143–6)

Rumours possess the people, and their condition is one of fantasy, of fearful imaginings like those John describes to Hubert and like the image Pembroke has seen living in Hubert's eye. Hubert himself soon reinforces the Bastard's tale of public dismay, reporting widespread rumours about 'Young Arthur's death', 'of a many thousand warlike French . . . ranked in Kent', and, again, 'of Arthur's death' (4.2.187, 199–200, 202). John's reply once more exploits the ambiguity of 'possess': 'Why seek'st thou to possess me with these fears?' (4.2.203). Here the dominant meaning plainly seems to be 'make [others'] fears possess me', since the alternative is the appropriate but banal 'communicate this information [about others' fears] to me'. In the next scene, Salisbury announces the nobles' defection and returns to the imagery (possession, clothing) he had used before:

> The King hath dispossessed himself of us;
> We will not line his thin bestainèd cloak
> With our pure honours, nor attend the foot
> That leaves the print of blood where'er it walks.
>
> (4.3.23–6)

These uses of 'possession' and its variants strongly recall the word's first appearance, when it also has an unequivocal meaning, 'ownership, control'. John stoutly declares his reasons for braving the French, 'Our strong possession and our right for us', but his mother advises,

> Your strong possession much more than your right,
> Or else it must go wrong with you and me;
> So much my conscience whispers in your ear,
> Which none but heaven, and you, and I, shall hear.
>
> (1.1.40–3)

By the end of Act 4, the word has become much less hard-edged, and the state of mind it represents much less certain. As evidence grows that the characters imagine themselves possessed, by vision or some fearful emotion, so too grows the sense that public meanings of 'possession' and 'dispossession' are being invoked. Notorious demonic possessions and dispossessions of the 1580s and 1590s made the words current and generated a bulky controversial literature which reached one climax in Dr (later Archbishop) Samuel Harsnett's *Declaration of Egregious Popish Impostures* (1603), a source for *King Lear*.[1] Shakespeare had earlier recognized that possession and exorcism make good theatre: when Adriana supposes her husband mad, Dr Pinch begins the ritual—'I charge thee, Satan, housed within this man, | To yield possession' (*The Comedy of Errors* 4.4.55–6)— and then declares 'both man and master is possessed' (l. 93).[2]

King John's language, construed as narrowly as the dialect of political negotiation or as widely as all the poet's verbal resources, points to a transient topicality and to a more permanent intimation that King John is represented as, or believes himself and is believed by others to be, possessed. Legendarily, the Plantagenets descended from 'the demon-countess of Anjou', and St. Bernard thought the family literally satanic: 'From the Devil they came, and to the Devil they will return'.[3] Less sensationally, the play's language develops the analogy between John's royal 'possession' *of* England (as he uses the word in Act 1) and his being possessed *by* an England conceived as a body suffering the physical torment of rebellion.

[1] Keith Thomas summarizes the public controversy over 'Possession and dispossession' in the late sixteenth century; see *Religion and the Decline of Magic* (New York and London, 1971), pp. 477–92. D. P. Walker discusses some case histories (1585–1616) and published English discussions (1584 *et seq.*) in *Unclean Spirits: Possession and Exorcism in France and England in the late sixteenth and early seventeenth centuries* (1981).

[2] Details from contemporary cases of possession appear in Jonson's *Volpone* and *The Devil is an Ass* (ibid., pp. 82–3, 109 n. 29).

[3] See *Giraldi Cambrensis Opera*, ed. J. S. Brewer *et al.* (1861–91), viii. 301 and viii. 309 (the latter translated in Warren, p. 2).

Accusing Hubert of murder, John defines the political effects on himself and on England as coterminous:

> My nobles leave me, and my state is braved,
> Even at my gates, with ranks of foreign powers;
> Nay, in the body of this fleshly land,
> This kingdom, this confine of blood and breath,
> Hostility and civil tumult reigns
> Between my conscience and my cousin's death.
>
> (4.2.243–8)

When he describes his dying father, Prince Henry again uses the imagery of fantasy and capture or possession:

> Death, having preyed upon the outward parts,
> Leaves them invisible, and his siege is now
> Against the mind, the which he pricks and wounds
> With many legions of strange fantasies,
> Which, in their throng and press to that last hold,
> Confound themselves.
>
> (5.7.15–20)

Salisbury, loyal once more, comforts the Prince,

> you are born
> To set a form upon that indigest
> Which he hath left so shapeless and so rude.
>
> (5.7.25–7)

And John continues the analogy between the 'indigest' of England and his own 'scribbled form', making himself England once and for all when he senses her seasons, her rivers, and her winds:

> There is so hot a summer in my bosom
> That all my bowels crumble up to dust;
> I am a scribbled form, drawn with a pen
> Upon a parchment, and against this fire
> Do I shrink up. . . .
> And none of you will bid the winter come
> To thrust his icy fingers in my maw,
> Nor let my kingdom's rivers take their course
> Through my burned bosom, nor entreat the north
> To make his bleak winds kiss my parchèd lips
> And comfort me with cold.
>
> (5.7.30–4, 36–41)

3. King John's tomb in Worcester Cathedral as it appeared in the early eighteenth century (the sculpture has since been slightly damaged); the tomb was opened and its contents described in August 1797. See Valentine Green, *An Account of the Discovery of the Body of King John . . .* (1797) and *The Gentleman's Magazine*, 67, pt. 2 (1797), 705 and 745–6.

These passages, among the last in the play, have a figurative history stretching back almost to John's first words and to the language of many moments in the political pattern that brings him to Swinstead Abbey and death. John begins the play possessing loyalty, crown, and a healthy nation. He ends possessing and possessed by 'mistempered lords', 'strangely fantasied' subjects, a devalued crown, and a shapeless, rude mass. John begins decisive, healthy, clear-sighted, 'God's wrathful agent' (2.1.87); at the end, 'fear and sad distrust | Govern the motion of a kingly eye' (5.1.46–7), a 'tyrant fever burns' him up and 'Weakness possesseth' him (5.3.14, 17), and he dies 'a clod | And module of confounded royalty' (5.7.57–8).

One way the play links this beginning and these ends, perhaps even the most persuasive way among those it offers, lies in the figurative discourse and unexpressed frameworks for that discourse I have examined here. Language, figures of speech, and latent concepts begin almost casually as common verbal coin and ridiculed conceit. They conclude in a terrible vision of John pieced into bloody footsteps and bloody fingers' ends, ripped up as England's womb and shrivelled as the 'indigest' he has created.

Wills and the Crown of England. In Act 1, the Earl of Essex invites King John to judge 'the strangest controversy' (1.1.44) between Philip Faulconbridge, 'eldest son . . . to Robert Faulconbridge' (1.1.51–2), and Robert Faulconbridge, 'son and heir to that same Faulconbridge' (l. 56). To an Elizabethan audience, the paradox would be plain: primogeniture, the eldest son's right to inherit his father's real property, makes Philip the heir; Robert the younger son adopts the legal formula, 'son and heir', that should describe Philip. The King assumes that old Sir Robert fathered a bastard:

> Is that [Philip] the elder, and art thou [Robert] the heir?
> You came not of one mother then, it seems.
>
> (ll. 57–8)

Legally the child of no one, a bastard could not inherit; should Robert succeed in having Philip declared illegitimate, the elder son's inheritance would fall to the younger. When Philip asserts that it is 'well known' that both are Lady Faulconbridge's sons, the King is again puzzled: 'Why, being younger born, | Doth he lay claim to thine inheritance?' (ll. 71–2).[1] Despite Robert's claim that Philip is a bastard, John knows the law is clear—'your brother is legitimate; | Your father's wife did after wedlock bear him' (ll. 116–17)—and he overrides Robert's protests:

> . . . let me have what is mine,
> My father's land, as was my father's will.
>
> (ll. 114–15)

> Shall then my father's will be of no force
> To dispossess that child which is not his?
>
> (ll. 130–1)[2]

As with so many other disputes in the play, a compromise is found: Robert inherits in the face of all law to the contrary;

[1] In his edn., Robert Smallwood comments, 'the question is redundant . . . King John is obviously unable to keep pace with the Bastard's mental, and verbal, agility' (1.1.71–4n), but John is right to be puzzled, as his later decision and the law concerning legitimacy show. The question is also a way of drawing further attention to the issue of inheritance.

[2] In *Shakespeare's Legal and Political Background* (1967), George W. Keeton finds John's judgement in the illegitimacy conflict 'good law' (p. 127). What appears to be an original note to ll. 130–1 in G. C. Verplanck's otherwise very unoriginal edn., *Shakespeare's Plays*, 3 vols. (New York, 1847), briefly remarks the historical legal changes in the disposition of real property by will that I discuss here.

Philip becomes an acknowledged bastard of Lady Faulconbridge and Richard Coeur-de-Lion.

Besides raising the issue of bastardy, so frequently emphasized in Philip Faulconbridge–Richard Plantagenet's later speeches, this dispute draws attention to a man's *will* in disposing of his real property, his land. Primogeniture became settled English law in the 'last years of Henry II',[1] and during the twelfth and thirteenth centuries was joined by another important common-law principle forbidding the testamentary disposition ('devising' in legal jargon) of real property.[2] Alongside these developments arose a compensatory rule that in most circumstances allowed an individual freely to 'alienate' (i.e., sell, give, dispose of) real property during his lifetime. In sum: 'Free alienation without the heir's consent will come in the wake of primogeniture' and 'from the end of the thirteenth century [i.e., the statute *Quia Emptores*, 1290] the law was settled. The ancestor could alienate as he pleased in his lifetime. He could not prevent the heir from inheriting what he had left at his death.'[3] That is, should Philip Faulconbridge insist upon his legally recognized and royally endorsed status as legitimate elder son, old Sir Robert Faulconbridge's *will* is moot.

One further chapter in legal history and one in political history will make the dramatic relevance of these matters clear. Individuals wishing complete freedom to dispose of their real property after their deaths naturally sought loopholes in the apparently rigid laws; one of the most popular, the conveying of land to one party for the 'use' of another, has its roots in the thirteenth century and became widespread.[4] The 'use' effectively permitted a father to bequeath land to the church or to heirs other than the eldest son or his representative in the line of

[1] Frederick Pollock and F. W. Maitland, *The History of English Law Before the Time of Edward I*, 2nd edn., reissued with a new introduction by S. F. C. Milsom, 2 vols. (1898; Cambridge, 1968), ii. 274.

[2] Ibid., ii. 325. Robert Faulconbridge's claim that his father 'Upon his death-bed . . . by will bequeathed | His lands to me' (1.1.109–10) makes his case impossible to sustain: 'the gift of land by a last will stood condemned; not because it infringes any feudal rule . . . but because it is a death-bed gift, wrung from a man in his agony' (Pollock and Maitland, ii. 328).

[3] Ibid., ii. 309 and W. S. Holdsworth, *A History of English Law*, 3rd edn., 7 vols. (Boston, 1923), iii. 76, respectively. My summary omits many distinctions, irrelevant here, among the kinds of 'tenure' in real property.

[4] Pollock and Maitland, ii. 231–2.

descent; it was so widely employed that under Henry VIII the
'Statute of Uses' (1535) was enacted in order to seize monastic
property and to recover various financial benefits that the Crown
had lost through this device. This statute did achieve Henry's
goal of 'securing the estates of the monasteries for the Crown',
but it was so sweepingly worded that 'public opinion compelled
the passing, in the year 1540, of a statute [of Wills] which openly
sanctioned the devise of legal interests' with some exceptions.[1]

Primogeniture brought with it the issue of 'representation in
inheritance', 'the principle which allows the children or remoter
descendants of a dead person to stand in that person's stead'.[2]
King John and Arthur form a clear historical case for the
application of these twinned principles, and English law would
regularly have preferred the nephew's claim before the uncle's;
indeed, during the reign of John's son, Henry III, the so-called
casus Regis—the precedent set by John's coronation and reign—
led the courts to withhold judgement in ordinary, everyday legal
conflicts between an uncle and a nephew over inheritance.[3]
Politically sensitive instances of uncle–nephew controversies
would have been known to Elizabethan students of dynastic
inheritance and to London theatre-goers alike. Jean Bodin noted
that the situation was rare in royal families—it arose 'in the
space of five or six hundred years . . . once in England, once in
Castile, twice in Portugal, and once in Sicily'; in his enormously
influential *Les six livres de la république* (Paris, 1576), Bodin none
the less concluded: 'let the sentence as well of the ancient as of
the later lawyers prevail for the nephew against the uncle'.[4] And

[1] Edward Jenks, *A Short History of English Law*, 6th edn. (1949), pp. 100
and 104–5. For a summary of Tudor–Stuart land law and its confusions, see
B. Coward, 'Disputed Inheritances: Some Difficulties of the Nobility in the Late
Sixteenth and Early Seventeenth Centuries', *Bulletin of the Institute of Historical
Research*, 44 (1971), 194–215; pp. 195–7.
[2] Pollock and Maitland, ii. 283.
[3] Ibid., ii. 284–5; 'from the Edwardian [i.e., Edward I] law books the *casus
Regis* had disappeared. The nephew can now recover the land from the
uncle . . .' (ibid., ii. 286).
[4] Jean Bodin, *The Six Books of a Commonweale*, trans. Richard Knolles (1606),
vi. 5, p. 740; the book also appeared in Latin (1586). The question of Elizabeth's
successor, if no other, would have made the book pertinent in late Tudor England;
for the popularity and early influence of Bodin in English political thought in the
late sixteenth and seventeenth centuries, see Ulrike Krautheim, *Die Souveränitäts-
konzeption in den englischen Verfassungskonflikten des 17. Jahrhunderts: Eine Studie
zur Rezeption der Lehre Bodins . . .* (Frankfurt am Main, 1977), pp. 44–69.

sometime in the mid-1590s Shakespeare himself dramatized a nephew's regular inheritance of the Crown: Richard II succeeded Edward III as the son of his grandfather's eldest son, the Black Prince, although others of Edward's sons, the 'seven vials' of Edward's 'sacred blood' (*Richard II* 1.2.12) who are Richard's uncles, were alive.[1]

According to Holinshed, John's claim rested with Richard I's will, or rather, his 'testament':

he [Richard] ordained his testament, or rather reformed and added sundry things unto the same which before he had made, at the time of his going forth towards the holy land. . . . Unto his brother John he assigned the crown of England, and all other his lands and dominions, causing the nobles there present [at his deathbed] to swear fealty unto him.[2]

Since *testament* (the disposition of chattels, of moveable property) and *will* (the disposition of real property) were still carefully distinguished terms, Holinshed's words acknowledge that contemporary Elizabethan law on 'willing' real property was in some confusion; he implies that Richard I treated England as his personal property to be disposed of by testament, rather than as real property to be inherited through primogeniture and the principle of representation. In *King John*, Queen Eleanor and Constance first attempt to impeach their sons' respective claims through asserting each other's infidelity and, respectively, John's and Arthur's illegitimacy (2.1.122–33); that is, they each retrace Robert Faulconbridge's eventually successful tack in his claim against Philip. In Shakespeare's carefully allusive treatment, Eleanor then refers to Richard I's bequest: 'I can produce | A will that bars the title of thy son' (2.1.191–2).

A *will* that bequeaths sovereignty would have been especially congenial to Shakespeare's understanding of royal succession:

Shakespeare's conception of the right to rule England is fundamentally

[1] By the principles of primogeniture and representation, Roger Mortimer had the superior claim to succeed Richard II, as the King himself is reported to have stipulated (*1 Henry IV* 1.3.143–5); since Roger died before Richard, his claim descended to his eldest son, Edmund, who traces it at length in *1 Henry VI* 2.5.63–92.

[2] Holinshed, 155b; O4–156a; O4^v. On his departure for the Holy Land in 1190, Richard 'named (as some suppose) his nephew Arthur, the son of his brother Geoffrey duke of Bretagne, to be his successor in the kingdom' (ibid., 122b; L5^v); note Holinshed's careful parenthesis.

dynastic. The Crown to him descends in the manner of real property, and he has best claim who can prove priority of descent. All others are usurpers. This is a view reflected in all the Histories.[1]

Whatever Shakespeare's private convictions, this view had significant consequences for his history plays and their contemporary appeal: it permitted a concise, logical, and affirmatively moral dramatic pattern for those plays, and it cohered both with Elizabeth's own claim on the Crown and with the claims of others to succeed her. Most serious sixteenth-century claims to the English throne depended upon the three Acts of Succession passed in Henry VIII's reign and upon his last will and testament. The second Act of Succession (1536) had legally bastardized Elizabeth in a clause that was never rescinded (as Catholic polemicists regularly noted), while the third Act (1543) stipulated that the Crown should devolve first through Henry's male and then through his female offspring if any one died without heirs (as all three, Edward, Mary, and Elizabeth, did). This Act gave Henry the authority to 'limit and appoint' the further succession 'by his letters patents . . . or by his last will in writing, signed with his Majesty's hand' (35 Henry VIII, c. 1), and his will named the heirs of his younger sister, Mary, Duchess of Suffolk, to succeed the heirs of his body.[2] This last clause contravened customary practice by ignoring descendants of Henry's elder sister, Margaret, Queen of Scots. Her heirs included Mary, Queen of Scots, and her son, James VI of Scotland, who eventually succeeded Elizabeth in despite of her father's will.[3]

Even during Henry's reign there were serious objections to his bequeathing the Crown by will—it was one of the complaints raised by Robert Aske, a leader of the Pilgrimage of Grace—

[1] Keeton, p. 249; see also p. 253 and the comment on *2 Henry VI* 1.3 at pp. 256–7. Keeton's Chapter 17, 'The Title to the Crown in the Histories', is of great interest.

[2] A full text of Henry's will appears in Thomas Rymer, comp., *Foedera*, 20 vols. (1704–32), xv. 110–17; for excerpts from this and many other relevant documents, see Mortimer Levine, *Tudor Dynastic Problems 1460–1571* (1973), pp. 125–84.

[3] On Henry's will and its Elizabethan and Jacobean ramifications, see Mortimer Levine, *The Early Elizabethan Succession Question* (Stanford, California, 1966), pp. 147–62 and Joel Hurstfield, 'The Succession Struggle in late Elizabethan England' in S. T. Bindoff *et al.*, eds., *Elizabethan Government and Society* (1961), pp. 369–96; pp. 372–5. For contemporary attitudes toward James VI's claim, see H. G. Stafford, *James VI of Scotland and the Throne of England* (New York, 1940).

and a later, pro-Stuart writer called it 'that extravagant and unparalleled liberty of appointing his successor by will and testament'.[1] While Elizabeth evidently considered her father's will valid, many writers attacked its authenticity or its legality.[2] Distressed by Parliamentary debate over the succession early in her reign, Elizabeth forbade public, and especially published, discussion of her title and her successor, but numerous manuscripts and a few printed pamphlets did circulate.[3] She could not control foreign presses as she did native ones. The exiled English Jesuit Robert Parsons and others, writing as 'R. Doleman', published the most comprehensive treatment, *A Conference concerning the next Succession* ('N.' [Antwerp], 1594 [1595]); this work refuted James's claim and settled on the Spanish Infanta as having the best title. English and Scottish writers generally scoffed at the Infanta's pretensions. They were forced, however, to rebut Parsons's historical examples, and chief among the English ones were John and Henry IV. Contradicting the Tudor chroniclers, many disputants were now driven to regard John as a usurper like Bolingbroke, to emphasize Richard I's original appointment of Arthur as successor, and to dismiss or ignore Richard's later will, the only 'possible precedent' for Henry VIII's.[4]

In March 1603, the customary pattern of dynastic succession

[1] See, respectively, Levine, *Problems*, pp. 68–9 and 157–8 (Aske's statement), and Thomas Craig, *The Right of Succession to the Kingdom of England* (1603), trans. J[ames]. G[atherer]. (1703), p. 131. On the contemporary and later political significance of objections to the Succession Acts, see in part, G. R. Elton, 'Politics and the Pilgrimage of Grace' (1980), reprinted in his *Studies in Tudor and Stuart Politics and Government*, 3 vols. (Cambridge, 1974–83), iii. 183–215; pp. 202, 205–6, 212–15.

[2] Elizabeth's view is hypothesized by Levine, *Problems*, p. 113. Mid-century debate over the will is summarized in Levine, *Succession*, pp. 151–9; later Elizabethan attacks on the will appear in: Craig, *Right of Succession*, pp. 343–5; Peter Wentworth, *A Pithy Exhortation . . . whereunto is added a Discourse . . . of the true and lawful successor* [written 1595] (1598), M1ᵛ–M2; [Henry Constable], *A Discovery of a Counterfeit Conference* (Collen [i.e., Paris?], 1600).

[3] See, respectively, Levine, *Succession*, pp. 89–98 and Stafford, pp. 323–4. The preface to John Hayward's *An Answer to the First Part of a certain Conference . . .* (1603), dedicated to James I, complains of 'the nimble ear which lately was borne to the touch of this string [i.e., the succession]' (A3 in the first of two signatures so signed).

[4] Levine, *Succession*, p. 32. For attacks on John, see, among many: John Leslie, *A Treatise touching the right . . . of . . . Mary, Queen of Scotland* ([Rouen,] 1584), D6 and E7ᵛ–E8ᵛ; Hayward, *An Answer*, S2ᵛ–S3; Craig, *Right of Succession*, pp. 179 and 281–2; John Harington, *A Tract on the Succession* (1602), ed. Clements R. Markham (1880), p. 59.

prevailed, but from the beginning to the end of Elizabeth's reign, loyal subjects and foreign controversialists debated her title and that of her rivals. Throughout the debate, King John and his reign were an explicit or implicit issue. Dramatizing that reign, Shakespeare largely forwent, as the author of *The Troublesome Reign of King John* did not, the obviously dramatic conflict with Rome because the dynastic struggle itself guaranteed contemporary attention. That struggle recalled the Tudor claim in general, it recalled the claim of Mary, Queen of Scots in particular, and it was most germane to an overriding intellectual and emotional preoccupation of the 1590s, the question of Elizabeth's successor.[1]

Legal and political history in the twelfth and sixteenth centuries clarify Shakespeare's treatment of his subject, and they make the conflict between Robert and Philip Faulconbridge a complex and impressive overture to the dynastic struggle between John and Arthur rather than a simple thematic analogy between Philip's illegitimacy and John's 'usurpation'.[2] Indeed, finding dramatic tension in John's conflict with Arthur was a more delicate problem than critics sometimes allow: analogies between the succession of Arthur and of Richard II recommend Arthur's claim; analogies between the wills of Richard I and Henry VIII recommend John's. Moreover, if the play overstressed Richard's will (and therefore John's claim), it might be understood as opposing the contemporary Stuart pretension to the English throne, denied by Henry VIII's will. And that position was a very dangerous one in the 1590s: as sternly as Elizabeth suppressed the succession debate, she was equally ambivalent, at least publicly, toward James's hopes.

[1] For an early attempt to find political topicality in *King John*, see Richard Simpson, 'The Politics of Shakspere's Historical Plays', *The New Shakspere Society's Transactions* (1874), 396–441; pp. 397–406. After listing eight major discrepancies between the chronicles and Shakespeare's play, Simpson asserts, 'All the changes seem made with a view to the controversy on the title to the crown. This was the standing trouble of Elizabeth's reign. Her own title was controverted, first because she was illegitimate, next because she was excommunicate' (p. 402). Campbell's chapter on *King John* develops Simpson's position in detail.

[2] See, e.g., Peter Saccio, *Shakespeare's English Kings: History, Chronicle, and Drama* (New York, 1977), p. 203: 'Illegitimacy, indeed, is a central idea in *King John*. Not only does it appear in the form of illegitimate rule (usurpation), but also as illegitimate birth (bastardy), and illegitimate honor (boastful pretensions).' Earlier, Saccio finds that 'Shakespeare's John is flatly a usurper', while noting 'Most Tudor historians do not question the legitimacy of John's crown' (p. 202).

Shakespeare responds with factual distortion and verbal obfuscation: Arthur is made unhistorically young, to enforce the dangers of a child-king; Eleanor is made melodramatically conscious that her son's claim is 'strong possession much more than . . . right' (1.1.40); Arthur is sometimes presented as Richard I's son rather than his nephew in order to simplify and exaggerate the issue of primogeniture (2.1.6 and 13); claims that John is a 'usurper' are placed in the mouths of national enemies, the French (e.g., 2.1.9), or of Constance, whose personal motive is manifest; the Roman Church, which was in fact continuously involved in the Anglo-French political disputes, is represented as seeking only that John agree to Stephen Langton's election as Archbishop of Canterbury.

Monarchs, Parents, and the Bastard. Patrilineal inheritance of the Crown and the commonplace analogy between monarch and parent—the English Parliament and James VI of Scotland, for instance, both referred to Elizabeth as 'mother'—mean that accession to the throne and succession of parents and children have deep metaphorical links.[1] In the histories, Shakespeare quite naturally and conventionally treats political and familial issues as twins: the second tetralogy is as plainly organized in terms of fathers and sons as it is in terms of usurpation, rebellion, and legitimate succession.[2] *King John* also takes up these forms of thought, but the presence of three mothers—Eleanor, Lady Faulconbridge, Constance—and of a peculiarly freakish 'son'— the Bastard—makes the play unique among the histories.[3]

---

[1] As the expression *Pater patriae* testifies, the parent–monarch, family–state equation is classical and might have been known to Shakespeare and his audience through Seneca (*Epistles* 47 and 90), Elyot (*The Governor*, 2.4), Hooker (*Laws of Ecclesiastical Polity*, 1.10.4), or Bodin (*Six Books of the Commonweal*, 1.5). See also Gordon J. Schochet, 'Patriarchalism, Politics and Mass Attitudes in Stuart England', *Historical Journal*, 12 (1969), 413–41, and the same author's *Patriarchalism in Political Thought* (Oxford, 1975), Chapters 2 and 3.

[2] For this view of *1* and *2 Henry IV*, see John Dover Wilson, *The Fortunes of Falstaff* (Cambridge, 1943), Chapters 2 and 4, and A. R. Humphreys, ed., *Henry IV, Part 1*, Arden Shakespeare (1960), pp. xlvi–xlix; the chapter devoted to *King John* in Robert B. Pierce's *Shakespeare's History Plays: The Family and the State* ([Athens, Ohio], 1971) explores the metaphorical connection through studying the figurative language and styles of speech in the play.

[3] Female characters are intermittently important as mothers in the first tetralogy, but no such separation between maternal and other dramatically important qualities can be drawn for the three adult female characters in *King John*.

The French royal family establishes the expected pattern in the play's first half. King Philip dominates his country's affairs and arranges an obedient son's expedient marriage. Toward the end of Act 3, however, Philip (quite unhistorically) loses his influence over Louis and vanishes from the play. Another member of the play's older generation, Pandulph, temporarily replaces Philip as Louis's 'surrogate' father, just as Worcester threatens to replace Northumberland as Hotspur's 'father' in *1 Henry IV*. Pandulph's influence is briefer than Philip's. Ashamed at the French defeat before Angers and sceptical of any future victory, rebuked as 'youthful' in mind and 'green . . . and fresh in this old world' (3.4.125, 145), Louis re-enters the play one act later as a mature political manipulator who brushes aside Pandulph's attempts to control him:

> I will not back.
> I am too high-born to be propertied,
> To be a secondary at control . . .
> (5.2.78—80)

Thereafter he makes his own way and his own mistakes. Through rearranging historical facts and redistributing historical emphases, Shakespeare creates a conventional sequence: the royal heir is first dominated by his father, then enters the social and political arena through marriage, submits to the guidance of another older male, and finally emerges as an independent character, striving to achieve a monarchy to rival his now-forgotten father's. The pattern is common in Shakespeare's plays. It may be tragic, if the father's displacement requires regicide, or comic, if the child's maturation into adult sexuality predominates.

Matters are ordered less well in England. Competition for monarchy and independence here cross generational lines more distinctly than in France: Arthur and John strive for the same imperium, and another member of the younger generation—Richard Coeur-de-Lion's illegitimate son—gradually comes to seem that king's most promising successor. Moreover, unlike the French father and son, each English competitor has a mother who appears in the play.[1] Lady Faulconbridge's acknowledged

[1] This symmetry seems to be a chief reason for Lady Faulconbridge's presence: the Bastard's parentage might have been more economically confirmed, though Shakespeare uses the episode to develop the Bastard's breezy self-confidence. Emrys Jones shows how this scene and the larger issues of generation and inheritance

liaison with Coeur-de-Lion puts any mother's fidelity into dramatic question: Constance and Eleanor soon accuse each other of bearing illegitimate sons (2.1.122–33).[1] Of the three, Lady Faulconbridge appears only briefly, but as generations of actresses confirm, Eleanor and especially Constance are exceptionally powerful roles. Eleanor exercises political power and sophisticated calculation through her son, much as Pandulph manoeuvres to do through Louis and later achieves to some degree through John. Less effectively, Constance promotes the political claims of *her* son, and Eleanor at least finds a mirror of her own behaviour in 'ambitious Constance' (1.1.32) who would 'be a queen and check the world' (2.1.123). Outflanked by John, who uses his niece, and by Philip, who uses his son, Constance becomes first the play's political conscience (with the Bastard) and then a mad and terrible figure lamenting the play's indifference to its younger generation.

The cross-currents of affection and self-interest are thoroughly developed in the Constance–Arthur relation, but we are invited to translate them imaginatively to the other principal mother–son relation. Whatever tenderness, whatever sense of human as opposed to political value, there exists between John and Eleanor is expressed once, fleetingly and with great theatrical force. Alone on stage, 'amazed | Under the tide' of bad news, and struggling to regain control of himself and events, John exclaims, 'My mother dead!' (4.2.181). Since Adrien Bonjour's essay on *King John*, it has become a critical commonplace to see John's instigating of Arthur's death in Act 3, Scene 3 as the turning point of the King's fortunes and, indeed, of his ability to rule successfully.[2] Certainly his 'order' and the death that stems from it cost John

in the play anticipate *Hamlet*; see *Scenic Form in Shakespeare* (Oxford, 1971), pp. 99–104.

[1] Kristian Smidt, in *Unconformities in Shakespeare's History Plays* (1982), treats this episode as evidence that Shakespeare abandoned an earlier plan to 'use the theme of bastardy in the main plot' (p. 77); I think the episode has sufficient integrity to meet the legal argument (see above, pp. 54–7) and the metaphorical one. See ibid., pp. 74–8.

[2] Adrien Bonjour, 'The Road to Swinstead Abbey: A Study of the Sense and Structure of *King John*', *ELH*, 18 (1951), 253–74. John's political fortunes, strictly construed, turn when Philip releases his hand in Act 3, Scene 1; see Jay L. Halio, 'Alternative Action: The Tragedy of Missed Opportunities in *King John*', *Hebrew University Studies in Literature and the Arts*, 11 (1983), 254–69, pp. 261–3, and 3.1.192n, below.

any moral standing he might have and perhaps even any claim to a pragmatic royal legitimacy, but the collapse of his ability to rule comes only, and immediately, after news of the death of his mother.

The symmetry between Constance–Arthur and Eleanor–John is not only emotional nor merely sentimental: a single messenger-speech reports the deaths of both women. In the brief dramatic span from the end of Act 3 to the end of Act 4, Scene 2, the play has lost three senior members of its cast—Philip, Constance, Eleanor—and we immediately witness Arthur's death as he tries to escape his uncle (Act 4, Scene 3). Coincidentally, Louis's violence has escaped his father's and Pandulph's control, and the Bastard has plainly begun the maturing of heart and head that will gain him 'the ordering of this present time' (5.1.77). The coiled spring of (masculine) violence—a violence that would first destroy Angers and then debate its ownership, a violence that willingly keeps a wedding feast with slaughtered men—has finally and completely been released from parental or quasi-parental restraint. And that violence sweeps Blanche and Arthur, Philip, Eleanor, and Constance out of the play. Two members of the younger generation have been used and discarded, but with them—almost simultaneously—have gone the elder manipulators,

> and England now is left
> To tug and scramble, and to part by th'teeth
> The unowed interest of proud-swelling state.
> (4.3.145–7)

The play's dramatic economy treats Eleanor and Constance almost as brutally as its political contrivance treats Blanche. No longer needed, all three are dismissed or forgotten. Blanche's fate demonstrates the pragmatism and emotional and moral emptiness of the Anglo-French reconciliation; her silent presence when Pandulph torments Philip's conscience, followed by her passionate and ineffectual claims for peace and some lingering shred of 'honour' (3.1.300 ff.), make Philip's dilemma seem almost as casuistical as Pandulph's speeches. Eleanor and Constance are made of sterner stuff. While they can exchange bawdy insult and misogynistically conceived shrewish rant, each has a less stereotyped role. Whether or not 'conscience' (1.1.42) dictates her advice, Eleanor serves John well as political counsellor (see especially 2.1.469–80) and as a Gertrude- or Lady Macbeth-like smoother of social conflicts (for example, in her early response to the Bastard, or her treatment of Arthur when John arranges his murder). Like Eleanor, Constance has political reasons to advance her son's claims; the same immaturity (exaggerated by Shakespeare) which makes Arthur an unlikely king would make him his mother's pawn were she to gain him the throne. Yet Constance is also the only character directly engaged in the succession conflict who echoes the Bastard's detached and be-mused fascination with the shuttlecock changes of allegiance, the swearing and forswearing, of her allies. Finally abandoned by those allies and stripped of her son, Constance becomes— perhaps inconsistently, but very theatrically—a madwoman, futilely claiming the human cost of political machination:

> I am not mad; I would to God I were,
> For then 'tis like I should forget myself.
> O, if I could, what grief should I forget!
> (3.4.48–50)

Her self-awareness anticipates Gloucester's, if not Lear's, and the similarity emphasizes the power of her claim even as it confirms its hopelessness.

The play's other female character, Lady Faulconbridge, is not treated quite so brusquely by Shakespeare's plot or his politicians. Her son's humorous insensitivity,

> Therefore, good mother,
> To whom am I beholden for these limbs?
> Sir Robert never holp to make this leg
> (1.1.238–40)

and his comic bawdry at her expense,

> Your fault was not your folly;
> Needs must you lay your heart at his dispose,
> Subjected tribute to commanding love,
> Against whose fury and unmatchèd force
> The aweless lion could not wage the fight,
> Nor keep his princely heart from Richard's hand
> (1.1.262–7)

sound uncomfortably like Gloucester's rough and ready account of Edmund's 'making' (*Tragedy of King Lear* 1.1.8 ff.),[1] but Lady Faulconbridge never achieves sufficient dramatic reality to lose the Bastard our affection when he leaps suddenly from country gentry to royal status. The manner of that leap, however, makes the Bastard an extraordinary exception to the patterns of family and state elsewhere in the play.

Given the political and legal importance of patrilineal descent, the Bastard's true parentage confers a metaphorical claim on the Crown, for it links him with Richard I, England's last undoubtedly legitimate king, here presented as a legendary warrior-hero, remembered for boldly taking what he wanted and praised even by his enemies (2.1.2–5). The play's references to Coeur-de-Lion are too few to justify John Danby's claim—'He is the only king Shakespeare knows who is completely without flaw. . . . the perfect Englishman', but Danby rightly stresses the importance of Richard's reputation, the way 'the Bastard re-incarnates, but in a changed time, the virtues of his father' and the 'sanction' that his descent gives 'this new type of man'.[2]

The Bastard receives that sanction and gains admission to high society and royal status only after his paradoxical social condition—actual illegitimacy, legal legitimacy—has been thoroughly analysed.[3] Accepting royal favour and landless prestige, he gives up rural security and ignominy for a chance at martial booty, life at the centre, and a new name. Some at least of Shakespeare's audience would have found the manner in which John dubs Philip Faulconbridge highly unusual:

> From henceforth bear his name whose form thou bearest:
> Kneel thou down Philip, but rise more great;
> Arise Sir Richard and Plantagenet.

> (1.1.160–2)

---

[1] The Bastard behaves less coarsely than Gloucester. Gloucester boasts of Edmund's parentage in his presence, the Bastard questions his mother only after dismissing James Gurney, who was introduced in order to be dismissed, thus 'pointing out the Bastard's delicacy of feeling' (Bonjour, pp. 266–7 n. 28). Emrys Jones examines verbal and structural relations between *King John* and *King Lear* in *Form*, pp. 167–70, 184–6, 193–4.

[2] John F. Danby, *Shakespeare's Doctrine of Nature: A Study of 'King Lear'* (1949), p. 77. Danby places the Bastard in the context of Richard III, Edmund, and the *Henry IV* plays (see pp. 57–101); in *Shakespeare* (1936), J. M. Murry had earlier remarked that Falstaff and Hotspur were 'in the imaginative order . . . the Bastard's direct descendants' (p. 155).

[3] See above, pp. 54–61.

Historical and literary accounts of dubbing ceremonies in Shakespeare's time and for centuries before include a recitation of the new knight's ancestry, just as Philip Faulconbridge's has been recalled in a slightly unusual way.[1] Like Philip Faulconbridge, knights of literary romance sometimes first appear as bumptious, uncouth, or rustic intruders at court, and they are sometimes nameless or only nicknamed until the moment of knighting.[2] Shakespeare's knighting ceremony departs sharply from historical and literary texts, however, when it includes the act of renaming.[3] Naming or renaming reminds us of baptism, or for an adult, the entry into a religious order, and knighting ceremonies had analogies with both: entry into the 'order' of knighthood; a fixed moment of maturation; the young male's entrance into full warrior status.[4] Shakespeare's ceremony accumulates romantic and religious and even anthropological resonances to 'give birth' to the Bastard, whose subsequent soliloquy (1.1.182–216) and conversation with his mother emphasize his new condition, a condition requiring learned, imitative behaviour.[5] That behaviour specifically includes, humorously or otherwise, new techniques of condescension and class discrimination, as well as new techniques of deceit, self-analysis, and self-protection.

---

[1] Contemporary discussions of the dubbing ceremony appear in: William Segar, *The Book of Honour and Arms* (1590), 5.4; the same author's *Honour Military and Civil* (1602), 2.1–3, 7–8, and 11; André Favyn, *The Theater of Honour and Knighthood* (1620), trans. A. M[unday?]. (1623), 1.6; John Selden, *Titles of Honour*, 2nd edn. (1631), 2.5.34–5. For a summary of historical and literary evidence on the dubbing ceremony, see Maurice Keen, *Chivalry* (1984), Chapter 4.

[2] The anonymous man who eventually becomes Sir Gareth is at first contemptuously nicknamed 'Beaumains' in Malory's *Morte*, but must reveal his true lineage upon being dubbed; Spenser's 'Letter to Ralegh' appended to *The Faerie Queene* (1590) describes Redcrosse Knight on his first appearance as 'a tall clownish young man' who 'rested him on the floor, unfit through his rusticity for a better place'. In *Mundus et Infans* (1508?, printed 1522), Mundus renames and reclothes Infans as he ages; when Infans reaches twenty-one, Mundus names him 'Manhood', introduces him to the Seven Deadly Sins, and concludes, 'here I dub thee a knight, | And haunt alway to chivalry' (ll. 199–200 in *Three Late Medieval Morality Plays*, ed. G. A. Lester (1981)).

[3] The renaming also occurs in *The Troublesome Reign*, but the episode is otherwise completely different.   [4] Keen, pp. 14, 66–7, and 71.

[5] In *Two Shakespearean Sequences* (1977), F. W. Brownlow says of the Bastard that 'Like a mythical hero, his birth is mysterious, his behaviour unpredictable; but the mystery is an open secret, the unpredictability predictable' (p. 82). The Bastard's remarks on 'habit', 'device', and 'accoutrement' (1.1.210–11) suggest that he expects a new coat of arms, the visible sign of his new status; for the taking of knighthood and of armorial bearings simultaneously, see Keen, p. 128.

The Bastard erupts into the play as a sourceless, unlocated character. The name by which he is first known does not accurately represent, as names customarily do, genetic relation; his social caste and his behaviour are equally incorrect or misleading. The play's plot-and-character dynamic explains or rationalizes these qualities as 'bastardy', and Philip is also figuratively a bastard:

> this is worshipful society
> And fits the mounting spirit like myself;
> For he is but a bastard to the time
> That doth not smack of observation,
> And so am I whether I smack or no . . .
>   (1.1.205–9)

In other ways, however, bastardy is a superficial, even mechanical, response to Philip's origins, for those origins include the Vice of the moral play and the hints of Raphael Holinshed's *Chronicles*. In the first three acts at least, the Bastard shares a number of characteristics with the Vice: intimacy with the audience; lengthy comic and satiric monologues; an individual verse form used by no other speaker; a joyful anarchism; indifference to rank and other social conventions; association with the devil (2.1.135 ff. and 4.3.95, 100).[1] Morality plays sometimes show the Vice, once he is defeated, becoming a sombre rather than a comic voice.[2] Faulconbridge also changes, as the French invasion proceeds and John increasingly fails to control or react to events. Deeper involvement with the political action requires a different and more maturely responsible character. The Bastard moves toward the action's centre by degrees—first as John's agent in sacking the monasteries and arresting Peter of Pomfret, then as emissary to the rebel lords—but a quite new 'character' appears when he foresees the consequences of Arthur's

---

[1] Julia C. Van de Water seems first to have associated the Bastard with the Vice; see 'The Bastard in *King John*', *SQ*, 11 (1960), 137–46; pp. 141 and 143. Jones, *Form*, pp. 240–1, mentions the Bastard's Vice descent in the context of his similarities to Enobarbus. On the dramaturgical uses of the Vice in post-morality drama, see my 'Early Shakespearian Tragedy and its Contemporary Context: Cause and Emotion in *Titus Andronicus*, *Richard III*, and *The Rape of Lucrece*', in *Shakespearian Tragedy*, ed. D. J. Palmer and Malcolm Bradbury, Stratford-upon-Avon Studies, 20 (1984), 96–128; pp. 109–10.

[2] For example, John Pickering, *Horestes* (1567), Malone Society Reprint prepared by Daniel Seltzer (Oxford, 1962), ll. 1232–42, 1254–60.

4. An Elizabethan three-farthing piece, one of the several coins that place a Tudor rose 'behind the ear' of the Queen's profile. See *King John* 1.1.142–3.

death (4.3.140–59) and then receives command of the English war effort: 'Have thou the ordering of this present time' (5.1.77).

These changes owe most, perhaps, to the needs of Shakespeare's plot, but the Bastard is also a dramatist's response to the chaos of motivation in Holinshed's account of the reign. Holinshed and Arthur Fleming, who made several additions to the *Chronicles* for the 1587 edition, provide neither a clear interpretation of John nor an unambiguous account of Arthur's death, a central event in the chronicle as it is in Shakespeare's play.[1] Noting the 'dizzying concentration of contrary evaluations and responses' in this part of the *Chronicles*, Stephen Booth finds that while Shakespeare simplified events and John's 'many moral identities', the play makes 'the events . . . as difficult to think about comfortably as those' in the chronicle. Booth concludes that Shakespeare 'seems to be trying to do to his audience what the *Chronicles* do to their reader. He succeeds, and the play therefore inevitably fails.'[2] Whether or not *King John* fails and if so for this reason, the Bastard, virtually unhistorical, is Shakespeare's response to the problem of interpreting history. An outsider to many of the play's overt concerns—law, family, politics—he embodies the

[1] For the inconclusive account of Arthur's death and its perpetrators, see Holinshed 165a–b; P3 (partly quoted at 3.3.66n, below).

[2] Stephen Booth, *The Book Called Holinshed's Chronicles* (San Francisco, 1969), pp. 78–9.

5. *King John*, Act 3, Scene 1, Stratford-upon-Avon, 1957 (directed by Douglas Seale); King John (Robert Harris) formally clasps the hand of King Philip (Cyril Luckham), stage left, in token of their new amity.

playwright's own practical need for an analytical consciousness and offers a focus for unifying disparate, uninterpreted events.[1]

The conflict over Angers in Act 2 illustrates the Bastard's amphibious, mediating role. For the only time in the play, a group of more or less common folk who have no interest vested with any single royal claimant but only in 'The King of England, when we know the King' (2.1.363) confront, but cannot determine, the sovereign competition. Their situation and their indecision make 'the walled town in France . . . an emblem of England itself'.[2] Those walls have, however, been described 'as a waist doth girdle you [the citizens] about' (2.1.217), and other metaphors establish the conventional analogy, common in Petrarchan love-poetry and prominent in *The Rape of Lucrece*, between the city and a woman's body (see especially 2.1.208–25). After an indecisive battle and the citizens' continued reluctance to choose

[1] Emrys Jones finds Faulconbridge a 'folk hero' and a 'spectator-surrogate' through whose 'responses the true meaning of the play is mediated to us'; see *The Origins of Shakespeare* (Oxford, 1977), pp. 244, 252, 246.

[2] Philip Edwards, *Threshold of a Nation: A Study in English and Irish Drama* (Cambridge, 1979), p. 117.

sides, Faulconbridge persuades John and Philip to follow his 'wild counsel' (2.1.395), the resolutely mad suggestion that the two Kings unite to destroy Angers before deciding who owns the city. Figuratively, then, the French and English forces agree to 'rape' Angers, just as Philip had earlier described John's usurpation as 'a rape | Upon the maiden virtue of the crown' (2.1.97–8), and Hubert will later compare Arthur's blood with that of a ruptured maidenhead (4.2.252–3). When Angers is saved through the sacrifice of Blanche to make a political–sexual alliance between France and England, when England is insistently personified as a woman and mother (see, for instance, 5.2.25–9, 33–6, 151–3), the metaphorical equation is complete.[1] Arthur, Blanche, Angers, England do not matter in themselves; they are pretexts— for violence, or political manipulation, or both. All this the Bastard instigates and decries. The behaviour of the Kings and their followers is so inconsistent, so unprincipled, that they can be persuaded to any contradiction and, so persuaded, condemned. The Bastard's fine concluding soliloquy (2.1.562 ff.) arraigns Philip and John as self-interested liars and treats their 'mad composition' as the equivalent of his own earlier 'wild counsel' that smacked 'something of the policy'. There are no victors before Angers, only losers, even Blanche, 'Who having no external thing to lose | But the word "maid" ', loses that, and Arthur, who loses his 'title in the whole' of England (2.1.572–3, 563).

  The Bastard is both a reader of the text of history and part of that text. He mediates between generations and between genders; he incorporates values, aims, desires, and qualities that separately define other characters in the play. We see his similarity with Arthur when his paternity is established by the very means, bodily appearance (1.1.85–90), that fail to establish Arthur's right to the throne (2.1.99–103); we see his similarity to Arthur and to Richard when John's mother claims him for her own grandson and follower (1.1.168, 148–9). He is the sole member of the play's younger generation who is both loyal to and critical of its parental generation. Initially, he represents King John (in sacking the church and placating the English noblemen, for

[1] Noting this personification of England in *Shakespeare's Imagery and What It Tells Us* (Cambridge, 1935), p. 247, Caroline Spurgeon cites its appearance in *Richard II* 2.3.[91–3] and 3.3.96[–7].

example), but gradually he comes to replace John in the military conflict, 'pretends', in fact, 'that his own stirring eloquence is an index of John's continued strength'.[1] Espousing England's cause in Act 4, Scene 3, he becomes Arthur's surrogate, a royal claimant unknown to history and therefore 'safe', who eventually proclaims his own and Arthur's replacement, a prince unmentioned until the play's final scene, a 'sweet self' to 'put on | The lineal state and glory of the land' (5.7.101–2). The Bastard's voice is a critical and subversive one like Constance's or Blanche's, and his character an old–young, legal–illegal, royal–common, male–female oxymoron.[2] He is Shakespeare's response to the problems of dramatizing chronicle history; he is, in many ways, Shakespeare's representative.

Patterns of Action in 'King John'. Studies that locate the play's political conflicts in the characters claim the 'plot of *King John* is built around the question of who should be King of England' and discuss the identity of the 'hero'.[3] This analysis produces an X-shaped, or chiastic, pattern similar to that in *Richard II*: like Richard, King John declines; like Bolingbroke, the Bastard rises.[4] John loses political sensitivity and his earlier decisiveness, and he decays first into physical illness and then into a near-hallucinatory frenzy. By keeping the Bastard separate from the plot to kill Arthur and by not dramatizing his sacking of the church, Shakespeare holds him aloof from John's destruction until the end of Act 4. The Bastard's summary speeches, which so frequently mark stages in the action (1.1.180 ff., 1.1.259 ff., 2.1.562 ff., 4.3.139 ff., 5.7.110 ff.), show how the character is changed from a witty, detached, even self-interested commentator into an increasingly thoughtful participant in, and eventually a major director of, the political action.[5]

As I have argued in the preceding section, the play's generations

---

[1] Edwards, p. 121.

[2] In 'Anti-Historians: Women's Roles in Shakespeare's Histories', *Theatre Journal*, 37 (1985), 329–44, Phyllis Rackin examines the 'subversive' power of female characters in *1 Henry VI* and (pp. 336 ff.) in *King John* very illuminatingly.

[3] See, respectively, William H. Matchett, 'Richard's Divided Heritage in *King John*', *Essays in Criticism*, 12 (1962), 231–53; p. 231, and Bonjour, pp. 255–8 *et passim*.

[4] Bonjour analyses this pattern, without the analogy with *Richard II*.

[5] Alexander Leggatt discusses these changes fully in 'Dramatic Perspective in *King John*', *English Studies in Canada*, 3 (1977), 1–17.

are also formally symmetrical: an older group of parents and politicians rather abruptly yields to younger characters about mid-way through the play, leaving only Pandulph and John of the original elder group. Authority melts from both. Although he appears in the first two scenes of Act 5 and is mentioned as having arranged the French withdrawal in the last scene, Pandulph's policies have earlier failed and his influence over events has all but vanished. Paradoxically, Shakespeare demonstrates how politically ineffectual the play's most inflammatory event, John's submission to the Pope in Act 5, Scene 1, really is. A new group representing institutional authority rises to replace the old: John's rebellious noblemen. Militarily, they hold the balance between John and the invading French; we are led to believe, certainly the Bastard believes, that the French are still the stronger force even at the play's end.

The nobles are thus central to a historical or literal 'shape' in the play, the pattern of competing armies, the answer to an almost constant question in the histories, 'Who is winning?' Like others, the nobles announce a stake in the chaos of competing moral and political positions. Unlike Constance or Philip or Eleanor or Pandulph, however, they represent themselves as voicing the populace's anxieties and doubts.[1] Salisbury eventually makes them avengers of Arthur's death:

> It is the shameful work of Hubert's hand,
> The practice and the purpose of the King—
> From whose obedience I forbid my soul,
> Kneeling before this ruin of sweet life,
> And breathing to his breathless excellence
> The incense of a vow, a holy vow,
> Never to taste the pleasures of the world,
> Never to be infected with delight,
> Nor conversant with ease and idleness,
> Till I have set a glory to this hand
> By giving it the worship of revenge.
>
> (4.3.62—72)

Despite this vow and Salisbury's magniloquent lament that he and his fellows should ever be forced to 'step after a stranger' (5.2.8–39), the English nobles' motives are very obscure. The issue is whether they have already decided to join Louis and

[1] See above, pp. 48–53.

simply seize Arthur's death as a pretext or whether their moral
revulsion leads them to prefer disclaiming infanticide to remaining
loyal. Are they like the barons of Marlowe's *Edward II*, who
expressly admit they object to Gaveston as an excuse for withdraw-
ing their allegiance, or are they 'in a terrible dilemma . . . good
men rebelling against an erring monarch for a righteous reason,
yet in so doing putting themselves in the wrong'?[1] The answer,
if there is one, has large consequences for our views of the
'immoral' John and the 'loyal' Bastard and for our estimate of
the play's pattern and its political content.

Believing Arthur dead, the noblemen angrily depart to 'find
th'inheritance of this poor child, | His little kingdom of a forcèd
grave' (4.2.97–8). We then hear Hubert report to John that
Arthur still lives (4.2.249 ff.), and soon thereafter we see his
death while trying to escape (4.3.1–10). The English lords enter
conversing:

> SALISBURY
>
> Lords, I will meet him at Saint Edmundsbury.
> It is our safety, and we must embrace
> This gentle offer of the perilous time.
>
> PEMBROKE
>
> Who brought that letter from the Cardinal?
>
> SALISBURY
>
> The Count Melun, a noble lord of France,
> Whose private with me of the Dauphin's love
> Is much more general than these lines import.
>
> BIGOT
>
> Tomorrow morning let us meet him then.
>
> SALISBURY
>
> Or rather then set forward, for 'twill be
> Two long days' journey, lords, or ere we meet.
>
> (4.3.11–20)

This exchange is ambiguous: to whom does Salisbury initially
refer, Pandulph or Louis or even Melun? What is the 'gentle
offer'? Has Salisbury or have all the nobles now decided not to
seek Arthur's grave, but to 'set forward' and meet 'him' at St.
Edmundsbury? Since the Bastard's greeting—'Once more today
well met, distempered lords' (4.3.21)—establishes that this
conversation takes place on the same day as Act 4, Scene 2,

---

[1] Bullough, iv. 21.

James L. Calderwood believes Salisbury has negotiated his treason with Louis before finding Arthur's body, perhaps even before begging Arthur's release in Act 4, Scene 2:

Either the nobles have been in communication with the Dauphin for some time then, or Melun's delivery of the letter to Salisbury represents Lewis' first overture. If the former is true, the nobles clearly were traitorous even before their criticism of John in scene 2, and if the latter is true, Lewis must have had some prior indication of their willingness to cooperate, else why send Melun to these particular nobles?[1]

The final question is over-naturalistic: Shakespeare had a restricted number of actors to serve as 'English lords', and he is not especially consistent in naming them or careful in differentiating among them.[2] If this letter represents 'Lewis' first overture' (as Pembroke's question and Salisbury's eagerness to inflate the French offer suggest), then the scene may be no more and no less than a coincidence between honourable distaste for John's crime and a welcome offer of seeming security. In short, it may be a version of the compromise worked out before Angers, where self-interest and superficially honourable conduct were also joined. Objecting that Calderwood combines 'a behind-the-scene analysis and . . . a rather naive approach to Shakespearean dramatic time-schemes', J. L. Simmons argues that 'Shakespeare gives us English noblemen motivated by the simplest moral feeling of revulsion from evil. There is no commodity in their action; they have nothing to gain.'[3] Shakespeare's time-schemes are generally synchronized with the play's forward movement, and it is also true, as Simmons points out, that only the nobles' revolt makes Arthur's death politically significant, and that they thereby contribute to what seems to have been a master-aim of the play.

When the dying Melun reveals Louis's plan to kill the English rebels as soon as their usefulness is over (5.4.10–48), they are shamed (and frightened) into renewed loyalty. This shame seems to be the reciprocal of an at least partly honourable anger: Melun's 'treason' teaches them something about their own, and once they return 'to our great King John' (5.4.57), the national

---

[1] James L. Calderwood, 'Commodity and Honour in *King John*', *University of Toronto Quarterly*, 29 (1959–60), 341–56; pp. 345–6; Matchett takes the same view ('Heritage', pp. 245–6).   [2] See above, pp. 22–5.

[3] Simmons, p. 67; he points out that both Holinshed and *The Troublesome Reign* attack the nobles as self-interested traitors.

danger almost magically evaporates.[1] My own view is that the nobles act from a mixture of honest anger at John's actions and plain self-interest, for the play often shows how seemingly opposite motives coincide, or appear to coincide, how peace-making before Angers is selfish and dishonourable and how loyalty demands a high ethical price from the Bastard at the end of Act 4, Scene 3. Finally, Shakespeare would also have every reason to make the lords' behaviour as ambiguous as possible: later acting texts take his obscurity the next step into voluntary (?) self-censorship and cut many of the references to native rebellion.[2]

Historical authority for the lords' defection comes from accounts of the events leading up to Magna Carta (1215) and the French invasion (1216), but Shakespeare telescopes this late period of John's reign with the much earlier period of the Battle of Mirabeau (Shakespeare's 'Angers') in 1202 and Arthur's death in 1203. Scenes 2 and 3 of Act 4 jumble events occurring over more than a decade and link the two epochs Shakespeare chose to dramatize. This function partly accounts for the emotional and theatrical interest of the scenes, because the playwright's resources are stretched and tingling as he welds drama to history. Shakespeare's factual material falls into two parts (almost 'halves'), and those two parts parallel other binary divisions: John triumphant and the Bastard detached in the first part, John indecisive and the Bastard confident in the second, for example, or domination by the older generation in the first and by the younger in the second, or female characters in the first, no female characters in the second, or lords loyal in the first part and disloyal in the second. Each division occurs or is announced or culminates in these two scenes, which might also be imagined as the 'crossing' of the chiastic structures I have already mentioned.[3]

Joining the two parts of the play's action may have posed dramaturgical problems, but the beginning did not. Isolated chronologically among Shakespeare's histories, *King John* has a theatrical beginning that does not, and need not, link the play to earlier events: 'Nothing essential has gone before; the very

---

[1] Jones, *Origins*, p. 257, ingeniously claims that Melun's 'love' for Hubert (5.4.41) makes the nobles understand John was not responsible for Arthur's death.

[2] See below, pp. 82–4.

[3] For other evidence that Shakespeare disposed 'his somewhat intractable material in two unequal parts', see Jones, *Form*, pp. 83–4.

opening of the play is the opening of a state occasion.'[1] Although
we first see John receiving an embassy from France, we may
easily imagine that his coronation as Richard I's successor has
only recently occurred; a new reign begins, and we watch how
the new King will handle his first crisis.[2] Origins are easier to
define, it seems, than closure. The play's conclusion is much less
emphatic, partly because Shakespeare fulfils the title's promise
(*The Life and Death* . . .) by ending with John's death rather than
the Treaty of Lambeth, which stipulated the French withdrawal
from England, and partly because he almost suppresses Prince
Henry's existence and keeps the psychological focus on the
unhistorical Bastard.

'Is Prince Henry a convenience of art, or another product of
the Bastard's extraordinary skill in creating a centre of loyalty
out of nothing?'[3] These are not exclusive questions, nor the only
ones prompted by the play's end, but they underscore how
completely our sense of closure depends upon the artistry and
manipulation of Shakespeare and of his representative, the
Bastard. Since the Bastard never existed, or never existed in this
hyperbolic form, only his rhetoric, not his deeds, can conclude
the play's historical action. As it is, Shakespeare's divided
allegiance to historical fact and dramatic reality produces a
curious hitch at the play's end, when the Bastard pursues his
earlier warmongering:

> instantly return with me again
> To push destruction and perpetual shame
> Out of the weak door of our fainting land.
> Straight let us seek, or straight we shall be sought;
> The Dauphin rages at our very heels.
>
> (5.7.76–80)

Salisbury intervenes as a slightly inaccurate Holinshed to draw
the play back toward its historical sources:

> It seems you know not, then, so much as we.
> The Cardinal Pandulph is within at rest,
> Who half an hour since came from the Dauphin,

---

[1] Holmes, p. 141. Virginia Mason Vaughan examines *K. John*'s relation to the
other histories in 'Between Tetralogies: *King John* as Transition', *SQ*, 35 (1984),
407–20.

[2] *1 Henry IV* and *Henry V*, for example, have similar opening scenes.

[3] Edwards, p. 121. The future Henry VII is similarly withheld from our view
until the last act of the first tetralogy.

> And brings from him such offers of our peace
> As we with honour and respect may take,
> With purpose presently to leave this war. . . .
> Nay, 'tis in a manner done already,
> For many carriages he hath dispatched
> To the seaside and put his cause and quarrel
> To the disposing of the Cardinal . . .
>
> (5.7.81–6, 89–92)

Dramatic invention and historical fact collide, and the Bastard looks a little silly. The further Shakespeare imposes the Bastard upon the plot of history, the more noticeable will be the discrepancies. However magnificent as patriotic appeal, the Bastard's final speech seals no final event; it 'is not evasive, and not ironic; but the last line is a conditional clause whose fulfilment the rest of the play and the rest of the Histories show to be pretty well impossible'.[1] The conclusion is also inconclusive because it reproduces with differences the political situation at the start: 'The Bastard, with his now proven political abilities, faces a child-king in circumstances little different from those that must have confronted John in the undramatized time prior to the play's opening.'[2]

The action of *King John* exhibits both chiastic and two-part patterns; it has a direct, strong opening, a complex transition between its two parts, and a conclusion mingling signs of finality with disturbing hints of a return to the *status quo ante* and an unspoken promise of the troubles to come in Henry III's reign. These patterns have unsettled audiences and critics; one critic supposes the confusion deliberate, another arraigns Shakespeare of boredom, indecision, and carelessness, another portrays him as searching for a 'modern' perspective on both his medieval source material and Elizabethan political beliefs and institutions.[3]

---

[1] Ibid.; 'The image [of John in 5.2] is not a mere fiction, however, for it is personified in the Bastard himself . . .' (Matchett, 'Heritage', p. 249).

[2] David Scott Kastan, *Shakespeare and the Shapes of Time* (1982), p. 54. See also Matchett: 'The Bastard is in the identical situation which faced John upon the death of Richard and the question is, will he, like John, usurp the throne' ('Heritage', p. 251; disputed by Jones, *Origins*, p. 259). Many critics are satisfied that the Bastard's speech does 'resolve' the play; see, e.g., M. M. Reese, *The Cease of Majesty* (1961), p. 278.

[3] See, respectively, Booth, *Holinshed*, Robert Ornstein, *A Kingdom for a Stage: The Achievement of Shakespeare's History Plays* (Cambridge, Mass., 1972), Chapter 4, and Burckhardt.

I have tried to show the marks of deliberate design in the play's language and action, as well as the contemporary legal and political forces that contributed to the play's obscurity, structural emphases, and diffused rather than concentrated effects. The historical 'facts' of John's reign as Shakespeare knew them and the contradictory Elizabethan views on the meaning of king and reign resisted formal resolution. Shakespeare's Bastard is only the most notable of the dramatic, unhistorical efforts he makes to impose shape and direct response. The Bastard's speech and action equally (and I would argue, appropriately) admit the unshaping energies in the play—energies dramatic, historical, and contemporary. Any imaginable dramatic 'resolution' would or could have placed the playwright in actual danger. A wise, belated Elizabethan wrote, 'No man can have in his mind a conception of the future, for the future is not yet. But of our conceptions of the past, we make a future; or rather, call past, future relatively.'[1] With Shakespeare's finest history plays, *King John* further suggests that the struggle between shape and unshaping force, between 'conception' and unmediated experience, is a struggle we all undergo when we confront history, because the history of 'then' is always somehow the history of 'now', Elizabethan or modern.

'King John' in the Theatre

Early Stage History. Besides Francis Meres's mention in 1598, allusions to *King John*, some more, some less convincing appear to confirm that it was performed in the 1590s and perhaps in the early seventeeth century. I offer a selection here.[2]

1. Pembroke's lines at 4.2.28–9 may have influenced a couplet

---

[1] Thomas Hobbes, *The Elements of Law*, ed. Ferdinand Tönnies, 2nd edn. (1969), 1.4.7, p. 15.

[2] Among the exclusions are Edmond Malone's paralleling of *King John* 2.1.458–66 with the anonymous *Captain Thomas Stukely* (*c.*1595?; printed 1605): 'Why here's a gallant, here's a king indeed; | He speaks all Mars, tut, let me follow such a | Lad as this. This is pure fire; | Every look he casts flasheth like lightning. | There's mettle in this boy; | He brings a breath that sets our sails on fire' (MSR, ll. 2548–53) and J. O. Halliwell-Phillipps's suggestion that the phrase 'pure unspotted brain' from Thomas Deloney's 'The death of King John poisoned by a Friar' in *Strange Histories of Kings, Princes, Dukes . . .* (1602), B4–5, imitates 'his pure brain' (*King John* 5.7.2); see Honigmann's edn., 5.7.2n.

in an unoriginal collection of verse, *Belvedere* (1600), attributed
to John Bodenham:

> Some men so strive in cunning to excel,
> That oft they mar the work before was well.[1]

2. In Thomas Heywood's *Edward IV, Part 2* (1600), King
Edward's charge to a herald contains lines that may derive from
King John 1.1.24–6:

> Be thy voice
> As fierce as thunder, to affright his soul.
> Herald, begone, I say! and be thy breath
> Piercing as lightning, and thy words as death![2]

Since Part 1 of the play very prominently includes 'the Bastard
Falconbridge' (i.e., the historical Thomas Neville), derived from
Holinshed and mentioned at *3 Henry VI* 1.1.240, Heywood might
have been thinking of another bastard Faulconbridge in *King
John*.[3]

3. Ernst Honigmann has suggested that George Chapman
imitated portions of the Bastard's speech on commodity (*King
John* 2.1.575 ff.) in *Bussy D'Ambois* (printed 1607, but probably
performed several years earlier), 5.1.153, 155–7:

> Now it is true, earth moves, and heaven stands still; . . .
> The too huge bias of this World hath sway'd
> Her back-part upwards, and with that she braves
> This Hemisphere . . .[4]

4. To the second edition of Sir John Hayward's *The Life and
Reign of King Edward the Sixth* (1636), the printer appended *The
Beginning of the Reign of Queen Elizabeth,* a work Hayward declared
he had finished before Prince Henry returned from a progress in
late August 1612.[5] After describing Londoners' eagerness to see

[1] Quoted from the reprint (Manchester, 1875), p. 54; see R. W. Dent's entry
for Tilley W260 in *Shakespeare's Proverbial Language: An Index* (Berkeley, Los
Angeles and London, 1981).

[2] Act 1, Scene 1 in Barron Field, ed., *The Dramatic Works of Thomas Heywood,*
2 vols. (1842–50), i. 97–8; for the 'parallel', see J. O. Halliwell-Phillipps,
Shakespeare Memoranda on Love's Labour's Lost . . . (1879), p. 89.

[3] August Sander, *Thomas Heywoods Historien King Edward IV und ihre Quellen*
(Jena, 1907) identifies numerous debts to Shakespeare's plays, but none to *King
John.*

[4] Quoted from *Bussy D'Ambois*, ed. Nicholas Brooke, The Revels Plays (1964);
see Honigmann's edn., 2.1.574n.

[5] John Hayward, *The Lives of the III Normans, Kings of England* (1613), A3,
where he does not specify a date; Prince Henry left London on 7 August to join

the new queen as she approached the city, Hayward dilates on her personal qualities in conventional language and euphuistic style. He concludes, 'Excellent Queen! What do my words but wrong thy work? What do I but gild gold? What, but show the sun with a candle, in attempting to praise thee . . .' (pp. 453–4). The sun–candle phrase, at least, is proverbial, and the gild–gold phrase had earlier appeared in Sidney's *Arcadia* (3.19).[1] Their combination, however, may echo Salisbury's celebrated speech: 'To gild refinèd gold . . . or with taper-light | To seek the beauteous eye of heaven to garnish . . .' (4.2.11, 14–15).[2]

5. Roland Mushat Frye discovered a peculiar testimony to *King John*'s doctrinal, if not its theatrical, interest in the first half of the seventeenth century. A copy of the second Folio (1632) 'at some time between 1641 and 1651 was expurgated by authority of the Holy Office by William Sankey, S.J., and then permitted by the same authority as reading matter for students in the English College at Valladolid, Spain'. Frye notes that 'some of the most interesting theological deletions come in connection with *King John*'; 'twenty-two lines or parts of lines' are deleted from the argument between John and Pandulph, 3.1.147–207, and the deletions 'point up the presence of more pronounced Anglican doctrine in the speeches of King John than has often been seen by modern commentators'.[3]

6. A list made on or about 12 January 1669 allots certain plays, including *King John*, to Thomas Killigrew and the King's Company; the plays are described as 'formerly acted at the Blackfriars and now allowed of to his Majesty's Servants'.[4] If *King John* was in fact acted by the King's Men at the Blackfriars, then that performance must have taken place some time after the

his father's progress and returned to Richmond on 31 August, already suffering, some thought, from his fatal illness (see John Nichols, *Progresses . . . of King James the First*, 4 vols. (1828), ii. 458 and *462).

[1] See Albert Feuillerat, ed., *Complete Works*, 4 vols. (Cambridge, 1922–6), i. 467.

[2] See John Bruce's edn. of Hayward's complete manuscript, *Annals of the first four years of the reign of Queen Elizabeth* (Harleian MS 6021), Camden Society Publications, 7 (1840), p. 8 n.

[3] Frye, pp. 276, 282, 285. For the claim that Shakespeare's treatment of Catholic doctrine and the Church's historical position is generally accurate and even-handed, see Greenewald, *passim*.

[4] Quoted (in modernized form) from the transcript in Allardyce Nicoll, *A History of Restoration Drama* (Cambridge, 1923), Appendix B.II.3 (pp. 315–16).

winter of 1609–10, when Shakespeare's company began acting there.

The Text in the Theatre. Unlike some more celebrated Shakespearian plays, *King John* survived in the post-Restoration theatre with only minor textual indignities. Actor–managers from David Garrick to John Philip Kemble to Charles Kean and William Charles Macready, it is true, all shortened the text, and from Garrick's time to Kean's the text shrank and, it seems, the length of performance grew, as the stage spectacle became more elaborate and time-consuming.[1] Charles H. Shattuck compared several important acting versions: against approximately 2,570 lines in the Folio, Garrick's version has 1,905; Kemble's 1,690; Macready's, 1,830.[2]

While published acting texts may not always accurately reflect the play as spoken,[3] several categories of theatrical cuts may none the less be identified: 'redundant' imagery; various forms of word-play, especially the Bastard's speeches as 'cracker' (2.1.147) and Constance's lamentations; some dialogue concerning political machinations, especially Pandulph's logic-chopping and his speeches advising Louis; many mentions of the English peers' alliance with the French.

[1] In this discussion of acting texts, I refer to the following: 'Garrick's version' in the first edn. of *Bell's Shakespeare* (1773–5), vol. 4, 'as performed at the Theatre-Royal, Drury Lane'; 'Kemble's version' in *The Kemble Promptbooks*, ed. Charles H. Shattuck, 11 vols. (Washington, DC, 1974), vol. 5 and essentially represented in souvenir editions 'Revised by J. P. Kemble' published from 1804 onward; the 'Macready' (1842) and 'Charles Kean' (1846) versions as represented by *William Charles Macready's 'King John': A facsimile prompt-book*, ed. Charles H. Shattuck (Urbana, Ill., 1962), including pencil markings of Charles Kean's changes for the 1846 New York production.

William P. Halstead collated forty-one acting editions and prompt-books of *King John* dating from the eighteenth century to the twentieth in his heroic *Shakespeare as Spoken: A Collation of 5000 Acting Editions and Promptbooks*, 12 vols. (Ann Arbor, Mich., 1977–80), vol. 5 (1979); vols. 13–14 (Washington, DC, 1983) of the same work contain a statistical summary.

[2] Shattuck, ed., *Macready's 'King John'*, p. 10; Charles Kean's changes in Macready's acting version were very minor, but seem to have added slightly to the length. Shattuck discusses *King John*'s various acting texts, especially the Victorian ones, and gives details of Macready's cuts and staging, ibid., pp. 9–11 and 23–30.

[3] Playbills often omit lesser characters and actors, but those for Mrs Cibber's benefit (16 March 1754) and a Haymarket performance of 20 August 1770 suggest radical cutting; see G. W. Stone, Jr., ed., *The London Stage, Part 4, 1747–1776*, 3 vols. (Carbondale, Ill., 1962), i. 414 and iii. 1491, respectively.

Scenes involving French characters and politics are regularly
diminished (Act 5, Scene 5 disappears from Garrick's, Macready's,
and Kean's texts, but remains in Kemble's, for example), as are
many references to native English unrest. Garrick and Kemble
excise Peter of Pomfret, incidentally making Hubert's appearance
in Act 4, Scene 2 much more logical and emotionally consecutive.
Blanche's part was often severely trimmed, and both Garrick and
Kemble reduce Pandulph's role as political commissar for Louis
in Act 3, Scene 3. Louis's stout rejection of Pandulph (5.2.79–
82, 97–107, 110–16) is cut, presumably to reduce his 'attractive'
anti-Papal stand. While the French side gets a reduced hearing,
John's and Eleanor's shiftiness and the English peers' eager self-
interest also diminish. At the very start, Eleanor's admission, 'So
much my conscience whispers in your ear, | Which none but
heaven, and you, and I, shall hear' (1.1.42–3) vanishes; later,
her manipulative urging of the Louis–Blanche marriage, 'Son,
list to this conjunction; make this match', and her mention of
John's 'unsured assurance to the crown' (2.1.469–80) disappear
entire.

Besides a few bridge passages to close wounds made by
cutting, a very few interpolations were deemed necessary. Garrick
evidently wished to motivate and clarify the Bastard's hostility
toward Austria, so he followed Pope's edition by adding this
exchange after 3.1.133:

> *Austria.* Methinks, that *Richard's* pride and *Richard's* fall
> Should be a precedent to fright you, Sir.
> *Faulconbridge.* What words are these! how do my sinews shake
> My father's foe clad in my father's spoil!
> How doth *Alecto* whisper in my ears,
> 'Delay not, *Richard*; kill the villain strait;
> 'Disrobe him of the matchless monument,
> 'Thy father's triumph o'er the savages.'—
> Now by his soul I swear, my father's soul,
> Twice will I not review the morning's rise,
> 'Till I have torn that trophy from thy back,
> And split thy heart, for wearing it so long.

Garrick also interpolated the vow's fulfilment after 3.2.3:

> Thus hath King *Richard's* son perform'd his vow,
> And offer'd *Austria's* blood for sacrifice,
> Unto his father's ever-living soul.

Both passages come from *The Troublesome Reign of King John*. Kemble jettisoned these additions but kept the theatrical 'Remember, Hubert' after 3.3.74[1] as well as agreeing with Garrick to shift 'Young Arthur is alive' (4.2.251) from the beginning of Hubert's last speech in Act 4, Scene 2 to its end. This change replaces Hubert's ironic and ignorant consolation (we know young Arthur is *not* alive) with a transient suspense; depending on the actors, the change could intensify the relation of monarch and loyal, honourable subject. Francophobia meant, however, that despite the toning down of English collaboration, Kemble replaced 5.1.74–6 with a piece of jingoism retained by most acting texts (basically Garrick–Kemble) until Macready's day:

> Sweep off these base invaders from the land:
> And above all exterminate those slaves,
> Those British slaves, whose prostituted souls,
> Under French banners, move in vile rebellion,
> Against their king, their country, and their God.

Theatrical Reputation and Stage History.[2] Popular, even controversial, from the early eighteenth century to the early twentieth, *King John* has since been relatively neglected.[3] This decline from frequent performance, prominent allusion, and status as a test play for new actors and trusted vehicle for established ones is often attributed to a parallel rise and fall in the audience's love of spectacle, particularly the sight of a crowded stage, detailed scenic sets, elaborate costuming, and pageant-like production.

[1] This repetition had clearly become an actor's 'point'; Macready omitted it, but Charles Kean followed tradition and restored it to his copy of Macready's prompt-book.

[2] Wilson's edn. includes an extensive stage history by Harold Child (pp. lxiii–lxxix), and Eugene Waith establishes some of the play's now unfashionable virtues through an excellent study of its eighteenth- and nineteenth-century staging in '*King John* and the Drama of History', *SQ*, 29 (1978), 192–211, with many valuable illustrations. To supplement these studies, I stress the theatrical and political elements in the play's stage history and add some comments on later twentieth-century productions.

[3] David Hirvela lists English productions, 1737–1970, and American, 1768–1967, in '*King John*: An Interpretation using its Stage History' (unpublished Ph.D. dissertation, University of Wisconsin, 1971; pp. 226–33). With some corrections and additions, and counting the reappearance of the same cast in a later season as a separate production, the tables illustrate the pattern of *King John*'s popularity: twenty-six English productions, 1737–95; thirty-one productions, 1800–99; eighteen productions, 1901–75.

This view claims corroboration in the supposed analogy of *Henry VIII*, another play susceptible to spectacular representation.

With *Henry VIII*, *King John* does indeed hold an important place, even a pre-eminent one, in a now unfashionable style of Shakespearian production, the so-called 'archaeological' style that sought costumes, sets, and props factually faithful to a play's fictional period. In the mid eighteenth century, Garrick could comfortably 'dress the characters [of *King John*] half old English, half modern, as in [William Shirley's] Edward the Black Prince',[1] but his most influential successors as actor–managers pursued historical, or antiquarian, accuracy as intensely as they eventually came to pursue a form of textual purity.

Despite the survival of John Philip Kemble's prompt-book for *King John*, it is difficult to reconstruct any major production before a series of three in the first half of the nineteenth century that set the seal on archaeological performances and contributed to the play's vast popularity. Following the lead of artists like John Singleton Copley (who in 1792 asked Edmond Malone for antiquarian help in reconstructing the event that thirteen years later Copley exhibited as 'Charles I Demanding the Arrest of the Five Impeached Members'),[2] Charles Kemble invited J. R. Planché to provide documented models for the appearance of *King John*'s historical characters. Depending heavily on Joseph Strutt's *A Complete View of the Dress and Habits of the People of England* (1796–9) and adducing evidence from funerary sculpture, manuscript illuminations, and other original sources, Planché complied to his own and the public's great satisfaction with a production at Covent Garden (24 November 1823).[3]

William Charles Macready, assisted by William Telbin's excellent scenic designs, advanced the antiquarian cause still further in a production of *King John* (24 October 1842) whose prompt-book became the basis for the Charles Kean productions (New

[1] Letter 93 (to James Lacy, 27 July 1750) in David M. Little and George M. Kahrl, eds., *The Letters of David Garrick*, 3 vols. (1963), i. 152; see Donald T. Mackintosh, 'New Dress'd in the Habits of the Times', *Times Literary Supplement*, 25 August 1927, p. 575. Shirley's pseudo-Elizabethan play was first performed 6 January 1750.

[2] See Roy Strong, *And When Did You Last See Your Father? The Victorian Painter and British History* (1978), p. 28.

[3] See, respectively, J. R. Planché, *Dramatic Costume, no. 1: Costume of Shakespeare's Historical Tragedy of King John* (1823) and Evelyn Richmond's note in *SQ*, 11 (1960), 233, where the playbill is reproduced.

York, 16 November 1846; revived in London, 9 February 1852 and 18 October 1858) that remain 'famous even to our own day [i.e., 1920]'.¹ A hint of Macready's concern for historical fact appears, for example, in his preparation copy (1842) when he identifies the location of Act 5, Scene 1 as 'The Temple Church actually at Dover but sup[posedly]. at Northampton'.²

From Garrick's haphazard dressing of the play to the anxious accuracy of Macready's production, *King John* moved from the analogous but slightly earlier periods in historical painting that Sir Roy Strong calls 'Gothick Picturesque' and 'Artist-Antiquarian' into a melding of 'Intimate Romantic' (especially clear in stagings of the Arthur–Hubert scene) with the high Victorian demand for untrammelled factual accuracy.

By the time Herbert Beerbohm Tree staged *King John* (for the second time) in 1899, Charles Kean's and Macready's archaeological innovations and spectacular staging had become *de rigueur*—'To-day the history and the rhetoric [that appealed to Elizabethan audiences] are felt in themselves to verge on the tiresome, so that a picturesque setting is of [*sic*] necessity, if only as a gilding to the pill' (*The Times*, 21 September 1899, p. 4); 'a play such as *King John* is to be regarded as a vehicle for stage pageant' (*The Athenaeum*, 23 September 1899, p. 427). Tree's production was in some ways the high-water mark of the archaeological style applied to *King John*.³ The play's episodic qualities could also be exaggerated to serve a style of production Martin Meisel calls 'serial discontinuity' and a 'pictorial drama-turgy . . . organizing a play as a series of achieved situations'.⁴ Consequently, *King John* did not escape the addition of tableaux, wordless business, and the like in Tree's production. The two great tableaux, faithfully pictured in the souvenir programme, represent the battle in Act 3 (see Fig. 6) and the signing of Magna

---

¹ George C. D. Odell, *Shakespeare from Betterton to Irving*, 2 vols. (New York, 1920), ii. 286; for dates of performance and a convincing argument that Charles Kean's production derives from Macready's, see Shattuck, ed., *Macready's 'King John'*, pp. 4–9.

² Quoted ibid., p. 29.

³ For the general point, see M. St Clare Byrne's valuable 'Fifty Years of Shakespearian Production: 1898–1948', *Shakespeare Survey 2* (Cambridge, 1949), 1–20; p. 1.

⁴ *Realizations: Narrative, Pictorial, and Theatrical Arts in Nineteenth-Century England* (Princeton, NJ, 1983), pp. 38 and 41; for an anticipation of this view specifically applied to *King John*, see Waith, pp. 198–200.

6. Tableau of the Battle of Angers (*King John*, Act 2, Scene 1) from Beerbohm Tree's 1899 production; the perspective painted backdrop continues the scene represented by the actors. Tree added a similar tableau illustrating the signing of Magna Carta.

Carta. In *The Saturday Review* of 30 September 1899, Tree's half-brother, Max Beerbohm, reviewed the production, emphasizing 'points of "business" and stage management' in part because he had 'never seen the play acted' and 'reading it, . . . had found it insufferably tedious'.[1] His description of Act 3, Scene 3 wonderfully achieves his aim of allowing 'readers to imagine the production at Her Majesty's Theatre':

In a glade of slim beeches, John communes with the faithful, grim Hubert. The old soldier stands immovable, while his master whispers in his ear. Beyond stands the queen mother, watching with her eyes of ill omen. Little Arthur is plucking the daisies. The king smiles down at him as he passes, and the child starts away. There are some daisies growing near the spot where the king has been whispering his behest. Lightly, he cuts the head off them with his sword.[2]

The staging of Shakespeare reflects, of course, legislation by the drama's patrons. Some of their laws and some of *King John*'s

[1] Max Beerbohm, *More Theatres 1898–1903* (1969), p. 193. (This review is mistakenly attributed to G. B. Shaw by A. C. Sprague in *Shakespeare and the Actors* (Cambridge, Mass., 1945), p. 377 n. 138.)

[2] Ibid., p. 192.

popularity arose less from love of Shakespeare or love of spectacle than from such powerful sentiments as Francophobia, anti-Catholicism, and arguments over constitutional monarchy. Certainly these forces combined when John Rich's recently-built Covent Garden revived *King John*, 'Never Acted there before' and 'As written by Shakespear', on 26 February 1737.[1] A rather mysterious group of advocates, 'The Shakespeare Ladies Club',[2] may have prompted this first recorded post-Restoration production, but aesthetic enthusiasm here meets literary dispute because Colley Cibber's tendentiously anti-Catholic, anti-Jacobite adaptation, *Papal Tyranny in the Reign of King John*, had recently made Shakespeare's play newsworthy. Even before *King John* graced Covent Garden, Cibber had written in the *Daily Advertiser* (4 February 1737) and other newspapers trying to deflect criticism of his adaptation, then in rehearsal; he explained, 'many of that Fam'd Author's Pieces, for these Hundred Years past, have lain dormant, from, perhaps, a just Suspicion, that they were too weak, for a compleat Entertainment'.[3] And Fielding's very popular *Historical Register for the Year 1736* (Haymarket, 21 March 1737) soon belaboured Cibber (as 'Ground-Ivy') and his son Theophilus ('Pistol') for thinking 'King John, as now writ, will not do—But . . . I will make him do' (1737, C5^v).

This controversy probably explains why *King John* became the main exhibit in the most notorious attack on the Licensing Act, the leading essay in *The Craftsman* for 2 July 1737. Perhaps by Nicholas Amhurst or by Fielding himself, this essay purports to come from 'C[olley]. C[ibber]. P[oet]. L[aureate].' and quotes *King John* extensively to demonstrate that even texts more than a century old may be found to 'reflect' upon Walpolian

---

[1] *The Craftsman* (2 July 1737) claims that 'Mr. R——h hath had the Presumption' to alter *King John*, so the claim of authenticity may be comparative rather than absolute.

[2] See Emmett L. Avery, 'The Shakespeare Ladies Club', *SQ*, 7 (1956), 152–8; p. 154, and the advertisement of a competing production at the Haymarket (4 March 1737): 'With a New Prologue . . . concluding with an Address to the Ladies of the Shakespear Club' (*London Daily Post and General Advertiser*). Fielding's *Historical Register for the Year 1736* (1737) ends by asking the ladies' approbation 'whether you be *Shakespear*'s Ladies, or *Beaumont* and *Fletcher*'s Ladies' (D1).

[3] See Emmett L. Avery, 'Cibber, *King John*, and the Students of the Law', *Modern Language Notes*, 53 (1938), 272–5. Cibber also mentions 'the same Sett of Ladies, two certain days every week so laudably attentive, to their own Choice of only *Shakespear*'s Plays'.

politics. Claiming that 'King John is represented through the whole Play as an *Usurper*', the essayist chose several passages 'capable of very bad Applications'. Constance's demand that 'it be lawful that law bar no wrong' (3.1.186 ff.) represents 'a *Parliamentary Tyranny*, or *legal Slavery*', for example. Two passages on rebellious citizens—'If but a dozen French | Were there in arms, they would be as a call | To train ten thousand English to their side . . .' (3.4.173 ff.) and 'Our discontented counties do revolt . . .' (5.1.8 ff.)—must be omitted, as should John's reflection on Hubert's apparent willingness to murder Arthur, 'It is the curse of kings to be attended | By slaves . . .' (4.2.208 ff.). These satiric choices precisely echo theatrical cuts: Garrick and Kemble omitted all but the last passage, at least partly, one assumes, on political grounds, and as late as the 1840s and 1850s Macready and Kean omitted the first and third 'sensitive' speeches.

Cibber lost the skirmish of 1737 and withdrew his play. Yet, despite Pope's confidence that 'King John in silence modestly expires' (*New Dunciad* [1742], i. 252), Cibber's adaptation responded to—or so a commercially sensitive management might think—current social and political concerns. *Papal Tyranny* consequently came before the public (Covent Garden, 15 February 1745, with nine more performances in February) when many audiences saw a parallel between Cibber's play and the Jacobite rebellion then threatening the north of England.[1] After the professional courtesy of a brief pause, Garrick (as King John) and Drury Lane crushed their rivals by performing Shakespeare's play, 'Not acted in 50 Years' on 20 February. Thereafter, *King John* appears in the repertory of both patent houses, earning disparate marks of popularity: for example, two royal command performances (31 January 1754, during a run when Garrick first played the Bastard, and 23 December 1760) and an adaptation at Cushing's booth in Bartholomew Fair (23 August 1748 and

[1] See Arthur H. Scouten, ed., *LS, Part 3, 1729–1747*, 2 vols. (Carbondale, Ill., 1961), ii. 1153–5; there were two further performances on 4 April 1745 and 8 February 1746 (ibid., ii. 1164–5, 1217). The adaptation was printed in 1745. Sensible contemporary criticism appeared in *A Letter to Colley Cibber, Esq.; on his Transformation of 'King John'* (1745), probably by the 'Occasional Prompter', who earlier (1736–7) published a series of letters in the *Daily Journal*; see Brian Vickers, ed., *Shakespeare: The Critical Heritage*, 6 vols. (1974–81), vol. 3 (1975), pp. 155–62 and 71–80, respectively.

after).[1] Old rivalries died hard; in the 1760–1 season, Covent Garden and Drury Lane—almost without precedent—performed the play in direct competition.[2]

The writer of the *Craftsman* essay promised 'to execute . . . with great Industry' the altering (or 'gutting') of '*other People's Works* . . . to the Confusion of all *Papists*, *Jacobites*, *Incendiaries*, and *Patriots*'. This civic concern, no less than the contemporary satire of the essay itself or Cibber's own religio-political comments in the epistle dedicatory to *Papal Tyranny* (1745), all testify to the play's potential as a controversial text. During the Seven Years' War, for example, feeling at a provincial performance ran so high that shouts and apples hurled from the gallery compelled King Philip, Louis, and the other French characters to remove the white cockades they wore as part of their (contemporary) French military costume.[3] In fact, the command performance at Drury Lane and the simultaneous presentation of *King John* at both houses in December 1760 almost certainly exploited the play's supposed patriotism both as an anti-French tract and as a mark of George III's accession.

The post-Restoration critical and theatrical consensus saw Shakespeare's histories (and, to a lesser extent, the historical tragedies like *Julius Caesar* and *Coriolanus*) as 'shewing us the Virtues and Vices of our Ancestors, with an honest and manly Freedom'.[4] That portrait might arouse patriotic enthusiasm or contemporary satiric reflection or anti-monarchical feeling. Thus, Nahum Tate's adaptation of *Richard II*, even disguised as *The Sicilian Usurper*, was—in his words—'*stifled on the* Stage' and suspected as '*a Disloyal or Reflecting* Play' (*The History of King Richard the Second* [1681], sig. A1) and, a century later, the Lord

---

[1] For a brief discussion and cast list, see Sybil Rosenfeld, *The Theatre of the London Fairs in the 18th Century* (Cambridge, 1960), p. 56; the droll was performed with 'The Adventures of Sir Lubberly Lackbrains and his Man Blunderbuss'. See also *LS, Part 4*, i. 130.

[2] Charles Beecher Hogan calls the twelve-night Garrick–Barry rivalry in *Romeo and Juliet* (September and October 1750) 'a unique, but premeditated, violation' of a custom that ensured 'the extreme rarity of the occasions on which the two houses acted the same play on the same night' (*LS, Part 5, 1776–1800*, 2 vols. (Carbondale, Ill., 1968), vol. i, pp. cxli–cxlii and n. 190). In 1760, Covent Garden presented *King John* on 9, 10, 17, and 23 December (and 3 January 1761); Drury Lane on 17, 20, and 23 December.

[3] See [Francis Gentleman,] *The Dramatic Censor*, 2 vols. (1770), ii. 172–3.

[4] James Ralph, *The Case of our Present Theatrical Disputes, Fairly Stated* (1743), D2ᵛ.

Chamberlain forbade performances of *King Lear* out of deference to George III's insanity.[1]

Even without the fortuitous (or otherwise) circumstance that *King John*'s first post-Restoration performances coincided with controversy over the Licensing Act, the play provides many opportunities for 'modern' social and political applications, as its later history shows. During the Napoleonic Wars and amid fears of a French invasion, J. P. Kemble chose to include the jingoistic claptrap quoted above, and the Reverend Richard Valpy's piously patriotic (and dreadful) adaptation was performed at Covent Garden (20 May 1803), where it received 'enthusiastic applause, expressive of the general feelings at the present awful crisis'.[2] Reviewing Charles Kean's production, *The Times* remarked, 'The determination to check Papal aggression met with all the *accustomed* cheers, and the "Italian priest" coming in for his due share of defiance from boxes, pit, and gallery' (10 February 1852; my italics). At century's end, *The Athenaeum* found Tree's production not only 'worthy of our modern stage', but 'opportune also, and there is no question that recent events will lend its patriotic language the utmost possible significance' (23 September 1899, p. 427). The 'recent events' were the dispatch, on 8 September, of ten thousand troops to South Africa and, on 22 September, the mobilization of troops based in Britain.

King John's potential for political comment has not been lost on twentieth-century audiences and producers. For example, reviewing Harcourt Williams's Sadler's Wells production of 1931 (with Robert Speaight as John, Ralph Richardson as the Bastard), *Punch* (16 September) quoted 5.7.112–17 and found 'a message

---

[1] See L. W. Conolly, *The Censorship of English Drama 1737–1824* (San Marino, Calif., 1976), p. 126 and p. 203 nn. 44–5. John Philip Kemble was forbidden (June 1817) to act in *King Lear* before his retirement, and Conolly cites a similar prohibition from 1814, but implies that the play had been suppressed for some considerable time before.

[2] Richard Valpy, DD, *King John, an Historical Tragedy . . . as it was acted at Reading School . . .*, 2nd edn. (Reading, 1803); the quoted passage comes from a paragraph dated May, 1803 and appended to the 'Advertisement' reprinted from the first edn. (1800). Evidence for an earlier school production survives: see George Keate's Prologue and Epilogue 'to the Play of King John acted at Mr. Newcomb's [school], at Hackney, in March MDCCLXIX' in *A Collection of Poems by Several Hands*, 4 vols. (1770), iii. 74–5 and 76–7. For further details of Keate and the Hackney school-plays, see: Kathryn Gilbert Dapp, *George Keate, Esq., Eighteenth-Century English Gentleman* (Philadelphia, 1939) and Alfred Jones, 'Newcome's Academy and Its Plays', *Library*, IV, 14 (1933), 339–97.

for us in our present crises, flights from the pound and the like'. International tensions, rather than economic troubles, soon regained their allegorical centrality; the *Sunday Express* reviewer of an OUDS production had no patience with the Oxford Union and its notorious 'King and Country' debate of 9 February 1933, but did remember Coward's *Cavalcade* (1931): 'Pacifism or no pacifism, warm applause greeted the final speech . . . with its famous lines, so reminiscent of Noel Coward' (26 February 1933). Six years later, Harold Neilson's travelling production prompted a reviewer to remind readers that 'Mr Chamberlain always travels with a pocket Shakespeare. In his speech at Blackburn last night he quoted . . . "Come the three corners of the world in arms | And we shall shock them" ' (*Daily Telegraph*, 23 February 1939). Advertising a BBC production with Ralph Richardson as the Bastard, *The Listener* claimed 'of all Shakespeare's plays, *King John* is probably, at this moment, the most topical' (22 December 1944), and right after the war's end, the *Birmingham Gazette* called Peter Brook's production at the Birmingham Repertory Theatre (with Paul Scofield as the Bastard) 'a tract for the times' (17 November 1945). An Old Vic production directed by Peter Potter and later to open in London prompted an Edinburgh reviewer to see an unusual parallel: 'Angiers, with its closed access, invested by two hostile Powers, stood for Berlin' (*The Scotsman*, 30 July 1961). The most recent Royal Shakespeare Company production (Stratford, 1974 and London, 1975; directed by John Barton) 'constantly emphasized the play's topicality', and once again a reviewer found 'a parable for our own times' (*Oxford Mail*, 21 March 1974).[1]

The play's stage history in the twentieth century is a melancholy record of fewer and fewer productions. At the Shakespeare Memorial–Royal Shakespeare Theatre, Stratford-upon-Avon, for example, it was presented in 1890 (directed by Osmond Tearle, who also took John), four times between 1901 and 1916 (all by F. R. Benson's company), and in 1925 (directed by W. A. Bridges-Adams), 1940 (Ben Iden Payne), 1948 (Michael Benthall), 1957 (Douglas Seale), 1970 (Buzz Goodbody), and 1974

---

[1] Quoted in Robert Smallwood, 'Shakespeare Unbalanced: The Royal Shakespeare Company's *King John*, 1974–5', *Shakespeare Jahrbuch* (*West*) 1976, 79–99; p. 91. Smallwood analyses this production thoroughly.

(John Barton).[1] Texts for these last two productions were severely cut and include many non-Shakespearian interpolations. The former was a 'Theatre-go-round' travelling production that omitted James Gurney and Lady Faulconbridge, for example, while the latter was 'the most severely altered Shakespearian text ever to be delivered at the Stratford theatre'.[2] Beside Shakespeare, audiences heard pieces of *The Troublesome Reign* and of Bale's *King Johan*, as well as lines written by John Barton.

King John was presented at the Old Vic, London, in 1918, 1921, 1926, 1953, and 1961. The 1953 production, directed by George Devine, appeared in the first season of the Old Vic's five-year-long programme to present all the Folio texts; Roger Wood and Mary Clarke preserved a valuable photographic and verbal record.[3] As with other twentieth-century productions, the audience at the Old Vic—'caught up, but able to laugh at the horrors . . . No one was much moved, but all conspired to attend with sympathy' (Philip Hope-Wallace, *The Guardian*, 29 October 1953)—had difficulty with the historical costumes and setting; decades earlier, James Agate named the style 'Norman Nondescript', and probably wounded it fatally in his review of the Harcourt Williams production at Sadler's Wells Theatre (*The Sunday Times*, 20 September 1931). Worse yet, the audience laughed outright at the unpersuasive battle scenes in Devine's production.[4] These reactions from critics and audiences alike underscore the change in theatrical fashion and convention since the high Victorian era.

[1] For cast lists, production personnel, and a listing of reviews, see Michael Mullin and Karen Morris Muriello, comp., *Theatre at Stratford-upon-Avon: A Catalogue-Index*, 2 vols. (Westport, Conn., 1980), i. 204–10.

[2] Smallwood, 'Shakespeare Unbalanced', p. 98. The two productions are also described, and attacked, in Kenneth McClellan, *Whatever Happened to Shakespeare?* (1978), pp. 205–7.

[3] *Shakespeare at the Old Vic* (1954), pp. 18–25 and 60–3.

[4] Ibid., p. 62, and see Alfred Harbage, *Theatre for Shakespeare* (Toronto, 1955), on the same production: 'the battle of Angiers was represented by the *usual* patterned and somewhat embarrassing manoeuvres of supers. . . . The battle had been so well behaved and Falconbridge [played by Richard Burton] had carried himself through it with such patronizing aplomb that the head of Austria seemed more plausible as a prize in a raffle than as a trophy of war' (p. 53; my emphasis).

EDITORIAL PROCEDURES

THE editorial procedures of the Oxford Shakespeare are discussed at length in Gary Taylor's edition of *Henry V* (Oxford, 1982), pp. 75–81. Here, I only state, rather than justify, the conventions of the series and add certain points relevant to the editing of *King John* in particular.

Quotations from early printed books in English have been silently modernized on the principles adopted for this edition and discussed at length by Stanley Wells, 'Modernizing Shakespeare's Spelling', in Stanley Wells and Gary Taylor, *Modernizing Shakespeare's Spelling, with Three Studies in the Text of 'Henry V'* (Oxford, 1979). Similarly, quotations from modern original-spelling editions (e.g., those of Dekker and of Chapman's comedies) have also been modernized. Texts originally printed in black letter with roman for emphasis are here represented in roman and italic, respectively, and those in italic with roman for emphasis are here represented in roman and italic, respectively.

Citations of Shakespeare's plays refer to *William Shakespeare: The Complete Works*, gen. eds. Stanley Wells and Gary Taylor (Oxford, 1986).[1] Unless otherwise noted, all quotations from the Bible refer to the Bishops' Bible (1568), and line numbers for classical Latin works refer to the respective Loeb editions. In the commentary, other editors' references have been silently normalized to these texts and editions.

Glosses and lexical discussions employ *OED*'s abbreviations for parts of speech (e.g., *sb.* for 'substantive', *v.* for 'verb') where a word may be used as more than one part of speech, and *OED*'s numbering system for different definitions. Thus, the note on 'dear' (1.1.257) reads in part 'heartfelt (Schmidt, quoted at *a.*[1] II.7a), but probably mixed with "fond, loving" (I.5b)' and refers to two of *OED*'s numbered definitions of *dear*, an adjective. Only in controversial places, or for clarity, is *OED*'s definition quoted directly; often it is cited without acknowledgement. The *OED*'s

---

[1] When citing a quarto or Folio reading that does not appear in the Wells–Taylor edn., I refer to signatures for quartos and to TLN for the Folio. The Wells–Taylor edn. refers to *2 Henry VI* and *3 Henry VI* as *The First Part of the Contention* and *Richard Duke of York* respectively, and to *Henry VIII* as *All is True*.

claims for chronological appearances of a word have been checked against numerous later sources, including Jürgen Schäfer, *Documentation in the O.E.D.: Shakespeare and Nashe as Test Cases* (Oxford, 1980).

Unless otherwise noted, citation of an earlier editor by name refers to that editor's text of *King John* listed in the 'Editions of Shakespeare'; a reference to an earlier editor by name and a citation in the form '1.2.34n' refer the reader to that editor's note on the specified line. Citation of other texts by an author's name refers the reader to the titles listed in 'Other Works and Abbreviations'. I have borrowed from many editors' work and, especially in the commentary, have sometimes silently added to or corrected the original references—for example, when a work was cited by title only.

In the collation, some features of the Folio's typography (for example, 'long' s, ligatures, and diagraphs) are ignored unless they are relevant to emendation and/or interpretation, but the Folio's spelling, capitalization, punctuation (for instance, hyphens), and use of italics are reproduced *literatim*. For example:

> 2.1.106 Geoffrey's; in the name of God] ROWE; *Geffreyes* in the name of God: F

> 2.1.425 near] F (neere); niece SINGER 1856 (*conj.* Collier, *Notes*)

Citations from Folios 2, 3, and 4 are modernized in the collation, and represented in the same way as texts whose editors' names are known, unless the original spelling is relevant to an emendation, modernization, or a probable error; for example,

> 2.1.335 run] F2 (runne); rome F1

Trevor Howard-Hill offers a conservative list of the Folio's misprints, turned letters, wrong-fount letters, etc.[1] These typographical errors have been silently corrected.

The appearance of the masculine pronoun after the word 'heaven' at 3.1.156 ('him') and 5.7.60 ('he') virtually proves that the Folio's text has been expurgated and the word *God*

---

[1] See Trevor Howard-Hill, *King John: A Concordance to the Text of the First Folio*, Oxford Shakespeare Concordances (Oxford, 1970), p. xii. The Norton facsimile prepared by Charlton Hinman (New York, 1968) appears to read 'gronnd' (for 'ground') at 2.1.577, but that is a flaw in the reproduction; Folger Folio 1, from which Hinman took this page, reads 'ground', although the *u* is clearly weak.

replaced with (monosyllabic) *heaven*.[1] These two lines require emendation on the principle that some agency other than Shakespeare has affected the text, but the expurgation evident here means, as William Matchett writes, 'each appearance of the word "heaven" in this play becomes suspect. . . . In phrases like "heaven and earth" (2.1.173), "clouds of heaven" (2.1.252), or "heaven or hell" (2.1.407), it is obvious that no change should be made. But this leaves a large group of doubtful instances.'[2] Where 'God' or 'heaven' appears in a common phrase (e.g., 'God knows', 'by heaven'), it is possible to study Shakespeare's habitual practice in the unexpurgated quartos (*Titus*, *Richard III*, *1* and *2 Henry IV*, *Romeo*, *Dream*, *Merchant*, *Much Ado*, and *Hamlet*) and in the Folio plays where oaths appear to have been least censored (*Errors*, *All's Well*, *Henry V*, *1*, *2*, *3 Henry VI*, and *Richard III*).[3] It seems clear that Shakespeare preferred 'God('s) sake' and 'God knows', but the asseveration 'by heaven' appears much more frequently than 'by God' even in unexpurgated texts. Evidence that Shakespeare personified 'heaven' is slight and inconclusive.[4] Consequently, I have not adopted the most thoroughgoing of emendations and conjectural emendations (represented by Matchett's edition). Where a convincing body of evidence from apparently unexpurgated texts exists, I have substituted 'God' for 'heaven'; it seems very likely that Shakespeare wrote, or would have chosen to write, 'God'

[1] These examples and this explanation are commonplaces of editorial comment on the play. The two most recent discussions are Matchett's edn., pp. 150–1 and Gary Taylor, 'Zounds'; each offers slightly different comparative statistics for the appearances of 'God' and 'heaven' in *King John* and other Shakespeare plays, but the unusual preponderance of 'heaven' in this play is a matter of universal agreement.

[2] Matchett's edn., p. 150. In addition to the two traditional emendations mentioned above, Matchett emends six other lines (see Collation); he lists ten lines 'where I would also prefer to make the change' (i.e., at 1.1.83, 1.1.84, 1.1.256, 2.1.373, 3.1.236, 3.1.242, 3.1.266 (twice), 4.1.55, 4.3.82, and 5.1.29 in this edn.) and eighteen 'other places where the change would be possible but where, for contextual reasons (with which others might disagree), I would not make it'.

[3] See Taylor, 'Zounds', for the reasons to regard these Folio plays as largely unexpurgated.

[4] For example, if we exclude one example where the metre requires disyllabic 'heaven' (*Richard II* 5.2.37), 'hand of God' or 'God's hand' appears four times in the quartos and the Folio and 'hand of heaven' thrice—too small and too inconclusive a sample to justify emending 'hand of heaven' at *King John* 5.2.66.

more frequently, and 'heaven' less frequently, than this edition indicates.

Not recorded in the collation are minor modernizations that distinguish usages that have developed distinct modern spellings where Elizabethan conventions were different or inconsistent: thus, the Folio *King John* never prints *than*, only *then*. Similarly, uncontroversial expansions of the Folio's rare contractions (e.g., y̔, frȯ) are not recorded. Also not recorded are earlier editors' printing of 'Oh'; both exclamation and vocative appear uniformly as 'O' in this edition. Some earlier editors treated modernization as if it were emendation; the Folio's reading is sometimes collated to indicate that a changed spelling is simply a modernization:

4.2.216 account] F (accompt)

Also not recorded are editorially introduced variants distinguishing syllabic and non-syllabic *-ed*: some editions differentiate these uses by *-ed* and *'d*, others (like this one) with accents over syllabic *-èd*, etc. The Folio text of *King John* is remarkably consistent and accurate in distinguishing between *-ed* (syllabic) and *'d* (syncopated).

Most editorial changes for metrical and grammatical purposes have not been recorded. Editors, especially in the eighteenth century, tended to fit Shakespeare's verse into a pentameter strait-jacket; emendations designed to regularize the metre (e.g., Alexander Pope's 'on his' for the Folio's 'on's' at 2.1.289 or his 'I'd' for the Folio's 'I would' three lines later) have not been recorded. Again especially in the eighteenth century, editors adjusted Shakespeare's grammar and syntax to the norms of their own day. For example, where the Folio reads 'The sea enraged is not halfe so deafe, | Lyons more confident, Mountaines and rockes | More free from motion' (2.1.452–4), Pope twice substituted *so* for *more* to regularize the grammar. Editors have similarly emended failures of concord between subject and verb; where the Folio reads, 'His grandames wrongs, and not his mothers shames | Drawes those heauen-mouing pearles fro[m] his poore eies' (2.1.168–9), Capell substituted 'Draw'. None of these 'improvements' has been recorded in the collation.

Changes in the Folio's punctuation have been recorded when they change the grammar or syntax or resolve an ambiguous syntactical structure. Although the Folio compositors had a sort for '!' (one appears at TLN 728), they commonly used '?' to represent both modern '?' and '!'; except for certain non-controversial categories, insertions of '!' have been collated because earlier editors tended to exaggerate the play's verbal violence.[1] On the rare occasions (2.1.533, 5.2.180) where it seems that the Folio has omitted a final mark of punctuation at the end of a character's speech, editors have supplied one; in *King John*, these occasions, which may merely be the result of a broken type or of a type's failure to print, are uncontroversial and have not been collated.

Many other classes of changed punctuation are not recorded; to do so would merely be to list historical changes in conventions of punctuation or to record individual editors' preferences among competing systems. The classes are:

1. Editorial punctuations of vocatives, of oaths, of 'O', and of quoted speech (e.g., at 1.1.185). The Folio rarely marks vocatives, but occasionally uses parentheses for that purpose—e.g., at 1.1.6: 'Silence (good mother) heare the Embassie' or at 3.1.51-2: 'at thy birth (deere boy) | Nature and Fortune ioyn'd'. In such cases, the parentheses have been replaced with commas according to modern convention, and the change has not been recorded in the collation.

2. Editorially introduced possessives (e.g., 'woman's' at 1.1.269).

3. Editorially introduced inverted commas to indicate imaginary, reported, or hypothetical speech (e.g., the Bastard's imaginary conversation at 1.1.185 ff.).

4. Editorially introduced capitalization and italics where they merely make Shakespeare's text conform to contemporary usage; capitals introduced to mark personification (again, e.g., 'Question' and 'Answer' in the Bastard's imaginary conversation at 1.1.195 ff.).

All directions for a character to speak *aside* or *to* another character are editorial; few are original with this edition. None

---

[1] The collation does not record editorial '!' in the following categories: calls to arms and battlefield exhortations (2.1.287, 2.1.299, 2.1.358, 2.1.416, 3.1.255, 3.1.347, 3.2.5, 3.3.6, 3.3.74, 3.4.181, 4.3.114, 5.1.73, 5.4.2, 5.4.60); formal greetings or the marking of a character's entrance using words such as 'Look' or 'Hail' (3.4.17, 4.3.21, 5.2.68); interjections and imprecations using words such as 'Out', 'What', 'Peace', 'be gone', 'Lo', and 'Avaunt' (1.1.64, 1.1.245, 2.1.122, 2.1.134, 3.1.36, 3.4.21, 4.3.77).

of these added directions has been recorded in the collation; debatable ones are discussed in the commentary. All other changes and additions to the Folio's stage directions have been recorded. Where I have adopted an earlier editor's exact language for a direction, the collation records the debt even if that editor is not the first to have introduced substantially the same direction; otherwise the collation merely records what stands (or does not stand) in the Folio. Debatable alterations or additions to the Folio's directions are enclosed in half-brackets (⌐ ⌐) in the text and collated if they derive from an earlier edition. Ordinarily, I have inserted (and collated) the characters' titles (King, Queen, Dauphin, etc.) in the opening stage directions of each scene, but have not added them to subsequent stage directions within scenes. This edition employs dashes to indicate a speaker's change of addressee or the interruption of one speaker by another; these changes are not recorded unless they seem debatable, nor are earlier editors' various conventions for indicating the same situations.

Speech headings have been silently normalized and are not collated unless the Folio's reading may provide evidence of the compositors' manuscript copy or physical conditions of the printing (e.g., long lines and/or crowded text, type shortages). Reassignments of speeches (in this or earlier editions) are recorded.

The Folio provides no list of the characters in *King John*; Nicholas Rowe was the first editor to supply such a list, and all subsequent ones are based on his. Personal names (e.g., 'Salisbury' for the Folio's 'Salsbury' at 4.3.81 and 5.2.19) and place-names (e.g., 'Anjou' and 'Touraine' for the Folio's *Aniowe* and *Torayne* at 1.1.11) have been silently normalized to their commonest modern French and English forms, with one exception. The exception is 'Britaine', the name of the French duchy held by Arthur's father, Geoffrey; the territory is more or less congruent with modern Brittany, but that trisyllable is metrically unacceptable as a modernization. To print 'Britain', however, invites the very confusion the French language avoids with the locution 'Grande Bretagne' and Spenser with the phrase 'greater Brytayne' (*Faerie Queene* 3.2.7). I join many editors in printing 'Bretagne', a disyllable that ensures that neither reader nor theatre audience will imagine that Arthur claims to be 'duke' of Great Britain.

I have not examined all editions of *King John* nor does the collation record all the variants in those I have examined.[1] Rather, the collated emendations and conjectures of earlier editors represent rejected but possible or plausible readings or readings (including punctuation) that produce interpretations of the text markedly different from that implied by the reading I adopt or retain (these readings are usually discussed in the commentary). I have attempted to attribute readings to their earliest proposers and/or to those editors who first accepted them in a published text. For my errors, oversights, and ignorance, I apologize to my predecessors and to the reader; it is regrettably true that 'This edition' appears more often than is justified.

The work of several earlier editors requires brief discussion. Alexander Pope placed at the foot of the page the Folio lines he thought spurious; these words he none the less 'edited', and I have attributed to him readings that appear in the ostracized passages. I have also examined the earliest of the three editions of Shakespeare known to have been annotated by Lewis Theobald's acquaintance Styan Thirlby (1686?–1753), a Cambridge don and editor of Justin Martyr.[2] Thirlby started annotating his copy of Pope's first edition (in quarto), I suppose, shortly after it appeared early in 1725. Theobald visited Thirlby in Cambridge in 1728, discussed the emendation of Shakespeare's text, and examined Thirlby's annotated copy, as he allusively explains in a draft of the introduction to his own edition:

I come now to speak of those kind Assistances, w[hi]ch I have met with from particular Friends, towards forwarding & compleating this Work. Soon after my Design [of 'publishing . . . *Emendations* and *Remarks* on our Poet'] was known [i.e., '[i]n the Middle of the Year 1728'], I had the Honour of an Invitation to Cambridge; & a generous Promise from the Learned & ingenious D.[r] Thirlby of Jesus-Colledge there, who had taken great Pains w[i]th my Author, that I should have the Liberty of collating his Copy of Shakespeare, mark'd thro' in the Margin with his

---

[1] The collation in Furness's edn. is untrustworthy.

[2] This set is now part of the Osborn Collection, Beinecke Library, Yale University, and was identified as Thirlby's by Stephen Parks, Curator of that collection, and Peter Blayney. For information on Thirlby and the two later editions (Theobald's first, 1733, and Warburton's, 1747) he annotated, see Christopher Spencer and John W. Velz, 'Styan Thirlby: A Forgotten "Editor" of Shakespeare', *ShakS*, 6 (1970), 327–33, and the helpful essay by John Hazel Smith, 'Styan Thirlby's Shakespearean Commentaries: A Corrective Analysis', *ShakS*, 11 (1978), 219–41. Some of Thirlby's marginalia suggest that he had originally begun his commentary in one of Rowe's editions, perhaps the first, 1709 (see Smith, p. 222).

own MSS References, & accurate [*deleted*: Emend] Observations. He not only made good this Promise, but favour'd me with a Sett of Emendations, interspers'd & distinguish'd [*deleted*: thro'] in his Name, thro' the Edition; & which can need no Recommendation here to the judicious Reader.[1]

The printed text of Theobald's introduction follows this corrected draft, and 'The ingenious Dr. *Thirlby*' appears in Theobald's note to *King John* 2.1.438, as well as elsewhere in his edition.

Styan Thirlby mentions both the Cambridge visit and his later list of emendations in a letter to Theobald:

At last I send you the list of such of my conjectures as I am at present not unwilling to own. I waited some time, in expectation of my Quarto [i.e., Pope's edition of 1725], which I wanted to consult about some places. . . . You will wonder perhaps at the shortness of the list, especially having, I suppose, transcribed from the margin of my book, many things I fancy you will think as certain as many, if not any, of those here inserted.[2]

This letter clearly implies that Theobald had taken away the annotated quarto edition, and 'I suppose, transcribed . . . many things'. Thirlby awaited the return of his quarto volume(s) before sending his selected emendations to Theobald.[3] At two places in *King John*, Thirlby has suggested readings (a hyphen in 'fast closed' at 2.1.448 and 'task' for 'tast' at 3.1.148) adopted by Theobald in his first edition (1733); in the margin beside these two changes, and in a different ink, Thirlby notes, 'Mr T. has it'.

---

[1] This draft appears in Theobald's letter to Warburton, 4 December 1731, British Library Egerton MS 1956, fol. 19ᵛ; 'accurate Observations' has been changed in darker ink from 'accurate Emendations'. For further details of the Cambridge visit, which seems to have lasted a week, see Smith, p. 227.

[2] Letter of 7 May 1729, Folger MS W.b. 74, fols. 32–3; it is reprinted, among many others in the Theobald–Warburton correspondence, in Nichols, *Illus.*, ii. 222–3. The only *King John* emendation in the list is one Theobald eventually accepted and attributed to Thirlby ('as she' for 'a she' at 2.1.439). Many of Theobald's letters attribute to Thirlby emendations not in Thirlby's list of 7 May 1729 (e.g., letters of 6 December 1729, 24 February 1730, 3 March 1730, 21 March 1730); presumably, these emendations are among those Theobald read in Thirlby's annotated copy of Pope's quarto edn. Sixty-eight letters from the Theobald–Warburton correspondence (1729–34) on Shakespeare are now in Folger MS W.b. 74–5 (formerly Phillipps MS 8565); I am grateful to Professor Gail Kern Paster for checking Nichols's sometimes inaccurate text against the originals.

[3] This also appears to be the interpretation of Thirlby's words in R. F. Jones, *Lewis Theobald: His Contribution to English Scholarship* (New York, 1919), p. 220, but see the more cautious remarks in Smith, n. 14.

This phrase apparently means that in their 1728 discussions Theobald stated he had earlier and independently made the same emendations.[1] In the letter of 1729, Thirlby refers to his marginal notation of Theobald's (probably verbal, possibly written) reaction: 'Finding in the margin of my book, *Mr. Theobald is dubious*, I have considered this over'.[2] As a result of these exchanges, Thirlby's contribution to Theobald's first edition is likely to have been minimized, deliberately (as Thirlby thought and as Theobald's draft introduction hints) or not. My collation therefore attributes to Thirlby the following material from his earliest known annotated copy of Shakespeare: independent conjectures that seem to have merit; manuscript conjectures that are first printed (without attribution to Thirlby) in Theobald's edition of 1733 but are absent from Theobald's *Shakespeare Restored* (1726).[3]

John Payne Collier published two editions of *Notes and Emendations* in 1853 and attributed the readings to 'the old corrector', purportedly an individual annotating a copy of F2 at some time in the seventeenth century. It seems very likely that Collier was himself largely responsible for annotating this book, the so-called 'Perkins' Folio now in the Huntington Library, and many of the readings had already appeared in print before 1853.[4] Readings that appear to originate with Collier's *Notes and Emendations* are

[1] See Smith, p. 230, where he continues, 'At that time Thirlby had accepted Theobald's assertions on faith, but he came to doubt their veracity . . .'. The marginal phrase could be interpreted as a later note when Thirlby had collated his annotated Pope against Theobald's first edition, but it seems that Thirlby had by then (1733, or more probably 1736–7) decided to make his copy of Theobald's edn. the principal repository of his own emendations, conjectures, and remarks (my inference from Smith, p. 220).

[2] The marginalium appears in vol. 6, p. 200 of Pope's first edn.

[3] This decision may exaggerate Thirlby's originality (he appears in my collation of eleven lines), but that seems small recompense for the years of near-anonymity his very interesting work has suffered. As Smith explains (pp. 223–5), Thirlby had an elaborate, Latin shorthand system for ranking his conjectures, but I have not (*pace* Smith, p. 226) attempted to distinguish them in the collation. Thirlby's various annotated editions seem to have circulated among editors of Shakespeare for many years after Thirlby's death (for details, see the essays of Spencer and Velz and of Smith and next n.), and it is entirely possible that readings credited to later editors in fact originated with Thirlby.

[4] For a survey of the debate over the Perkins Folio, see John W. Velz's review article of Dewey Ganzel, *Fortune and Men's Eyes: The Career of John Payne Collier*, 'The Collier Controversy Redivivus', *SQ*, 36 (1985), 106–15; Velz speculates that Collier had seen some of Thirlby's manuscript annotations (p. 114).

collated as conjectures and attributed to 'Collier, *Notes*'; many of them were first printed in, respectively, S. W. Singer's (1856) and Collier's (1858) own second editions of the complete works.

This edition was prepared independently of John Jowett's in *William Shakespeare: The Complete Works* (Oxford, 1986). I have consulted that text, and it is represented in the collation.

Abbreviations and References

Prompt-books and acting texts of *King John* are entered under 'Other Works'. Place of publication is London unless otherwise noted.

EDITIONS OF SHAKESPEARE

F	The First Folio, 1623
F2	The Second Folio, 1632
F3	The Third Folio, 1663
F4	The Fourth Folio, 1685
Alexander	Peter Alexander, *Complete Works* (1951)
Boswell	James Boswell, *Plays and Poems*, 21 vols. (1821), vol. 15
Cambridge	W. G. Clark and W. A. Wright, *Works*, The Cambridge Shakespeare, 9 vols. (New York, 1891–3), vol. 4
Capell	Edward Capell, *Mr. William Shakespeare his Comedies, Histories, and Tragedies . . .*, 10 vols., vol. 5 (1767)
Clarke	Charles and Mary Cowden Clarke, *Plays*, Cassell's Illustrated Shakespeare, 3 vols. in 60 parts (1864–8), parts 22–3 (December 1865–January 1866)
Collier	J. Payne Collier, *Works*, 8 vols. (1842–4), vol. 4 (1842)
Collier 1858	J. Payne Collier, *Shakespeare's Comedies, Histories, Tragedies and Poems*, new edn., 6 vols. (1858), vol. 3
Delius	Nicolaus Delius, *Werke*, 7 vols. (Elberfeld, 1854–60), vol. 3 (1857)
Donovan	Thomas Donovan, comp., *English Historical Plays . . . Arranged for Acting as well as Reading*, 2 vols. (1896), vol. 1
Dyce	Alexander Dyce, *Works*, 6 vols. (1857), vol. 3
Dyce 1864	Alexander Dyce, *Works*, 2nd edn., 9 vols. (1864–67), vol. 4 (1864)
Fleay	F. G. Fleay, *King John*, Collins Classics (1878)

Furness	Horace Howard Furness, Jr., *King John*, A New Variorum Edition, vol. 19 (Philadelphia, 1919)
Furnivall	F. J. Furnivall, *King Iohn*, Old-Spelling Shakespeare, The Shakespeare Library (1911)
Halliwell	J. O. Halliwell, *Works*, 16 vols. (1853–65), vol. 8 (1859)
Hanmer	[Thomas Hanmer,] *Works*, Revised and Corrected, 6 vols. (Oxford, 1743–4), vol. 3 (1743)
Honigmann	E. A. J. Honigmann, *King John*, Arden Shakespeare, rev. 4th edn. (1954)
Hudson 1881	Henry N. Hudson, *Complete Works*, Harvard Edition, 20 vols. (Boston, 1881), vol. 10
I. John	Ivor B. John, *The Life and Death of King John*, Arden Shakespeare (1907)
Johnson	Samuel Johnson, *Plays*, 8 vols. (1765), vol. 3
Keightley	Thomas Keightley, *Plays*, 6 vols. (1864), vol. 3
Knight	Charles Knight, *Works*, Pictorial Edition, 7 vols. (1838–43), Histories, vol. 1 (1838)
Malone	Edmond Malone, *Plays and Poems*, 10 vols. (1790), vol. 4
Matchett	William H. Matchett, *King John*, The Signet Shakespeare (New York, 1966)
Neilson	William Allan Neilson, *Complete Works*, Student's Cambridge Edition, 3rd edn. (Boston, 1910)
Moore Smith	G. C. Moore Smith, *King John*, The Warwick Shakespeare (1900)
Oxford	John Jowett, *King John*, in Stanley Wells and Gary Taylor, gen. eds., *Complete Works* (Oxford, 1986)
Pope	Alexander Pope, *Works*, 6 vols. (1725), vol. 3
Pope 1728	Alexander Pope, *Works*, 10 vols. (1728), vol. 4
Rann	Joseph Rann, *Works*, 6 vols. (Oxford, 1786–94), vol. 3 (1789)
Reed	*Plays* . . . 6th edn., Revised and augmented by Isaac Reed, 21 vols. (1813), vol. 10
Rolfe	William J. Rolfe, *Shakespeare's History of the Life and Death of King John*, English Classics (New York, 1887)
Rowe	Nicholas Rowe, *Works*, 6 vols. (1709), vol. 3
Rowe 1714	Nicholas Rowe, *Works*, Revis'd and Corrected, 8 vols. (1714), vol. 3

Singer	Samuel Weller Singer, *Dramatic Works*, 10 vols. (Chiswick, 1826), vol. 4
Singer 1856	Samuel Weller Singer, *Dramatic Works*, 2nd edn., 10 vols. (1856), vol. 4
Smallwood	R. L. Smallwood, *King John*, New Penguin Shakespeare (Harmondsworth, 1974)
Staunton	Howard Staunton, *Plays*, 50 parts in 3 vols. (1858–60), parts 6–8 (May and June 1857)
Steevens	Samuel Johnson and George Steevens, *Plays*, 10 vols. (1773), vol. 5
Steevens 1778	Samuel Johnson and George Steevens, *Plays*, 10 vols. (1778), vol. 5
Theobald	Lewis Theobald, *Works*, 7 vols. (1733), vol. 3
Theobald 1740	Lewis Theobald, *Works*, 2nd edn., 8 vols. (1740), vol. 3
Warburton	William Warburton, *Works*, 8 vols. (1747), vol. 3
White	Richard Grant White, *Works*, 12 vols. (Boston, 1857–61), vol. 6 (1859)
Wilson	John Dover Wilson, *King John*, The New Shakespeare (Cambridge, 1936)
Wright	William Aldis Wright, *King John*, Clarendon Press Series (Oxford, 1886)

OTHER WORKS AND ABBREVIATIONS

Abbott	E. A. Abbott, *A Shakespearian Grammar*, 3rd edn. (1891); reference is by section (§) number
Apocrypha	C. F. Tucker Brooke, ed., *The Shakespeare Apocrypha* (Oxford, 1908)
Beaumont and Fletcher	Fredson Bowers, gen. ed., *The Dramatic Works in the Beaumont and Fletcher Canon* (Cambridge, 1966–)
Bevington	David Bevington, *Action is Eloquence: Shakespeare's Language of Gesture* (Cambridge, Mass., 1984)
Bonjour	Adrien Bonjour, 'The Road to Swinestead Abbey: A Study of the Sense and Structure of *King John*', *ELH*, 18 (1951), 253–74
Booth	Stephen Booth, *Shakespeare's Sonnets* (New Haven, Conn., 1977)
Booth, *Holinshed*	Stephen Booth, *The Book Called Holinshed's Chronicles* (San Francisco, 1969)

Bowers	Fredson Bowers, 'Authority, Copy, and Transmission in Shakespeare's Texts' in *Shakespeare Study Today*, ed. Georgianna Ziegler (New York, 1986), pp. 7–36
Branam	George C. Branam, *Eighteenth-Century Adaptations of Shakespearean Tragedy*, English Studies, 14 (Berkeley and Los Angeles, 1956)
Bullough	Geoffrey Bullough, *Narrative and Dramatic Sources of Shakespeare*, 8 vols. (1957–75)
Burckhardt	Sigurd Burckhardt, *Shakespearean Meanings* (Princeton, NJ, 1968)
Campbell	Lily Bess Campbell, *Shakespeare's Histories: Mirrors of Elizabethan Policy* (San Marino, Calif., 1947)
Capell, *Notes*	Edward Capell, *Notes and Various Readings to Shakespeare*, 3 vols. (1779–83), vol. 1 (1779)
Carter	Thomas T. Carter, *Shakespeare and Holy Scripture* (1905)
Cercignani	Fausto Cercignani, *Shakespeare's Works and Elizabethan Pronunciation* (Oxford, 1981)
Chambers	E. K. Chambers, *William Shakespeare: Facts and Problems*, 2 vols. (Oxford, 1930)
Chapman	George Chapman's comedies are cited from Allan Holaday, gen. ed., *The Plays of George Chapman: The Comedies* (Urbana, Ill., 1970) and his tragedies from T. M. Parrott, ed., *The Plays of George Chapman: The Tragedies* (1910), except for *Bussy D'Ambois*, ed. Nicholas Brooke, The Revels Plays (1964)
Collier, *Notes*	J. Payne Collier, *Notes and Emendations to the Text of Shakespeare's Plays from Early Manuscript Corrections in . . . Folio, 1632 . . .*, 2nd edn. (1853)
conj.	conjecture, conjectured by
Cotgrave	Randle Cotgrave, *A Dictionarie of the French and English Tongues* (1611)
Dekker	Fredson Bowers, ed., *The Dramatic Works of Thomas Dekker*, 4 vols. (Cambridge, 1953–61)
Dent	R. W. Dent, *Shakespeare's Proverbial Language: An Index* (Berkeley, Los Angeles, and London, 1981); reference is by proverb number
Dent, *PLED*	R. W. Dent, *Proverbial Language in English Drama Exclusive of Shakespeare, 1495–1616* (Berkeley, Los Angeles, and London, 1984); reference is by proverb number

Diary	Philip Henslowe, *Henslowe's Diary*, eds. R. A. Foakes and R. T. Rickert (Cambridge, 1961)
Division	*The Division of the Kingdoms: Shakespeare's Two Versions of 'King Lear'*, eds. Gary Taylor and Michael Warren (Oxford, 1983)
Edward III	*The Raigne of . . . Edward the Third* in *Apocrypha*
EETS	Early English Text Society
Edwards	Philip Edwards, *Threshold of a Nation: A Study in English and Irish Drama* (Cambridge, 1979)
Farmer	Richard Farmer, 'Appendix II' in Samuel Johnson and George Steevens, eds., Shakespeare, *Plays* (1773), vol. 10
Ford	John Ford, *The Broken Heart*, ed. T. J. B. Spencer, The Revels Plays (Manchester, 1980)
Frye	R. M. Frye, *Shakespeare and Christian Doctrine* (Princeton, NJ, 1963)
Garrick	David Garrick's acting version of *King John* ('As performed at the Theatre-Royal, Drury-Lane Regulated from the Prompt-Book'), as represented in *Bell's Shakespeare*, 9 vols. (1773–5), vol. 4
Gentleman	[Francis Gentleman,] *The Dramatic Censor; or, Critical Companion*, 2 vols. (London and York, 1770)
Greenewald	Gerald M. Greenewald, OM, *Shakespeare's Attitude towards the Catholic Church in 'King John'* (Washington, DC, 1938)
Greg, *Ed. Prob.*	W. W. Greg, *The Editorial Problem in Shakespeare*, 3rd edn. (Oxford, 1954)
Greg, *Folio*	W. W. Greg, *The Shakespeare First Folio* (Oxford, 1955)
Harbage	Alfred Harbage, *Theatre for Shakespeare* (Toronto, 1955)
Hart	Alfred Hart, *Shakespeare and the Homilies* (Melbourne, 1934)
Heath	Benjamin Heath, *A Revisal of Shakespear's Text* (1765)
Heuser	Georg Heuser, *Die aktlose Dramaturgie William Shakespeares* (Marburg, 1956)
Hinman	Charlton Hinman, *The Printing and Proof-Reading of the First Folio of Shakespeare*, 2 vols. (Oxford, 1963)
Holinshed	Raphael Holinshed, *The Third Volume of Chronicles, beginning at Duke William the Norman . . .* (1587); reference is by page and column (a or b) and by signature
Holmes	Martin Holmes, *Shakespeare and Burbage* (1978)

Honigmann, *Impact*   E. A. J. Honigmann, *Shakespeare's Impact on his Contemporaries* (1982)

Hoy   Cyrus Hoy, *Introductions, Notes, and Commentaries to . . . 'Dramatic Works of Thomas Dekker'*, 4 vols. (Cambridge, 1980)

Hughes and Larkin   Paul L. Hughes and James F. Larkin, CSV, eds., *Tudor Royal Proclamations*, 3 vols. (New Haven, Conn., 1964–9); reference is by proclamation number and year

Hulme   Hilda Hulme, *Explorations in Shakespeare's Language* (1962; repr. 1977)

Irving   Henry Irving's proposed performance text of *King John* as represented in Henry Irving and Frank A. Marshall, eds., *The Works of William Shakespeare*, The Irving Shakespeare, 2nd edn., 8 vols. (1898), vol. 3

Jackson   MacD. P. Jackson, *Studies in Attribution: Middleton and Shakespeare*, Jacobean Drama Series, 79 (Salzburg, 1979)

Jewkes   W. T. Jewkes, *Act Division in Elizabethan and Jacobean Plays 1591–1616* (Hamden, Conn., 1958)

Jones, *Form*   Emrys Jones, *Scenic Form in Shakespeare* (Oxford, 1971)

Jones, *Origins*   Emrys Jones, *The Origins of Shakespeare* (Oxford, 1977)

Jonson   Ben Jonson, *The Alchemist*, ed. F. H. Mares, The Revels Plays (1967); *Every Man in his Humour*, ed. G. B. Jackson, The Yale Ben Jonson (New Haven, Conn., 1969)

Kean   Charles Kean's prompt-book for *King John*, as represented in Charles H. Shattuck, ed., *William Charles Macready's 'King John': A facsimile prompt-book* (Urbana, Ill., 1962)

Keen   Maurice Keen, *Chivalry* (1984)

Keeton   George W. Keeton, *Shakespeare's Legal and Political Background* (1967)

Kellner   Leon Kellner, *Restoring Shakespeare: A Critical Analysis of the Misreadings in Shakespeare's Works* (1925); reference is by section (§) number

Kemble   John Philip Kemble's prompt-book for *King John* in Charles H. Shattuck, ed., *The Kemble Promptbooks*, 11 vols. (Charlottesville, Va., 1974), vol. 5

Kinsmen   John Fletcher and William Shakespeare, *The Two Noble Kinsmen*, ed. G. R. Proudfoot, Regents Renaissance Drama (Lincoln, Nebr., 1970)

Kyd	F. S. Boas, ed., *The Works of Thomas Kyd*, rev. edn. (Oxford, 1955) except for *The Spanish Tragedy*, ed. Philip Edwards, The Revels Plays (1959)
Levine, *Problems*	Mortimer Levine, *Tudor Dynastic Problems 1460–1571* (1973)
Levine, *Succession*	Mortimer Levine, *The Early Elizabethan Succession Question* (Stanford, Calif., 1966)
Linthicum	M. Channing Linthicum, *Costume in the Drama of Shakespeare and his Contemporaries* (Oxford, 1936)
LS	Emmett L. Avery, Charles Beecher Hogan, A. H. Scouten, George Winchester Stone, and William Van Lennep, eds., *The London Stage 1660–1800: A Calendar of Plays, Entertainments, and Afterpieces*, 11 vols. (Carbondale, Ill., 1960–8)
Lyly	R. Warwick Bond, ed., *The Complete Works of John Lyly*, 3 vols. (Oxford, 1902); reference is by act-, scene-, and line-numbers for dramatic works, by volume and page for non-dramatic works
Macready	Charles H. Shattuck, ed., *William Charles Macready's 'King John': A facsimile prompt-book* (Urbana, Ill., 1962)
Mahood	M. M. Mahood, *Shakespeare's Wordplay* (1957)
Malone, *Supp.*	Edmond Malone, *Supplement to the Edition of Shakespeare's Plays Published in 1778*, 2 vols. (1780), vol. 1
Marlowe	Fredson Bowers, ed., *Complete Works of Christopher Marlowe*, 2nd edn., 2 vols. (Cambridge, 1981) except for *Tamburlaine the Great* [*Parts 1* and *2*], ed. J. S. Cunningham, The Revels Plays (Manchester, 1981)
Mason	John Monck Mason, *Comments on the Last Edition of Shakespeare's Plays* [i.e., Steevens 1778] (Dublin, 1785)
Mason[2]	John Monck Mason, *Comments on the Several Editions of Shakespeare's Plays* (Dublin, 1807)
Matchett, 'Heritage'	William H. Matchett, 'Richard's Divided Heritage in *King John*', *Essays in Criticism*, 12 (1962), 231–53
Maxwell	J. C. Maxwell, 'Notes on *King John*', *N. & Q.*, 195 (18 February 1950), 75–6
Maxwell[2]	J. C. Maxwell, '*King John*—Textual Notes', *N. & Q.*, 195 (28 October 1950), 473–4
MLN	*Modern Language Notes*
MLR	*Modern Language Review*

MSR	Malone Society Reprint (Oxford)
N. & Q.	*Notes and Queries*
Nares	Robert Nares, *A Glossary of Words, Phrases, Names, and Allusions*, ed. J. O. Halliwell and T. Wright (1905)
Nashe	R. B. McKerrow, ed., *The Works of Thomas Nashe*, revised by F. P. Wilson, 5 vols. (Oxford, 1958)
Nichols, *Illus.*	John Nichols, *Illustrations of the Literary History of the Eighteenth Century*, 2 vols. (1817)
Noble	Richmond Noble, *Shakespeare's Biblical Knowledge and Use of the Book of Common Prayer* (1935)
O'Connor	John S. O'Connor, 'A Qualitative Analysis of Compositors C and D in the Shakespeare First Folio', *SB*, 28 (1977), 57–74
OED	*Oxford English Dictionary*
Partridge	Eric Partridge, *Shakespeare's Bawdy* (1947)
Peele	C. T. Prouty, gen. ed., *The Life and Works of George Peele*, 3 vols. (New Haven, Conn., 1952–70)
Pollock and Maitland	Frederick Pollock and F. W. Maitland, *The History of English Law Before the Time of Edward I*, 2nd edn., reissued with a new introduction by S. F. C. Milsom, 2 vols. (1898; Cambridge, 1968)
Rastell	[John Rastell,] *Les Termes de la Ley . . . newly imprinted . . .* (1624); this work is arranged alphabetically
Roderick	Richard Roderick, *Remarks on Shakespear*, in Thomas Edwards, *The Canons of Criticism . . . and Sonnets* (1765), pp. 260–76
Schäfer	Jürgen Schäfer, *Documentation in the O.E.D.: Shakespeare and Nashe as Test Cases* (Oxford, 1980)
SB	*Studies in Bibliography*
Schmidt	Alexander Schmidt, *Shakespeare Lexicon and Quotation Dictionary*, 3rd rev. edn. Gregor Sarrazin, 2 vols. (1902; repr. New York, 1971)
ShakS	*Shakespeare Studies* (USA)
Shakespeare's England	C. T. Onions, comp., *Shakespeare's England*, 2 vols. (Oxford, 1916)
Sider	John W. Sider, ed., *The Troublesome Raigne of King John* (New York, 1979)

Simmons	J. L. Simmons, 'Shakespeare's *King John* and Its Source: Coherence, Pattern, and Vision', *Tulane Studies in English*, 17 (1969), 53–72
Sisson	C. J. Sisson, *New Readings in Shakespeare*, 2 vols. (Cambridge, 1955), vol. 2
Slater	Ann Pasternak Slater, *Shakespeare the Director* (Brighton, 1982)
Smith	John Hazel Smith, 'Styan Thirlby's Shakespearean Commentaries: A Corrective Analysis', *ShakS*, 11 (1978), 219–41
Sprague	Arthur Colby Sprague, *Shakespeare's Histories: Plays for the Stage* (1964)
SQ	*Shakespeare Quarterly*
SR	The Stationers' Register
Stafford	H. G. Stafford, *James VI of Scotland and the Throne of England* (New York, 1940)
subs.	substantively
Sugden	Edward H. Sugden, *A Topographical Dictionary to the Works of Shakespeare and his Fellow Dramatists* (Manchester, 1925)
Taylor, 'Zounds'	Gary Taylor, '"Zounds" Revisited: Theatrical, Editorial, and Literary Expurgation' in Gary Taylor and John Jowett, *Shakespeare Reshaped 1606–1623* (forthcoming)
Textual Companion	Stanley Wells and Gary Taylor with John Jowett and William Montgomery, *William Shakespeare: A Textual Companion* (Oxford, 1987)
Thirlby	Styan Thirlby, manuscript annotations in a copy of Pope's edition, vol. 3 (1725), Osborn Collection, Beinecke Library, Yale University (shelfmark: fpc 13)
Thomas	Keith Thomas, *Religion and the Decline of Magic* (New York and London, 1971)
Tilley	Morris Palmer Tilley, *A Dictionary of the Proverbs in England in the Sixteenth and Seventeenth Centuries* (Ann Arbor, Mich., 1950); reference is by proverb number
Tillyard	E. M. W. Tillyard, *Shakespeare's History Plays* (1944)
TLN	T[hrough] L[ine] N[umber(s)] as found in the Norton facsimile of the Folio prepared by Charlton Hinman (New York, 1968)

TR	*The Troublesome Reign of King John*, in Bullough, vol. 4 (1962); cited by part and line number(s)
Tyndale	William Tyndale, *The Obedience of a Christian Man* (1528)
Tyrwhitt	Thomas Tyrwhitt, *Observations and Conjectures upon Some Passages of Shakespeare* (Oxford, 1766)
Vaughan	Henry Halford Vaughan, *New Readings and New Renderings of Shakespeare's Tragedies* [*sic*], 2nd edn., 3 vols. (1886), vol. 1
Waith	Eugene M. Waith, '*King John* and the Drama of History', *SQ*, 29 (1978), 192–211
Walker	William Sidney Walker, *A Critical Examination of the Text of Shakespeare* . . ., ed. W. N. Lettsom, 3 vols. (1860)
Warren	W. L. Warren, *King John*, 2nd edn. (1978)
Webster	John Webster, *The Duchess of Malfi*, ed. J. R. Brown, The Revels Plays (1964) and *The White Devil*, ed. J. R. Brown, The Revels Plays (1960)
Whiting	B. J. and H. W. Whiting, *Proverbs, Sentences, and Proverbial Phrases; from English Writings mainly before 1500* (Cambridge, Mass., 1968)
Williams	W. W[illiams]., 'Notes on *King John*', *The Parthenon: a Weekly Journal of Literature, Science and Art*, no. 16 (16 August 1862), p. 506
Wilson, *ODEP*	*Oxford Dictionary of English Proverbs*, 3rd edn., rev. F. P. Wilson (Oxford, 1970)

The Life and Death of King John

THE PERSONS OF THE PLAY

KING JOHN of England

QUEEN ELEANOR, his mother, widow of Henry II

PRINCE HENRY, his son and later Henry III of England

BLANCHE of Castile, his niece and later wife of Louis the Dauphin of
France

Geoffrey Fitz Peter, Earl of ESSEX

William 'Long-Sword', Earl of SALISBURY   English nobles, sometimes

William Marshall, Earl of PEMBROKE   allied with France

Roger, Lord BIGOT, Earl of Norfolk

PETER OF POMFRET, an English 'prophet'

EXECUTIONERS, two servants of King John

ENGLISH HERALD

MESSENGER, of the English party

PHILIP FAULCONBRIDGE, also known as THE BASTARD and Sir Richard
Plantagenet, illegitimate son of Richard I of England ('Coeur-de-
Lion') and Lady Faulconbridge

ROBERT FAULCONBRIDGE, legitimate son of the deceased Sir Robert
Faulconbridge and Lady Faulconbridge

LADY FAULCONBRIDGE, their mother

JAMES GURNEY, servant of the Faulconbridge family

KING PHILIP the Second of France

LOUIS THE DAUPHIN, his son

Viscount of MELUN, a French nobleman

CHATILLON, French nobleman and ambassador to John

FRENCH HERALD

MESSENGER, of the French party

CONSTANCE, wife of Geoffrey, deceased son of Henry II of England

ARTHUR, her son and nephew of John, claimant to the throne of England
and eventually Duke of Bretagne (Brittany)

Duke of AUSTRIA, also called 'Limoges', an ally of King Philip of France

CARDINAL PANDULPH, representative of Pope Innocent III

HUBERT, a citizen of Angers and later supporter of the English cause

CITIZEN of the city of Angers

Sheriff, of an English county

English lords

English soldiers

English attendants

French lords

French soldiers

French attendants

The Life and Death of King John

<hr/>

1.1   ⌈*Flourish.*⌉ *Enter King John, Queen Eleanor, the*
       Earls of Pembroke, Essex, and Salisbury, with
       Chatillon, the French Ambassador

KING JOHN
   Now say, Chatillon, what would France with us?
CHATILLON
   Thus, after greeting, speaks the King of France,

The Life and Death of King John] F (*table of contents, title-page, and running titles throughout*)
   1.1] F (*Actus Primus, Scæna Prima.*)   0.1 *Flourish.*] OXFORD; *not in* F. *See note.*   0.1–3
Enter . . . Ambassador] F (*Enter King Iohn, Queene Elinor, Pembroke, Essex, and Salisbury, with
the Chattylion of France.*) *See note.*   1 Chatillon] F (*Chatillion and thus throughout except*
Chattillon *at 1.1.30 and* Chattilion *at 2.1.49.1*)

1.1 Location: The royal court, somewhere
   in England, perhaps London (see l. 45:
   'Come from the country'). In John's
   reign, to a much greater extent than in
   Elizabeth's, all the institutions of central
   government travelled with the monarch;
   on the 'authority' of *TR*, this scene is
   sometimes imagined as being in Norfolk.
   Historically, John was usually on the
   continent; he 'could not by any stretch
   of the imagination be called an Englishman. . . . If all John's sojourns in England
   were added together, it seems improbable
   that they would reach a total of five
   years' (Sidney Painter, *The Reign of King
   John* (Baltimore, 1949), p. 4).
0.1 *Flourish* F apparently lacks a number
   of sound-cues; see Appendix C.
0.1–3 *King John . . . Ambassador* Protocol
   or a convention of F's editors may dictate
   the order of the list (royalty, native aristocrats, foreign aristocrat), but it may indicate the order of the characters' entry
   on stage; see Appendix D. F evidently
   regards 'Chattylion' as a title rather than
   a personal name (see 1.1.0.2n below);
   Honigmann hypothesizes an overlooked
   tittle in 'thē' and reads 'with them'. For
   the English lords named here, see Introduction, pp. 22–3.
0.1 *King John* Born 1166, reigned 1199–
   1216; the fifth and youngest son of
   Eleanor and Henry II, who nicknamed
   him 'Sans Terre' or 'Lack-land'.

Queen Eleanor Daughter and heir of
   William V, Duke of Aquitaine; she mar-
   ried and was divorced from Louis VII of
   France and then married Henry II of
   England; see 4.2.120n.
0.2 *Pembroke* Historically, William Marshall, and loyal to John; he served as
   regent at the beginning of Henry III's
   reign and concluded the Treaty of Lambeth with Louis in 1217.
   Essex The historically appropriate Earl of
   Essex is Geoffrey Fitz Peter, Justicier of
   England from 1198 until his death in
   1213.
   Salisbury Called 'William Longespee'
   (Long-Sword) and historically a very important nobleman loyal to John; Henry
   II's bastard (but not, as late Tudor legend
   had it, by 'Fair' Rosamond Clifford) and
   therefore John's half-brother.
   Chatillon A member of a noble family
   prominent in John's day; the character
   appears in *TR* ('Chattilion') and the name
   in *Edward III* and *Henry V* ('Chattillion'
   at TLN 1422; 'Chatilion, Admirall of
   France' at TLN 2812), but Chatillon
   would be most familiar to Elizabethans
   as the family name of the assassinated
   Huguenot leader, Admiral Coligny, who
   appears in Marlowe's *Massacre at Paris*
   (named as 'Shatillian' at 5.312) and as
   'the Ghost of . . . Shattilion' in Chapman's
   Revenge of Bussy (1613), K3.

119

In my behaviour, to the majesty,
The borrowed majesty, of England here.
QUEEN ELEANOR
A strange beginning—'borrowed majesty'?
KING JOHN
Silence, good mother; hear the embassy.
CHATILLON
Philip of France, in right and true behalf
Of thy deceasèd brother Geoffrey's son,
Arthur Plantagenet, lays most lawful claim
To this fair island and the territories—   10
To Ireland, Poitiers, Anjou, Touraine, Maine—
Desiring thee to lay aside the sword
Which sways usurpingly these several titles,
And put the same into young Arthur's hand,
Thy nephew and right royal sovereign.
KING JOHN
What follows if we disallow of this?
CHATILLON
The proud control of fierce and bloody war
To enforce these rights so forcibly withheld—
KING JOHN
Here have we war for war and blood for blood,
Controlment for controlment. So answer France.   20

18 withheld—] OXFORD; with-held, F

3 **behaviour** bearing the character of another, personification (so 1c giving this
line as the sole citation)
4 **borrowed majesty, of England** A com-
pactly insulting phrase: *borrowed* =
'usurped'; *majesty* = 'sovereignty' and
'external magnificence befitting a sovereign' (*sb.* 1 and 3); *England* = the nation
and King John.
6 **embassy** an ambassador's message (earliest citation for *sb.* 2). The modern meaning appears at 1.1.22 and 99.
7 **Philip of France** Philip II, or 'Philip Augustus' (1165–1223), son of Louis VII;
he substantially increased the territory
controlled by the Capetian dynasty (so
named after Hugh Capet, a tenth-century
ruler whose descendants ruled France
until 1848).
8 **Geoffrey** Count or Duke of Brittany and
Earl of Richmond (1158–86), fourth son
of Henry II.
9 **Arthur Plantagenet** See 2.1.13n.

10 **territories** 'feudal dependencies' (Wright)
11 **Poitiers** Elizabethan orthography did not
distinguish Poitiers (the city) from Poitou
(the province), employing 'Poyctiers' (F's
reading here) or some variant for both;
see 2.1.152n.
12 **sword** i.e., sword of state
13 **sways** rules, governs (earliest citation for
v. 9). See 2.1.344.
   several individual, separate
15 **right** 'very', but with the implication of
'by right' or 'in justice'
17 **control** rebuke or restraint, check. See
'his raging eye . . . | Without control,
listed to make a prey' (*Richard III* 3.5.
81–2).
19 **Here** both 'in England' and 'in response'
   blood for blood Tilley B458, 'Blood will
have blood' (citing Genesis 9: 6 and
examples from *c.*1560 onward). Whiting
has examples of this extremely popular
idea from *c.*1395 onward.

CHATILLON

Then take my king's defiance from my mouth,
The farthest limit of my embassy.

KING JOHN

Bear mine to him, and so depart in peace.
Be thou as lightning in the eyes of France,
For ere thou canst report, I will be there;
The thunder of my cannon shall be heard.
So hence. Be thou the trumpet of our wrath
And sullen presage of your own decay.—
An honourable conduct let him have.
Pembroke, look to't.—Farewell, Chatillon.   30

Exeunt Chatillon and Pembroke

QUEEN ELEANOR

What now, my son? Have I not ever said
How that ambitious Constance would not cease
Till she had kindled France and all the world
Upon the right and party of her son?

30.1 *Exeunt . . . Pembroke*] F (*Exit Chat<illon>. and Pem<broke>.*)

---

22 **farthest limit of my embassy** Two closely
related meanings: full extent (= *farthest
limit*) of what I was instructed to say as
part of my diplomatic mission (= *embassy*); bound beyond which I, acting on
my mission, am not permitted to go.

24–6 **Be thou as lightning . . . shall be heard**
Proverbially, 'There is lightning lightly
before thunder' (Tilley L281); Wilson,
ODEP, lists examples from 1545 onward,
and Dent cites Ecclesiasticus 32: 10, but
a pun on 'report' (l. 25)—Chatillon's
message, the sound of Chatillon's voice,
the noise of John's cannon, the thunder
that follows lightning—unifies John's
threat: Chatillon, like lightning, may be
seen by King Philip, but John will move
so swiftly that the English army will have
arrived before either the ambassador's
message or the thunder that follows a
lightning flash. A similar punning on
'report' appears at *Bussy D'Ambois*
2.1.107–12, in response to the Nuntius'
speech. Thunder, lightning, and cannon
are often associated; see, e.g., 'Have I
not heard great ordnance in the field, |
And heaven's artillery thunder in the
skies?' (*Shrew* 1.2.202–3) and the title-
page woodcut of *Look Up and See Wonders*
(1628).

28 **sullen** Applied to sounds or musical in-
struments, *sullen* means 'Of a deep, dull,
or mournful tone' (*a., adv.,* and *sb.* 3b),
but the context also seems to suggest
'baleful, malignant' (1d, first cited from
1676). Shakespeare often uses the word
in funereal contexts, as John may intend
here; see 'No longer mourn for me when
I am dead | Than you shall hear the surly
sullen bell | Give warning to the world
that I am fled' (Sonnet 71.1–3) and 'Our
solemn hymns to sullen dirges change'
(*Romeo* 4.4.115).
presage Accent on first syllable here and
at 3.4.158, although the word is accented on the second syllable elsewhere
in Shakespeare.

29 **conduct** escort, company of attendants;
perhaps also a document guaranteeing
Chatillon's safe passage (accent on first
syllable)

32 **Constance** She inherited the territory of
Richmond (Yorkshire) from her father,
Conan IV, Duke of Brittany, and married
Geoffrey in 1181; after his death, she
remarried twice. See 4.2.122–3n.

33 **France** i.e., the King of France, as well
as the French nation

34 **party** side, cause, interest

This might have been prevented and made whole
With very easy arguments of love,
Which now the manage of two kingdoms must
With fearful bloody issue arbitrate.

KING JOHN
Our strong possession and our right for us.

QUEEN ELEANOR (*aside to John*)
Your strong possession much more than your right,   40
Or else it must go wrong with you and me;
So much my conscience whispers in your ear,
Which none but heaven, and you, and I, shall hear.
    Enter a sheriff

ESSEX
My liege, here is the strangest controversy,
Come from the country to be judged by you,
That e'er I heard. Shall I produce the men?

KING JOHN (*to Essex*) Let them approach.—   [*Exit sheriff*]
Our abbeys and our priories shall pay
This expeditious charge.—

43 heaven] F (heauen); God MATCHETT   43.1 *Enter a sheriff*] F (*Sheriffe*); *Enter the Sheriff of* Northamptonshire, *and whispers* Essex CAPELL   47 *Exit sheriff*] CAPELL; *not in* F   49 expeditious] F1; expeditions F2

35 **made whole** i.e., satisfactorily agreed, a union worked out; perhaps from *make*, *v.*¹ V.59 ('with substantives expressing the action of verbs') and the obsolete *whole, v.* II.3, 'to make into a whole; to assemble or unite'

36 **arguments** tokens, manifestations

37 **manage** 'conduct, administration' (Steevens; Moore Smith quotes *Edward III* 3.3.223–4: 'That courage and experience join'd in one, | Your manage may be second unto none'; see *sb.* 5), or 'proceeding, taking of measures, contriving of means' (Schmidt). Yet 'bloody issue' (l. 38, where *issue* = event, consequence, but could also = birth, progeny) suggests a play on words: 'manage' as 'male population' or 'male soldiers'; this meaning does not appear in *OED*, but see the obsolete (citations 1611–74) 'manage' for 'majority', the age at which one becomes a man. Shakespeare allowed Julia to describe her decorous male disguise as 'mannerly' (*Two Gentlemen* 2.7.58) and Lance soon puns on 'unmannerly' as both 'impolite' and 'not an adult

male' (3.1.371); see 5.2.131n. *OED* offers no support for Smallwood's useful gloss, 'rulers', which suits 'Till I had with an unresisted shock | Controlled the mannage [*sic*] of proud Angers' walls' (*TR* 1.432–3).

40 **to John** Lines 42–3 indicate that Eleanor 'whispers' the entire speech.

43.1 **Enter a sheriff** Editors have moved this entry and have added stage directions to recreate *TR*'s whispered conversation between Essex and the sheriff, balancing Eleanor and John's low-voiced conversation (1.1.31 ff., and see the two conversations, one heard, the other not, at 2.1.469 ff.), but it seems just as likely that the sheriff's arrival simply and economically prompts Essex to raise the next order of business for the court.

49 **expeditious** Believing that F's *expeditious* includes a 'turned' *n*, editors have emended to 'expedition's', but *expeditious* (= speedy) suits both the suddenness of the French threat and John's quick response. 'Expedition', 'expedience', 'expedient', and 'expeditious' all derive from Latin

Enter Robert Faulconbridge and Philip Faulconbridge
What men are you?

PHILIP FAULCONBRIDGE

Your faithful subject I, a gentleman,   50
Born in Northamptonshire and eldest son,
As I suppose, to Robert Faulconbridge,
A soldier, by the honour-giving hand
Of Coeur-de-Lion knighted in the field.

KING JOHN (*to Robert Faulconbridge*) What art thou?

ROBERT FAULCONBRIDGE

The son and heir to that same Faulconbridge.

KING JOHN

Is that the elder, and art thou the heir?
You came not of one mother then, it seems.

PHILIP FAULCONBRIDGE

Most certain of one mother, mighty King,
That is well known; and, as I think, one father.   60
But for the certain knowledge of that truth
I put you o'er to heaven and to my mother;
Of that I doubt, as all men's children may.

49 *Enter Robert Faulconbridge and Philip Faulconbridge*] F (*Enter Robert Faulconbridge, and Philip* after 'you?'); *Exit Sheriff; and Re-enters, with* Philip, *the Bastard* Faulconbridge, *and* ROBERT *his Brother* CAPELL (*after* 'approach', *l. 47*)   50 subject I, a] CAPELL; subiect, I a F   53 honour-giving hand] F (Honor-giuing-hand)   54 Coeur-de-Lion] F (*Cordelion throughout*) 62 heaven] F (heauen); God MATCHETT

expedire, and all seem to have connoted haste or to have been used to intensify that connotation for Shakespeare; see, for example: 'expedient march' (2.1.223); 'expedient haste' (4.2.268); 'A breach that craves a quick expedient stop!' (*2 Henry VI* 3.1.288).

Philip Faulconbridge Holinshed mentions 'Philip bastard son to King Richard' who 'killed the Viscount of Limoges in revenge of his father's death' (160b; O6ᵛ, and see 1.1.54n and 3.1.114n). Editors who stigmatize Philip Faulconbridge as 'his [Robert's] bastard brother' are mistaken: John declares him legally legitimate (1.1.116), and Philip becomes officially and dramatically a bastard only after 1.1.162 (or perhaps at 1.1.138, when F's speech-prefix changes to '*Bast.*'). Capell's stage direction reflects the novelizing bent of many editors.

54 **Coeur-de-Lion** Richard I (1157–99), a

figure around whom many romantic legends quickly gathered, including the story of his wresting the heart from a still-living lion; the epithet is probably contemporary, although the story is not. **knighted in the field** An honour for instant bravery (as at *Titus* 1.1.195–6), somewhat diminished in Elizabethan times by Leicester's and Essex's wholesale knightings in Holland and Ireland, respectively.

58 **You came not of one mother** 'John assumes paternal infidelity' (Smallwood); see Introduction, pp. 54–9.

60–2 **as I think . . . mother** A proverbial attitude: see Tilley M1193, 'Ask the mother if the child be like his father'.

62 **put . . . o'er** hand over, refer; sole citation for *put*, *v.*¹ B.IV.49f

63 **doubt** am uncertain. The doubt is proverbial: Tilley C309, 'It is a wise child that knows his own father'.

QUEEN ELEANOR

Out on thee, rude man! Thou dost shame thy mother
And wound her honour with this diffidence.

PHILIP FAULCONBRIDGE

I, madam? No, I have no reason for it.
That is my brother's plea and none of mine,
The which if he can prove, a pops me out
At least from fair five hundred pound a year.
Heaven guard my mother's honour and my land.   70

KING JOHN ⌈*aside*⌉

A good blunt fellow.—Why, being younger born,
Doth he lay claim to thine inheritance?

PHILIP FAULCONBRIDGE

I know not why, except to get the land;
But once he slandered me with bastardy.
But whe'er I be as true begot or no,
That still I lay upon my mother's head.
But that I am as well begot, my liege—
Fair fall the bones that took the pains for me—
Compare our faces and be judge yourself.
If old Sir Robert did beget us both   80
And were our father, and this son like him,
O old Sir Robert, father, on my knee
I give heaven thanks I was not like to thee.

KING JOHN

Why, what a madcap hath heaven lent us here!

QUEEN ELEANOR (*to John*)

He hath a trick of Coeur-de-Lion's face;

75 But] F; Now (*conj.* WRIGHT); And (*conj.* KELLNER)   79 yourself.] ROWE; your selfe‸ F
84 here!] F (∼ ?)

64 **Out** A common (Dent OO3) and angry
interjection: 'Get out!', 'Go away!'
65 **diffidence** reluctance (to state your
parentage)
68 **a** he
69 **fair** fully (*adv.* 9c), at the least. The sum
is attractive (= *fair*), but the Bastard also
implies that the estate may be worth
more than £500.
75 **whe'er** whether
78 **Fair fall** i.e., may good fortune befall, but
perhaps with a pun on the physical and
moral *fall* his mother took when she

conceived him
84 **madcap** reckless or impulsive person
85 **trick** characteristic quality, trait, as in
'the fox, | Who, ne'er so tame, so cher-
ished, and locked up, | Will have a wild
trick of his ancestors' (*1 Henry IV* 5.2.9–
11). Steevens (in Malone) points out that
the word literally means 'the tracing of
a drawing' (see 2.1.101n and Helen of
Bertram in *All's Well* 1.1.92–5: 'to sit
and draw | His archèd brows . . . | In our
heart's table—heart too capable | Of
every line and trick of his sweet favour').

The accent of his tongue affecteth him.
Do you not read some tokens of my son
In the large composition of this man?

KING JOHN (*to Eleanor*)

Mine eye hath well examinèd his parts
And finds them perfect Richard.—Sirrah, speak.   90
What doth move you to claim your brother's land?

PHILIP FAULCONBRIDGE

Because he hath a half-face like my father!
With half that face would he have all my land—
A half-faced groat—five hundred pound a year!

ROBERT FAULCONBRIDGE

My gracious liege, when that my father lived,
Your brother did employ my father much—

PHILIP FAULCONBRIDGE

Well, sir, by this you cannot get my land;
Your tale must be how he employed my mother.

ROBERT FAULCONBRIDGE

And once dispatched him in an embassy
To Germany, there with the Emperor   100
To treat of high affairs touching that time.
Th'advantage of his absence took the King,

92 father!] DELIUS; ∼? FI; ∼, F2   93 half that face] F; that half face THEOBALD   94
year!] JOHNSON; yeere? F   96 much—] ROWE; ∼. F

86 **affecteth** i.e., has the character or quality of, but without the modern sense of 'affectation'
him Coeur-de-Lion

87 **tokens** 'sign[s] by which something is perceived' (Schmidt)

88 **composition** bodily and/or mental constitution

90 **Sirrah** A slighting form of address, expressing John's superior status and authority.

92 **half-face** thin face; the face in profile, as on a coin. See 1.1.94n, 1.1.142–3n, and Fig. 4.

94 **half-faced groat** The small Elizabethan half-groat coin bore the Queen's image in profile; see 1.1.142–3n. 'Half-faced' could also mean 'unfinished, imperfect'; the phrase appears in Munday's *The Downfall of Robert Earl of Huntingdon* (MSR), l. 2320 (*K. John* shares several important historical characters with

this play and its sequel, *The Death of Robert Earl of Huntingdon*).

97–8 **Well, sir . . . my mother** Philip (the Bastard) tends to interrupt other characters with Vice-like insouciance, and they tend to ignore the interruptions; see the two Kings' determinedly regular pentameters at 2.1.276 ff.

98 **tale** narrative, but quibbling on 'tail' = penis, pudendum (*sb.*[1] 5c); Robert's tale concerns tail(s)
employed used the services of, but with the additional, bawdy sense 'had sexual relations with'

100 **Emperor** According to Holinshed (148a; N6ᵛ), Richard I sent an embassy to the Holy Roman Emperor, Henry VI (reigned 1191–7) in 1195.

102 **advantage** The first use of a word which will become (with 'vantage') a motif of the play in sexual, military, and ethical matters.

And in the mean time sojourned at my father's;
Where how he did prevail, I shame to speak.
But truth is truth: large lengths of seas and shores
Between my father and my mother lay,
As I have heard my father speak himself,
When this same lusty gentleman was got.
Upon his death-bed he by will bequeathed
His lands to me, and took it on his death   110
That this, my mother's son, was none of his;
And if he were, he came into the world
Full fourteen weeks before the course of time.
Then, good my liege, let me have what is mine,
My father's land, as was my father's will.

KING JOHN

Sirrah, your brother is legitimate;
Your father's wife did after wedlock bear him.
And if she did play false, the fault was hers,
Which fault lies on the hazards of all husbands
That marry wives. Tell me, how if my brother,   120
Who as you say took pains to get this son,
Had of your father claimed this son for his?
In sooth, good friend, your father might have kept
This calf bred from his cow from all the world;

122 his?] THEOBALD; ~, F

105 **truth is truth** Tilley T581

110 **took it on his death** staked his life on it
(so *take*, *v*. VI.40b, quoting *2 Henry VI*
2.3.93–4: 'I will take my death I never
meant him any ill'; see Dent TT1). Since
old Sir Robert is dying, Shakespeare perhaps mocks young Robert's callous indifference or his verbal ineptitude.

113 **course of time** usual or ordinary dur-
ation (here, nine months' gestation; see
time, *sb.* I.7b *spec.* a)

115 **will** In legal terminology, *will* = an individual's declaration of how his real property (i.e., land) is to be disposed of after
his death; 'testament' is the analogous
declaration concerning personal or 'mov-
able' property; for other meanings see
I.I.133n.

118 **fault** wrong, defect, or vice; another
meaning, 'crevice', led, through 'rough
anatomical analogy' to bawdy slang:
'vagina' (John Astington, '"Fault" in

Shakespeare', *SQ*, 36 (1985), 330–4;
p. 330). For phonic echo between 'false'
and 'fault', see Booth, p. 481 (commentary on Sonnet 138.14) and *passim*.

119 **on the hazards of** on the perils of; *hazard*
here derives from the obstacles to be
overcome in various games (dice, tennis,
billiards). *OED* defines 'on the hazard' as
'at stake', but does not cite this line;
see below 2.1.71n, 5.6.7, and Hotspur's
avowal 'for I will ease my heart, | Al-
though it be with hazard of my head' (*1
Henry IV* 1.3.125–6).

120 **my brother** i.e., Richard Coeur-de-Lion

123–4 **kept . . . from all the world** i.e., the
owner of the cow keeps any calf, no
matter who owns the bull. See Tilley
C765, 'Who bulls the cow must keep
the calf'; Tilley and Dent, *PLED*, cite
Chapman, *May Day* 3.3.125: 'If my bull
leap your cow, is not the calf yours?'

In sooth he might. Then if he were my brother's,
My brother might not claim him, nor your father,
Being none of his, refuse him. This concludes:
My mother's son did get your father's heir;
Your father's heir must have your father's land.

ROBERT FAULCONBRIDGE
Shall then my father's will be of no force   130
To dispossess that child which is not his?

PHILIP FAULCONBRIDGE
Of no more force to dispossess me, sir,
Than was his will to get me, as I think.

QUEEN ELEANOR
Whether hadst thou rather—be a Faulconbridge
And like thy brother to enjoy thy land,
Or the reputed son of Coeur-de-Lion,
Lord of thy presence, and no land beside?

BASTARD
Madam, an if my brother had my shape
And I had his, Sir Robert's his like him,
And if my legs were two such riding-rods,   140
My arms such eel-skins stuffed, my face so thin
That in mine ear I durst not stick a rose,

---

134 rather—] CAPELL (*subs.*); rather‸ F   138 BASTARD] F (*Bast⟨ard⟩.; and thus until 3.1.131*)
an if] F (and if)

125-7 **if he were . . . refuse him** i.e., if Philip
Faulconbridge were Richard I's son,
Richard could not legally claim him, nor
could Sir Robert refuse to acknowledge
Philip as his son, even if he were not
130 **will** testament; determination
133 **will** At least three meanings: aim, inclination; lust, sexual desire; penis. For all
three, see Booth, pp. 466-7.
134 **Whether hadst thou rather—be** i.e.,
which of the two (= *Whether*) would you
prefer: [to] be ('a Faulconbridge' [or [to
be] 'the reputed son of Coeur-de-Lion').
Compare 'Whether had you rather[, to]
lead mine eyes, or [to] eye your master's
heels?' (*Merry Wives* 3.2.3–4). The obsolete grammatical construction (*had* +
dative + comparative adjective) evolved
from *be* + dative + comparative adjective, as in 'Poor lady, she were better
love a dream' (*Twelfth Night* 2.2.26),
eventually producing such phrases as

'Me rather had' (*Richard II* 3.3.190) to
express choice or preference with *as well*,
as good, *liefer*, *rather* and the like words
and phrases followed by *that*, *than*, or the
infinitive. See *have*, v. II. 22 a–c and,
for the omission of *to* in the subsequent
infinitives, Abbott §350.
136 **reputed** supposed, reckoned
137 **presence** 'demeanour or carriage' (5)
mixed with 'immediate vicinity, the space
you occupy' (2)
138 **an if** if
139 **Sir Robert's his like him** The double
possessive makes the phrase confusing:
Sir Robert's shape is like Robert Faulconbridge's shape.
140 **riding–rods** thin rods or switches used
by horsemen
142-3 **That . . . goes** Elizabethans sometimes
wore roses behind the ear as adornment;
see C[yril]. T[ourneur]., *Laugh and Lie
Down, or The World's Folly* (1605), D3,

Lest men should say, 'Look where three-farthings goes',
And to his shape were heir to all this land,
Would I might never stir from off this place.
I would give it every foot to have this face;
It would not be Sir Nob in any case.

QUEEN ELEANOR

I like thee well. Wilt thou forsake thy fortune,
Bequeath thy land to him, and follow me?
I am a soldier and now bound to France.   150

BASTARD

Brother, take you my land; I'll take my chance.
Your face hath got five hundred pound a year;
Yet sell your face for fivepence and 'tis dear.
Madam, I'll follow you unto the death.

QUEEN ELEANOR

Nay, I would have you go before me thither.

147 It] F1 ; I F2   Sir Nob] F4 (Sir Nobbe), *after* F1 (sir nobbe); sir Nob CAPELL

describing a 'nimble-witted and glib-tongued fellow' in the House of Folly, 'The picktooth in the mouth, the flower in the ear, the brush upon the beard, the kiss of the hand . . .'. Elizabeth's profile on the three-farthings was rather thin and stiff, and the coin, like several others of small denomination, also bore a Tudor rose more or less behind the Queen's ear to distinguish it from coins of similar size and weight. See Fig. 4.

145 **Would I might never stir** Tilley S861, 'I would I might never stir else'. Dent, *PLED*, shows that the expression was common from at least 1596, but this line seems to be the earliest use so far discovered.

145–7 **Would . . . case** a triplet

147 **It . . . case** The compositor may have remembered *it* from the previous line, and editors (following Ff2–4) have emended *It* to *I*, but F's sentence may be paraphrased: My face (*It*) would never look like his *nob* (= head) no matter what my appearance (*case* = face, external appearance) or the circumstances (*case* = situation), i.e., no matter how ugly I might become, my ugliness could never equal his. Since *case* was slang for 'vagina', the Bastard may have wandered into hyperbolic insult.

Sir Nob A contemptuous title and a nickname, 'Nob' for 'Robert' (see E. G. Withycombe, *Oxford Dictionary of English Christian Names*, 3rd edn. (Oxford, 1977), p. 254), but—since Robert Faulconbridge's facial appearance concerns the Bastard here—the sarcasm probably embraces (*k*)*nob* as slang for 'head' (earliest *OED* citation, *nob*, *sb.*¹, about 1700); a 'noddy' is a fool or a simpleton (*sb.*¹ 1), and there may be some hint of that meaning here since English slang favors a phonetic shape of (k)n + vowel + stopped fricative for a bump, the head, and a fool (see *knub*; *noddle*, *sb.*¹ 2b; *noodle*, *sb.*¹, from 1753; *nub*, *sb.* 2; *nub*, *v.*¹, from 1610).

152–3 **Your face . . . 'tis dear** a couplet, perhaps to point the sarcasm

153 **dear** expensive; five pence is more than your face is worth

154–6 **I'll follow . . . betters way** Although the Bastard makes a joke about the difference between courtly and rustic manners, his caution is proverbial: Tilley P89, 'At an ill passage honour thy companion' (i.e., let another take the greater risk). See 'Finding their enemy to be so curst, | They all strain court'sy who shall cope him first' (*Venus* 887–8).

BASTARD

Our country manners give our betters way.

KING JOHN What is thy name?

BASTARD

'Philip', my liege, so is my name begun;

Philip, good old Sir Robert's wife's eldest son.

KING JOHN

From henceforth bear his name whose form thou
    bearest: 160

Kneel thou down Philip, but rise more great;
    He knights the Bastard

Arise Sir Richard and Plantagenet.

BASTARD

Brother by th' mother's side, give me your hand;

My father gave me honour, yours gave land.

Now blessèd be the hour by night or day

When I was got, Sir Robert was away.

QUEEN ELEANOR

The very spirit of Plantagenet!

I am thy grandam, Richard; call me so.

BASTARD

Madam, by chance but not by truth, what though?

Something about a little from the right,   170

    In at the window, or else o'er the hatch;

159 wife's] F (wiues)   160] POPE's *lineation*; *as two lines, breaking after* 'name' F   161.1
He knights the Bastard] *not in* F; *knighting him* CAPELL, *after l. 162*   167 Plantagenet!]
THEOBALD; ∼ : F

158–9 **'Philip' . . . son** The couplet under-
    lines the sing-song quality of a children's
    rhyme.
159 **wife's eldest son** 'My lady's eldest son'
    (Dent L30.1) may be proverbial for 'a
    bastard'; Dent compares *Much Ado* 2.1.9
    and *The Puritan* 1.2.54–7 in *Apocrypha*.
160 **From . . . bearest** The compositor broke
    this pentameter into two lines because
    as one it is too long for the measure.
161 **Kneel . . . great** a common antithesis
    in Shakespeare and contemporary
    dramatists
162 **Arise . . . Plantagenet** Elizabethan de-
    scriptions of the knighting ceremony do
    not include the renaming of the new
    knight; see Introduction, pp. 66–7.
    Plantagenet Originally a nickname for
    John's grandfather, Geoffrey of Anjou,

derived from his habit of wearing a sprig
of broom (= *planta genista*) in his cap;
Richard Duke of York first treated it as a
family name in the mid-fifteenth century.
165–6 **Now blessèd . . . away** F's punctu-
    ation, retained here, makes two slightly
    different interpretations possible: the Bas-
    tard regards as *blessèd* either the moment
    of his birth or the time of his legal father's
    absence that permitted his mother's
    affair.
165 **hour** Possibly with a pun on 'whore'
    (see 3.1.56n).
170–5 **Something about . . . begot** The
    stanza form used in *Venus*.
170 **about** 'near', but perhaps mixed with
    the nautical meaning of 'on an opposite
    course or tack'
171 **In at the window . . . hatch** Both

Who dares not stir by day must walk by night,
    And have is have, however men do catch;
Nea'er or farre off, well won is still well shot,
And I am I, howe'er I was begot.

KING JOHN

Go, Faulconbridge. Now hast thou thy desire;
A landless knight makes thee a landed squire.
Come madam, and come Richard, we must speed
For France, for France, for it is more than need.

BASTARD

Brother, adieu. Good fortune come to thee,   180
For thou wast got i'th' way of honesty.

Exeunt all but Bastard

A foot of honour better than I was,
But many a many foot of land the worse.
Well, now can I make any Joan a lady;
'Good den, Sir Richard', 'God-a-mercy, fellow' —

174 Nea'er] F (Neere)   181.1 *Bastard*] F (*bastard*)   182] *speech continued* ROWE; *Bast⟨ard⟩.*
F

phrases impute bastardy. The first can be instanced from 1551 (Tilley W456); Dent notes that *K. John* is the first text known to add *hatch* which later appears in *Northward Ho* (*c.*1605; printed 1607) and *Family of Love* (printed 1608).

173 **have is have** Earliest known instance of Tilley H215, but Whiting records 'Own is own' (= Tilley O100) from *c.*1250; see I.1.40.

174 **Nea'er ... shot** i.e., whether an archer stands closer to or farther from his target, an accurate arrow deserves praise. The Bastard also quibbles on his mother's having been *won* sexually by Coeur-de-Lion who *shot* (performed sexually) *well*. **Nea'er** This modernization tries to preserve F's *Neere*, a comparative (= modern *nearer*).

farre farther (an archaic comparative).

179 **it is more than need** it is urgently necessary. The same phrase occurs at *LLL* 4.3.287. *OED*, *need*, *sb.* 4a, lists 'it is need' only before infinitives and without citations between 1556 and 1676.

180–1 **Brother . . . honesty** The couplet mockingly dismisses Robert Faulconbridge.

181 **i'th' way of honesty** A phrase common

from at least 1594; see Dent and Dent, *PLED*, on Tilley W155.

183 **many a many** Emphatic phrase for 'many' and *OED*'s sole citation.

184 **make any Joan a lady** See Tilley J57, 'Joan is as good as my lady (in the dark)'; the proverb exists in two forms (with *Joan*, without *dark*; with *dark*, without *Joan*) before they are combined in an example known from 1611, and Dent, *PLED*, suggests that the 'bawdy sense should perhaps constitute a separate entry'. See *LLL* 3.1.200 and *As You Like It* 3.5.39 f.

Joan Type-name for a rural woman, mockingly regarded as the hardest task for the Bastard's new power of social advancement; see 'And greasy Joan doth keel the pot' (*LLL* 5.2.913).

185 **Good den** A colloquial greeting and contraction (= 'God give you good even') virtually synonymous with 'Good day' (see *Much Ado* 5.1.46) and used at any time after noon (as *Romeo* 2.3.101–5 demonstrates); in Shakespearian usage, the phrase does not seem to be 'the salutation of an inferior' (Rann): Don Pedro uses it to Don John and to Leonato in *Much Ado*, the tribunes use it to the people in *Coriolanus*, Tybalt — with

An if his name be George, I'll call him 'Peter',
For new-made honour doth forget men's names,
'Tis too respective and too sociable
For your conversion. Now your traveller,
He and his toothpick at my worship's mess;   190
And when my knightly stomach is sufficed,
Why then I suck my teeth and catechize
My pickèd man of countries: 'My dear sir'—
Thus leaning on mine elbow I begin—
'I shall beseech you'. That is Question now,
And then comes Answer like an Absey book:
'O sir,' says Answer, 'at your best command,
At your employment, at your service, sir.'
'No, sir,' says Question, 'I, sweet sir, at yours.'
And so, ere Answer knows what Question would,   200
Saving in dialogue of compliment

---

186 An if] F (And if)   189 conversion.] CAPELL; conuersion, F

'Gentlemen'—uses it to Romeo and Mer-cutio.

God-a-mercy God have mercy (on you), an expression of thanks, sometimes used ironically or condescendingly

186 **An if** if

187 **new-made honour doth forget men's names** A proverbial conviction; see Tilley H583, 'Honours change manners' (examples from 1548 onward).

188–9 **'Tis ... conversion** i.e., (understood: to remember men's proper names) would be too respectful (= *respective*) and friendly (= *sociable*) to suit a negligent substitution (= *conversion*) of one name for another. Shakespeare uses *conversion* on only one other occasion (*As You Like It* 4.3.137, where the word connotes a spiritual transformation), and it may here refer, as Steevens first suggested, to the Bastard himself: 'one thus changed in status' (Smallwood). Both uses of *your* in l. 189 are the contemptuous 'that you know of' similar to the ethical dative *you*; see 3.4.146n and 'Your serpent of Egypt is bred now of your mud by the operation of your sun; so is your croco-dile' (*Antony* 2.7.26–7). Honigmann quotes Halliwell's gloss on *conversion* as 'converse (= conversation)', but *OED* provides no support.

189–93 **Now your traveller . . . countries**

Travellers were expected to 'sing for their supper'; Gaveston agrees to employ one 'To wait at my trencher and tell me lies at dinner-time' (*Edward II* 1.1.31).

190 **toothpick** Still a sign of (pretended) sophistication, Elizabethan toothpicks were usually made of precious metal; see 1.1.142–3n.

my worship's mess i.e., the company of diners I (who now bear the honorific 'your worship') have gathered

193 **pickèd** A triple quibble: spruce, over-refined (see *LLL* 5.1.12–13, 'He is too picked, too spruce'); having used a tooth-pick; elected, chosen.

of countries concerning foreign lands (but puns on *pickèd* may continue: 'selec-ted from (many) countries')

196 **Absey book** i.e., ABC-book, an introduc-tory book or manual, often in dialogue form; not limited to hornbook or primer (earliest citation for *sb.* 4). F's archaic form is required metrically.

201 **dialogue of compliment** '[T]he affected, magniloquent, periphrastic discourse of those who imitate, or think they are imitating, the court' (J. Barish, *Ben Jonson and the Language of Prose Comedy* (Berk-eley and Los Angeles, 1960), p. 117). Jaques says 'that they call compliment is like th'encounter of two dog-apes' (*As You Like It* 2.5.23–4); Hoy, i. 154, col-

And talking of the Alps and Apennines,
The Pyrenean and the River Po,
It draws toward supper in conclusion so.
But this is worshipful society
And fits the mounting spirit like myself;
For he is but a bastard to the time
That doth not smack of observation,
And so am I whether I smack or no;
And not alone in habit and device,   210
Exterior form, outward accoutrement,
But from the inward motion to deliver
Sweet, sweet, sweet poison for the age's tooth,
Which though I will not practise to deceive,
Yet to avoid deceit I mean to learn,

203 Pyrenean] F (Perennean)   208 smack] F (smoake)   212 motion to deliver] F; motion too, deliver CAPELL; motion—to deliver SMALLWOOD

lects other contemporary comments on the word. F's *Complement* may, however, indicate the Bastard's joking reference to the way Question and Answer 'complete' (*complement, sb.* I. 1 and II. 6–7), without advancing, the conversation; the King of Navarre describes Armado as 'A man of complements, whom right and wrong | Have chose as umpire of their mutiny' (*LLL* 1.1.166–7) where 'courtesy', 'accomplishment', and 'fulfilment' in the sense of 'resolution or reconciliation' are all present.

204 **draws toward supper** i.e., the time passes between mid-day and evening meals

so Thus, in this fashion; the rhyme with 'Po' begs the actor to punctuate the couplet with an exaggeratedly polite or satiric gesture.

206 **mounting** rising, aspiring

207 **bastard to the time** i.e., not a legitimate or successful participant in current affairs

208 **smack of** participate in, have the flavour of, but *smoke* and *smack*, whose spellings were not yet distinguished (Honigmann 1.1.208–9n), also connoted 'observe, suspect'

observation paying attention, noticing, but also 'the habit of paying personal attention or court' (Wright)

209 **And so . . . or no** i.e., I am literally a bastard whether or not I escape being a figurative one

210 **habit** dress, clothing

device Heraldic or emblematic figure; the 'mounting' Bastard will now adopt, e.g., a coat of arms. See next n.

211 **accoutrement** apparel. Comments on dress and the words *device* and *accoutrement* appear in Rosalind's criticism of Orlando's failure to imitate the conventional lover (*As You Like It* 3.2.369–70); *accoutrement* may have been a fashionable and pretentious word in the 1590s: a character in Dekker's *Patient Grissil* says of *accoutrements* 'that's one of their fustian outlandish phrases too' (2.1.62).

213 **sweet poison** Dent F349.1, 'Flattery is sweet poison', citing among other examples 'What drink'st thou oft, instead of homage sweet, | But poisoned flattery' (*Henry V* 4.1.247–8); Dent, *PLED*, has examples from 1557 onward.

214 **practise** act or proceed, often in the sense of acting typically or habitually. In Elizabethan English both noun and verb could carry connotations of deceit (see 4.1.20 and 4.3.63), but the Bastard specifically excludes them here. See Walter Scott, *Marmion* VI.xvii, 'O what a tangled web we weave, | When first we practise to deceive!'

215 **Yet . . . learn** i.e., I must study how to avoid the deception I expect to meet, but the line also implies 'I must study how to deceive in order to avoid being harmed by the deceit of others'; see Chapman,

For it shall strew the footsteps of my rising.
      Enter Lady Faulconbridge and James Gurney
But who comes in such haste in riding-robes?
What woman-post is this? Hath she no husband
That will take pains to blow a horn before her?
O me, 'tis my mother. How now, good lady?   220
What brings you here to court so hastily?

LADY FAULCONBRIDGE

Where is that slave thy brother? Where is he
That holds in chase mine honour up and down?

BASTARD

My brother Robert, old Sir Robert's son—
Colbrand the Giant, that same mighty man—
Is it Sir Robert's son that you seek so?

216.1] *as here*, This edition; *after l. 221*, F (*Iames*); *after l. 220*, CAPELL   222 LADY
FAULCONBRIDGE] F (*Lady.; and thus throughout*)   222–3 he | . . . down?] THEOBALD (*subs.*);
he? | . . . downe. F

Bussy D'Ambois 1.1.102–3: 'And (hearing villainies preached) t'unfold their
art | Learn to commit them—'Tis a
great man's part'
216.1 **James Gurney** Shakespeare rarely
names plebian characters so precisely
unless there is an ulterior motive. Perhaps the precision here hints that the
Bastard has been 'democratically'
friendly with his mother's servants, as
does Gurney's addressing him by his
first name (l. 231); his cheerful and
unpompous jesting immediately belies
the preceding soliloquy and ensures that
we know it was self-mockery. Holinshed
mentions a 'Hugh Gourney' (144b;
N4ᵛ), who eventually revolted from John
(166b; P3ᵛ).
217 **riding-robes** Lady Faulconbridge enters
in a costume that conventionally indicates haste and travel; she has not
paused to don more formal clothing.
For this costuming, see Alan Dessen,
Elizabethan Stage Conventions (Cambridge,
1985), pp. 39–40.
219 **blow a horn before her** The post or an
assistant blew a horn to draw attention
to his arrival (see the stage direction,
'Post blowing a horn within' at 3 *Henry
VI* 3.3.160.1, and *Merchant* 5.1.46–7);
since old Sir Robert has been publicly
branded a cuckold, he has the proper
equipment, a horn, the badge of his

dishonour. Tilley H618, 'Wear a horn
and blow it not', may or may not refer
to cuckoldry, although the proverb could
be used allusively that way: Gonstanzo
advises the convinced cuckold Cornelio,
'Yet if there come no proofs, but that
her actions were cleanly, or indiscreet
private[ly] . . . will you blow the horn
yourself, when you may keep it to yourself?' (Chapman, *All Fools, c.*1599,
printed 1605, 5.2.173–5). *OED* first cites
post-horn from 1675.
223 **holds in chase** Pursues; the metaphor is from hunting, as in 'Spies of the
Volsces | Held me in chase' (*Coriolanus*
1.7.18–19).
      up and down entirely. A common phrase:
see Dent UU1.
225 **Colbrand the Giant** Colbrand was
brought to England as part of an invading
Danish army and was defeated by the
eponymous hero of *Guy of Warwick*, a
fourteenth-century romance; for the episode, see Julius Zupitza, ed., *The Romance
of Guy of Warwick*, EETS, extra series, 42,
49, 59 (1883, 1887, 1891), pp. 576–
607. Guy and his legends remained immensely popular in chronicle, chapbook,
ballad, and even drama; see R. S. Crane,
'The Vogue of *Guy of Warwick* from the
Close of the Middle Ages to the Romantic
Revival', *PMLA*, 30 (1915), 125–94.
During the sixteenth century, Guy's

LADY FAULCONBRIDGE

'Sir Robert's son'? Ay, thou unreverent boy.
Sir Robert's son? Why scorn'st thou at Sir Robert?
He is Sir Robert's son, and so art thou.

BASTARD

James Gurney, wilt thou give us leave a while?   230

JAMES GURNEY

Good leave, good Philip.

BASTARD   'Philip Sparrow', James,
There's toys abroad; anon I'll tell thee more.

                                                    Exit Gurney

Madam, I was not old Sir Robert's son;
Sir Robert might have eat his part in me
Upon Good Friday and ne'er broke his fast.
Sir Robert could do well, marry, to confess;
Could get me, Sir Robert could not do it.

227 son'?] F3; sonne, FI   231 JAMES GURNEY] F (*Gour⟨ney⟩*.)   'Philip Sparrow',] WILSON
(*subs.*); *Philip*, sparrow, F; Philip! sparrow: CAPELL; Philip?—Sparrow! RANN   232.1 *Exit
Gurney*] F (*Exit Iames.*)   236 do well, marry, to confess;] This Edition; doe well, marrie, to
confesse‸ F; do well, marry, to confess! ROWE; do well: marry, to confess‸ CAMBRIDGE; do
well—marry, to confess— WILSON; do: well—marry, to confess—ALEXANDER   237 Could get
me, Sir] This edition; Could get me sir F; Could he get me? Sir POPE; Could not get me; Sir
DYCE (*conj.* Collier, *Notes*); Could he get me. Sir WILSON; Could . . . get me? Sir HONIGMANN;
Could he get me! Sir SMALLWOOD; Could a get me! Sir OXFORD (*conj.* Maxwell)

sword was preserved at Warwick Castle
(not far from Shakespeare's home town
of Stratford), and various chapels and
statues were associated with his name in
the Tudor period (Crane, pp. 135–6).
Colbrand and Guy appear together in
another comic dialogue (*All is True*
5.3.21), and Drayton recounts the tale
(*Polyolbion* 12.129–334).

227 **Ay** an interjection, expressing surprise,
anger, or distress
unreverent irreverent

230 **give us leave** A common expression
(Dent L167.1) as a request for privacy.

231 **'Philip Sparrow'** Philip was a common
name for pet sparrows (as in, for example,
John Skelton's poem, *Philip Sparrow*);
since Philip Faulconbridge is now Sir
Richard Plantagenet, the name 'Philip'
is better applied to a pet bird than to him,
and he jokingly rejects it.

232 **toys** antics, fantastic or unexpected
tricks (perhaps the Bastard's unexpected
knighthood)

234–5 **eat his part . . . fast** Tilley P75,

'He may his part on Good Friday eat and
fast never the worse for ought he shall
get'; Tilley, Wilson, *ODEP*, and Dent
cite only John Heywood, *A Dialogue of
Proverbs* (1546) and this instance; *eat* is
an archaic past participle, pronounced
'et'.

236 **do well, marry, to confess** two senses:
act prudently or sensibly (= *do well*), I
admit; perform intercourse (= *do well*),
I agree. For the ironic, bawdy use of *do
well*, see *well*, *adv.* II.5c; *marry* is a
weakened interjection (from 'by the
Virgin Mary').

237 **Could get . . . do it** The Bastard conceded
(l. 236) Sir Robert's ability to *do well*,
to fornicate; he now considers the consequences and claims Sir Robert could not
father (= [be]*get me*), Philip, only thin
and ugly Robert ('his handiwork', l. 238).
As *it* (= *get me*) indicates, the Bastard's
grammar treats *get me* as a noun, the
object of *could*; like *do well* (l. 236), *do
it* refers to intercourse and conception
(see *employed* in l. 98).

We know his handiwork. Therefore, good mother,
To whom am I beholden for these limbs?
Sir Robert never holp to make this leg.   240

LADY FAULCONBRIDGE

Hast thou conspirèd with thy brother too,
That for thine own gain shouldst defend mine honour?
What means this scorn, thou most untoward knave?

BASTARD

'Knight, knight', good mother, Basilisco-like!
What! I am dubbed, I have it on my shoulder.
But, mother, I am not Sir Robert's son;
I have disclaimed Sir Robert and my land;
Legitimation, name, and all is gone.
Then, good my mother, let me know my father—
Some proper man I hope—who was it, mother?   250

LADY FAULCONBRIDGE

Hast thou denied thyself a Faulconbridge?

BASTARD

As faithfully as I deny the devil.

LADY FAULCONBRIDGE

King Richard Coeur-de-Lion was thy father;
By long and vehement suit I was seduced
To make room for him in my husband's bed.
Heaven lay not my transgression to my charge;
Thou art the issue of my dear offence
Which was so strongly urged past my defence.

BASTARD

Now by this light, were I to get again,

239 beholden] F (beholding)   244 'Knight . . . Basilisco-like!] SMALLWOOD (*subs.*); Knight, knight good mother, Basilisco-like: F   256 Heaven₍₎] F (Heauen); ~ ! KNIGHT; ~ , SINGER my charge;] F (my charge,); my charge! POPE; thy charge₍₎ WILSON (*conj.* Staunton)   257 Thou] F2; That F1

238 **his handiwork** i.e., Robert Faulcon-
    bridge
240 **holp** helped
243 **untoward** indecorous, unseemly (5a;
    earliest citation, 1628–9)
244 **Basilisco-like** Basilisco, a coward, de-
    mands his correct title, 'Knight', in Kyd's
    Soliman and Perseda 1.3.169; see Intro-
    duction, pp. 14–15.
249 **good** A conventional epithet signifying
    respect, here used placatingly.
252 **deny** repudiate, renounce
257–8 **Thou . . . defence** The couplet under-

scores the antithesis (*offence/defence*).
257 **Thou** Honigmann defends F's *That*, but
    at the cost of making *Heaven* (l. 256) an
    interjection, although it appears to be
    the subject of *lay not*; *That* and *Thou*
    abbreviated in manuscript might easily
    be confused. F treats all of l. 256 as an
    interjection or plea to *Heaven*.
    dear heartfelt (Schmidt, quoted at *a.*¹
    II.7a), but probably mixed with 'fond,
    loving' (I.5b) and 'dire, grievous' (*a.*² 2)
259 **by this light** 'a petty oath' (Wright)
    get be begotten

Madam, I would not wish a better father.   260
Some sins do bear their privilege on earth,
And so doth yours. Your fault was not your folly;
Needs must you lay your heart at his dispose,
Subjected tribute to commanding love,
Against whose fury and unmatchèd force
The aweless lion could not wage the fight,
Nor keep his princely heart from Richard's hand.
He that perforce robs lions of their hearts
May easily win a woman's. Ay, my mother,
With all my heart I thank thee for my father.   270
Who lives and dares but say thou didst not well
When I was got, I'll send his soul to hell.
Come, lady, I will show thee to my kin,
    And they shall say when Richard me begot,
If thou hadst said him nay, it had been sin.
    Who says it was, he lies; I say 'twas not.   *Exeunt*

2.1   ⌈*Flourish.*⌉ *Enter before Angers, King Philip of*
          France, Louis the Dauphin, Constance, Arthur, and

269 Ay] F (aye)
    2.1] ROWE 1714's *act-division*; *Scaena Secunda* F   0.1 *Flourish.*] OXFORD; *not in* F   0.1–4
Enter . . . other] This edition; *Enter before Angiers, Philip King of France, Lewis, Daulphin,*
Austria, Constance, Arthur. F

261 **privilege** dispensation, specifically from
    divine punishment as 'on earth' makes
    clear (*sb.* 2b, without citations between
    *c.*1380 and 1754)
262 **fault** See 1.1.118n.
266 **aweless** unawed (the passive for the
    active form; see Abbott §3)
268 **perforce** forcibly
269 **Ay** yes
271–6 **Who lives . . . not** The couplet and
    quatrain (an 'inverted' *Venus*-stanza) sig-
    nal the scene's conclusion and add a final
    flourish to the Bastard's verbal inventive-
    ness.
276 **Who says . . . 'twas not** Perhaps a comic
    gag line directed at the audience; see,
    e.g., the Fool's scene-closing couplet,
    'She that's a maid now, and laughs at
    my departure, | Shall not be a maid long,
    unless things be cut shorter' (*Tragedy of
    Lear* 1.5.49–50).
2.1.0.1–3 Line 1 indicates that two groups
    of characters meet, and the Elizabethan

public theatre provided at least two up-
stage doors that could be imagined as
entrances from different locations; l. 2
indicates that Arthur accompanies the
French group.
0.1. *Angers* F's *Angiers* (throughout, except
    Angires at 2.1.536) suggests an attempt
    to soften the English hard *g* (producing
    the Elizabethan pronunciation 'Anjers');
    the city lies on the Loire between Nantes
    and Saumur. Some of the details here
    and in Act 3 derive from Holinshed's
    account of the battle of Mirabeau (1202).
    This act received extravagant scenic
    treatment on the nineteenth-century
    stage (see Fig. 6), and some more recent
    productions treat the act's latter half
    (after the Kings' return at l. 333.1) as
    comic satire on the entire political project.
0.1 *King Philip* See 1.1.7n.
0.2 *Louis the Dauphin* Born 1187 and
    reigned, as Louis VIII, 1223–6; the title,

their forces ⌐*on one side*⌐*; Duke of Austria (wearing a lion's skin) and forces* ⌐*on the other*⌐

KING PHILIP

Before Angers well met, brave Austria.
Arthur: that great forerunner of thy blood,
Richard that robbed the lion of his heart
And fought the holy wars in Palestine,
By this brave Duke came early to his grave.
And for amends to his posterity,
At our importance hither is he come
To spread his colours, boy, in thy behalf,
And to rebuke the usurpation
Of thy unnatural uncle, English John.   10
Embrace him, love him, give him welcome hither.

ARTHUR

God shall forgive you Coeur-de-Lion's death
The rather that you give his offspring life,
Shadowing their right under your wings of war.

---

1 KING PHILIP] DYCE 1864 (*conj.* Theobald; *see note*); Lewis [*the Dauphin*]. F   2] *speech continued*
F; *K⟨ing⟩. Phi⟨lip⟩.* HONIGMANN   Arthur:] This edition; *Arthur*∧ F   12 ARTHUR] F (*Arth⟨ur⟩.*;
and thus subs. (*Ar., Art.*) *for remainder of play*)

which dates from 1349, is a common
Elizabethan anachronism.
  Constance See 1.1.32n and 4.2.122–3n.
  Arthur Posthumous son of Geoffrey (see
1.1.8n) and Constance; also called Duke
of Brittany (1187–1203). In the eighteenth and nineteenth centuries, the part
was usually taken by an actress; see
4.3.143n.
0.3 *Duke of Austria* This historical figure,
who captured and held to ransom Richard Coeur-de-Lion in 1192, was Leopold
V, Duke of Austria (died 1194), a member
of the powerful Babenberg family. Editors
sometimes mistitle the character 'Arch-
duke', but that title dates through forgery
from 1359 and legally from 1453; it
would be familiar to Shakespeare and his
audience as the title of the heir apparent
to the Holy Roman Emperor; see
3.1.114n.
1 KING PHILIP F's entry stage directions
often list first (here, King Philip) the
character who speaks first following the
entry (see Appendix D), and protocol
would seem to urge that Philip, rather
than his son (to whom F assigns this
speech), introduce Austria to Arthur; the

use of the royal plural, *our* (l. 7), also
supports the reassignment of the speech.
Theobald's conjectural reassignment appears in his letter to Warburton, 6 January 1730, repr. in John Nichols,
*Illustrations of the Literary History of the
Eighteenth Century*, 2 vols. (1817), ii.
388.
4 holy wars in Palestine i.e., the Crusades
6 posterity Either 'descendants' or 'suc-
ceeding generation'; Shakespeare here
begins the genealogical confusion made
plain in l. 13.
7 importance importunity
8 spread his colours display his personal
flag or other insignia (indicating Austria's presence and willingness to do
battle). The same phrase appears at *Tamburlaine, Part 1* 4.1.7.
13 his offspring Richard's progeny, his descendants; the singular for plural (see
their in l. 14) was common. Shakespeare
(or Philip) apparently regards Arthur as
Richard's (rather than Geoffrey's) des-
cendant here.
14 Shadowing sheltering, protecting (*v.* 2:
'chiefly in Biblical use')

I give you welcome with a powerless hand,
But with a heart full of unstainèd love.
Welcome before the gates of Angers, Duke.

LOUIS THE DAUPHIN

A noble boy, who would not do thee right?

AUSTRIA (*to Arthur*)

Upon thy cheek lay I this zealous kiss,
As seal to this indenture of my love: 20
That to my home I will no more return
Till Angers and the right thou hast in France,
Together with that pale, that white-faced shore,
Whose foot spurns back the ocean's roaring tides
And coops from other lands her islanders,
Even till that England hedged in with the main,
That water-wallèd bulwark, still secure
And confident from foreign purposes,
Even till that utmost corner of the west
Salute thee for her king. Till then, fair boy,   30
Will I not think of home, but follow arms.

CONSTANCE

O, take his mother's thanks, a widow's thanks,

18 LOUIS THE DAUPHIN] F (*Lewis.*); King Philip. DYCE 1864 (*conj.* Theobald)   A] F; Ah,
HONIGMANN (*conj.* Fleay)

15 **powerless** i.e., unsupported by a 'power',
by troops or armed force
16 **unstainèd** pure, unspotted. The metaphor
and sentiment are a little surprising;
Kellner, §150, argues for a misreading
of manuscript 'unfained' (= unfeigned),
proposed by Samuel Bailey, *The Received
Text of Shakespeare's Dramatic Writings*, 2
vols. (1862–6), ii. 244.
18 **A noble boy** Louis's tone is patronizing;
he may address this phrase to Constance
or to the company at large, the remainder
of the line to Arthur himself. F's *A*
might be the archaic interjection 'Ah';
although *OED*'s latest examples are from
the fifteenth century, the usage occurs
much later (e.g., in Marlowe's *Edward II*
and in *The True Tragedy of Richard III*,
both printed 1594).
19 **zealous** intensely earnest, enthusiastic
20 **seal to this indenture** i.e., Austria's im-
printed kiss resembles his seal set in the

wax of a covenant or contract (= *indenture*) in which he vows his support for
Arthur's cause. 'Set thy seal manual on
my wax-red lips' (*Venus* 516) makes the
metaphor clear. An 'inevitable quibble'
(Wilson, 2.1.477–9n) has been seen in
zeal-/seal.
23 **white-faced** i.e., the chalk cliffs of the
south-eastern coast of England
25 **coops** 'shuts off, divides protectively',
but probably without the implication
(endorsed by *v.*[1] 2) of irksome confinement
28 **confident** 'Bold, self-reliant, assured', but
thoroughly mixed in Shakespeare's time
with the negative possibility of over-
confidence; for the former meaning, see
2.1.61 and 452.
purposes 'aims, designs', but probably
with the further idea of movement or
motion (of an army) to achieve those
aims (see *sb.* 1b)

Till your strong hand shall help to give him strength
To make a more requital to your love.

AUSTRIA

The peace of heaven is theirs that lift their swords
In such a just and charitable war.

KING PHILIP

Well then, to work. Our cannon shall be bent
Against the brows of this resisting town.
Call for our chiefest men of discipline
To cull the plots of best advantages.   40
We'll lay before this town our royal bones,
Wade to the market-place in Frenchmen's blood,
But we will make it subject to this boy.

CONSTANCE

Stay for an answer to your embassy,
Lest unadvised you stain your swords with blood.
My lord Chatillon may from England bring
That right in peace which here we urge in war,
And then we shall repent each drop of blood
That hot rash haste so indirectly shed.

Enter Chatillon

KING PHILIP

A wonder, lady! Lo, upon thy wish   50
Our messenger Chatillon is arrived.
What England says, say briefly, gentle lord;
We coldly pause for thee. Chatillon, speak.

CHATILLON

Then turn your forces from this paltry siege
And stir them up against a mightier task;

37 KING PHILIP] F (*King.; and thus subs. (Kin.) until 2.1.89*)   work. Our] COLLIER; worke_∧
our F   50 lady!] ROWE; ~ : F

34 **more requital** greater (see Abbott §17) return (for kindness done)
37 **to work. Our cannon shall be bent** F's punctuation might represent an inversion (i.e., 'our cannon shall be bent to work'), but *OED* offers no examples of an infinitive after 'bend'.
39 **discipline** military skill or experience (*sb.* 3b)
40 **cull** select, pick out
   plots sites, pieces of ground
42 **Wade . . . blood** A popular image; see *Tamburlaine, Part* 2 1.3.84, or Peele, *Battle of Alcazar* (*c.*1589), ll. 1079–81: 'myself

will lead the way, | And make a passage with my conquering sword | Knee deep in blood of these accursed Moors'.
43 **But** unless
44 **Stay** wait, pause
45 **unadvised** thoughtless, headstrong (Moore Smith)
49 **indirectly** pointlessly, irrelevantly (not covered by *adv.* 1c)
52 **England** i.e., King John
53 **coldly** calmly, dispassionately
55 **stir them up** rouse or encourage them
   against towards, in a direction facing

England, impatient of your just demands,
Hath put himself in arms. The adverse winds,
Whose leisure I have stayed, have given him time
To land his legions all as soon as I.
His marches are expedient to this town,   60
His forces strong, his soldiers confident.
With him along is come the Mother Queen,
An Ate stirring him to blood and strife;
With her her niece, the Lady Blanche of Spain;
With them a bastard of the King's deceased;
And all th'unsettled humours of the land—
Rash, inconsiderate, fiery voluntaries
With ladies' faces and fierce dragons' spleens—
Have sold their fortunes at their native homes,
Bearing their birthrights proudly on their backs,   70
To make a hazard of new fortunes here.

62 Mother Queen] F1; Mother-Queen F4; mother-queen CAPELL   63 Ate] ROWE; Ace F
65 King's] F1 (Kings); King F2   deceased;] CAMBRIDGE; deceast, F (*see note*)

56 **impatient of** made impatient by, not heeding

58 **Whose leisure I have stayed** whose permission or inactivity (= *leisure*) I have awaited (= *stayed*)

60 **marches** course or direction of orderly movement
   expedient direct (see A.I.1)

62 **Mother Queen** Queen Mother (not hyphenated according to *sb*. IV.16); F's speech-prefixes later in this scene use this designation for Eleanor.

63 **Ate** The goddess of revenge, who made a celebrated appearance in the Prologue and in Act 2 of Peele's *The Arraignment of Paris* (*c.*1581, printed 1584), to which 'More Ates, more Ates—stir them on, stir them on!' (*LLL* 5.2.682–3) may directly allude. See Introduction, p. 22.

65–6 **With . . . land** F's punctuation suggests that 'th'unsettled humours' are part of Chatillon's catalogue, although the grammar subsequently ('have sold . . . to make') suggests that l. 66 begins a new and independent clause.

66 **humours** A periphrasis for John's gentlemen followers, but the image depends upon contemporary medical theory: the humours were technically the four bodily fluids (blood, choler, phlegm, and black choler or melancholy) believed to con-

trol an individual's temperament. In a healthy body, these humours are in equilibrium; in an unhealthy one, they are *unsettled*. Chatillon's metaphor of England as a medically unbalanced body continues in the next two lines and recurs in 5.1.12–13 (see n.).

67 **inconsiderate** careless, reckless (earliest citation in *OED*)
   voluntaries volunteers (= F4's reading); such gentlemen-soldiers often served without pay. See 'Ajax was here the voluntary, and you as under an impress' (*Troilus* 2.1.98–9).

68 **fierce dragons' spleens** 'Spleen' may be an image either of speed or of anger; see 2.1.449n, 5.7.50n; and 'Our ancient word of courage, fair Saint George, | Inspire us with the spleen of fiery dragons' (*Richard III* 5.6.79–80).

70 **birthrights . . . on their backs** i.e., they have spent their patrimonies to purchase clothes. See Tilley W61, 'All his wardrobe on his back' (earliest example, Lyly's *Endymion*, 1588, 4.2.38) and Tilley L452, 'He wears a whole lordship on his back' (Wilson, *ODEP*, has examples from 1576 onward).

71 **make a hazard** risk, gamble for. See 1.1.119n and 5.6.7.

In brief, a braver choice of dauntless spirits
Than now the English bottoms have waft o'er
Did never float upon the swelling tide
To do offence and scathe in Christendom.
          Drum beats
The interruption of their churlish drums
Cuts off more circumstance; they are at hand,
To parley or to fight, therefore prepare.

KING PHILIP

How much unlooked-for is this expedition!

AUSTRIA

By how much unexpected, by so much   80
We must awake endeavour for defence,
For courage mounteth with occasion.
Let them be welcome, then; we are prepared.
          Enter King John, Bastard, Queen Eleanor, Blanche,
          the Earl of Pembroke, and English forces

KING JOHN

Peace be to France, if France in peace permit
Our just and lineal entrance to our own;

75.1 *Drum beats*] F (*after l. 78*)   79 expedition!] F4; expedition. F1   83.1–2 *Enter King John . . . forces*] F (*Enter K. of England, Bastard, Queene, Blanch, Pembroke, and others.*)

72 **In brief** in short, in few words
  braver choice more splendid, beautiful (Schmidt) selection. 'Brave' in various parts of speech appears many times in the play, often mingling the meanings of courage, defiance, fine display, and ostentation.
73 **bottoms** ships
  waft Acceptable Elizabethan usage for 'wafted' (Abbott §341); the verb conveys the ease and speed of John's voyage in comparison with Chatillon's. Shakespeare uses this form ('waft') and transitive meaning exclusively, but only in *K. John*, 2 and 3 *Henry VI*, and *Merchant*.
75 **scathe** harm, damage
75.1 **Drum beats** A cue for an off-stage sound effect as in the 'plot' of 1 *Tamar Cam*, 'Drum a far off'; see W. W. Greg, ed., *Dramatic Documents from the Elizabethan Playhouse: Reproductions and Transcripts* (Oxford, 1931), item VII.
77 **circumstance** subordinate matters, details
77–8 **they . . . prepare** F's punctuation allows 'to parley or to fight' to serve as the

object of both the preceding and the following clauses.
79 **expedition** two meanings: invading army; speed
82 **courage mounteth with occasion** Dent, *PLED* C15a, 'Calamity (Extremity) is the touchstone of a brave mind (unto wit)', cites 'Brave minds are strongest in extremes' (Peele, *The Battle of Alcazar*, l. 544) as the earliest example.
  occasion circumstance calling for action; pretext
83.1–2 **Enter . . . forces** The order of names in F may indicate the Bastard's changed social and (presumably) dramatic status (see Appendix D). Concerning F's *Pembroke, and others*, see Introduction, pp. 22–3.
83.1 **Blanche** Daughter of John's sister Eleanor and Alfonso VIII, King of Castile, she is often called 'Blanche of Spain' (see 2.1.64 and 424).
85 **lineal** i.e., according to the legitimate authority conferred by direct (= *lineal*) descent from one's ancestors
  entrance Both the act of physical entry

The Life and Death of King John

If not, bleed France, and peace ascend to heaven,
Whiles we, God's wrathful agent, do correct
Their proud contempt that beats his peace to heaven.
KING PHILIP
Peace be to England, if that war return
From France to England, there to live in peace.   90
England we love, and for that England's sake
With burden of our armour here we sweat.
This toil of ours should be a work of thine;
But thou from loving England art so far
That thou hast underwrought his lawful king,
Cut off the sequence of posterity,
Outfacèd infant state, and done a rape
Upon the maiden virtue of the crown.
Look here upon thy brother Geoffrey's face.
These eyes, these brows, were moulded out of his;   100
This little abstract doth contain that large
Which died in Geoffrey, and the hand of time
Shall draw this brief into as huge a volume.
That Geoffrey was thy elder brother born,
And this his son; England was Geoffrey's right,
And this is Geoffrey's; in the name of God

89 KING PHILIP] F (*Fran⟨ce⟩.; and thus subs.* (*Fra.*, *France.*) *for remainder of play*)   106
Geoffrey's; in the name of God] ROWE; *Geffreyes* in the name of God: F. *See note.*

and entering into an office or duty (of
king and ruler over Angers); the latter
meaning explains the slightly strained
metaphor of *lineal*.
86 **peace ascend to heaven** Alluding perhaps
to the classical myth of Astraea; see
4.3.145n.
87 **Whiles** while (not archaic according to
adv. II.4, but last cited from 1858 and
perhaps now only poetical diction)
89 **if that** if
95 **underwrought** undermined, worked to
destroy from beneath or underhandedly
his its
96–8 **Cut . . . crown** The imagery reverses
the chronology of procreation by moving
from 'sequence of posterity' to 'infant' to
'rape' to 'maiden'.
97 **Outfacèd** defied, confronted impudently
99–103 **Look here . . . volume** This appeal
to appearance as evidence of descent and
inheritance parallels that by which the
Bastard was identified in 1.1.

101 **abstract** Epitome, but there is a further,
etymological, sense of someone 'drawn
from' another person (the sense of *trick*
at 1.1.85).
103 **brief** The use of *abstract*, *large*, and
volume suggests that Philip's analogy
refers to written documents or books, in
which case *brief* would mean 'note, pré-
cis, written outline' (see *sb.* III.5b, citing
this line); very similar language appears
in *Edward III*: 'Whose body is an abstract
or a brief, | Contains each general virtue
in the world' (2.1.82–3).
105 **England was Geoffrey's right** Smallwood rightly sees 'some distortion of
history in order to emphasize the validity
of Arthur's claim; England was never in
fact *Geoffrey's right* since he died before
his father and elder brother' (2.1.105n).
106 **And this is . . . God** The line is a
confusing one; *this* may refer (as it did
in l. 105) to Arthur, or it may refer to
right (and hence *England*), or it may refer

How comes it then that thou art called a king,
When living blood doth in these temples beat
Which own the crown that thou o'ermasterest?

KING JOHN

From whom hast thou this great commission, France,　　110
To draw my answer from thy articles?

KING PHILIP

From that supernal judge that stirs good thoughts
In any breast of strong authority
To look into the blots and stains of right;
That judge hath made me guardian to this boy:
Under whose warrant I impeach thy wrong
And by whose help I mean to chastise it.

KING JOHN

Alack, thou dost usurp authority.

KING PHILIP

Excuse it is to beat usurping down.

QUEEN ELEANOR

Who is it thou dost call usurper, France?　　120

109 own] F (owe)　　113 breast] F2; beast F1　　120 QUEEN ELEANOR] F (*Queen.; and thus until 2.1.166*)

to Angers itself. Editors have repunctuated and added directions to emphasize these possibilities; my choice assumes that 'this is Geoffrey's' refers to Arthur. Edwards, p. 116, discusses the line and offers two conjectures: 'And it was Geoffrey's in the name of God' and 'And thus is Arthur's in the name of God'.

108 **living blood** The first hint that if Arthur were not 'living' John might rule unopposed.

110 **commission** 'the Warrant or Letters Patents which all men using Jurisdiction . . . have for their power to . . . determine any matter' (Rastell)

111 **articles** Counts or charges in an indictment; see the deposition scene in *Richard II*: 'My lord, dispatch; read o'er these articles' (4.1.233). John reacts similarly and with similar legal language to Pandulph's demands (3.1.147 ff.).

112 **supernal judge** God. *Supernal* = existing or dwelling in the heavens; Shakespeare's only use of the word.

113 **breast** This reading from F2 makes more conventional and immediate sense than F1's *beast*, and the conventionality might argue against emendation, but Composi-

tor C, who set this line, probably omitted *r* from F1's *fiends* (3.4.64), usually emended to *friends*. He may have made the same error here, and/or it may be that a confusing manuscript form stood in both places. Honigmann defends F1 as Philip's sarcastic hyperbole.

116 **whose** God's, not—as the grammar might suggest—Arthur's
　　impeach challenge, accuse. The word concludes a series of legal and judicial terms begun by John's *commission* (2.1.110) and continued in *answer*, *articles*, and *warrant*.

117 **chastise** accented on the first syllable

119 **Excuse . . . down** i.e., 'It is sufficient excuse for my usurpation of authority that I am fighting against usurpation' (Percy Simpson, *N. & Q.*, 101 (1900), 164). Simpson's proposed punctuation, a comma after *is*, seems unnecessary.

120 **Who . . . France** Eleanor's question initiates a raucous argument with Constance, sometimes called 'the Billingsgate scene' but 'best understood . . . as a variation on the formal defiances before battle, so frequent on the Elizabethan stage' (Sprague, p. 14).

CONSTANCE

Let me make answer. (*To Eleanor*) Thy usurping son.

QUEEN ELEANOR

Out, insolent! Thy bastard shall be king

That thou mayst be a queen and check the world.

CONSTANCE

My bed was ever to thy son as true

As thine was to thy husband, and this boy

Liker in feature to his father Geoffrey

Than thou and John, in manners being as like

As rain to water, or devil to his dam.

My boy a bastard! By my soul, I think

His father never was so true begot.   130

It cannot be an if thou wert his mother.

QUEEN ELEANOR (*to Arthur*)

There's a good mother, boy, that blots thy father.

CONSTANCE (*to Arthur*)

There's a good grandam, boy, that would blot thee.

AUSTRIA

Peace!

BASTARD Hear the crier!

AUSTRIA   What the devil art thou?

---

127 John, in manners being] F; John in manners; being CAPELL (*conj.* Roderick)   129
bastard!] ROWE; ~ ? F   131 an if] F (and if)   133] POPE's *punctuation*; *as two lines, breaking
after* 'boy' F   134 crier!] HALLIWELL; Cryer. F

---

122 **Out** See 1.1.64n.
   insolent A presumptuous, overbearing
   person (*OED*'s earliest citation for the
   sb.); the use of 'insolence' in this construction would be Shakespearian, and
   that word may have appeared in his
   manuscript. See Introduction p. 22 and
   n. 1.
123 **queen and check** *Check* has both the
   general sense of 'rebuke, chastize, control' and the more specific sense, drawn
   from chess, of 'challenge, put in danger';
   the former sense also introduces the pun
   on *queen* and 'quean' (= strumpet, a
   proverbially shrewish woman); Constance reacts to this aspersion at
   2.1.124 ff.
125 **As thine . . . husband** 'Elinor had been
   divorced from her first husband, Louis
   VII of France, for infidelity' (Wright).
125–6 **this boy | Liker** i.e., this boy is more

like
126–7 **in feature . . . in manners** The contrast
   is between physical appearance and daily
   behaviour.
127–8 **as like | . . . devil to his dam** A
   common comparison (Tilley D225, 'The
   devil and his dam'); Whiting has many
   instances from *c.*1350 onward.
130 **His father** i.e., Geoffrey, Constance's
   dead husband
131 **an if** if
133 **There's . . . thee** The compositor broke
   this line because it was too long for the
   measure; the preceding line required a
   turnover.
134 **crier** 'Alluding to the usual proclamation for *silence*, made by criers in
   courts of justice' (Malone).
   What the devil *OED* cites this common
   phrase (Dent DD12) sixteen times from
   *c.*1385.

BASTARD

One that will play the devil, sir, with you,
An a may catch your hide and you alone.
You are the hare of whom the proverb goes,
Whose valour plucks dead lions by the beard.
I'll smoke your skin-coat an I catch you right!
Sirrah, look to't, i'faith I will, i'faith!   140

BLANCHE

O, well did he become that lion's robe
That did disrobe the lion of that robe.

BASTARD

It lies as sightly on the back of him
As great Alcides' shoes upon an ass.
But, ass, I'll take that burden from your back,
Or lay on that shall make your shoulders crack.

AUSTRIA

What cracker is this same that deafs our ears
With this abundance of superfluous breath?

136 An] F (And)   139 an] F (and)   right!] CAMBRIDGE; ～, F   140 i'faith!] SMALLWOOD;
～. F   141 BLANCHE] F (Blan⟨che⟩.; and thus until 3.1.207); Const⟨ance⟩. CLARKE conj.   144
Alcides' shoes] F (Alcides shooes); Alcides' shews THEOBALD (conj. Thirlby); Alcides' shows
KEIGHTLEY; Alcides' shew'd CAMBRIDGE

135 **play the devil** A common phrase: see
  Dent PP13, showing that *OED*'s entry
  for the phrase, at *play, v.* VI.34 may be
  antedated from *c.*1790 to an instance
  from 1519. See also *devil, sb.* II.22k, for
  an instance in 1542.
136 **An a** if he
137–8 **the hare . . . beard** Tilley H165, 'So
  hares may pull dead lions by the beard'
  (examples in English from 1580 onward;
  also in Erasmus, *Adagia* (1500), 1118A).
  See Introduction, pp. 14–15.
139 **smoke** i.e., stupefy you by exposing
  your coat (and you) to smoke (so *v.* II.5b,
  quoting this line). Schmidt (2c) defines
  as 'curry', perhaps recalling Cotgrave's
  definition of *en*: 'J'en aurai (blows being
  understood) I shall be well-beaten; my
  skin-coat will be soundly curried'.
  an I if I
141 **become** merit, earn, grace. See 5.1.55
  and n.
144 **As great . . . an ass** This insult combines
  two proverbial expressions: Tilley A351,
  'An ass in a lion's skin', and Tilley S366,
  'A great (Hercules') shoe will not fit a
  little (a child's) foot'. The second proverb

appears in Erasmus' *Adagia* (1500),
566D, and entered English use in 1548;
ridiculing allegorical readings of Homer,
Stephen Gosson combined the two expressions: 'You will smile . . . to see how
this moral philosopher [Maximus of Tyre]
toils to draw the lion's skin upon Aesop's
ass, Hercules' shoes on a child's feet' (*The
School of Abuse* (1579), A3ᵛ). In Gosson
and *K. John*, the phrase describes an
incongruous mixture of great and small,
important and trivial.
Alcides Hercules
shoes F's *shooes* (= shoes) makes proverbial sense; Theobald's emendation,
shews (= shows, distinctive garb, hence
the lion's skin) also makes sense. Both
'shoes' and 'shows' could be represented typographically by *sho(o)es* (see
Maxwell). Although the compositor may
have adjusted the spelling away from
manuscript and toward the common
proverb, Honigmann thinks that both
meanings are present.
145–6 **But . . . crack** Rhyme summarizes
  the insulting threat.
147 **cracker** A boaster or braggart and also

KING PHILIP

Louis, determine what we shall do straight.

LOUIS THE DAUPHIN

Women and fools, break off your conference.   150

King John, this is the very sum of all:

England and Ireland, Angers, Touraine, Maine,

In right of Arthur do I claim of thee.

Wilt thou resign them and lay down thy arms?

KING JOHN

My life as soon. I do defy thee, France.

Arthur of Bretagne, yield thee to my hand,

And out of my dear love I'll give thee more

Than e'er the coward hand of France can win.

Submit thee, boy.

QUEEN ELEANOR (*to Arthur*) Come to thy grandam, child.

CONSTANCE

Do, child, go to it grandam, child.   160

Give grandam kingdom, and it grandam will

---

149 KING PHILIP] CAPELL's *speech assignment*; *speech continues* F (King *Lewis*, . . .)   150 LOUIS
THE DAUPHIN] F (*Lew⟨is⟩.*); THEOBALD *assigns speech to Philip*   151] *speech continues* F; *K⟨ing⟩.
Phil⟨ip⟩.* HONIGMANN   152 Angers] F; Anjou THEOBALD

word-play on *crack* (l. 146), but probably
alluding to 'firework which explodes with
a sharp report or a succession of sharp
reports' (6); the only use in Shakespeare.
deafs deafens

149 **KING PHILIP** See Appendix A1 for an
explanation of how F's text became confused and of the dramatic value of this
reassignment.

152 **Angers** Like Chatillon's original list
(1.1.11) and the one at 2.1.528–9, this
list mingles a city (here Angers) with
provinces, although it omits *Poyctiers*
(i.e., Poitiers, for 'Poitou'). John's list at
2.1.488 also contains *Angiers*, although
his following lines make clear that the
city is not part of Blanche's dowry. There
are thus either factual errors or confusing
place-names in all four lists (Poitiers for
Poitou, at 1.1.11 and 2.1.529; Angers
for Anjou, at 2.1.152 and 2.1.488); all
four occur in Compositor C's work and
may be his mistaken expansions of a
manuscript abbreviation or scribble.
Since these provinces and cities might be
only slightly more familiar to Eliza-

bethans than to either Compositor C or
most modern audiences, at least three of
the place-names are unlikely to jar and
probably do not need editorial emendation on principle; indeed, emendation
cannot produce factual accuracy because
Shakespeare has exaggerated the historically agreed dowry. The dramatic value
of all the lists is how much (not which)
territory is in dispute: thus, for example,
the two French demands include England
and Ireland (1.1.11 and 2.1.152), but
John just as regularly omits them without
even passing patriotic comment. The only
'error' likely to confuse the audience is
Angiers at 2.1.488, and that requires
emendation.

160–1 **it . . . it** its . . . its. *It* is 'an early
provincial form . . . for *its*, especially
when a child is mentioned, or when any
one is contemptuously spoken of as a
child' (Abbott §228); see *Tragedy of Lear*
1.4.198–9: 'The hedge-sparrow fed the
cuckoo so long | That it's had it head bit
off by it young'.

Give it a plum, a cherry, and a fig.
There's a good grandam.
ARTHUR   Good my mother, peace.
I would that I were low laid in my grave;
I am not worth this coil that's made for me.
QUEEN ELEANOR
His mother shames him so, poor boy, he weeps.
CONSTANCE
Now shame upon you whe'er she does or no!
His grandam's wrongs, and not his mother's shames,
Draws those heaven-moving pearls from his poor eyes,
Which heaven shall take in nature of a fee.   170
Ay, with these crystal beads heaven shall be bribed
To do him justice and revenge on you.
QUEEN ELEANOR
Thou monstrous slanderer of heaven and earth!
CONSTANCE
Thou monstrous injurer of heaven and earth,
Call not me slanderer; thou and thine usurp
The dominations, royalties, and rights
Of this oppressèd boy. This is thy eldest son's son,

---

166 QUEEN ELEANOR] F (*Qu⟨een⟩. Mo⟨ther⟩.*)   167 no!] THEOBALD; no, F   171 Ay] F (I)
173 QUEEN ELEANOR] F (*Qu⟨een⟩.*)   earth!] THEOBALD; ∼. F

---

162 **fig** Three meanings are possible: poisoned fruit (*sb.*¹ 2, citing 'an Italian figge'
from 1589); anything small, valueless
or contemptible (*sb.*¹ 4); a contemptuous
or obscene gesture (*sb.*²). The first meaning may predominate here. The latter
two meanings, both figurative, appear in
the citations for Tilley F213, 'To give one
a fig' (Wilson, *ODEP*, includes figurative
uses from 1565–6 and the literal use for
poisoned fruit from 1585).
163 **Good** See 1.1.249n.
165 **coil** trouble, commotion
166 **shames** disgraces; makes ashamed
167 **whe'er** whether
169 **Draws** Such failures of agreement are
frequent in Elizabethan writing.
170 **Which ... fee** Arthur's tears will serve
as a lawyer's *fee* to purchase heavenly
intervention; see *bribed* (l. 171). The
grammar also permits, especially for the
listening audience, a slight wavering between *Which* = 'heaven-moving pearls'

and *Which* = 'his poor eyes' (a price
almost exacted in 4.1).
171 **Ay** yes
beads figuratively, the *beads* used to count
prayers
173 **slanderer** From Eleanor's point of view,
it is slanderous to believe that heaven
would do the wrong of supporting
Arthur's claim.
174 **injurer** *OED*'s earliest citation for the
sb.
176 **dominations** lordships or sovereignty
(1b)
royalties a monarch's prerogatives or
privileges (5, citing this line). For a different meaning of 'royalty', see 5.2.129.
177 **eldest son's son** This phrase could mean
'eldest grandson' (Honigmann cites Deu-
teronomy 6: 2: 'thou, and thy son, and
thy son's son'), but it may be further
genealogical confusion (as at 2.1.2 ff. and
see 2.1.13n).

Infortunate in nothing but in thee.
Thy sins are visited in this poor child;
The canon of the Law is laid on him,   180
Being but the second generation
Removèd from thy sin-conceiving womb.

KING JOHN

Bedlam, have done.

CONSTANCE   I have but this to say:
That he is not only plaguèd for her sin,
But God hath made her sin and her the plague
On this removèd issue, plagued for her,
And with her plague her sin; his injury
Her injury the beadle to her sin,
All punished in the person of this child
And all for her. A plague upon her!   190

QUEEN ELEANOR

Thou unadvisèd scold, I can produce
A will that bars the title of thy son.

187 plague her sin; his] POPE; plague her sin: his F; plagued; her sin his DYCE 1864 (*conj.*
Roderick); plague; her sin his CAMBRIDGE (*conj.* Roby); plague, her sin; his WILSON   190
her!] THEOBALD; ∼ . F   191 QUEEN ELEANOR] F (*Que⟨en⟩.*)

178 **Infortunate** unfortunate. Shakespeare's
word is obsolete.
179 **visited** punished (especially by divine
judgement; see *v.* II.6, although *OED*
quotes this line at I.5b, 'to avenge, or
inflict punishment on'). Similarly biblical
phrasing appears at 2.1.14.
179–82 **Thy sins . . . womb** Alluding to
the Catechism's version of the second
Commandment (in the Book of Common
Prayer): 'and visit the sins of the fathers
upon the children unto the third and
fourth generation of them that hate me'
(Noble, p. 114; see Exodus 20: 5).
180 **canon of the Law** i.e., an ecclesiastical
rule, law or decree (= *canon*), part of the
Ten Commandments (= *the Law*). The
same combination of words appears in
the Countess of Salisbury's lament, 'Blot
out the strict forbidding of the law, | And
cancel every canon that prescribes | A
shame for shame or penance for offence'
(*Edward III* 2.1.424–6).
182 **Removèd** distant in relationship (by two
generations)
sin-conceiving i.e., Eleanor breeds sins,
not sons. Noble (p. 114) compares 'and
in sin hath my mother conceived me'
(Psalms 51:5).
183 **Bedlam** lunatic (derived from the Hospi-
tal of the Priory of St. Mary of Bethlehem,
a contemporary London asylum)
185–90 **But God . . . upon her** The lines are
confusing because of Constance's 'witty'
use of *plague* as both noun and verb; the
punctuation chosen here assumes that
God hath made (l. 185) serves as subject
and verb controlling *her plague* and *his
injury* (ll. 187–8).
187 **And with her plague her sin** i.e., with
her person torment (*plague*) the sin she
committed
187–8 **his injury . . . her sin** i.e., Constance's
wrong (*injury*) harms Arthur (becomes
his injury) and thus rebounds to punish,
as a parish constable (*beadle*) would punish, her original sin
191 **unadvisèd**   'rash,   inconsiderate'
(Wright)
192 **A will that bars the title** A *will* and a
son's *title* were similarly at stake between
Philip and Robert Faulconbridge (see
I.I.II4–I5 and I30–I and Introduction, pp. 54–60); John ruled by virtue of
Richard I's *will* (Holinshed, 155b–156a;
O4–O4ᵛ).

CONSTANCE

Ay, who doubts that? A will—a wicked will,

A woman's will, a cankered grandam's will!

KING PHILIP

Peace, lady. Pause, or be more temperate;

It ill beseems this presence to cry aim

To these ill-tunèd repetitions.

Some trumpet summon hither to the walls

These men of Angers; let us hear them speak

Whose title they admit, Arthur's or John's.   200

   Trumpet sounds.

   Enter Citizen⌈s⌉ of Angers, ⌈including Hubert,⌉ upon

   the walls

CITIZEN

Who is it that hath warned us to the walls?

KING PHILIP

'Tis France, for England.

KING JOHN   England, for itself.

You men of Angers, and my loving subjects—

KING PHILIP

You loving men of Angers, Arthur's subjects,

Our trumpet called you to this gentle parle—

KING JOHN

For our advantage; therefore hear us first.

193 Ay] F (I)   194 will!] REED 1813; ∼. F   200.2–3 *Enter . . . walls*] This edition; *Enter a Citizen vpon the walles.* F; *Enter certain Citizens on the Walls* CAPELL. *See Appendix A2.*   203 subjects—] ROWE (*subs.*); subiects. F   205 parle—] ROWE (*subs.*); ∼. F

bars In legal language, a bar 'is when the defendant . . . pleadeth a plea which is a sufficient answer and that destroyeth the action of the plaintiff forever' (Rastell).

194 **A woman's will** See Tilley W723, 'Women will have their wills'.

196 **presence** assembly of important or royal individuals (a mixture of 2 and 3)
cry aim abet, encourage (from the signal, 'aim', in an archery contest)

198 **trumpet** Metonymy for 'trumpeter'; stage directions often replaced agent with instrument; see, e.g., 'Enter Talbot with Trumpe and Drumme, | before Burdeaux' (*1 Henry VI* TLN 1948–9), 'Enter Yorke | with Trumpet, and many Souldiers' (ibid. TLN 2008–9), and below,

2.1.299.2–3: 'Enter the Herald of France with Trumpets to the gates' (F1).

200.2 **including Hubert** See Appendix A2 for a discussion of this added stage direction.

201 **warned** 'summoned' (Wright)

204 **loving men . . . subjects** Philip's rhetoric echoes John's to emphasize the substitution of 'Arthur's subjects' for 'my loving subjects'.

205 **parle** parley, conference under truce; the verse requires F's archaic but monosyllabic *parle* here and at 2.1.226, the disyllabic and modern *parley* at 2.1.78 (F: *parlie*), 4.2.238 and 5.1.68 (both *parley* in F), respectively. Elsewhere, F prints *parlee* (*LLL* 5.2.123).

206 **advantage** benefit

These flags of France that are advancèd here
Before the eye and prospect of your town
Have hither marched to your endamagement.
The cannons have their bowels full of wrath,   210
And ready mounted are they to spit forth
Their iron indignation 'gainst your walls.
All preparation for a bloody siege
And merciless proceeding by these French
Confronts your city's eyes, your winking gates.
And but for our approach, those sleeping stones,
That as a waist doth girdle you about,
By the compulsion of their ordinance
By this time from their fixèd beds of lime
Had been dishabited, and wide havoc made   220
For bloody power to rush upon your peace.
But on the sight of us your lawful King,
Who painfully with much expedient march
Have brought a countercheck before your gates,
To save unscratched your city's threatened cheeks,
Behold the French, amazed, vouchsafe a parle.
And now, instead of bullets wrapped in fire
To make a shaking fever in your walls,

214 French$_\Lambda$] CAMBRIDGE; ~ . F   215 Confronts] CAPELL; Comfort F   your city's] ROWE;
yours ~ F

207 **advancèd** 'raised, lifted up' (Wright)
215 **Confronts . . . gates** F's line probably
    has one common printing error, an *s*
    attached to the wrong word (*yours*).
    Comfort(s) misread from manuscript *Con-*
    front(s) is not impossible (Compositor B
    set this line, but Compositor C seems to
    have been especially prone to omit an *r*
    after a consonant, as may have happened
    here; see 2.1.113n and 3.1.259n).
    Honigmann (2.1.215n) defends *Com-*
    fort(s) as irony and instances *winking* as
    'very playful', but 'winking' here means
    'shut' (see Schmidt), and Shakespeare
    associates *winking* with foolish, not
    playful, self-destruction: Lord Bardolph
    recalls that Hotspur 'with great imagin-
    ation | Proper to madmen, led his powers
    to death, | And winking leapt into de-
    struction' (2 *Henry IV* 1.3.31–3), and
    Orléans criticizes English mastiffs (and
    by implication English soldiers), 'Foolish
    curs, that run winking into the mouth

of a Russian bear' (*Henry V* 3.7.139–
40).
    winking gates i.e., gates 'that fear to
    open, gates that are in the state of an
    eye that fears annoyance' (Capell, *Notes*)
218 **ordinance** military equipment. In mod-
    ern English, the trisyllabic spelling has
    been replaced by *ordnance* (so *ordinance*,
    sb. 4c).
220 **dishabited** dislodged, violently removed
    from their places (*OED*'s only citation for
    this meaning). Fleay reads 'dishabit' with
    support from Kellner, §205.
223 **expedient** quick, speedy. See 1.1.49n.
225 **unscratched** This line is *OED*'s earliest
    citation for the *ppl. a.*
227 **bullets wrapped in fire** The same or very
    similar phrases appear in numerous texts
    from the late 1580s onward, for instance,
    'We'll send thee bullets wrapt in smoke
    and fire' (Marlowe, *The Jew of Malta*
    2.2.54).

They shoot but calm words folded up in smoke
To make a faithless error in your ears,   230
Which trust accordingly, kind citizens,
And let us in. Your King, whose laboured spirits
Forwearied in this action of swift speed,
Craves harbourage within your city walls.
KING PHILIP
When I have said, make answer to us both.
Lo, in this right hand, whose protection
Is most divinely vowed upon the right
Of him it holds, stands young Plantagenet,
Son to the elder brother of this man,
And king o'er him and all that he enjoys.   240
For this downtrodden equity we tread
In warlike march these greens before your town,
Being no further enemy to you
Than the constraint of hospitable zeal
In the relief of this oppressèd child
Religiously provokes. Be pleasèd then
To pay that duty which you truly owe
To him that owns it, namely, this young Prince.
And then our arms, like to a muzzled bear
Save in aspect, hath all offence sealed up;   250
Our cannons' malice vainly shall be spent
Against th'invulnerable clouds of heaven,
And with a blessèd and unvexed retire,
With unhacked swords and helmets all unbruised,
We will bear home that lusty blood again

248 owns] F (owes)

229 **words folded up in smoke** words enclosed in (deceitful) obscurity (*smoke, sb.* I.4d, e), but playing on 'wrapped in fire' (l. 227). See 'This helpless smoke of words doth me no right' (*Lucrece* 1027) and 'Sweet smoke of rhetoric' (*LLL* 3.1.61).
231 **trust** i.e., distrust
232–4 **Your King . . . walls** The subordinate clause ('whose . . . speed') lacks a verb, and Pope emended to make 'Craves' a plural verb.
233 **Forwearied** Exhausted, completely tired out; F does not consistently distinguish between two prefixes: *for-* (in senses such

as prohibition or excess) and *fore-* (in the sense of temporal or spatial priority). Thus, F's *Fore-wearied* could mean 'wearied before, tired by previous acts', but that meaning would be a Shakespearian coinage, whereas the now archaic sense adopted here was then current.
241 **tread** word-play on 'downtrodden'
250 **aspect** accent on second syllable
252 **invulnerable** incapable of being injured. *OED*'s earliest citation for *a.* 1.
254 **unhacked** uncut or undamaged through use in battle. *OED* cites only this line and *Antony* 2.6.38 for the *ppl. a.*

Which here we came to spout against your town,
And leave your children, wives, and you in peace.
But if you fondly pass our proffered offer,
'Tis not the roundure of your old-faced walls
Can hide you from our messengers of war,   260
Though all these English and their discipline
Were harboured in their rude circumference.
Then tell us: shall your city call us lord
In that behalf which we have challenged it,
Or shall we give the signal to our rage
And stalk in blood to our possession?

CITIZEN
In brief, we are the King of England's subjects.
For him, and in his right, we hold this town.

KING JOHN
Acknowledge then the King, and let me in.

CITIZEN
That can we not. But he that proves the King,   270
To him will we prove loyal; till that time
Have we rammed up our gates against the world.

KING JOHN
Doth not the crown of England prove the King?
And if not that, I bring you witnesses,
Twice fifteen thousand hearts of England's breed—

BASTARD (*aside*) Bastards and else.

---

258 offer] F; love DYCE 1864 (*conj.* Walker)   259 roundure] F (rounder)   275 breed—]
CAMBRIDGE; ∼ . F

---

258 **fondly pass** foolishly neglect or disregard
259 **roundure** 'Roundness; rounded form or
space' (*OED, roundure*). *OED* considers
F's *rounder* an exceptional spelling and
cites only three uses through 1623, the
next from Keats, and two (in the *Supplement*) from the twentieth century.
Steevens found the word in Rowley's
All's Lost by Lust (1633): 'Will she be
woman? will she meet our arms | With
an alternate roundure? will she do?'
(A4), which incidentally antedates *OED*'s
earliest citation for *alternate* (= reciprocal) by almost a century. F's spelling
might indicate pronunciation, and it may
convey a vaguely French linguistic ambi-
ence (Cotgrave has 'rondeur'), although

the English translator of André Favyn's
Le Théâtre d'honneur (1620) wrote *rounder*
without any obvious cognate in his
original (see *The Theatre of Honour and
Knighthood*, 1623, p. 12). If 'rondure'
(Sonnet 21.8) is the same word, as *OED*
suggests, it is less uncommon than
sometimes thought (Booth, p. 169).
261 **discipline** i.e., individuals skilled in warfare (a transferred sense of *sb.* 3b; see
2.1.39n).
264 **In that behalf which** in respect
of which, in reference to which (that
is, Arthur's claim to sovereignty over
Angers)
267 **brief** few words

KING JOHN

To verify our title with their lives.

KING PHILIP

As many and as well-born bloods as those—

BASTARD (*aside*) Some bastards too.

KING PHILIP

Stand in his face to contradict his claim.   280

CITIZEN

Till you compound whose right is worthiest,

We for the worthiest hold the right from both.

KING JOHN

Then God forgive the sin of all those souls

That to their everlasting residence

Before the dew of evening fall shall fleet

In dreadful trial of our kingdom's king.

KING PHILIP

Amen, amen. Mount, chevaliers. To arms!

BASTARD

Saint George that swinged the dragon, and e'er since

Sits on's horseback at mine hostess' door,

Teach us some fence! (*To Austria*) Sirrah, were I at
    home   290

At your den, sirrah, with your lioness,

I would set an ox-head to your lion's hide

And make a monster of you.

278 those—] ROWE; ~. F   288–89] POPE; *as two lines, breaking after* 'dragon' F   290
fence!] CAPELL; ~. F

281 **compound** settle, determine
282 **hold** While the Citizen may mean 'occupy' or 'retain' (an office, or the privileges of the town), the context seems
to demand 'withhold' or 'keep back',
although *OED* provides no precisely apposite definition.
287 **chevaliers** Mounted soldiers, knights;
the word was in native English use since
the Middle Ages, pronounced as if spelled
'chivalers'.
288–9 **Saint George . . . hostess' door** See
Tilley S42, 'Like Saint George, who is
ever on horseback yet never rides' (because the figure appears on a tavern- or
inn-sign and with bawdy senses of a man
'riding' a woman sexually); Lyly uses
the proverb (i. 260 and 313) as a criticism
of idleness, and in Chapman's *Gentleman*

Usher, a reference to 'the English sign of
great Saint George' (1.2.93) is regarded
as a 'gross enough' (1.2.144) imputation
of cowardice. J. L. Brereton thought that
Chapman's reference might be 'to some
London sign-board of particular notor-
iety' (*MLR*, 3 (1907–8), 398); the Bastard's reference may initiate the bawdy
jokes of the following lines to Austria.
288 **swinged** thrashed
289 **on's** on his
290 **fence** use of the sword
291 **lioness** i.e., Austria's wife (because
of the lion-skin he wears), but *lioness*
also = prostitute (Honigmann 2.1.291n)
292–3 **set . . . monster** Given a chance,
the Bastard would place the cuckold's
horns on Austria's forehead, thus making
him a monster to masculine pride and a

AUSTRIA   Peace, no more.
BASTARD

O, tremble, for you hear the lion roar.

KING JOHN

Up higher to the plain, where we'll set forth
In best appointment all our regiments.

BASTARD

Speed then to take advantage of the field.

KING PHILIP

It shall be so, and at the other hill
Command the rest to stand. God and our right!

> *Exeunt, severally, the English and French forces*
> *Here, after excursions, enter the Herald of France*
> *with trumpeters to the gates*

FRENCH HERALD

You men of Angers, open wide your gates   300
And let young Arthur Duke of Bretagne in,
Who by the hand of France this day hath made
Much work for tears in many an English mother,
Whose sons lie scattered on the bleeding ground;
Many a widow's husband grovelling lies,
Coldly embracing the discoloured earth;
And victory with little loss doth play
Upon the dancing banners of the French,
Who are at hand, triumphantly displayed,
To enter conquerors and to proclaim   310
Arthur of Bretagne England's king and yours.

299.1 *Exeunt . . . forces*] Exeunt F   299.2–3 *Here . . . gates*] F (*trumpets*). *See note.*

monstrous combination of ox and lion; see Dent C876.1, 'A cuckold is a beast (monster)', citing *Hamlet* 3.1.141 f. and *Othello* 4.1.60 among others. Line 292 is *OED*'s earliest citation for *ox-head*, *sb.* 1.

296 **appointment** equipment
regiments large units of armed force

297 **advantage** Both 'superior position, a place of vantage' and 'opportunity or chance' (Hulme, pp. 307–8); see 'the best part of my power, | As I upon advantage did remove' (5.7.61–2).

299.2–3 *enter . . . gates* Heralds delivered messages, but did not themselves carry or sound the attention-getting trumpet:

see *Tragedy of Lear* 5.3.100 ff. and C. W. Scott-Giles, *Shakespeare's Heraldry* (1950), p. 53.

305 **grovelling lies** lies prone, belly downward

309 **Who are . . . displayed** Although the French *banners* are more likely to be *displayed* than the French themselves, two meanings are possible: 'the French troops are spread out to form an extended line' (i.e., 'deployed'; see *display, v.* 1b) and 'the French army has made a great show, has acted ostentatiously' (see 5b, quoting *Tragedy of Lear* 2.2.216–17: 'the . . . fellow which . . . Displayed so saucily against your highness').

Enter English Herald with trumpeter

ENGLISH HERALD

Rejoice, you men of Angers, ring your bells;
King John, your king and England's, doth approach,
Commander of this hot malicious day.
Their armours that marched hence so silver-bright
Hither return all gilt with Frenchmen's blood;
There stuck no plume in any English crest
That is removèd by a staff of France;
Our colours do return in those same hands
That did display them when we first marched forth,   320
And like a jolly troop of huntsmen come
Our lusty English, all with purpled hands,
Dyed in the dying slaughter of their foes.
Open your gates and give the victors way.

HUBERT

Heralds, from off our towers we might behold
From first to last the onset and retire
Of both your armies, whose equality
By our best eyes cannot be censurèd.
Blood hath bought blood, and blows have answered
        blows;
Strength matched with strength, and power confronted
        power.   330
Both are alike, and both alike we like.
One must prove greatest. While they weigh so even,
We hold our town for neither, yet for both.

311.1 *Enter . . . trumpeter*] F (*Trumpet*)   315 silver-bright] POPE; *not hyphenated in* F   323 Dyed] F (*Dide*)   325 HUBERT] F (*Hubert.*); Citi⟨zen⟩. ROWE; I. C⟨itizen⟩. CAPELL

315 **silver-bright** a common analogy (Dent S453.1; Whiting has instances from about 1420 onward)
316 **gilt . . . with blood** smeared . . . with blood, but playing upon 'covered with a layer of gold'. For the association of gold with red, see 3.1.85–6n.
317 **plume** perhaps word-play on 'Plantagenet' (see 1.1.162n)
321–3 **troop of huntsmen . . . dying slaughter** 'It was, I think, one of the savage practices of the chase for all to stain their hands in the blood of the deer as a trophy' (Johnson); the 'savage practice' is explicit at *Caesar* 3.1.206–7: 'here thy hunters stand | Signed in thy spoil and crimsoned

in thy lethe'; for other evidence, see Honigmann 2.1.321n.
323 **dying** word-play: expiring; changing an object from one colour to another
325 **HUBERT** F's speech assignment; see Appendix A2. For the historical Hubert de Burgh, see ibid., n. 3.
328 **censurèd** estimated, judged (according to v. 3, a recent meaning in Shakespeare's day, but Latin *censeo* was an extremely common verb with the same meaning)
329 **Blood hath bought blood** See 1.1.19n.
331 **both alike we like** i.e., we approve both sides equally. 'You like not all alike' appears in Chapman's *Gentleman Usher* 4.2.62.

Enter on one side King John, Queen Eleanor, Blanche,
the Bastard, the Earl of Salisbury, and English forces;
on the other side King Philip, Louis the Dauphin,
Austria, and French forces

KING JOHN

France, hast thou yet more blood to cast away?
Say, shall the current of our right run on,
Whose passage, vexed with thy impediment,
Shall leave his native channel and o'erswell
With course disturbed even thy confining shores,
Unless thou let his silver water keep
A peaceful progress to the ocean?   340

KING PHILIP

England, thou hast not saved one drop of blood
In this hot trial more than we of France;
Rather, lost more. And by this hand I swear
That sways the earth this climate overlooks:
Before we will lay down our just-borne arms,
We'll put thee down, 'gainst whom these arms we bear,
Or add a royal number to the dead,
Gracing the scroll that tells of this war's loss
With slaughter coupled to the name of kings.

BASTARD

Ha, majesty! How high thy glory towers   350
When the rich blood of kings is set on fire.

333.1–4 *Enter . . . French forces*] *Enter the two Kings with their powers, at seuerall doores.* F
335 run] F2 (runne); *rome* F1   337 o'erswell] F (ore-swell)   339 water‸] F4; Water, F1
350 Ha, majesty!] CAPELL (*subs.*); Ha Maiesty: F

335 **run** flow (see 5.4.53–7); *rome* (F1's
     reading, modernized as 'roam') is restric-
     ted to variations on the sense of 'walk'
     (see *1 Henry VI* 3.1.52) and could have
     been misread from manuscript *run*(n)(*e*)
335–40 **shall the current . . . to the ocean**
     See Tilley S929, 'The stream (current,
     tide) stopped swells the higher' (Wilson,
     ODEP, cites an example from 1563).
338 **confining** This line is *OED*'s earliest
     citation for the *ppl. a.* meaning 'bounding,
     limiting'.
340 **progress** Journey, travel, but perhaps
     with the additional meaning of a state
     journey or visit, as at 5.2.46, a passage
     that also refers to dew (tears) and silver.
     ocean? Although the speech is techni-
     cally a question (*Say*, l. 335), it is effec-

     tively a threat. 'Ocean' is here trisyllabic.
343 **this hand** Either Philip's own hand or
     Arthur's; see 4.3.71n.
344 **climate** portion of the sky (Honigmann).
     Not in *OED*, but I. John quotes Cotgrave,
     '*Climat* . . . a division in the sky . . .'.
345 **just-borne** recently carried; rightly
     (*just-* = justly) carried
346 **put . . . down** 'crush, extirpate', but
     perhaps with the sense 'add to the list,
     write down'
347 **royal number** 'a royal item [or entry]
     in the list [of dead]' (Moore Smith)
351 **blood . . . set on fire** A common image;
     Dent F287.1, '(To set) (one's heart) on
     fire', cites five other Shakespearian in-
     stances and Dent, *PLED*, has instances
     from *c*.1516.

O, now doth Death line his dread chops with steel;
The swords of soldiers are his teeth, his fangs,
And now he feasts, mousing the flesh of men,
In undetermined differences of kings.
Why stand these royal fronts amazèd thus?
Cry havoc, Kings! Back to the stainèd field,
You equal potents, fiery kindled spirits!
Then let confusion of one part confirm
The other's peace. Till then, blows, blood, and death!   360

KING JOHN

Whose party do the townsmen yet admit?

KING PHILIP

Speak, citizens, for England. Who's your king?

HUBERT

The King of England, when we know the King.

KING PHILIP

Know him in us that here hold up his right—

KING JOHN

In us that are our own great deputy
And bear possession of our person here,
Lord of our presence, Angers, and of you.

HUBERT

A greater power than we denies all this.

352 dread] This edition (*conj.* Mull); dead F chops] F (chaps)   357 Kings!] CAPELL; ∼, F
358 equal potents] F; equal-potent DYCE 1864 (*conj.* Walker, *withdrawn*); equal-potents
MOORE SMITH   360 death!] HANMER; ∼. F   362 Who's] F (whose)   363 HUBERT] F
(*Hub⟨ert⟩*.)   368 HUBERT] HONIGMANN (*conj.* Macmillan MS in Cambridge); *Fra⟨nce⟩*. F;
Citi⟨zen⟩. ROWE; 1. C⟨*itizen*⟩. CAPELL

352–4 **Death . . . feasts** See Tilley W47,
   'War is death's feast' (from 1623), and
   Dent D138.1, 'Death devours all things'
   (instances from 1557, including *Romeo*
   2.5.7); the idea returns at 5.2.176–8.
352 **dread** F's *dead* is curiously flat and
   redundant, making Mull's conjecture
   (recorded in Cambridge) attractive. This
   line was set by Compositor B, although
   elsewhere it is Compositor C who may
   have omitted *r* after an initial consonant
   (see 2.1.113n, 3.1.259n, 3.4.64n).
   chops the jaws, often used to describe
   beasts of prey. F's *chaps* has been superseded by *chops* in this usage.
354 **mousing** 'tearing, biting', as a cat does
   a mouse
355 **undetermined** unresolved
356 **fronts** foreheads

357 **Cry havoc** give the order, 'Havoc' (i.e.,
   seize the spoils of war)
358 **potents** Powerful individuals (adjective
   for noun, see Abbott §433); the only
   appearance of the noun in Shakespeare.
   Similar usages appear in 'discontents at
   home' (4.3.151), 'ingrate revolts'
   (5.2.151), and 'revolts of England'
   (5.4.7).
359 **part** party, side
365 **our own great deputy** That is, 'The
   King of England does not need a deputy'
   (Honigmann), but the line anticipates
   3.1.136 and 155 and suggests that
   John's sovereignty derives from himself
   alone.
367 **Lord of our presence** See 1.1.137n.
368–72 **A greater power . . . deposed** This
   speech responds to the symmetrical royal

And till it be undoubted, we do lock
Our former scruple in our strong-barred gates.   370
Kings of our fear, until our fears resolved
Be by some certain king, purged and deposed.

BASTARD

By heaven, these scroyles of Angers flout you, Kings,
And stand securely on their battlements
As in a theatre, whence they gape and point
At your industrious scenes and acts of death.
Your royal presences, be ruled by me:
Do like the mutines of Jerusalem,
Be friends a while, and both conjointly bend
Your sharpest deeds of malice on this town.   380
By east and west let France and England mount
Their battering cannon chargèd to the mouths,
Till their soul-fearing clamours have brawled down
The flinty ribs of this contemptuous city.
I'd play incessantly upon these jades
Even till unfencèd desolation

370 strong-barred] POPE; *not hyphenated in* F   371 Kings] F; King'd TYRWHITT   373
scroyles] F; scroils HALLIWELL   377 Your] F; You ROWE   381 mount∧] F2; mount. F1

demands and therefore belongs to a
character who speaks from the walls of
Angers; see Appendix A2 and 3.
371–2 **Kings . . . purged and deposed** i.e.,
(we will remain) ruled by (= *Kings of*; see
Abbott §168) our apprehensive doubts
(= *fear*, *fears*) until the legitimate monarch (= *some certain king*) banishes those
fears, that is, purges and deposes the
monarch, Fear, who rules Angers now.
This compact passage has been often
repunctuated and elicited Tyrwhitt's
graphically plausible but unnecessary
emendation. Like John's nobles in 4.2,
Hubert is anxious to remain both uncom-
mitted and inoffensive; the effort strains
his syntax.
373 **scroyles** wretches, scoundrels (earliest
citation in *OED*)
376 **industrious scenes and acts of death**
The Bastard puns on the theatrical meanings of 'scenes and acts'; see 'Why stand
we like soft-hearted women here, | Wail-
ing our losses, whiles the foe doth rage; |
And look upon, as if the tragedy | Were
played in jest by counterfeiting actors?'
(3 *Henry VI* 2.3.25–8) and 'For all my

reign hath been but as a scene | Acting
that argument' (*2 Henry IV* 4.3.326–7).
377 **presences** 'persons', but with the sense
of 'embodied selves'
378 **mutines of Jerusalem** mutineers of Jerusalem. About AD 70, civil factions in
Jerusalem united to fight the Romans
under Titus (Josephus, *Jewish Wars* 5.6.4,
in *Works*, rev. edn. by A. R. Shilleto, 5
vols. (1889–1911), v. 33–4); several
Elizabethan plays that survive only as
titles suggest that the episode was well
known (Wilson, 2.1.378n), as does Bara-
bas' casual allusion (*Jew of Malta* 2.3.10).
The spelling *mutines* appears in both Q2
and F *Hamlet* (5.2.6) and in *More* Add.
II. D, l. 129 (where the *n* has been added
above the line to *mutyes*).
381 **mount** raise in preparation for firing
382 **chargèd** loaded
383 **soul-fearing** soul-frightening
     brawled down driven or forced down.
Brawl has the more specific sense of
'quarrel noisily' and may have been
suggested by *clamours*.
385 **jades** broken-down horses
386 **unfencèd** unlimited, uncontained

Leave them as naked as the vulgar air.
That done, dissever your united strengths
And part your mingled colours once again;
Turn face to face and bloody point to point.   390
Then, in a moment, Fortune shall cull forth
Out of one side her happy minion,
To whom in favour she shall give the day
And kiss him with a glorious victory.
How like you this wild counsel, mighty states?
Smacks it not something of the policy?

KING JOHN
Now, by the sky that hangs above our heads,
I like it well. France, shall we knit our powers
And lay this Angers even with the ground,
Then after fight who shall be king of it?   400

BASTARD (*to Philip*)
An if thou hast the mettle of a king,
Being wronged as we are by this peevish town,
Turn thou the mouth of thy artillery,
As we will ours, against these saucy walls.
And when that we have dashed them to the ground,
Why, then defy each other and pell-mell
Make work upon ourselves, for heaven or hell.

KING PHILIP
Let it be so. Say, where will you assault?

KING JOHN
We from the west will send destruction
Into this city's bosom.   410

AUSTRIA I from the north.

---

401 An] F (And)

---

387 **vulgar** common, universal
389 **colours** flags, insignia of war
390 **point to point** i.e., sword- or lance-point
  against sword- or lance-point. The same
  expression occurs at *Romeo* 3.1.159 and
  'point against point' at *Macbeth* 1.2.56.
392 **minion** darling. Henry IV enviously
  describes Hotspur as 'sweet Fortune's
  minion' (*1 Henry IV* 1.1.82).
395 **states** 'persons of rank' (Honigmann)
396 **Smacks** savours, tastes. See 1.1.208
  and n.

401 **An if** if
402 **peevish** 'foolish, childish, wayward'
  (Wright)
406–7 **Why . . . hell** The couplet summarizes
  the Bastard's advice.
406 **pell-mell** 'headlong', but with the more
  specific military sense of 'hand-to-hand
  combat'
407 **heaven or hell** The phrase, which
  means 'either eternal life or eternal damnation', also appears at *Macbeth* 2.1.64.

KING PHILIP Our thunder from the south
  Shall rain their drift of bullets on this town.
BASTARD (*aside*)
  O prudent discipline! From north to south,
  Austria and France shoot in each other's mouth.
  I'll stir them to it.—Come, away, away!
HUBERT
  Hear us, great Kings. Vouchsafe a while to stay,
  And I shall show you peace and fair-faced league.
  Win you this city without stroke or wound;
  Rescue those breathing lives to die in beds   420
  That here come sacrifices for the field.
  Persever not, but hear me, mighty Kings!
KING JOHN
  Speak on with favour; we are bent to hear.
HUBERT
  That daughter there of Spain, the Lady Blanche,
  Is near to England. Look upon the years
  Of Louis the Dauphin and that lovely maid.
  If lusty love should go in quest of beauty,
  Where should he find it fairer than in Blanche?
  If zealous love should go in search of virtue,
  Where should he find it purer than in Blanche?   430
  If love ambitious sought a match of birth,
  Whose veins bound richer blood than Lady Blanche?
  Such as she is in beauty, virtue, birth,

412 thunder] F; thunders WHITE (*conj.* Capell, *Notes*)   422 Kings!] HONIGMANN; ~ . F   425
near] F (neere); niece SINGER 1856 (*conj.* Collier, *Notes*)   426 Dauphin] F (Dolphin *throughout
except* Dolphine *at 3.4.177, 5.7.80*)

413 **their** Another failure of grammatical
  agreement (see *thunder*, l. 411).
  drift shower, driven mass (so *sb.* II.8,
  quoting this line), but perhaps with the
  added meaning of 'flock' (*sb.* II.7)
414 **discipline** See 2.1.39n.
420 **breathing lives** individuals now living
422 **Persever** F's consistent spelling, with
  the accent on the second syllable; the
  preferred modern spelling is 'persevere',
  with the accent on the third syllable.
423 **favour** approving permission
424 **That daughter . . . of Spain** See
  2.1.83.1n.
425 **near to** closely related in blood to,
  favourably regarded by. F's *neere* could

easily arise from Compositor B's misreading of manuscript *neece* (Blanche's true
  relation to John, who so addresses her at
  2.1.522, although Chatillon calls her
  Eleanor's niece at 2.1.64 and 470; these
  three lines were set by Compositor C).
429 **zealous love** Earlier, the French party's
  support of Arthur was represented by
  a 'zealous kiss' (2.1.19); here, Hubert
  proposes the abandonment of Arthur in
  the name of 'zealous love'.
430 **purer than in Blanche** Perhaps a pun
  on *blanche* (= white).
431 **birth** high birth, as *ambitious* and the
  comparatives 'fairer' (l. 428) and 'purer'
  (l. 430) suggest

Is the young Dauphin every way complete.
If not complete of, say he is not she,
And she again wants nothing to name want,
If want it be not, that she is not he.
He is the half part of a blessèd man,
Left to be finishèd by such as she,
And she a fair divided excellence,   440
Whose fullness of perfection lies in him.
O, two such silver currents when they join
Do glorify the banks that bound them in,
And two such shores to two such streams made one,
Two such controlling bounds shall you be, Kings,
To these two princes if you marry them.
This union shall do more than battery can
To our fast-closèd gates; for at this match,
With swifter spleen than powder can enforce,
The mouth of passage shall we fling wide ope   450
And give you entrance. But without this match,
The sea enragèd is not half so deaf,

448 fast-closèd] THEOBALD (*conj.* Thirlby); *not hyphenated in* F

434 **complete** perfect, fully equipped
435 **complete of** full of, perfected in. Hubert
does not repeat the qualities he has just
listed for Blanche (l. 433); see *of, prep.*
IX.30 for analogous uses and *complete,*
a. 6, on 'complete with' as parallel to
'replete with'; Honigmann notes that
of sometimes represents 'oh' (a reading
proposed by Hanmer).
436–7 **And she . . . not he** F's punctuation
permits two closely related interpretations: 'She lacks nothing one could call
a "lack" unless we consider it a lack
that she is not he'; 'She lacks nothing,
although if one were to inquire for a
deficiency one might say that she is not
he'.
436 **wants** lacks
438 **blessèd** Perhaps slang for 'sexually satisfied' (see *bliss*, Partridge, p. 75).
440–1 **divided excellence** | . . . **perfection lies**
in him See Tilley W718, 'Women receive
perfection by men'; 'Women grow by
men' (*Romeo* 1.3.97) suggests a bawdy
possibility in these lines (*fullness* =
pregnancy).
442–5 **O, two . . . bounds** Hubert echoes the
imagery of ll. 335–40 and portrays the

reconciled Kings as jointly controlling
the united lovers.
446 **princes** The word was used of either
sex.
447 **battery** Some elision ('batt'ry') is needed
for the metre.
448 **match** 'Betrothal, marriage', but punning—alas—on the match that lights
the powder (l. 449) in a cannon (see
2.1.463n).
449 **spleen** Impetuosity, eagerness (so 5b,
citing only this line and 5.7.50), but in
both lines there are overtones of anger
and heated temper; see 2.1.68n and
5.7.50n.
452–6 **The sea . . . city** L. A. Beaurline, cited
in Gordon Braden, *Renaissance Tragedy
and the Senecan Tradition* (New Haven,
Conn., 1985), pp. 176–7 and 250 n.,
compares Seneca's *Medea* 404–14 (*dum
siccas polus . . .*), which Braden in turn
compares with Othello's 'Like to the Pon-
tic Sea . . .' (3.3.456–65).
452 **sea enragèd is not half so deaf** Dent
S169.2, 'As deaf as the sea'; Dent, *PLED,*
cites Arthur Golding's translation of Ovid
(1567).

Lions more confident, mountains and rocks
More free from motion, no, not death himself
In mortal fury half so peremptory,
As we to keep this city.

BASTARD   Here's a stay
That shakes the rotten carcass of old death
Out of his rags. Here's a large mouth indeed
That spits forth death and mountains, rocks and seas;
Talks as familiarly of roaring lions   460
As maids of thirteen do of puppy-dogs.
What cannoneer begot this lusty blood?
He speaks plain cannon—fire, and smoke, and bounce;
He gives the bastinado with his tongue.
Our ears are cudgelled; not a word of his
But buffets better than a fist of France.
Zounds, I was never so bethumped with words
Since I first called my brother's father Dad.

QUEEN ELEANOR
Son, list to this conjunction; make this match.
Give with our niece a dowry large enough,   470
For by this knot thou shalt so surely tie
Thy now unsured assurance to the crown

463 cannon—fire,] DYCE; Cannon fire, F; cannon-fire POPE   469 QUEEN ELEANOR] F (*Old Qu⟨een⟩.*)

453 **Lions more confident** A conventional analogy: Dent L307.1 'As bold(ly) as (any, a) lion'. Whiting has four instances beginning *c*.1325, and Dent adds two Shakespearian uses.

453–4 **mountains . . . free from motion** Further conventional language: see Dent M1214.1, 'A mountain might be sooner (re)moved', and Tilley R151, 'As fixed (firm) as a rock'.

456–68 **Here's a stay . . . Dad** This speech may be spoken aside, but since the French party has apparently moved away (l. 476) to discuss Hubert's offer, the Bastard may speak to the audience or to the English party generally.

458 **mouth** Echoing the cannon *mouths* (l. 382) that threaten Angers.

461 **puppy-dogs** This line is *OED*'s earliest citation for the word.

463 **plain cannon** i.e., his language resembles the 'speech' or firing of a cannon

smoke See 2.1.229n.

bounce explosive noise

464 **bastinado** a blow with a stick or cudgel

467–8 **Zounds . . . Dad** The Bastard means either that ll. 451–6 are the worst scolding he has heard since he was a child or, more likely, that 'old Sir Robert' did not like his illegitimate son to address him as 'Dad'.

467 **Zounds** i.e., '(by) God's wounds', a strong oath

bethumped This line is *OED*'s earliest citation for the word.

469–80 **Son . . . it was** Capell marked this speech as an aside to John.

469 **list** listen

conjunction union in marriage (2a), but in view of *sun* (l. 473) perhaps mixed with the astrological sense of two planets in apparent proximity (3)

472 **unsured** uncertain; only citation for *ppl. a.*

That yon green boy shall have no sun to ripe
The bloom that promiseth a mighty fruit.
I see a yielding in the looks of France.
Mark how they whisper. Urge them while their souls
Are capable of this ambition,
Lest zeal now, melted by the windy breath
Of soft petitions, pity, and remorse,
Cool and congeal again to what it was.   480

HUBERT

Why answer not the double majesties
This friendly treaty of our threatened town?

KING PHILIP

Speak England first, that hath been forward first
To speak unto this city. What say you?

KING JOHN

If that the Dauphin there, thy princely son,
Can in this book of beauty read, 'I love',
Her dowry shall weigh equal with a queen.
For Anjou and fair Touraine, Maine, Poitiers,

---

478 Lest] F (Least)   zeal now, melted] This edition; *not punctuated in* F; zeal, now melted, HANMER; zeal, now melted‸ COLLIER   488 Anjou] POPE 1728 (*conj.* Theobald); *Angiers* F

---

473 **sun** (punning, as do ll. 500–1, on *sun* = royal support or favour)
476 **Mark** notice. The sentence serves as a direction to the other actors.
477 **capable of** open to, susceptible to
478–80 **Lest zeal . . . it was** F's lack of punctuation leaves open how much of the phrase following *zeal* may be construed in apposition to it. The choices made here assume that *zeal* refers to Philip's interest in advancing the proposed marriage, that *soft petitions* are the future and hypothetical pleas of Constance, and that (despite the surrounding imagery of hot and cold) *melt* means 'transform, change'. 'Zeal' has several times been used of the French commitment to Arthur although it also 'suggests exaggerated fervour masking self-interest' (Smallwood, 2.1.19n); if *zeal* here were to mean the commitment to Arthur rather than to the marriage, however, the *soft petitions* that Eleanor worries about would have to be understood as Hubert's aggressive 'bastinado with his tongue' (l. 464), a ridiculous anticlimax

that makes the conventional punctuation unacceptable. No doubt zeal is usually a 'hot' emotion in Shakespeare (at 3.4.150, for instance) and therefore unlikely to 'melt', but in a very similar dramatic situation Marlowe wrote 'Let us have hope that their unspotted prayers . . . Will melt his fury into some remorse' (*Tamburlaine, Part 1* 5.1.20, 22), and Shakespeare also uses the verb figuratively, especially with abstractions: with 'manhood' (*Much Ado* 4.1.319–20) and with 'honour' (*Tempest* 4.1.27–8). This abstract meaning suits the transformation of *zeal* into the vague 'what it was'. A paraphrase: (Encourage them) for fear that what is now enthusiasm (= *zeal*) will change (= *melt*), through pleas and a sense of compassion, into the earlier enmity.
479 **remorse** sorrow, compassion
482 **treaty** conference, negotiation
483 **forward** eager
487 **queen** i.e., queen's
488 **Anjou** For the emendation, see 2.1.152n.

And all that we upon this side the sea—
Except this city now by us besieged—   490
Find liable to our crown and dignity,
Shall gild her bridal bed and make her rich
In titles, honours, and promotions,
As she in beauty, education, blood,
Holds hand with any princess of the world.

KING PHILIP
What sayst thou, boy? Look in the lady's face.

LOUIS THE DAUPHIN
I do, my lord, and in her eye I find
A wonder, or a wondrous miracle,
The shadow of my self formed in her eye,
Which being but the shadow of your son,   500
Becomes a sun and makes your son a shadow.
I do protest I never loved my self
Till now infixèd I beheld myself,
Drawn in the flattering table of her eye.
        He whispers with Blanche

499 my self] F; myself THEOBALD   502 my self] F; myself THEOBALD   504.1 *He . . . Blanche*]
F (*Whispers with Blanch.*)

491 **liable to** subject or subservient to (so
    OED, quoting this line)
493 **promotions** elevations in rank or digni-
    ties
495 **Holds hand** is equal to, matches (only
    citation for this meaning at *hold*, *v.*
    III.29b)
497–504 **I do . . . her eye** J. M. Murry,
    Shakespeare (1936), pp. 163–4, thinks
    Shakespeare here laughs at his own Son-
    net 24.
500–1 **son . . . sun . . . son** Louis smoothly
    manipulates the son (= male offspring)/
    sun (= shining star and royal nature or
    favour) pun (see Sonnets 7.13–14 and
    33.14); F prints *sonne* for all three ap-
    pearances of the word here, and the twin
    meanings are closely intertwined. The
    end of l. 501 also activates the common-
    place analogy of *sun* with 'eye'; see
    Sonnets 7 (especially ll. 1–2), 33, and
    49.6.
500 **shadow of your son** i.e., reflection of
    your son's image; reflection of your
    royal, sun-like glory
501 **Becomes a sun** i.e., the reflection

('shadow') turns into the light ('sun')
that casts shadows. Duplicated in Blanche's bright eye, Louis's reflected image
is the offspring ('son') of himself. The line
may also exploit *Becomes* = suits, befits.
makes your son a shadow i.e., my image
in her eye is not the same as my self,
but a reflection (= *shadow*, the common
Shakespearian usage); she is so sun-like
that she outshines your royal brilliance,
making it comparatively *a shadow*. The
idea that Louis's reflection in Blanche's
eye is also his 'son', the product of
his (pro)creative act, here produces the
topsy-turvy idea (for an Elizabethan) of
the son outshining the father (= 'makes
your *sun* a shadow'). As this politically
and socially explosive possibility suggests, this line and its predecessor are far
from being mere, and timeworn, Petrarchan gymnastics.
503 **infixèd** fastened, implanted. For the
    idea, see 4.2.71–2n.
504 **flattering** Some elision ('flatt'ring') is
    needed for the metre.
    table writing tablet

164

BASTARD (*aside*)

'Drawn in the flattering table of her eye'?
  Hanged in the frowning wrinkle of her brow
And quartered in her heart, he doth espy
  Himself love's traitor. This is pity now,
That hanged, and drawn, and quartered, there should
    be
In such a love so vile a lout as he.   510

BLANCHE (*to Louis*)

My uncle's will in this respect is mine.
If he see aught in you that makes him like,
That anything he sees which moves his liking,
I can with ease translate it to my will.
Or if you will, to speak more properly,
I will enforce it eas'ly to my love.
Further I will not flatter you, my lord,
That all I see in you is worthy love
Than this, that nothing do I see in you,
Though churlish thoughts themselves should be
    your judge,   520
That I can find should merit any hate.

KING JOHN

What say these young ones? What say you, my niece?

BLANCHE

That she is bound in honour still to do
What you in wisdom still vouchsafe to say.

---

524 still] F; shall REED

505–10 **'Drawn . . . as he** The Bastard's stanza, the same used in *Venus* (see 1.1.170–5), appropriately reflects the sonnet language he chooses.
505 **drawn** word-play: written or sketched; disemboweled. See 2.1.508n.
507 **quartered** located, domiciled
508 **love's traitor** A traitor in love, not a traitor to love. The image is suggested by the traditional punishment for treason: hanging, drawing, quartering. *OED*'s earliest citation for 'drawn' as a *ppl. a.* in this sense in 1789.
511 **will** determination (but see 1.1.115, 130, and 133)
512 **aught** anything
514 **translate** Etymologically, the word means 'carry over'; since Blanche is

playing upon the difference between John's *liking* and her *will*, she may have a specifically verbal 'translation' in mind; rhetoricians sometimes associated the word with metaphor (hence *OED*'s figurative definition, *v.* II.3, 'to interpret . . . to express (one thing) in terms of another').
will desire (as well as determination)
515 **if you will** if you choose or determine (not = 'in other words')
properly decorously
516 **eas'ly** F's *easlie* is disyllabic.
517–18 **Further . . . love** i.e., I will flatter you no further in saying that everything (= *all*) I detect in you merits my love; *That* (l. 518) is a subordinate conjunction, not a demonstrative adjective
523 **still** always

KING JOHN

Speak then, Prince Dauphin. Can you love this lady?

LOUIS THE DAUPHIN

Nay, ask me if I can refrain from love,
For I do love her most unfeignedly.

KING JOHN

Then do I give Volquessen, Touraine, Maine,
Poitiers, and Anjou, these five provinces
With her to thee and this addition more,   530
Full thirty thousand marks of English coin.
Philip of France, if thou be pleased withal,
Command thy son and daughter to join hands.

KING PHILIP

It likes us well. Young princes, close your hands.

AUSTRIA

And your lips too, for I am well assured
That I did so when I was first assured.

⌈*Louis and Blanche join hands and kiss*⌉

KING PHILIP

Now, citizens of Angers, ope your gates;
Let in that amity which you have made,
For at Saint Mary's Chapel presently
The rites of marriage shall be solemnized.   540
Is not the Lady Constance in this troop?
I know she is not, for this match made up
Her presence would have interrupted much.
Where is she and her son? Tell me, who knows.

LOUIS THE DAUPHIN

She is sad and passionate at your highness' tent.

534 well. . . . princes,] COLLIER (*subs.*); well‸ . . . Princes: F   536.1 *Louis . . . kiss*] OXFORD
(*subs.*); *not in* F   544 son? . . . knows.] STEEVENS; sonne, . . . knowes? F

526–7 **Nay . . . unfeignedly** Phonic echo
(*refrain/unfeignedly*) makes the lines
sound like a couplet.
529 **Poitiers** Probably modern Poitou; see
1.1.11n and 2.1.152n.
531 **Full** no less than
    marks The mark was a coin worth
    two-thirds of a pound sterling. Thirty
    thousand marks is a very large sum;
    according to Holinshed, twenty-eight
    thousand marks was sufficient 'to levy
    and wage thirty thousand men' (168b,
    P4ᵛ).

534 **likes us well** pleases us (the royal plural)
    close join, clasp
535 **well assured** quite certain, very con-
    fident
536 **assured** Betrothed, engaged; Austria
    plays clumsily on the word.
539 **presently** immediately. Historically,
    Blanche married Louis in 1200 and lived
    happily with him.
542 **made up** agreed
545 **passionate** grieved, sorrowful (so 5,
    quoting this line)

KING PHILIP

And, by my faith, this league that we have made
Will give her sadness very little cure.
Brother of England, how may we content
This widow lady? In her right we came,
Which we, God knows, have turned another way,   550
To our own vantage.

KING JOHN   We will heal up all,
For we'll create young Arthur Duke of Bretagne
And Earl of Richmond, and this rich fair town
We make him lord of. Call the Lady Constance.—
Some speedy messenger bid her repair
To our solemnity.   *Exit Salisbury*
          I trust we shall,
If not fill up the measure of her will,
Yet in some measure satisfy her so
That we shall stop her exclamation.
Go we as well as haste will suffer us   560
To this unlooked-for, unprepparèd pomp.
          Exeunt all but Bastard

BASTARD

Mad world, mad kings, mad composition!
John, to stop Arthur's title in the whole,
Hath willingly departed with a part,
And France, whose armour conscience buckled on,
Whom zeal and charity brought to the field
As God's own soldier, rounded in the ear
With that same purpose-changer, that sly devil,
That broker that still breaks the pate of faith,
That daily break-vow, he that wins of all,   570

556 *Exit Salisbury*] not in F   561 unlooked-for] CAPELL; *not hyphenated in* F   561.1 *Exeunt all but Bastard*] ROWE; *Exeunt.* F; *Flourish. Exeunt . . . the Bastard* OXFORD   562 world, . . . kings,] F; ~ ! . . . ~ ! CAPELL   composition!] POPE; ~ : F

557 **measure** *Fill up* suggests that *measure* = vessel (used in quantifying liquids), although a more general sense, 'extent or limit', is not far away.
558 **in some measure** to some degree
560 **suffer** permit, allow
562–99 **Mad world . . . worship thee** Like the play's first scene, this one ends with the Bastard's commentary.
562 **composition** 'Agreement, compact', but

perhaps including 'compromise' and a sense that a payment of money has brought about the result (see 22–5).
564 **departed with** surrendered, given away (so v. III.12b, citing this line)
567 **rounded** whispered
569 **broker** middleman, go-between, but with the contemptuous sense of 'bawd, pimp'

Of kings, of beggars, old men, young men, maids—
Who having no external thing to lose
But the word 'maid'—cheats the poor maid of that—
That smooth-faced gentleman, tickling Commodity.
Commodity, the bias of the world;
The world who of itself is peisèd well,
Made to run even upon even ground
Till this advantage, this vile-drawing bias,
This sway of motion, this Commodity,
Makes it take head from all indifferency,   580
From all direction, purpose, course, intent.
And this same bias, this Commodity,
This bawd, this broker, this all-changing word,
Clapped on the outward eye of fickle France,
Hath drawn him from his own determined aid,
From a resolved and honourable war,
To a most base and vile-concluded peace.
And why rail I on this Commodity?
But for because he hath not wooed me yet.
Not that I have the power to clutch my hand   590
When his fair angels would salute my palm,

571 maids—] MALONE (*subs.*); ~, F   573 that—] This edition; ~. F   578 vile-drawing]
POPE; *not hyphenated in* F   583 all-changing word] F (all-changing-word); all-changing
w(h)ore KELLNER *conj.*   585 aid] F (ayd); aim SINGER 1856 (*conj.* Mason); end THIRLBY *conj.*

573 **'maid'** The Bastard may refer specifically to Blanche.
574 **smooth-faced** closely-shaven, hence
'plausible, ingratiating'. The adjective is
used of 'wooers' in *LLL* 5.2.815 and of
'peace' in *Richard III* 5.8.33.
 Commodity 'advantage, self-interest,
gain' (Wright)
575 **bias** swaying influence. The figure
comes from the weight (= *bias*) added
asymmetrically to the ball used in the
game of bowls so that it rolls on an
oblique path.
576 **peisèd** balanced, in equilibrium
577 **even ... even** in a straight line, undevi-
atingly . . . level
578 **advantage** Figuratively, favourable circumstance, or the prospect of some
benefit (I.5 and II.6–7), but perhaps
literally, a change, especially a rise, in
the surface upon which the bowl runs
(see I.3); see 2.1.297n.
 vile-drawing attracting toward the dis-

creditable. The *bias* causes the bowl (or
earth, or individual) to deviate from a
straight (and morally proper) line of
motion.
579 **motion** movement
580 **take head** 'rush away' (Honigmann)
 indifferency impartiality, equitable judgement or behaviour
584 **Clapped on the outward eye** 'Suddenly
presented to the eye' (Moore Smith; see
clap, v.[1] IV.10); *eye* = the hole in the
bowl in which the lead weight was inserted; *outward eye* = physical eye (as
opposed to the 'inward eye' of conscience).
588 **rail . . . on** abuse
590 **clutch** close (thereby refusing)
591 **angels** gold coins worth slightly more
than half a pound sterling. See Appendix
C and Fig. 7.
 salute greet. Sandra K. Fischer finds a
pun on *salut(e) d'or*, a French gold coin
well known in England (see *Econolingua*:

But for my hand, as unattempted yet,
Like a poor beggar raileth on the rich.
Well, whiles I am a beggar, I will rail
And say there is no sin but to be rich;
And being rich, my virtue then shall be
To say there is no vice but beggary.
Since kings break faith upon commodity,
Gain, be my lord, for I will worship thee!   *Exit*

3.1   *Enter Constance, Arthur, and the Earl of Salisbury*
CONSTANCE (*to Salisbury*)
Gone to be married? Gone to swear a peace?
False blood to false blood joined? Gone to be friends?
Shall Louis have Blanche, and Blanche those provinces?
It is not so; thou hast misspoke, misheard.
Be well advised, tell o'er thy tale again.
It cannot be; thou dost but say 'tis so.
I trust I may not trust thee, for thy word
Is but the vain breath of a common man.
Believe me, I do not believe thee, man;
I have a king's oath to the contrary.   10
Thou shalt be punished for thus frighting me,
For I am sick and capable of fears,
Oppressed with wrongs and therefore full of fears,
A widow, husbandless, subject to fears,
A woman naturally born to fears.
And though thou now confess thou didst but jest,
With my vexed spirits I cannot take a truce,

---

599 thee!] THEOBALD; ~. F

3.1] THEOBALD's *act-division*; *Actus Secundus* F   0.1 *the Earl of*] *not in* F   2 joined?] This edition; ioyn'd. F; ~ ! ROWE. *See note.*   16–17 jest, | . . . spirits‸] ROWE; iest‸ | . . . spirits, F

A Glossary of Coins and Economic Language in Renaissance Drama (Newark, Del., 1985), p. 22).

594 **whiles** See 2.1.87n.

596 **my virtue** i.e., my ostensibly virtuous behaviour. The slightly strained use is evoked by *sin* and *vice* (ll. 595, 597).

3.1 Location: the French royal camp near Angers.

1–2 **Gone . . . friends?** Rowe converted all of F's '?' here to '!', and most editors have followed him.

8 **common man** *common* by comparison

with a king; not 'commoner'

11 **frighting** Not archaic as a *vbl. sb.* according to *OED*, but cited only 1631–74.

12 **capable** See 2.1.477n.

14 **subject** accent on second syllable

17 **take a truce** conclude a peaceful agreement (*take, v.* VIII.54). See 'Betwixt mine eye and heart a league is took' (Sonnet 47.1). Constance implies a failed analogy between the political *truce* the Kings have agreed and her own emotional strife that cannot be compounded.

But they will quake and tremble all this day.
What dost thou mean by shaking of thy head?
Why dost thou look so sadly on my son?   20
What means that hand upon that breast of thine?
Why holds thine eye that lamentable rheum,
Like a proud river peering o'er his bounds?
Be these sad signs confirmers of thy words?
Then speak again: not all thy former tale,
But this one word, whether thy tale be true.

SALISBURY

As true as I believe you think them false
That give you cause to prove my saying true.

CONSTANCE

O, if thou teach me to believe this sorrow,
Teach thou this sorrow how to make me die,   30
And let belief and life encounter so
As doth the fury of two desperate men,
Which in the very meeting fall and die.
Louis marry Blanche? O boy, then where art thou?
France friend with England, what becomes of me?
Fellow, be gone! I cannot brook thy sight;
This news hath made thee a most ugly man.

SALISBURY

What other harm have I, good lady, done,
But spoke the harm that is by others done?

CONSTANCE

Which harm within itself so heinous is   40
As it makes harmful all that speak of it.

ARTHUR

I do beseech you, madam, be content.

CONSTANCE

If thou that bidd'st me be content wert grim,

19–24 **What dost . . . thy words?** Slater
(pp. 23–4) criticizes these 'baldly imperative questions' as 'clumsy' implicit stage
directions, and Bevington (p. 209
n. 33) compares 4.2.106–8.

20 **sadly** solemnly

22 **lamentable** lamenting (see Abbott §3)

23 **proud river . . . o'er his bounds** Imagery
of rivers and their banks appears often
in Act 2 (e.g., 335 ff., 442 ff.) to represent
the conflict of reason and emotion,

authority and wilful private conduct.

24 **confirmers** This line is *OED*'s earliest
citation for the *sb*.

28 **prove** Find out by experience (*v*. B.I.1
and 3) rather than 'make good, establish'
(B.II); Salisbury sadly acknowledges Constance's suffering discovery of the truth
rather than claiming that her suffering
demonstrates that truth.

31 **encounter** meet as adversaries

43–9 **If thou . . . not love thee** Constance's

Ugly and sland'rous to thy mother's womb,
Full of unpleasing blots and sightless stains,
Lame, foolish, crookèd, swart, prodigious,
Patched with foul moles and eye-offending marks,
I would not care; I then would be content,
For then I should not love thee. No, nor thou
Become thy great birth, nor deserve a crown.   50
But thou art fair, and at thy birth, dear boy,
Nature and Fortune joined to make thee great.
Of Nature's gifts thou mayst with lilies boast
And with the half-blown rose. But Fortune, O,
She is corrupted, changed, and won from thee;
Sh'adulterates hourly with thine uncle John,
And with her golden hand hath plucked on France
To tread down fair respect of sovereignty
And made his majesty the bawd to theirs.

rhetorical scheme (definition by denied negatives) and her language are similar to Venus' plea to Adonis at *Venus* 133–8.

44 **sland'rous** F's *slandrous* indicates an appropriate pronunciation.

45 **sightless** unsightly (so *a.* 3, quoting this line as the first of two examples). The word could also mean 'invisible, unseen' (see Abbott §3). In *Richard III* 3.7.217 ff., Richard of Gloucester hypocritically justifies the 'impure blots and stains' to come in his reign.

46 **swart** dark complexion, with the typically Shakespearian figurative implication of 'malign, evil'. See *fair* (l. 51).
   prodigious 'Monstrous', but perhaps also with the (here ironic) sense of 'ominous': Arthur's actual youth and appearance portend well, not ill as his condition now is; the same meaning appears in Lady Anne's curse on the murderer of Henry VI: 'If ever he have child, abortive be it, | Prodigious, . . . | Whose ugly and unnatural aspect | May fright the hopeful mother' (*Richard III* 1.2.21–4).

47 **foul moles** Moles were regarded as blemishes and exterior expressions of inward faults; see Lyly, *Endymion* 2.1.63–5, where dissembling in women is like 'spots upon doves, moles upon faces, caterpillars upon sweet apples, cobwebs upon fair windows'; *Tempest* 1.2.283, of Caliban: 'A freckl'd whelp, hag-born';

Robert Greene, *Pandosto*: 'One mole staineth the whole face' (*Complete Works*, ed. A. B. Grosart, 15 vols. (1881–6), iv. 250).

52 **Nature and Fortune joined** The two were conventionally enemies and the subject of classical debate (in Seneca, Plutarch, Boethius) and, later, schoolroom rhetorical exercises; see *As You Like It* 1.2.40–41 where Rosalind claims that 'Fortune reigns in gifts of the world, not in the lineaments of nature'.

54 **half-blown** half-blossomed

56 **Sh'adulterates** she commits adultery (because Fortune should lawfully be joined with Arthur, as his 'wife'). F's elision is needed, along with some such pronunciation as 'adult'rates'.
   hourly often. Perhaps with a pun on 'whore-ly' (the evidence for the pun is disputed: see Cercignani, pp. 191 ff., especially p. 194).

57 **her golden hand** Not a conventional attribute of the goddess; the phrase may be 'reverse' hendiadys (= gold and hand, where Constance implies that John has purchased his peace with Philip). Peele's mayoral pageant *Descensus Astraeae* (performed 29 October 1591 and probably in print at that time) mentions 'Fortune . . . With golden hands' (ll. 35–6).

59 **his majesty the bawd to theirs** Constance means that Philip and his *majesty* have pimped for John in arranging the mar-

France is a bawd to Fortune and King John,   60
That strumpet Fortune, that usurping John.
Tell me, thou fellow, is not France forsworn?
Envenom him with words, or get thee gone
And leave those woes alone which I alone
Am bound to underbear.

SALISBURY   Pardon me, madam,
I may not go without you to the Kings.

CONSTANCE

Thou mayst; thou shalt. I will not go with thee.
I will instruct my sorrows to be proud,
For grief is proud and makes his owner stoop.
To me and to the state of my great grief   70
Let kings assemble, for my grief's so great
That no supporter but the huge firm earth
Can hold it up. Here I and sorrows sit.

     She sits

Here is my throne; bid kings come bow to it.

                   Exit Salisbury with Arthur

     Constance remains seated.

73 sit.] This edition; ~ , F   73.1 *She sits*] *not in* F; *after l.* 69 SMALLWOOD   74.1–2 *Exit Salisbury . . . seated*] *not in* F

riage of Blanche and Louis; in effect, she repeats the Bastard's views (2.1.569 ff.) and language (see *broker* at 2.1.569, 583 and *bawd* at 2.1.583).

60–1 **France . . . John** i.e., King Philip is the hired go-between conveying Fortune's whorish bounty (the kingship) to her favourite, John. For *strumpet Fortune*, see Dent F603.1, 'Fortune is a strumpet (whore, huswife)', citing seven other Shakespearian uses.

62 **thou fellow** a contemptuous use of the pronoun (1b)

65 **underbear** sustain, endure

70 **state** Condition, but also in the limited sense of 'throne' or 'chamber of state' as in the play-scene between Falstaff and Hal: 'This chair shall be my state' (*1 Henry IV* 2.5.381). Constance's speech is threaded with ideas and images of collapse, support, bearing, and burden; see Edgar's too-quick consolation: 'How light and portable my pain seems now, |

When that which makes me bend, makes the King bow' (*History of Lear*, 13.101–2, Q only).

72 **supporter** Perhaps word-play on one of the figures (= *supporters*) holding up a heraldic shield or coat of arms (e.g., the lion and unicorn in the English royal arms).

73 **Here I and sorrows sit** Sitting or lying on the stage seems conventionally to have denoted grief; Slater (p. 46) instances Queen Margaret's lines, 'I must take like seat unto my fortune | And to my humble state [F: seat] conform myself' (*3 Henry VI* 3.3.10–11). For other examples, see the Portuguese Viceroy in Kyd's *The Spanish Tragedy* 1.3.5 ff., the Duchess of York's command to herself: 'Rest thy unrest on England's lawful earth' (*Richard III* 4.4.29), and *Richard II* 3.2.151 ff.

74.1–2 *Exit Salisbury . . . seated* On F's silence here and the puzzling entry

⌈*Flourish.*⌉ *Enter King John, King Philip, Louis the*
Dauphin, Blanche, Queen Eleanor, ⌈*Bastard*⌉, *Austria*

KING PHILIP (*to Blanche*)

'Tis true, fair daughter, and this blessèd day
Ever in France shall be kept festival.
To solemnize this day the glorious sun
Stays in his course and plays the alchemist,
Turning with splendour of his precious eye
The meagre cloddy earth to glittering gold.   80
The yearly course that brings this day about
Shall never see it but a holiday.

CONSTANCE (*rising*)

A wicked day and not a holy day!
What hath this day deserved? What hath it done,
That it in golden letters should be set

74.3] THEOBALD *continues scene*; *Actus Tertius, Scaena prima* F   Flourish.] OXFORD; *not in* F
74.3–4 *Enter King John . . . Austria*] MALONE (*subs.*); *Enter King Iohn, France, Dolphin, Blanch,*
Elianor, Philip, Austria, Constance. F   82 holiday] F (holy day)   83 *rising*] THEOBALD (*after*
'holy day'); *not in* F   day!] MALONE; ~. F

direction that follows, see Introduction,
pp. 32–5.

74.3–4 *Louis the Dauphin, Blanche* Philip's
speech (ll. 75 ff.) indicates that the marriage planned for 'St. Mary's Chapel' has
now been 'solemnized' (2.1.539–40),
and the actors' costume and manner
should indicate their new relation.

75 **daughter** i.e., daughter-in-law

77–8 **sun | Stays in his course** Pursuing the
Amorites, Joshua asked that the sun and
moon stand still, 'And the sun abode,
and the moon stood still, until the people
had avenged themselves upon their
enemies' (Joshua 10: 12–13); Philip's
allusion anticipates the warfare to come.

78 **plays the alchemist** The image depends
upon the pseudo-scientific belief that the
sun's warmth transmutes baser metals
into gold, as human alchemists sought
to do by other means; Moore Smith
compared Sonnet 33.

80 **cloddy** characterized by, or abounding
in, clods (*OED*). Shakespeare's only use
of the word.
glittering Some elision ('glitt'ring') is
needed for the metre.

82 **holiday** Festive occasion; the word was
not yet orthographically distinguished
from *holy day*, a specifically religious

festival (as at l. 86, where Constance's
'high tides in the calendar' makes the
meaning clear).

83–95 **A wicked day . . . falsehood change**
Superstitions about, and lists of, lucky
and unlucky days for such events as
birth, travel, changing employment, and
making bargains were widespread in
the Elizabethan period; see Thomas,
pp. 615–23.

85–6 **golden letters . . . calendar** Elizabethan
broadsides used rubrics to get attention
(see Jonson, *The Alchemist* 1.1.98, for
example); almanacs (see *calendar, sb.* 2
and *Richard III* 5.6.6–9) usually printed
dominical letters (used chiefly for finding
the date of Easter) in red, and calendars
used red for feast days (see Chapman,
Monsieur D'Olive 4.2.104–5: 'Saint Dennis shall be rased out of the calendar,
and the day of our instalment entered in
red letters'). Calendars and prayer books
also mention the 'golden number', like-
wise used in computing the date of mov-
able feasts. Red and gold, letters and
numbers, seem to have been inter-
changeable for Shakespeare: see 'My red
dominical, my golden letter' (*LLL* 5.2.44)
and 'His silver skin laced with his golden
blood' (*Macbeth* 2.3.112). 'When beauty

Among the high tides in the calendar?
Nay, rather turn this day out of the week,
This day of shame, oppression, perjury.
Or, if it must stand still, let wives with child
Pray that their burdens may not fall this day,   90
Lest that their hopes prodigiously be crossed.
But on this day let seamen fear no wreck;
No bargains break that are not this day made;
This day all things begun come to ill end;
Yea, faith itself to hollow falsehood change.

KING PHILIP

By heaven, lady, you shall have no cause
To curse the fair proceedings of this day.
Have I not pawned to you my majesty?

CONSTANCE

You have beguiled me with a counterfeit
Resembling majesty, which being touched and tried,   100
Proves valueless. You are forsworn, forsworn!

92 wreck] F (wracke)   101 forsworn!] STEEVENS; forsworne, F

boasted blushes, in despite | Virtue would stain that or [Q: ore] with silver white' (*Lucrece* 55–6) is probably another example (*ore* = heraldic 'or' = gold = the red of a blush).

86 **high tides** great festivals (as in Christmastide, Shrovetide, Eastertide)

87 **turn . . . week** Job, among others, 'cursed his day' and asked that 'the day perish wherein' he 'was born' and that 'it not be joined unto the days of the year, nor counted in the number of the months' (Job 3: 1–3, 6; Noble, p. 115).

89–90 **Or . . . this day** Commentators have suggested a reminiscence of Jesus' account of the last days (e.g., Matthew 24: 19: 'Woe shall be in those days to them that are with child, and to them that give suck'), and Shakespeare's memory might have been prompted by matters astronomical: 'Immediately, after the tribulation of those days, shall the sun be darkened, and the moon shall not give her light, and the stars shall fall from heaven and the powers of the heavens shall be shaken' (Matthew 24: 29; see 3.1.77–8n).

91 **prodigiously . . . crossed** Transferred usage; a mother's hope for a healthy child will be disappointed (= *crossed*) by

the birth of a monster, an ill-formed child, a 'prodigy'; see 3.1.46n. This line is *OED*'s earliest citation for *prodigiously* = portentously, ominously.

92 **But** except
   wreck shipwreck. F's *wrack* has been superseded.

93 **No . . . not . . . made** a double negative: break only those bargains made on this day

98 **pawned** pledged (as a guarantee of his vowed assistance)
   majesty sovereign dignity

99 **counterfeit** 'i.e., a false coin. A *counterfeit* formerly signified also a *portrait*.—A representation of the king being usually impressed on the coin, the word seems to be here used equivocally' (Malone).

100 **touched and tried** *Touched* derives from the use of a touchstone to measure the fineness (or worthlessness) of gold or silver objects (v. 1.8, quoting this line); *tried* principally means 'tested' (*try*, v. 7), but with the further implication, perhaps, of 'experienced' (v. 14). Constance has experienced the falsity of Philip's newly-tested honour.

101 **valueless** This line is *OED*'s earliest citation for the word.

174

You came in arms to spill mine enemy's blood,
But now in arms you strengthen it with yours.
The grappling vigour and rough frown of war
Is cold in amity and painted peace,
And our oppression hath made up this league.
Arm, arm, you heavens, against these perjured Kings!
A widow cries, be husband to me, heavens.
Let not the hours of this ungodly day
Wear out the days in peace, but ere sun set,   110
Set armèd discord 'twixt these perjured Kings.
Hear me, O, hear me!

AUSTRIA   Lady Constance, peace.

CONSTANCE

War! War! No peace! Peace is to me a war.
O Limoges, O Austria, thou dost shame
That bloody spoil. Thou slave, thou wretch, thou
        coward,

107 Kings!] CAPELL; Kings, F   108 heavens.] This edition; (heauens)ᴧ F; heav'ns, ROWE;
heavens! CAPELL; God! OXFORD; Lord! OXFORD *conj.*   110 days] F; day THEOBALD (*conj.*
Thirlby)   sun set] F (Sun-set)   112 me!] THEOBALD; ~. F   113 War! War! No peace!]
STEEVENS; War, war, no peace, F

102 **enemy's** F's *enemies* could be either
    singular or plural possessive, but 'enemy'
    may be regarded as a collective noun; the
    difference would not be heard in the theatre.
103 **arms** Constance puns on 'weapons, in-
    struments of war', on 'embraces' (as
    Johnson noted), and on 'coat of arms,
    heraldic bearing'; the armorial bearings
    of Blanche and Louis will now mingle
    (technically, 'quarter') the heraldic
    symbols of France and of England.
    yours your arms, your 'blood', your line
105 **painted peace** 'painted is peculiarly
    happy, as including the idea of gaudiness
    and hypocrisy jointly' (Capell, *Notes*)
106 **our** i.e., Constance and Arthur's; a
    small hint that Arthur may still be on
    stage here (see 3.1.74.1 and Introduc-
    tion, p. 33).
    made up composed, helped to produce,
    brought to completion
108 **A widow cries . . . heavens** Constance
    has reason to hope: 'yea, thou shalt for-
    get the shame of thy youth, and shalt not
    remember the dishonour of thy widow-
    hood. For he that made thee, shall be
    thy Lord and husband' (Isaiah 54: 4–5);
    see Judges 9: 3 (Carter, p. 208; Noble,
    p. 115).

110 **Wear out the days** Theobald's emen-
    dation has been very popular, mainly
    because it rationalizes the line by restrict-
    ing Constance's demand to this single
    day. F's *daies*, however, is an unlikely
    compositorial error so soon after *day*
    unless the phrase 'wear out the days'
    had some independent status for the
    compositor, as it might if he remembered
    Job 36: 11, 'If they now will take heed
    and serve him, they shall wear out their
    days in prosperity, and their years in
    pleasure', where the Bishops' Bible gener-
    ally follows Coverdale's translation. Of
    course, Shakespeare himself might have
    remembered the biblical phrase, in which
    case F's reading would be an accurate
    one.
114 **O Limoges, O Austria** Shakespeare has
    conflated two historical individuals:
    Duke Leopold of Austria (see 2.1.0.3n)
    and Viscount Vidomar of Limoges
    (whose castle Richard Coeur-de-Lion was
    attacking when he received his fatal
    wound); the same conflation appears
    in *TR*.
115 **bloody spoil** 'martial prize', specifically
    an enemy's arms and/or armour (*spoil*,
    sb. II.5); here, the lion's-skin

Thou little valiant, great in villainy,
Thou ever strong upon the stronger side;
Thou Fortune's champion that dost never fight
But when her humorous ladyship is by
To teach thee safety. Thou art perjured too,   120
And sooth'st up greatness. What a fool art thou,
A ramping fool, to brag and stamp and swear
Upon my party. Thou cold-blooded slave,
Hast thou not spoke like thunder on my side,
Been sworn my soldier, bidding me depend
Upon thy stars, thy fortune, and thy strength,
And dost thou now fall over to my foes?
Thou wear a lion's hide! Doff it for shame,
And hang a calf's-skin on those recreant limbs.

AUSTRIA

O that a man should speak those words to me!   130

BASTARD

And hang a calf's-skin on those recreant limbs.

AUSTRIA

Thou dar'st not say so, villain, for thy life!

BASTARD

And hang a calf's-skin on those recreant limbs.

KING JOHN

We like not this; thou dost forget thyself.

123 cold-blooded] ROWE; *not hyphenated in* F   128 hide!] CAPELL; ∼, F   129 calf's-skin]
F (Calues skin *and thus throughout, lacking hyphen only here and at 3.1.220)*   130 me!]
THEOBALD; ∼. F   131 BASTARD] F (*Phil⟨ip⟩.; and thus until 3.1.199)*   132 life!] THEOBALD;
∼. F

118 **champion** i.e., one who acts or fights
on behalf of another person or cause
121 **sooth'st up greatness** i.e., humour
powerful persons through agreement or
assent (*v.* 5b; first citation 1616). Since
the earliest meanings for this verb concern declaring something true (and later,
declaring true something that is false),
perjured may have suggested this word,
and Constance implies that Philip has
flattered John by agreeing to a falsehood.
The verb is pronounced as a single syllable.
122 **ramping** storming or raging with violent gestures (*v.*¹ 4); Constance implies
that Austria's protests are bluster, brag-
gadocio.

stamp and swear Alliterating and rhym-
ing phrases variously employing *ramp*,
brag, *stamp*, *swear*, and *stare* are common
and ancient; for examples, see *stare, v.*
3a; *staring, vbl. sb.*; Dent SS19, 'To stamp
and stare' (comparing Dent F672.1, 'To
fret and fume'); Dent SS21, 'Swearing
and staring'.
122–3 **swear | Upon my party** i.e., take an
oath appealing to my interests (see *v.* 16,
13a). Constance claims that Austria has
no right to invoke her name and demands
as guarantors of his oath; she does not
mean that he swears at her party.
127 **fall over** go over (only citation for this
meaning at *v.* XI.95c)
128–33 **a lion's hide … limbs** See 2.1.144n.

Enter Pandulph

KING PHILIP

Here comes the holy legate of the Pope.

CARDINAL PANDULPH

Hail, you anointed deputies of God!
To thee, King John, my holy errand is.
I, Pandulph, of fair Milan Cardinal
And from Pope Innocent the legate here,
Do in his name religiously demand   140
Why thou against the church, our holy mother,
So wilfully dost spurn and force perforce
Keep Stephen Langton, chosen Archbishop
Of Canterbury, from that holy see?
This, in our foresaid Holy Father's name,
Pope Innocent, I do demand of thee.

KING JOHN

What earthy name to interrogatories
Can test the free breath of a sacred king?

134.1 Pandulph] F (*throughout except 'Pandulpho' at 3.4.0.1, 5.2.64.1*)   136 God!] This edition; heauen; F; heaven! CAPELL. *See note.*   142 spurn₍] This edition; spurne; F   148 test] F (tast). *See note.*

134.1 **Pandulph** Shakespeare has apparently fused two historical individuals: Pandulphus, a native of Lucca, who was made Cardinal in 1182 and the Pandulph (d. 1226), never Cardinal but eventually Bishop of Norwich, who was appointed nuncio to John in 1211 and legate in 1218. Other versions of John's history make Pandulph a cardinal (*TR*, and see Honigmann, p. xxv), and a cardinal's costume would have great theatrical appeal. In Act 3, the historically appropriate cardinal-legate is Peter of Capua (mentioned by Holinshed), and in Act 5, Shakespeare gives to 'Pandulph' the historical role played by another legate, Cardinal Guala Bicchieri.

136 **God** Although Matchett (p. 150) tentatively opposes this emendation, it is justified on the following grounds: Shakespeare's other references to a king as 'deputy' and 'anointed' also mention 'God' (*Richard II* 1.2.37–8 and 4.1.116–18) or 'the Lord' (*Richard II* 3.2.50–3); the palpable expurgation of 'God' at l. 155 (for which this line prepares us); the strengthening of the verbal and political conflict between God's deputy, John, and

Christ's vicar, the Pope (see, e.g., 'earthy' and 'sacred' at ll. 147, 148).

139 **Pope Innocent** Innocent III (Pope, 1198–1216)

142 **spurn** reject contemptuously
force perforce by violent coercion (see *force, sb.*¹ 5b, citing the phrase but giving no examples. Dent PP6 lists three other Shakespearian examples and Kyd, *The Spanish Tragedy*, from *c.*1587).

143 **Stephen Langton** An Englishman, Langton was consecrated Archbishop of Canterbury in 1207; when John refused to accept the election, Langton took refuge—like Becket before him—at Pontigny in France; he returned to England in 1213 and died in 1228.

147 **earthy** existing on the earth (as opposed to heaven). Editors have emended to 'earthly'.
name to interrogatories *Interrogatories* has the legal sense of 'questions put to an accused person' in the *name* of some legal authority; John denies that the Pope's name has sufficient authority to validate Pandulph's questioning.

148 **test** F's *tast* is cited as a form of 'test' at *sb.*¹; all emendations have sought to

Thou canst not, Cardinal, devise a name
So slight, unworthy, and ridiculous   150
To charge me to an answer, as the Pope.
Tell him this tale, and from the mouth of England
Add thus much more: that no Italian priest
Shall tithe or toll in our dominions.
But as we, under God, are supreme head,
So, under Him, that great supremacy
Where we do reign, we will alone uphold
Without th'assistance of a mortal hand.
So tell the Pope, all reverence set apart
To him and his usurped authority.   160
KING PHILIP
Brother of England, you blaspheme in this.
KING JOHN
Though you and all the kings of Christendom
Are led so grossly by this meddling priest,
Dreading the curse that money may buy out,
And by the merit of vile gold, dross, dust,
Purchase corrupted pardon of a man
Who in that sale sells pardon from himself;
Though you and all the rest so grossly led
This juggling witchcraft with revenue cherish,
Yet I alone, alone do me oppose   170
Against the Pope and count his friends my foes.

---

155 God] HONIGMANN (*conj.* Collier, *Notes*); heauen F   156 So, under Him,] THEOBALD; So
vnder him F

produce the meaning 'put to the proof,
try' (*taste*, *v.* I.2). Printing 'taste' would,
through recourse to an archaic definition, conclude with the meaning 'test',
but the connotations of modern 'taste'
would be recalled unnecessarily and dis-
tractingly.
154 **tithe** Collect a 'tithe' or tenth of an
individual's goods or possessions for the
church's support; this intransitive use
for the collecting, as opposed to the
paying (see *v.*² 2), of a tithe is not
represented in the *OED* until 1822 (*v.*²
3c). See next n.
toll to exact or levy money. 'Tolled' and
'tithed' appear in *TR* I.1505.
155 **supreme head** Parliament gave Henry

VIII the title 'Supreme Head of the Church
of England' in 1534 and Elizabeth the
title 'Supreme Governor' in 1559.
156 **supremacy** position of highest authority
157 **Where** in which (see II.5, 11a and b)
159 **set apart** dismissed from consideration;
set aside
164 **buy out** ransom, redeem
167 **from himself** 'i.e., not from God' (Wilson)
169 **juggling** cheating, deceptive
revenue accent on second syllable
cherish foster
170–1 **Yet I alone . . . my foes** The couplet
and a rhetorical figure, anadiplosis (*alone*,
alone), in the first line give an aphoristic
and conclusive force to John's words.

CARDINAL PANDULPH

Then, by the lawful power that I have,
Thou shalt stand cursed and excommunicate,
And blessèd shall he be that doth revolt
From his allegiance to an heretic,
And meritorious shall that hand be called,
Canonizèd and worshipped as a saint,
That takes away by any secret course
Thy hateful life.

CONSTANCE   O, lawful let it be
That I have room with Rome to curse awhile.   180
Good father Cardinal, cry thou 'Amen'
To my keen curses, for without my wrong
There is no tongue hath power to curse him right.

CARDINAL PANDULPH

There's law and warrant, lady, for my curse.

CONSTANCE

And for mine too; when law can do no right,
Let it be lawful that law bar no wrong.

185 too; . . . right,] ROWE 1714; ~, . . . ~. F

173–9 **cursed and excommunicate . . . hateful life** In Marlowe's *Edward II*, the nobles simply assert that if Edward is excommunicated, 'then may we | Depose him and elect another king' (1.4.54–5). Pius V's bull, 'Regnans in Excelsis' (February 1570), had excommunicated and deposed Queen Elizabeth, absolved Roman Catholics of all oaths to her, and encouraged armed rebellion. Gregory XIII (Pope, 1572–85) explicitly endorsed Elizabeth's assassination. Elizabeth and Parliament responded with two proclamations (Hughes and Larkin, 577 and 580, both 1570) and a statute (1571) against possessing, circulating, or reading such 'Bulls and other Instruments from the See of Rome'. Cardinal William Allen's *A True, Sincere and Modest Defence of English Catholics* (Ingolstadt, 1584), Chap. 5, gives the Roman Catholic view of the excommunication, along with an historical survey that mentions John (p. 111).

173 **excommunicate** excommunicated (Abbott §342)

174–5 **blessèd . . . heretic** See Tilley F33, 'No faith with heretics' (Wilson, *ODEP*,

antedates Tilley's instances to 1555). Jean Bodin, *Les six livres . . . république* (1576), trans. Richard Knolles, *The Six Books of a Commonweal* (1606), Book 1, Chap. 9, pp. 139–40, explains the doctrine, citing King John among other examples; Protestant controversialists regarded the doctrine as typical of Roman Catholic treachery (see the citations at N. W. Bawcutt, ed., *The Jew of Malta*, The Revels Plays (1978), 2.3.313n).

177 **Canonizèd** accent on the second syllable, as at 3.4.52

180 **room with Rome** The two nouns were homophones in Elizabethan pronunciation.

181–2 **cry thou 'Amen' | To . . . curses** In the Commination service of Ash Wednesday, the congregation is directed to say 'Amen' after each of ten curses (see Noble, pp. 83 and 116).

185–9 **when law . . . perfect wrong** Constance's views were paradoxical in the Renaissance; very similar issues (impotent or debased law, the individual a law unto himself) are elaborately explored in Chapman's *Bussy D'Ambois*, especially 2.1.165–204.

Law cannot give my child his kingdom here,
For he that holds his kingdom, holds the law.
Therefore since law itself is perfect wrong,
How can the law forbid my tongue to curse?   190
        ⌜*Philip takes John's hand*⌝
CARDINAL PANDULPH
    Philip of France, on peril of a curse,
    Let go the hand of that arch-heretic
    And raise the power of France upon his head,
    Unless he do submit himself to Rome.
QUEEN ELEANOR
    Look'st thou pale, France? Do not let go thy hand.
CONSTANCE
    Look to that, devil, lest that France repent
    And by disjoining hands, hell lose a soul.
AUSTRIA
    King Philip, listen to the Cardinal.
BASTARD
    And hang a calf's-skin on his recreant limbs.
AUSTRIA
    Well, ruffian, I must pocket up these wrongs   200
    Because—
BASTARD   Your breeches best may carry them.
KING JOHN
    Philip, what sayst thou to the Cardinal?
CONSTANCE
    What should he say, but as the Cardinal?
LOUIS THE DAUPHIN
    Bethink you, father, for the difference

190.1 Philip . . . hand] FURNIVALL (*subs.*); *not in* F   196 that,] POPE; ~ ∧ F; it, SMALLWOOD (*conj.* Maxwell)   199 BASTARD] F (*Bast⟨ard⟩. and thus until* 4.3.116)

188 **his** i.e., Arthur's
190.1 ***Philip takes John's hand*** Although the text (at ll. 192, 226, 240, and 261–2) virtually stipulates this gesture, Furnivall and Jowett alone among the play's editors specify the action; Philip might take John's hand even earlier (as he speaks l. 161) in an attempt to restrain his new ally; see next n. and Fig. 5.
192 **Let go the hand** This handclasp recalls that of Blanche and Louis (2.1.534 ff.); here, it images royal unity and later,

broken, the enmity of England and France. Slater (pp. 60–1) sees an 'ironic reversal' of this gesture in Blanche's words at 3.1.327–30.
195 **Look'st . . . hand** A hypermetric line probably requiring some slurring or elision in speech; the line is very full in F.
200 **pocket up these wrongs** A common expression: Tilley I70.
203 **as the Cardinal** i.e., as the Cardinal says

Is purchase of a heavy curse from Rome,
Or the light loss of England for a friend.
Forgo the easier.

BLANCHE   That's the curse of Rome.

CONSTANCE

O Louis, stand fast; the devil tempts thee here
In likeness of a new untrimmèd bride.

BLANCHE

The Lady Constance speaks not from her faith,   210
But from her need.

CONSTANCE   O, if thou grant my need,
Which only lives but by the death of faith,
That need must needs infer this principle:
That faith would live again by death of need.
O then tread down my need, and faith mounts up;
Keep my need up, and faith is trodden down.

KING JOHN

The King is moved and answers not to this.

CONSTANCE (*to Philip*)

O, be removed from him and answer well.

AUSTRIA

Do so, King Philip; hang no more in doubt.

BASTARD

Hang nothing but a calf's-skin, most sweet lout.   220

KING PHILIP

I am perplexed and know not what to say.

---

209 **untrimmèd** Unadorned, often applied to loose hair without ornaments; see 'What means this gorgeous glittering head attire | How ill beseem these billaments [habiliments] of gold | Thy mournful widowhood? away with them, | So let thy tresses flaring in the wind | Untrimmed hang about thy bared neck' (*Tancred and Gismund*, MSR, ll. 1664–8) and 3.4.61n. An extended sense of *untrimmèd* might be 'naked', making possible an allusion to the temptation of St. Anthony by the devil in the shape of a naked woman, but citations of this line in support of 'Undevirginated' (Partridge, p. 213) and of *Titus* 5.1.93–5 for *trim* = 'allusive to sexual intercourse' (ibid., p. 207) are unconvincing.

211–16 **if thou grant . . . trodden down** Constance's characteristic logic-chopping turns on the idea that satisfying her *need*, her request for assistance, depends upon Philip and Austria keeping their pledged faith: if that faith is *dead*, her *need* continues unsatisfied (= *lives*); that faith 'would live again' if her need died by being satisfied. The submerged image in ll. 215–16 is of scales, or of buckets in a well, or of a treadwheel.

213 **infer** imply, lead to as a conclusion

217 **moved** perturbed, angered. Note Constance's word-play (*removed*) in the next l.

220 **lout** Rhyme stiffens the Bastard's insult.

221 **I am . . . what to say** The line has the rhythm and phrasing of Hermia's 'I am amazed, and know not what to say' (*Dream* 3.2.345); Philip is now puzzled much as the citizens of Angers were in 2.1.

CARDINAL PANDULPH
> What canst thou say, but will perplex thee more
> If thou stand excommunicate and cursed?

KING PHILIP
> Good reverend father, make my person yours,
> And tell me how you would bestow yourself.
> This royal hand and mine are newly knit,
> And the conjunction of our inward souls
> Married in league, coupled and linked together
> With all religious strength of sacred vows.
> The latest breath that gave the sound of words   230
> Was deep-sworn faith, peace, amity, true love
> Between our kingdoms and our royal selves;
> And even before this truce, but new before,
> No longer than we well could wash our hands
> To clap this royal bargain up of peace,
> God knows they were besmeared and overstained
> With slaughter's pencil where revenge did paint
> The fearful difference of incensèd kings.
> And shall these hands so lately purged of blood,
> So newly joined in love, so strong in both,   240
> Unyoke this seizure and this kind regreet?

222 more‸] DONOVAN; ∼ ? F; ∼ , ROWE   229 vows.] JOHNSON; vowes, F   236 God] This edition (*conj.* Matchett); Heauen F

222–3 **What canst . . . cursed?** F's punctuation makes two questions, the first implying that further debate will only cloud
the issue, the second elliptically remind-
ing Philip of the threat of excommuni-
cation; repunctuation attaches the idea
of further perplexity to the state of being
excommunicated.

222 **perplex** 'Confuse, puzzle' (so *v*. 1, citing
this line as its earliest example; Nashe's
use of the word in *Christ's Tears over
Jerusalem*, ii. 61, l. 31, cited by Schäfer
as an antedating, does not meet *OED*'s
definition).

227–9 **conjunction . . . vows** Philip uses
conjunction metaphorically to emphasize
that the literal marriage (= *conjunction*;
see 2.1.469n) of Blanche and Louis,
solemnized with *sacred vows*, has similarly *Married* the two Kings.

230 **latest** last, most recent

233 **new before** immediately preceding

235 **clap this bargain . . . up** Perhaps alluding

to an idiomatic expression: Dent H109.1,
'Clap hands and a bargain' (from 1580;
Dent lists two other Shakespearian instances); 'clap up' means specifically to
settle or concoct hastily (so *OED*, citing
this line as its earliest example).

236 **overstained** coloured all over

237 **pencil** brush for painting

238 **fearful** inducing fear, fearsome (Abbott
§3)

241 **seizure** grasp (here, handclasp)
   this kind regreet *OED* cites this line as its
earliest example of *regreet*, *sb*.¹, '(return
of) a salutation', and presumably regards
kind as an adjective and *regreet* as the
object of *Unyoke*. It would, however, be
Shakespearian to balance *Unyoke* with a
verb, *regreet* (= to greet again or anew),
also a late sixteenth-century formation.
In the latter case, the phrase would mean
'greet again this sort or category (= *kind*,
a less concrete sense of II.13) of behaviour' (i.e., battle); the Kings' un-

Play fast and loose with faith? So jest with heaven,
Make such unconstant children of ourselves,
As now again to snatch our palm from palm,
Unswear faith sworn, and on the marriage-bed
Of smiling peace to march a bloody host,
And make a riot on the gentle brow
Of true sincerity? O holy sir,
My reverend father, let it not be so.
Out of your grace, devise, ordain, impose   250
Some gentle order, and then we shall be blessed
To do your pleasure and continue friends.

CARDINAL PANDULPH

All form is formless, order orderless,
Save what is opposite to England's love.
Therefore to arms! Be champion of our church,
Or let the church our mother breathe her curse,
A mother's curse, on her revolting son.
France, thou mayst hold a serpent by the tongue,
A casèd lion by the mortal paw,

259 casèd] F (cafed); chafed THEOBALD (*conj.* Thirlby); chased POPE; caged COLLIER 1858; crased OXFORD

clasped hands may now 'shake hands' with renewed battle.

242 **Play fast and loose** A common expression (Tilley P401), derived from a confidence trick in which the victim bets whether a coiled strap or rope is pinned (= *fast*) or not (= *loose*) to a table by a knife. For illustrations of the trick, see appendix in I. John's edn.

jest with heaven See Dent J45.1 'It is ill jesting with gods' (citing this line and other examples from 1603–33).

250 **devise, ordain, impose** common legal synonyms (Honigmann, 3.1.176–7n)

255 **champion of our church** 'The King of France was styled the Eldest Son of the Church and the Most Christian King' (Wright, 3.1.267n).

257 **A mother's curse** Pandulph means 'the curse of the church our mother' (l. 256), but that curse will effectively also be the curse of another mother, Constance.

258 **hold a serpent by the tongue** Dent S228.1, 'To take (hold) a serpent by the tongue', comparing Tilley W603, 'He holds a wolf by the ears'; serpents' venom supposedly resided in their tongues.

259 **casèd** F's puzzling word may be ex-

plained: 'a *cased* lion is one still wearing his *case* (= skin), i.e., a live lion' (Honigmann, 3.1.185n). This line is, however, *OED*'s earliest citation for the *ppl. a.*, 'enclosed in or furnished with a case, put into a case'. The word may have been prompted (in Shakespeare's, or the copyist's, or the compositor's mind) by the frequent references to animal skins in the scene. Dyce drew attention to *Philaster* 5.3.64–5: 'what there is of vengeance in a lion | Chafed among dogs or robbed of his dear young' where Q1 reads 'Chaft', Qq2–5 and 9 read 'Chast', and Qq6–8 read 'Cast'. Theobald's emendation is thus graphically plausible (*h* overlooked, *f* misread as long *s*) and produces a platitudinous phrase (four of the eight appearances of 'chaf'd' and 'chafed' in Shakespeare refer to animals) suitable to speaker and context. The word was set by Compositor C, who made the common *c*:*t* error at 2.1.63 and who may have omitted *r* after the initial consonants in 'beast' (2.1.113) and 'fiends' (3.4.64); *crased* ('crazed'), adopted in the Oxford edition, or *traced* (= pursued, hunted) may therefore have stood

A fasting tiger safer by the tooth,   260
Than keep in peace that hand which thou dost hold.

KING PHILIP

I may disjoin my hand, but not my faith.

⌈*He releases John's hand*⌉

CARDINAL PANDULPH

So mak'st thou faith an enemy to faith,
And like a civil war sett'st oath to oath,
Thy tongue against thy tongue. O, let thy vow
First made to heaven, first be to heaven performed;
That is, to be the champion of our church.
What since thou swor'st is sworn against thyself
And may not be performèd by thyself.
For that which thou hast sworn to do amiss   270
Is not amiss when it is truly done.
And being not done, where doing tends to ill,
The truth is then most done not doing it.
The better act of purposes mistook
Is to mistake again; though indirect,
Yet indirection thereby grows direct,
And falsehood falsehood cures, as fire cools fire
Within the scorchèd veins of one new burned.

262.1 *He . . . hand*] FURNIVALL (*subs.*); *not in* F   267 church.] ROWE; Church, F   271 not]
F; but COLLIER 1858   275 again;] THEOBALD; ∼, F

in manuscript and would make good
Shakespearian sense here.
　mortal fatal, death-dealing (a transferred
adjective)
262.1 *He . . . hand* It is possible that Philip
does not release John's hand until he
says, 'England, I will fall from thee'
(l. 320); see 3.1.190.1n.
268 **What since thou swor'st** i.e., the oath
you made (to John) since you swore to
be 'champion of our church' (l. 267)
270–3 **that which thou hast sworn . . . not
doing it** Pandulph begins a series of
pseudo-paradoxes that would have appealed to an Elizabethan suspicion of
Catholic casuistry. Here, the paradox lies
in saying that a wrong act 'not done'
(l. 272) is 'truly done' (l. 271).
270–8 **thou hast sworn . . . new burned** See
Tilley O7, 'An unlawful oath is better
broken than kept' (varied instances from
1481 and numerous Shakespearian examples); *2 Henry VI* 5.1.180–1 clarifies

Pandulph's premiss: 'It is great sin to
swear unto a sin, | But greater sin to
keep a sinful oath'. See Introduction,
p. 41.
274 **act** acting
　purposes mistook The phrase appears at
Hamlet 5.2.338.
275 **though indirect** i.e., while this course
of action is oblique
276 **indirection** deceit, dishonest act (*OED*'s
earliest citation for this meaning).
Polonius plans 'By indirections [to] find
directions out' (*Hamlet* 2.1.65).
277 **falsehood falsehood cures** See Tilley
D174, 'One deceit (falsehood) drives out
another' (*deceit* appears from *c.*1520;
falsehood occurs only here and at *Kinsmen*
4.3.90–1 among known examples).
277–8 **fire cools . . . burned** See Tilley
F277, 'One fire (heat) drives out another',
'referring to the old belief that a burn
was cured by warming it' (Smallwood).

It is religion that doth make vows kept,
But thou hast sworn against religion: 280
By what thou swear'st against the thing thou swear'st,
And mak'st an oath the surety for thy truth,
Against an oath the truth; thou art unsure
To swear, swears only not to be forsworn,
Else what a mockery should it be to swear?
But thou dost swear only to be forsworn,
And most forsworn to keep what thou dost swear.
Therefore thy later vows against thy first
Is in thyself rebellion to thyself.
And better conquest never canst thou make   290
Than arm thy constant and thy nobler parts
Against these giddy loose suggestions;
Upon which better part our prayers come in,
If thou vouchsafe them. But if not, then know
The peril of our curses light on thee
So heavy as thou shalt not shake them off,
But in despair die under their black weight.

AUSTRIA
Rebellion, flat rebellion!
BASTARD   Will't not be?
Will not a calf's-skin stop that mouth of thine?

281 what] F; which CAPELL   282 truth] F; troth OXFORD   283 oath‚] F; ~. JOHNSON
(*conj.* Heath)   truth;] ROWE 1714; ~, F   284 swears] F (sweares); swear'st OXFORD   296
heavy‚ . . . off‚] CAMBRIDGE; heauy‚ . . . off‚ F   298 rebellion!] STEEVENS 1778; ~. F

281 **By what thou swear'st . . . swear'st** i.e.,
you have sworn against the very faith
by which you swear. The line amplifies
'against religion' (l. 280).
282–3 **And mak'st . . . the truth** These lines
amplify and repeat the preceding two
lines; in each pair of lines the second
depends elliptically upon the verb in the
first ('hast sworn'; 'mak'st'): you make
an oath to guarantee the truth of what
you swear, but the oath itself violates the
truth. Many editors end a sentence at
'an oath' (l. 283).
283 **unsure** lacking confidence, uncertain
(*a.* 5), and therefore 'hesitant'
284 **swears only not to be forsworn** i.e., you
make oaths that you plan to keep. *Swears*
is a northern inflection for the 2nd person
singular.
293 **part** side, party to a controversy (see
2.1.359), but word-play on 'nobler parts'

(l. 291)
294 **vouchsafe** receive graciously, deign to
accept (*v.* I.3b). Courtesy precedes the
threat of ll. 294–7.
295 **light** fall or descend on (but introducing
the antithetical *heavy* of the next line)
297 **black** deadly, baneful
298 **Rebellion, flat rebellion** Austria echoes
Pandulph (l. 289); as Furness saw,
Philip's silence here testifies to the
speech's baffling effect.
flat plain, absolute
298 **Will't not be?** 'Is everything in vain?'
(Honigmann, 3.1.224n); the exclamation is common (Dent B112.2; Dent,
PLED, cites examples from *c.*1495 onward): Talbot uses it when he fails to
rally his troops (*1 Henry VI* 1.7.33), the
Nurse when she fails to rouse Juliet
(*Romeo* 4.4.38).
299 **stop that mouth of thine** Tilley M1264,

LOUIS THE DAUPHIN
    Father, to arms!
BLANCHE   Upon thy wedding-day?   300
    Against the blood that thou hast marrièd?
    What, shall our feast be kept with slaughtered men?
    Shall braying trumpets and loud churlish drums,
    Clamours of hell, be measures to our pomp?
    O husband, hear me! Ay, alack, how new
    Is 'husband' in my mouth! Even for that name
    Which till this time my tongue did ne'er pronounce,
    Upon my knee I beg: go not to arms
    Against mine uncle.
CONSTANCE   O, upon my knee,
    Made hard with kneeling, I do pray to thee,   310
    Thou virtuous Dauphin, alter not the doom
    Forethought by heaven.
BLANCHE
    Now shall I see thy love. What motive may
    Be stronger with thee than the name of wife?
CONSTANCE
    That which upholdeth him that thee upholds:
    His honour. O, thine honour, Louis, thine honour!

300 arms!] HANMER; Armes. F   305 me!] CAPELL; ∼ : F   306 mouth!] F (∼ ?)   309–
12] POPE; *as four lines, breaking after* 'Uncle', 'kneeling', 'Dauphin', 'heaven' F   312 heaven]
F (heauen); God MATCHETT   316 honour!] THEOBALD; Honor. F

'To stop one's mouth' (earliest example from John Heywood, *A Dialogue of Proverbs*, 1546).

302 **kept** celebrated (*v.* II.12)
    slaughtered men Blanche conjures a scene in which men, not beasts, supply the wedding banquet; Philip imagines a similarly paradoxical scene at ll. 245–6.
304 **measures** tunes, melodies
305 **Ay, alack** The two words may form a single interjection (see *Ay, int.* 2).
308 **Upon my knee** Blanche may speak figuratively, as Constance may in her response (l. 309), but modern productions treat the lines literally (Sprague, pp. 12–13, and see the illustration of the 1948 Stratford production, *Shakespeare Survey* 2 (Cambridge, 1949), plate VIII.B); if the actresses do kneel, Constance might rise when she wins her point at l. 321 ('O fair return'), and Delius suggested that Louis ('him that thee upholds') might raise Blanche at l. 315.

309–12 **Against . . . heaven** Pope's lineation produces regular iambic pentameters; under normal circumstances, the compositor would not have had to crowd text here (as he appears to have done), but Hinman (ii. 474–5) records an interruption in the printing after this page was set, so carrying extra text over to the next page would have been more than usually difficult.

311 **doom | Forethought by heaven** judgement or sentence premeditated by God. Constance apparently believes Pandulph has pronounced a premeditated divine judgement on John, as 3.1.172 ff. imply. Honigmann suggests that Constance warns the 'virtuous Dauphin' not to forfeit (= *alter*) his predestinate salvation (= *doom | Forethought by heaven*) through a sinful act (as Catholic doctrine held possible), but this idea appears nowhere else in the dialogue while divine judgement of John is a common topic.

LOUIS THE DAUPHIN

I muse your majesty doth seem so cold
When such profound respects do pull you on.

CARDINAL PANDULPH

I will denounce a curse upon his head.

KING PHILIP

Thou shalt not need. England, I will fall from thee.   320

CONSTANCE

O fair return of banished majesty!

QUEEN ELEANOR

O foul revolt of French inconstancy!

KING JOHN

France, thou shalt rue this hour within this hour.

BASTARD

Old Time the clock-setter, that bald sexton Time,
Is it as he will? Well then, France shall rue.

BLANCHE

The sun's o'ercast with blood; fair day, adieu!
Which is the side that I must go withal?
I am with both; each army hath a hand,
And in their rage, I having hold of both,
They whirl asunder and dismember me.   330
Husband, I cannot pray that thou mayst win;
Uncle, I needs must pray that thou mayst lose;
Father, I may not wish the fortune thine;
Grandam, I will not wish thy wishes thrive.
Whoever wins, on that side shall I lose—
Assurèd loss before the match be played.

LOUIS THE DAUPHIN

Lady, with me, with me thy fortune lies.

---

318 on.] HANMER; ∼ ? F   321 majesty!] POPE; Maiestie. F   322 inconstancy!] POPE; ∼.
F   323 KING JOHN] F (*Eng⟨land⟩*.)   324 clock-setter] F3; *not hyphenated in* F1   326 adieu!]
THEOBALD; ∼, F

---

319 **denounce** proclaim, declare publicly
320 **fall from thee** i.e., 'sever the alliance',
but perhaps also 'let fall our handclasp'.
See 3.1.262.1n.
321-2 **O fair return . . . inconstancy** The
shared couplet forms an antithetical
choric comment.
324-5 **Old Time . . . shall rue** A pun on

'thyme' and 'rue' (both herbs); see Kyd,
The Spanish Tragedy 2.1.7-8 and Dent,
p. 19 n. 3.
324 **bald sexton Time** See Tilley T311, 'Take
time (occasion) by the forelock, for she
is bald behind' (varied from 1539; many
Shakespearian examples); see 4.2.125n.
333 **Father** i.e., father-in-law

BLANCHE

There where my fortune lives, there my life dies.

KING JOHN

Cousin, go draw our puissance together.   *Exit Bastard*

France, I am burned up with inflaming wrath,   340

A rage whose heat hath this condition

That nothing can allay, nothing but blood,

The blood and dearest-valued blood of France.

KING PHILIP

Thy rage shall burn thee up, and thou shalt turn

To ashes ere our blood shall quench that fire.

Look to thyself, thou art in jeopardy.

KING JOHN

No more than he that threats. To arms let's hie!

Exeunt

3.2   *Alarums, excursions.*
       Enter Bastard with Austria's head

339 *Exit Bastard*] POPE; *not in* F   342 allay] F; allay't DYCE 1864 (*conj.* Capell, *Notes*)   343
The blood] F; The best WALKER *conj.*   dearest-valued] THEOBALD; *not hyphenated in* F
    3.2] F (*Scoena Secunda*)

338 **dies** The rhyme helps convey the finality
of Blanche's dilemma.

339 **puissance** military forces (pronounced
as either a disyllable or a trisyllable)
    Exit Bastard The Bastard's individual exit
seems unnecessary so shortly before the
general *Exeunt*, but the actor has to
collect the prop head with which he will
immediately re-enter.

340–3 **inflaming wrath . . . blood** See Dent
B465.1, 'Only blood can quench the fire'
(Dent, *PLED*, has examples from 1566
onward), *Romeo* 1.1.80–2, and the
closely similar expressions at *Tambur-
laine, Part 1* 2.6.32–3 and 4.1.56.
Imagery of heat and blood returns in
John's dying speeches, 5.7.30 ff.

342–3 **nothing but blood, | The blood** The
repetition of *blood* suits the play's verbal
style, although one or more of the repetitions could also be a compositor's or
copyist's substitution; the first line scans
well enough with a breath-pause after
allay.

343 **dearest-valued** Either 'most highly
prized' (i.e., royal blood) or 'required for
life' (see the threat of death in Chapman, *Bussy D'Ambois* 1.2.191–2: 'your

buffoonly laughters will cost ye the best
blood in your bodies'). Shakespeare uses
'dearest' of 'blood' only here and in
the first tetralogy (*3 Henry VI* 1.1.224,
5.1.69, *1 Henry VI* 3.8.40).

346 **in jeopardy** in danger or peril. The noun
derives from games of chance and may
have been suggested by the imagery of
ll. 335–6.

347 **hie** hasten, hurry

3.2 Location: a place of relative safety (like
that mentioned in l. 8) near the field of
battle, but not the English royal camp
(see l. 6).

0.1 *Alarums* sounds on drum, trumpet, or
other instrument warning of attack or
danger (probably a conventional and
recognizable tune or rhythm is called for)
excursions sorties, raids. The word in a
direction may indicate that the audience
sees skirmishes on stage, or it may merely
require off-stage sound effects. For both
alarums and *excursions*, see Harbage,
pp. 52–3.

0.2 *with Austria's head* A head seems to
have been a stock property; see *Richard
III* 3.5.19.1 and Henslowe's now-lost
inventories (*Diary*, pp. 318, l. 27; 319,

BASTARD

Now, by my life, this day grows wondrous hot;
Some airy devil hovers in the sky
And pours down mischief. Austria's head lie there,
While Philip breathes.

He puts down Austria's head.
Enter King John, Arthur, Hubert

KING JOHN

Hubert, keep this boy.—Philip, make up!
My mother is assailèd in our tent,
And ta'en, I fear.

BASTARD   My lord, I rescued her;
Her highness is in safety, fear you not.
But on, my liege, for very little pains
Will bring this labour to an happy end.   10

Exeunt ⌜King John and the Bastard
(carrying Austria's head) at one door,
Hubert and Arthur at another door⌝

3.3   *Alarums, excursions, retreat.*
       Enter King John, Queen Eleanor, Arthur, Bastard,
       Hubert, lords

3 pours] F4; pour's F1   4.1 *He . . . head*] This edition; *not in* F   4.2 *Enter . . . Hubert*]
CAPELL; *after l.* 3 F (*Iohn*)   10.1–3 *Exeunt . . . another door*] OXFORD (*subs.*); *Exit.* F
3.3] CAPELL's *scene-division* F   0.1–3 *Alarums . . . lords*] F (*Alarums,*
excursions, Retreat. Enter Iohn, Eleanor, Arthur∧ *Bastard, Hubert, Lords.*)

ll. 65, 67; 320, l. 70); fearing laughter,
producers from Garrick's time to the
present have often rewritten and substituted Austria's lion-skin for his head.
2 **airy devil** Antonio comments to Bosola:
'You would look up to heaven, but I
think | The devil, that rules i'th' air,
stands in your light' (*The Duchess of Malfi*
2.1.94–5; in his note to this line, J. R.
Brown cites Ephesians 2: 2, where the
devil 'ruleth in the air'). Wilson regards
the line as referring to the devils of the air
especially responsible for thunderstorms,
but 'Legions of spirits fleeting in the air |
Direct our bullets and our weapons'
points' (*Tamburlaine, Part 1* 3.3.156–
7) suggests the idea may be generally
connected with battle.
4, 5 **Philip** i.e., the Bastard, here given his
original name as he is in F's direction
at 3.1.74.3. See Appendix A2 for the

Bastard's varied nomenclature.
5 **keep this boy** Arthur has evidently just
been captured.
  make up advance in a certain direction
(so *make*, v.[1] VIII. 96n, citing this line as
earliest instance)
7 **ta'en** F's *tane* (=taken) is an obsolete
past participle, but apparently not a syncopated form; as a graphic form, however, the seventeenth-century spelling
ta'en is more immediately understand-
able.
9–10 **little pains . . . labour** The Bastard
alludes to birth-pains (= *labour*), but may
deliver the line sardonically as he hefts
Austria's head.
3.3 Location: perhaps the English royal
camp. Ordinarily, Elizabethan battles
represented by sound effects, actors running on- and off-stage, etc. (see 3.2.0.1n)
and, like those in Act 2, do not interrupt

KING JOHN ⌜*to Eleanor*⌝

  So shall it be. Your grace shall stay behind,
  So strongly guarded.—(*To Arthur*) Cousin, look not sad;
  Thy grandam loves thee, and thy uncle will
  As dear be to thee as thy father was.

ARTHUR

  O, this will make my mother die with grief!

KING JOHN (*to Bastard*)

  Cousin, away for England! Haste before,
  And ere our coming see thou shake the bags
  Of hoarding abbots; imprisoned angels
  Set at liberty. The fat ribs of peace
  Must by the hungry now be fed upon.   10
  Use our commission in his utmost force.

BASTARD

  Bell, book, and candle shall not drive me back
  When gold and silver becks me to come on.

---

5 grief!] DYCE; griefe. F   8–9 imprisoned angels | Set at liberty] F; their imprisoned angels
| Set at liberty POPE; set at liberty | Imprisoned angels KEIGHTLEY (*conj.* Walker)   9 Set at
liberty] F; Set thou at liberty THEOBALD (*conj.* Thirlby)

---

the continuity of time or place sufficiently
to justify a scene-break. The re-entry of
the Bastard also argues for continuity
here. The battle mentioned at 3.2.9–10
has, however, apparently been won (the
sound effects of 3.3.0.1 representing perhaps a conclusive skirmish, perhaps the
French withdrawal), and enough time
has passed for John and his allies to
prepare the army's departure (l. 74) and
to concert the future plans they have
evidently just finished discussing as they
enter.

0.1 *retreat* sounds on drum, trumpet, or
other instrument recalling troops from
battle

0.3 *lords* This scene, like so many in *K.
John*, begins with a crowded stage that
gradually empties. Rather than to
Eleanor, John's first sentence might be
addressed to some of F's *Lords* (or to lords
and soldiers unmentioned in F), dismissing
them; some might exit with the Bastard
at l. 17, but others presumably remain
to dignify John's 'On toward Calais, ho!'
(l. 74). Those who remain must be relatively unobtrusive, however, to give full
effect to the contrast between John's
temptation of Hubert and Eleanor's un-

heard conversation with Arthur (l. 18).
See Introduction, pp. 22–3 and 87.
6–11 **away for England . . . utmost force**
Shakespeare uses John's historical pillag-
ing of the church to motivate the Bastard's exit and separate him from the plot
to murder Arthur.
8 **hoarding** This line is *OED*'s earliest
citation for the *ppl. a.*
angels Coins (see 2.1.591n, 5.2.64, Appendix C, and Fig. 7), but with the anti-
Catholic implication that the *abbots* are
unsuitable guardians of faith.
8–9 **imprisoned . . . liberty** Malone rewrote
to rectify the metre: 'angels imprisoned |
Set thou at liberty', and other suggestions
have been made; F may be defective, but
there is no obvious emendation.
9–10 **The fat . . . fed upon** These lines
continue the imagery of 2.1.352–4.
11 **commission** delegated authority, here
perhaps specifically the document (a warrant) conferring that authority. See
2.1.110n.
his its
12 **Bell, book, and candle** Tilley B276, 'To
curse with bell, book, and candle' (from
c.1470; only Shakespearian use).

I leave your highness.—Grandam, I will pray—
If ever I remember to be holy—
For your fair safety. So I kiss your hand.

QUEEN ELEANOR
Farewell, gentle cousin.

KING JOHN   Coz, farewell.   *Exit Bastard*

QUEEN ELEANOR (*to Arthur*)
Come hither, little kinsman. Hark, a word.
      She takes Arthur aside

KING JOHN
Come hither, Hubert.
      He takes Hubert aside
                                 O my gentle Hubert,
We owe thee much. Within this wall of flesh   20
There is a soul counts thee her creditor,
And with advantage means to pay thy love.
And, my good friend, thy voluntary oath
Lives in this bosom, dearly cherishèd.
Give me thy hand. I had a thing to say,
But I will fit it with some better tune.

---

17 *Exit Bastard*] POPE; *not in* F   18.1 *She . . . aside*] POPE (*subs.*); *not in* F   19 *He . . . aside*]
OXFORD; *not in* F   26 tune] F; time POPE

16 **kiss your hand** i.e., bid you farewell
respectfully. The action did not necessarily accompany this polite formula. See
1.1.142–3n.

18.1 **She . . . aside** The division of principal
actors into two groups, one heard, the
other unheard, occurs fairly frequently
in *K. John*; see, for example: the debate
over Hubert's proposal before Angers
(2.1.469 ff.; see especially 2.1.476);
John's unheard conference with Hubert
(4.2.68 ff.); and, more distantly, the
sequence of state affairs, intimate comment, and comic familial controversy
that opens Act 1.

20 **We owe thee much** The audience has
seen Hubert compromise the Anglo-
French conflict by suggesting the marriage of Louis and Blanche, but John may
refer to some (unseen) help in the recent
battle; see Appendix A2.

22 **advantage** interest (John will repay both
principal and interest on Hubert's loan
to him)

23 **voluntary oath** vow offered freely, with-

out persuasion. This is the first and only
time we hear of Hubert's volunteering
for John's service; for discussion of this
phrase and of other events mentioned
but not dramatized, see Appendix A2.

25 **Give me thy hand** John substitutes a
conventional gesture of farewell for the
conversation he is (or pretends to be)
reluctant to begin; Slater exaggerates the
hypocrisy as John's attempt to 'force an
unwilling acceptance' of 'a bond between
two people' (p. 55). This handclasp
dooms Arthur, as the earlier one in 3.1
between John and Philip seemed to save
him.

26 **tune** In manuscript, between the *t* and
the *e* of both *tune* and *time* would appear
four minims, and the words would therefore be easy to confuse, but Pope's emendation substitutes a falsehood (John
speaks his mind to Hubert at this, not
another, *time*) for a slightly strained
metaphor (*tune* = 'speech' or 'rhetorical
context'). John soon describes the context
appropriate to his speech in terms of the

By heaven, Hubert, I am almost ashamed
To say what good respect I have of thee.

HUBERT

I am much bounden to your majesty.

KING JOHN

Good friend, thou hast no cause to say so yet,   30
But thou shalt have, and creep time ne'er so slow,
Yet it shall come, for me to do thee good.
I had a thing to say, but let it go.
The sun is in the heaven, and the proud day,
Attended with the pleasures of the world,
Is all too wanton and too full of gauds
To give me audience. If the midnight bell
Did with his iron tongue and brazen mouth
Sound on into the drowsy race of night;
If this same were a churchyard where we stand,   40
And thou possessèd with a thousand wrongs;
Or if that surly spirit, melancholy,
Had baked thy blood and made it heavy, thick,
Which else runs tickling up and down the veins,

39 on into] F; one unto THEOBALD (*conj.* Thirlby)   race] F; ear DYCE (*conj.* Walker)   43
heavy, thick] F; heavy-thick POPE

midnight bell's 'iron tongue and brazen
mouth', i.e., in terms of sound (*tune*) not
occasion (*time*).

28 **respect** esteem, regard

29 **much bounden** deeply indebted

36 **wanton** 'sportive, merry'; perhaps also,
in view of later metaphors, 'amorous'
(OED offers no definitions that fully meet
the usage here)
    gauds playthings, toys

37–53 The speech is a series of alternative
protases or conditions ('If . . . If . . . Or
if . . . Or if . . .') leading to an apodosis
('Then . . . I would . . .'). One of the
conditions—that it be midnight (ll. 57–
9)—is of course logically inconsistent
with the last, existing condition, 'in despite of day', and it seems clear that
John (or Shakespeare) construes the full
apodosis only in conjunction with the
last condition (ll. 48–51). See 3.3.52n.

37 **midnight bell** bell marking the midnight
hour; perhaps by figurative extension, a
bell ringing late at night. Honigmann's
association (3.2.49n) of this phrase with
'passing-bell' (tolled when a parishioner
is dying) is unsupported by OED and

contradicted by Theseus' 'The iron
tongue of midnight hath told twelve'
(*Dream* 5.1.356; see *iron tongue* in next
line).

38 **brazen** i.e., because bells were made of
bronze (but perhaps with the further
sense of 'shameless, impudent')

39 **on** *Dream* 5.1.356 (quoted in 3.3.37n)
makes Theobald's popular reading less
plausible.
    race Course of time (so *sb.*¹ II.5c, citing
this line), but if *race of night* is parallel
with *gauds* (i.e., things or activities associated with the time), then *race* may =
offspring (*sb.*²), the beings or events to
which night gives birth or which night
encourages (hence, 'night's black agents',
Macbeth 3.2.54).

41 **possessèd with** Owning; but the grammar here, as elsewhere when this verb
appears, allows the sense of Hubert's
being owned by the wrongs (see 4.2.9,
145, 203).

44 **tickling** tingling (Honigmann, 3.2.54n)
    the veins As John manoeuvres toward
proposing murder, his language hovers

Making that idiot, laughter, keep men's eyes
And strain their cheeks to idle merriment,
A passion hateful to my purposes;
Or if that thou couldst see me without eyes,
Hear me without thine ears, and make reply
Without a tongue, using conceit alone,   50
Without eyes, ears, and harmful sound of words—
Then, in despite of broad-eyed watchful day,
I would into thy bosom pour my thoughts.
But, ah, I will not. Yet I love thee well,
And, by my troth, I think thou lov'st me well.

HUBERT

So well that what you bid me undertake,
Though that my death were adjunct to my act,
By heaven I would do it.

KING JOHN   Do not I know thou wouldst?
Good Hubert! Hubert, Hubert, throw thine eye
On yon young boy. I'll tell thee what, my friend,   60
He is a very serpent in my way,
And wheresoe'er this foot of mine doth tread,

---

45 idiot, laughter,] CAPELL; idiot‸ laughter‸ F   52 broad-eyed] POPE; brooded F   59
Hubert!] COLLIER; *Hubert,* F

between the general (see l. 45, 'men's eyes') and the personal, where *the* = your and denotes a 'part of the body of a person previously named' (*dem. adj.* and *pron.* 12).

50 **conceit** imagination; mental, not physical, senses

51 **harmful** painful, but implying 'full of harm' (the harm John invites Hubert to commit). See Abbott § 3.

52 **broad-eyed** with eyes wide open. Pope's graphically plausible emendation emphasizes the contrast between the physically vigilant (= *watchful*) 'day' and Hubert's entirely mental comprehension 'using conceit alone' (l. 50) of John's desires. *OED, broad, comb.* D.2a, lists two seventeenth-century uses of the adjective, and see Thomas Heywood, *If You Know Not Me* (Q1606), 'Thus in the face of heaven, and broad eye of all the multitude, | We give a welcome to the Spanish prince' (B2). F's *brooded* could = having a brood (chicks or other, more figurative offspring). The latent

image would then be that of a mother (= *day*) concerned for her offspring (see *wanton* and *race*) and therefore *watchful*. These metaphorical possibilities link the speech closely with *Macbeth* 3.2.47–54.

53 **into thy bosom pour my thoughts** A common image: Dent B546.2 (examples from 1582 onward).

55 **by my troth** by my truth (an asseveration)

57 **adjunct to** annexed to, 'consequent upon' (Wright)

58 **By heaven . . . wouldst** This shared line becomes a hexameter with a single contraction in the speaking (e.g., do't, or I'd, or heav'n).

59 **eye** Perhaps an archaic plural which appears elsewhere in the play (e.g., 4.1.66, 121, and 5.7.51).

61 **He . . . way** Jacob described the tribe of Dan as 'a serpent in the way, an adder in the path' (Genesis 49: 17; see Carter, p. 210 and Noble, p. 116); the Bishops' Bible explains marginally: 'The tribe of Dan should overcome his enemies, rather by craft than manhood'.

He lies before me. Dost thou understand me?
Thou art his keeper.
HUBERT   And I'll keep him so
That he shall not offend your majesty.
KING JOHN
    Death.
HUBERT My lord.
KING JOHN   A grave.
HUBERT
    He shall not live.
KING JOHN   Enough.
I could be merry now; Hubert, I love thee.
Well, I'll not say what I intend for thee.
Remember.—Madam, fare you well;   70
I'll send those powers o'er to your majesty.
QUEEN ELEANOR
    My blessing go with thee.
KING JOHN (*to Arthur*)   For England, cousin, go.
Hubert shall be your man, attend on you
With all true duty.—On toward Calais, ho!
            Exeunt ⌈Eleanor and attendants at one
                door, the rest at another door⌉

66–7] *as two lines,* This edition; *as five lines, breaking after* 'Death', 'lord', 'grave', 'live', 'enough' F; *as one line* STEEVENS. *See note.*   66 My lord.] F; My Lord? ROWE   74.1–2 *Eleanor . . . another door*] OXFORD (*subs.*); *not in* F

66–7 **Death . . . Enough** F gives each speech
    a separate line, as it often does when
    several short speeches follow one an-
    other; since the eighteenth century,
    however, editors have treated the five
    speeches as a single pentameter line,
    arranged like a staircase descending ac-
    ross the page. Few actors would willingly
    deliver the lines rapidly enough to allow
    an audience to perceive their united effect
    as a pentameter because to do so would
    destroy the tension and interest of this
    moment. The speeches are much more
    likely to be spoken with enough pauses
    (or 'silent' poetic feet) to equal the 'hear-
    ing time' of at least two ordinary penta-
    meters. The relineation offered here
    attempts to reproduce those pauses
    graphically while it also allows a reader
    to perceive the pentameter.
66 **Death** Holinshed reports the conflicting
    tales of Arthur's death and John's re-
    sponsibility for it; 'some affirm that King
    John secretly caused him to be murdered

and made away, so as it is not thoroughly
agreed upon in what sort he finished his
days, but verily King John was had in
great suspicion, whether worthily or not,
the Lord knoweth' (165b; P3).
    My Lord. 'Editors all read *My Lord?* It is
    a small point, but of much significance
    in the acting and interpretation, and the
    Folio *My Lord.* seems to me right. The
    trend of John's thought has become clear
    to Hubert already. His *My Lord* is not an
    exclamation or surprised question. It is
    submissive, understanding, and decisive,
    and follows naturally what has gone
    before' (Sisson, p. 10).
72 **For England, cousin, go** The line at
    first seems over-explanatory, since John,
    Arthur, and Hubert are all travelling to
    England *via* Calais, but John's words
    emphasize Arthur's inferior status as a
    captured enemy.
73 **man** personal servant
74 **true duty** Angevin and more than Ange-
    vin irony caps the scene: John quibbles

3.4   ⌈*Flourish.*⌉ *Enter King Philip, Louis the Dauphin,*
         Pandulph, Attendants

KING PHILIP

So by a roaring tempest on the flood

A whole armada of convected sail

Is scattered and disjoined from fellowship.

CARDINAL PANDULPH

Courage and comfort! All shall yet go well.

KING PHILIP

What can go well, when we have run so ill?

Are we not beaten? Is not Angers lost?

Arthur ta'en prisoner? Divers dear friends slain?

And bloody England into England gone,

O'erbearing interruption, spite of France?

LOUIS THE DAUPHIN

What he hath won, that hath he fortified.   10

So hot a speed, with such advice disposed,

Such temperate order in so fierce a cause,

Doth want example. Who hath read or heard

Of any kindred action like to this?

KING PHILIP

Well could I bear that England had this praise,

So we could find some pattern of our shame.

3.4] CAPELL; *Scaena Tertia* F   0.1 *Flourish*] This edition; *not in* F   0.1–2 *Enter . . .*
Attendants] F (*Enter France, Dolphin, Pandulpho, Attendants.*)   2 armada] F (Armado)
convected] FLEAY (*conj.* Dyce, *withdrawn*; *conj.* Hulme); conuicted F; collected POPE; convented
SINGER 1856 (*conj.* Mason²); connected DELIUS (*conj.* Malone, *Supp.*); conjuncted MAXWELL²
conj.   4 comfort!] CAPELL; ∼, F   14 kindred action] THEOBALD; *hyphenated in* F

on Hubert's 'duty' as Arthur's 'man'
(l. 73) and Hubert's sworn 'duty' to kill
his prisoner; a further definition of 'true
duty' (compassion for Arthur) will be the
central issue when we next see Arthur
and Hubert in 4.1.

3.4 Location: the French royal camp, somewhere in France.

1 **So** To insert a comma after this word, as
many editors do, makes Philip more
ruminative than distraught and diminishes the sense that the characters enter
in the midst of a conversation.
flood sea, ocean

2 **armada** fleet of warships. F's *armado* is
obsolete.
convected F's *conuicted*, which might
mean 'vanquished, defeated' (so *OED* and
many editors), is more likely to be a

Latinism for 'sailing together' (*con-
vectus*); 'as long as an "Armado" is
"whole", no part of it is "conuicted"
in the sense of "vanquished"' (Hulme,
pp. 220–1, apparently unaware of Dyce
and Fleay).

5 **run so ill** Ended in being, or grown, so
unfortunate (*v.* B.I.31b), but probably
mixed with other senses: flight from
battle and steering a ship poorly (ll. 1–
3); there is a mild antithetical play on
go (= walk) and *run*.

7 **ta'en** See 3.2.7n.
prisoner (disyllabic)

11 **So hot a speed** See 2.1.449n and 5.7.50n.
advice prudence, wisdom

13 **want example** lack precedent

16 **pattern** precedent, an instance appealed
to (so *OED*, citing this line). Evidently,

> *Enter Constance, distracted, with her hair about*
> *her ears*

Look who comes here! A grave unto a soul,
Holding th'eternal spirit against her will
In the vile prison of afflicted breath.
I prithee, lady, go away with me.   20
CONSTANCE
Lo, now, now see the issue of your peace!
KING PHILIP
Patience, good lady. Comfort, gentle Constance.
CONSTANCE
No, I defy all counsel, all redress,
But that which ends all counsel, true redress.
Death, death, O amiable, lovely death,
Thou odoriferous stench, sound rottenness,
Arise forth from the couch of lasting night,
Thou hate and terror to prosperity,
And I will kiss thy detestable bones,
And put my eyeballs in thy vaulty brows,   30
And ring these fingers with thy household worms,
And stop this gap of breath with fulsome dust,
And be a carrion monster like thyself.
Come, grin on me, and I will think thou smil'st
And buss thee as thy wife. Misery's love,
O, come to me!
KING PHILIP   O fair affliction, peace!

16.1–2 *distracted . . . ears*] OXFORD; *not in* F   21 peace!] CAPELL; ~. F   36 me!] THEOBALD;
~. F   peace!] COLLIER; ~. F

Philip is further downcast because he has
no historical fellowship in woe.

17–19 **grave . . . prison** See Tilley B497,
'The body is the prison of the soul' (Dent
cites earliest example from 1547 and
adds numerous dramatic examples);
Mason noted uses of the idea at 4.2.
245–6 and 4.3.136–7, but John has
already alluded to it at 3.3.20–1.

21 **issue of your peace** i.e., consequence
(= *issue*, with a pun on 'offspring') of
the Louis–Blanche marriage. Constance
unfairly ignores Philip's decision to 'fall
from' John.

23–36 **No, I defy . . . to me** In *Shakespeare:*
Leben, Umwelt, Kunst, 3rd edn. (Witten-
berg, 1923), p. 211, Alois Brandl records

the suggestion that Constance's speeches
in this scene are parallel with and might
be derived from Andromache's speeches
to Ulysses on behalf of Astyanax in
Seneca's *Troades* 739 ff., but the argument of influence is unconvincing.

23 **defy** 'renounce' (Wright; *OED*'s entry
does not precisely include the usage here)

26 **odoriferous stench** fragrant stink, an oxymoron

29 **detestable** accent on first syllable

30 **vaulty** i.e., resembling a vault, perhaps
alluding to the 'vile prison' (l. 19 and
explicit at *Lucrece* 119) or to a burial
vault (l. 17: 'a grave unto a soul')

35 **Misery's** accent on second syllable

CONSTANCE

No, no, I will not, having breath to cry!
O, that my tongue were in the thunder's mouth!
Then with a passion would I shake the world
And rouse from sleep that fell anatomy   40
Which cannot hear a lady's feeble voice,
Which scorns a modern invocation.

CARDINAL PANDULPH

Lady, you utter madness and not sorrow.

CONSTANCE

Thou art not holy to belie me so;
I am not mad. This hair I tear is mine;
My name is Constance; I was Geoffrey's wife;
Young Arthur is my son, and he is lost!
I am not mad; I would to God I were,
For then 'tis like I should forget myself.
O, if I could, what grief should I forget!   50
Preach some philosophy to make me mad,
And thou shalt be canonized, Cardinal.
For, being not mad, but sensible of grief,
My reasonable part produces reason
How I may be delivered of these woes
And teaches me to kill or hang myself.
If I were mad, I should forget my son,
Or madly think a babe of clouts were he.
I am not mad. Too well, too well I feel
The different plague of each calamity.   60

37 cry!] SMALLWOOD; ~ : F   38 mouth!] CAPELL; ~ , F   44 not holy] F4; holy F1; unholy
STAUNTON (*conj.* Steevens); too holy MAXWELL² *conj.*   47 lost!] POPE; ~ : F   48 God] OXFORD;
heauen F   50 forget!] F (~ ?)

40 **fell** dire
   anatomy skeleton (so *OED*, quoting this
   line)
42 **modern** ordinary, commonplace (the
   usual Shakespearian sense)
44 **holy** The word may be used absolutely
   (producing the sense of Maxwell's emendation): Pandulph's status (his faith, his
   office, his holy orders) forbid him to deny
   Constance. F4's reading may, however,
   restore the original, since compositors
   omit *not* fairly often: see Randall McLeod,
   'Gon. No more, the text is foolish' in

Division, pp. 153–93; p. 168 and n. 16.
49 **forget myself** i.e., lose consciousness (*v.*
   5d). The idea that mad persons were
   insensible to physical pain was common:
   see Dent F480, *Tragedy of Lear* 4.5.281–
   4, and Strozza's succinct assertion, 'mad-
   men, | By pains ungoverned, have no
   sense of pain' (Chapman, *Gentleman
   Usher* 4.3.55–6).
52 **canonized** accent on second syllable
53 **sensible** aware, conscious
58 **babe of clouts** doll (*clouts* = cloths, especially rags). See Dent CC13.

KING PHILIP

Bind up those tresses.—O, what love I note
In the fair multitude of those her hairs;
Where but by chance a silver drop hath fall'n,
Even to that drop ten thousand wiry friends
Do glue themselves in sociable grief,
Like true, inseparable, faithful loves,
Sticking together in calamity.

CONSTANCE

To England, if you will.

KING PHILIP   Bind up your hairs.

CONSTANCE

Yes, that I will. And wherefore will I do it?
I tore them from their bonds and cried aloud,   70
'O, that these hands could so redeem my son
As they have given these hairs their liberty!'
But now I envy at their liberty
And will again commit them to their bonds,
Because my poor child is a prisoner.

She binds up her hair

And, father Cardinal, I have heard you say
That we shall see and know our friends in heaven.
If that be true, I shall see my boy again,
For since the birth of Cain, the first male child,

64 friends] ROWE 1714; fiends F   66 loves] F; lovers COLLIER 1858   72 liberty!] THEOBALD; libertie: F   75.1 *She . . . hair*] OXFORD; *not in* F   79 male child] POPE; *hyphenated in* F

61 **Bind up those tresses** Loose or disheveled hair could signify a virgin bride, at least in Jacobean times (see the opening direction of *Kinsmen*: '. . . Hippolyta, *the bride*, . . . *her tresses . . . hanging*' and *The White Devil* 4.1.2 and n.), but more commonly signified a widow's or bereaved lover's grief: see, e.g., *Tancred and Gismund*, MSR, ll. 1664–8 (quoted above, 3.1.209n), F's stage direction for the widowed Queen Elizabeth, '*with her hair about her ears*' (*Richard III* 2.2.33.1), and Bevington, pp. 84–5, citing other verbal and visual examples.

64 **wiry** perhaps = 'tough', 'strong', but probably transferred from the common Elizabethan metaphor of hair = wires
friends F's *fiends* might be possible were Philip matching Constance's grotesque images, but Rowe's emendation suits *love*, *fair*, *sociable*, and *loves* (ll. 61–2, 65–6).

68 **To England, if you will** This incongruous reply may represent Constance's distraction. It does, however, respond logically to Philip's request at l. 20, and it may therefore indicate a revision or an interpolation (i.e., ll. 21–67); see Introduction, pp. 36–7.

71–4 **these hands . . . bonds** Slater (pp. 143–4) regards these lines as explicit directions to the actress, but Philip has already established the metaphor at ll. 61 ff.

73 **envy at** begrudge

78 **If that . . . again** The metre requires some elision (e.g., *I shall* becoming 'I'll'); Capell omitted *true*.

To him that did but yesterday suspire,   80
There was not such a gracious creature born.
But now will canker-sorrow eat my bud
And chase the native beauty from his cheek,
And he will look as hollow as a ghost,
As dim and meagre as an ague's fit,
And so he'll die; and, rising so again,
When I shall meet him in the court of heaven,
I shall not know him. Therefore never, never
Must I behold my pretty Arthur more.

CARDINAL PANDULPH

You hold too heinous a respect of grief.   90

CONSTANCE

He talks to me that never had a son.

KING PHILIP

You are as fond of grief as of your child.

CONSTANCE

Grief fills the room up of my absent child,
Lies in his bed, walks up and down with me,
Puts on his pretty looks, repeats his words,
Remembers me of all his gracious parts,
Stuffs out his vacant garments with his form.
Then have I reason to be fond of grief?
Fare you well. Had you such a loss as I,
I could give better comfort than you do.   100

⌈*She unbinds her hair*⌉

I will not keep this form upon my head

85 ague's fit] F (Agues fitte); ague-fit DYCE 1864   100.1 *She . . . hair*] OXFORD; *not in* F

80 **suspire** breathe
81 **gracious** graceful, graced (as at l. 96)
82 **my bud** i.e., Arthur, the 'half-blown rose' of 3.1.54, not—as reminiscence of *Twelfth Night* 2.4.111–12 ('But let concealment, like a worm i'th' bud | Feed on her damask cheek') might suggest—Constance herself. 'Canker' and 'bud' are associated twice in *Two Gentlemen* and in Sonnets 35.4 and 70.7. See Tilley C56, 'The canker soonest eats the fairest rose' (examples from 1576; Dent cites three in Shakespeare).
85 **ague's fit** the shaking occasioned by chills (or chills and fever)

86 **so . . . so** i.e., 'in that condition' (*conj.* and *adv.* B.I.4), not 'then' or 'thereafter'
91 **He talks . . . a son** Because Pandulph is celibate; the line's syntax, rhythm, and sentiment recall Romeo's response to Mercutio: 'He jests at scars that never felt a wound' (*Romeo* 2.1.43).
92 **fond of** feel tenderness toward or desire, but perhaps punning on *fond* = mad (i.e., 'you are mad from grief and you are loving toward your child'). See l. 98.
96 **Remembers** reminds
101 **form** due shape, good order (so *sb.* I.8, citing this line as its earliest example)

When there is such disorder in my wit.
O Lord! My boy, my Arthur, my fair son!
My life, my joy, my food, my all the world!
My widow-comfort, and my sorrows' cure!   *Exit*
KING PHILIP
I fear some outrage, and I'll follow her.   *Exit*
LOUIS THE DAUPHIN
There's nothing in this world can make me joy.
Life is as tedious as a twice-told tale,
Vexing the dull ear of a drowsy man,
And bitter shame hath spoiled the sweet word's taste,   110
That it yields naught but shame and bitterness.
CARDINAL PANDULPH
Before the curing of a strong disease,
Even in the instant of repair and health,
The fit is strongest. Evils that take leave,
On their departure most of all show evil.
What have you lost by losing of this day?
LOUIS THE DAUPHIN
All days of glory, joy, and happiness.
CARDINAL PANDULPH
If you had won it, certainly you had.
No, no. When Fortune means to men most good,
She looks upon them with a threat'ning eye.   120
'Tis strange to think how much King John hath lost
In this which he accounts so clearly won.
Are not you grieved that Arthur is his prisoner?

---

103 Lord!] CAPELL; ~, F   son!] ROWE 1714; ~, F   104 world!] THEOBALD; ~: F   105
sorrows'] F (sorrowes)   cure!] ROWE 1714; ~. F   110 word's] F (words); world's POPE
111 naught] F (nought)   114–15 leave, . . . departure‿] CAPELL; leaue‿ . . . departure, F

---

105 **sorrows'** For the plural possessive, see
  3.1.102n and 3.4.110n.
108 **tedious as a twice-told tale** Perhaps
  proverbial: Dent T53.1, 'Tales twice told
  are ungrateful' (a plausible citation from
  1586 and see below, 4.2.18–19); for the
  reverse, see Tilley T39, 'A good tale is
  none the worse to be twice told'.
110 **word's** F's *words* could be either singular
  or plural possessive, i.e., referring to the
  word *life* or to the words of the 'twice-told
  tale'; the pronoun *it* (3.4.111) probably

refers to *life* (hence my choice of *word's*),
but it may refer to *taste*, in which case
words' is a possible interpretation. The
difference would be undetectable in the
theatre. Although Pope presumably did
not know it, his popular emendation
reflects a pronunciational variant in Elizabethan English (see Hulme, pp. 207–8).
113 **repair** restoration to soundness or
  health (*sb.²*, citing this line as its earliest
  example)
122 **clearly** manifestly, evidently

LOUIS THE DAUPHIN

As heartily as he is glad he hath him.

CARDINAL PANDULPH

Your mind is all as youthful as your blood.

Now hear me speak with a prophetic spirit;

For even the breath of what I mean to speak

Shall blow each dust, each straw, each little rub,

Out of the path which shall directly lead

Thy foot to England's throne. And therefore mark: 130

John hath seized Arthur, and it cannot be

That whiles warm life plays in that infant's veins,

The misplaced John should entertain an hour,

One minute, nay, one quiet breath, of rest.

A sceptre snatched with an unruly hand

Must be as boisterously maintained as gained.

And he that stands upon a slipp'ry place

Makes nice of no vile hold to stay him up.

That John may stand, then Arthur needs must fall.

So be it, for it cannot be but so.   140

LOUIS THE DAUPHIN

But what shall I gain by young Arthur's fall?

CARDINAL PANDULPH

You, in the right of Lady Blanche your wife,

May then make all the claim that Arthur did.

LOUIS THE DAUPHIN

And lose it, life and all, as Arthur did.

---

133 misplaced John] ROWE; mis-plac'd-*Iohn* F   an] F; one COLLIER 1858

---

126 **prophetic** predictive, presageful (so *a.* 2, citing this line as its earliest example)

128 **dust** grain of dust (Honigmann, 3.3.128n)
   rub variation in the surface of a bowling green (recalling the Bastard's imagery at 2.1.575–84)

132 **infant's** Describing Arthur thus is part of Shakespeare's effort to intensify John's crime, but *infant* in the common law meant 'minor' and 'in the case of a ruler, one who has not reached the age at which he becomes constitutionally capable of exercising sovereignty' (*sb.*[1] 2); in Spenser and other writers of epic

romance, 'infant' means simply 'a youth of noble or gentle birth' (3).

133 **misplaced** This line is *OED*'s earliest citation for the *ppl. a.*

136 **boisterously** violently. Some elision ('boist'rously') is needed for the metre.

137 **slipp'ry place** As Honigmann notes, the phrase 'slippery places' occurs in Psalms 73: 18; early Tudor usage (e.g., in Wyatt) especially associates the adjective with high estate and hence with the turning of Fortune's wheel (see *stand* and *fall*, l. 139).

138 **Makes nice** displays reluctance, makes scruple
   stay support, maintain

CARDINAL PANDULPH

How green you are and fresh in this old world!
John lays you plots. The times conspire with you,
For he that steeps his safety in true blood
Shall find but bloody safety and untrue.
This act, so evilly borne, shall cool the hearts
Of all his people and freeze up their zeal,   150
That none so small advantage shall step forth
To check his reign, but they will cherish it.
No natural exhalation in the sky,
No scope of nature, no distempered day,
No common wind, no customèd event,
But they will pluck away his natural cause
And call them meteors, prodigies, and signs,
Abortives, presages, and tongues of heaven,
Plainly denouncing vengeance upon John.

LOUIS THE DAUPHIN

Maybe he will not touch young Arthur's life,   160
But hold himself safe in his prisonment.

145 world!] F (~ ?)   149 evilly borne] F (euilly borne); vilely born OXFORD

146 **lays you plots** i.e., intrigues on your behalf rather than his own, as he supposes (*you* = an ethical dative)

147–8 **steeps his safety . . . untrue** Noble (p. 117) sees an allusion to Genesis 9: 6 ('Whoso sheddeth men's blood . . .'), but the related and proverbial 4.2.104–5, below, make the biblical parallel less persuasive; antimetabole (safety . . . blood | bloody safety) gives the lines a sententious quality.

149 **borne** sustained, carried through. F's *borne* could also represent modern 'born' (the reading of Ff3–4), in which case a paraphrase might be, 'This act will be born in evil and mature into the populace's disaffection'.

151 **None so small** not the tiniest

153–9 **No natural exhalation . . . vengeance upon John** Pandulph's prediction is fulfilled; see 4.2.182–6.

153 **exhalation** meteor

154 **No scope of nature** i.e., 'Nothing within the limits of nature's power' (Smallwood)

155 **customèd** accustomed, common, ordinary

158 **Abortives** 'things produced contrary to the common course of nature, like monstrous births' (Wright; *OED*'s entry does not include the usage here)
   presages See 1.1.28n.

159 **denouncing** See 3.1.319n.

161 **hold himself safe in his prisonment** i.e., John will regard himself as being safe while Arthur is imprisoned. This reflexive meaning does not appear in *OED* (for example, *hold, v.* 7c: 'To keep oneself; to adhere, remain, keep' or 27: 'To restrain oneself, refrain, forbear'). A more strained interpretation would understand *himself* to mean 'him' (i.e., Arthur) in which case *safe* would have the meaning 'secured, kept in custody; not at present dangerous' (*safe, adj.* 10, from c.1600), but 'himself' for 'him' is un-Shakespearian, although the reverse ('him' for 'himself', 'her' for 'herself', etc.) is not (see, e.g., *Romeo* 3.5.143: 'Doth she not count her blest', and Abbott §223).

CARDINAL PANDULPH

   O sir, when he shall hear of your approach—
   If that young Arthur be not gone already—
   Even at that news he dies. And then the hearts
   Of all his people shall revolt from him,
   And kiss the lips of unacquainted change,
   And pick strong matter of revolt and wrath
   Out of the bloody fingers' ends of John.
   Methinks I see this hurly all on foot;
   And O, what better matter breeds for you   170
   Than I have named. The bastard Faulconbridge
   Is now in England ransacking the church,
   Offending charity. If but a dozen French
   Were there in arms, they would be as a call
   To train ten thousand English to their side,
   Or, as a little snow, tumbled about,
   Anon becomes a mountain. O noble Dauphin,
   Go with me to the King. 'Tis wonderful
   What may be wrought out of their discontent,
   Now that their souls are topfull of offence.   180
   For England, go! I will whet on the King.

LOUIS THE DAUPHIN

   Strong reasons make strange actions. Let us go,
   If you say ay, the King will not say no.   *Exeunt*

---

182 make] CAPELL; makes F   strange] F1; strong F2   183 ay] F (I)

167–8 **pick . . . fingers' ends** Moore Smith
paraphrases: 'And find good cause for
revolt in John's bloody finger-tips, viz. in
the crimes which John has instigated or
touched with his finger-tips, though he
has not performed them with his own
hands'. See Tilley F244, 'I sucked
(picked) not this (To suck, pick) out of
my fingers' ends'.

167 **matter** word-play: 'corrupt matter, pus;
argument' (Honigmann, 3.3.167n)

169 **Methinks I see** Pandulph continues to
speak 'with a prophetic spirit' (3.4.126).
hurly commotion; strife

173 **French** French persons (earliest citation
for *a.* and *sb.* B.2)

174 **call** decoy (as in bird-hunting)

175 **train** allure, entice

176–7 **a little snow . . . becomes a mountain**

Earliest known instance of Tilley S595,
'Like a snowball, that rolling becomes
bigger' (Dent adds instances that pre-
date Tilley's earliest).

180 **topfull** brim-full

182 **make** As the Oxford edition notes, the
compositor who set 'makes' probably
anticipated the first letter of 'strange'.
strange actions Foolish or unexpected
military deeds; Honigmann draws attention to this same sentiment in the Bastard's earlier soliloquies (at the end of
Acts 1 and 2); there may also be a
hint of *strange* = foreign (i.e., the French
invasion of England). Ff2–4 simplify and
coarsen the line: Pandulph has per-
suaded Louis to act against his own
earlier convictions.

183 **ay** yes

4.1   *Enter Hubert and Executioners* ⌈*with a rope and irons*⌉

HUBERT

Heat me these irons hot, and look thou stand
Within the arras. When I strike my foot
Upon the bosom of the ground, rush forth
And bind the boy which you shall find with me
Fast to the chair. Be heedful. Hence, and watch.

AN EXECUTIONER

I hope your warrant will bear out the deed.

HUBERT

Uncleanly scruples fear not you. Look to't.

                                        Exeunt Executioners

Young lad, come forth; I have to say with you.
     Enter Arthur

ARTHUR

Good morrow, Hubert.

HUBERT   Good morrow, little prince.

ARTHUR

As little prince, having so great a title   10
To be more prince, as may be. You are sad.

HUBERT

Indeed, I have been merrier.

4.1] F (*Actus Quartus, Scaena prima*); *Actus Quintus, Scaena prima* Ff2–4   0.1 *with . . . irons*] OXFORD; *not in* F   7 scruples₍] F1; ~, F4; ~! ROWE 1714; ~: OXFORD   *Exeunt Executioners*] CAMBRIDGE; *not in* F

4.1 Location: a prison, historically in Rouen, but fictively somewhere in England. The time references suggest morning, perhaps very early morning. For historical accounts of the various reported threats to Arthur, see 3.3.66n and Introduction, pp. 45–6 and n. 1.

0.1 *Executioners* Persons who carry out, who put into effect, a command, design, or instruction; the Elizabethan sense was not limited to persons who carry out a death sentence or who kill on instruction. *irons* metal branding or cauterizing tools

1 **Heat me these irons hot** Hubert plans to burn Arthur's eyes (see ll. 39, 61), and illustrations of this scene (e.g., the superb one by James Northcote, Fig. 1) often copy post-Restoration staging and include a brazier. Elizabethan public theatre practice, however, would probably direct Hubert to hand the irons to an executioner for off-stage 'heating'.

2 **Within the arras** i.e., hidden behind a tapestry hanging on the walls. In practice, the *arras* may have been a curtain hung before one of the doors in the façade of the Elizabethan public theatre; Schmidt, *arras*, lists Shakespeare's numerous usages of the arras as a hiding place.

6 **bear out** sustain, justify

7 **Uncleanly scruples** A transferred adjective: scruples about being unclean (i.e., morally defiled).
   fear frighten

8 **have to say** am obliged to speak (*have*, v. B.I.7c)

10–11 **As little . . . as may be** i.e., I have few of the privileges of being a prince despite having claim to an even greater title, 'king'

11 **sad** serious, solemn, as well as 'sorrowful, mournful' (*adj.* A.5)

ARTHUR   'Mercy on me!
Methinks nobody should be sad but I.
Yet I remember, when I was in France,
Young gentlemen would be as sad as night
Only for wantonness. By my christendom,
So I were out of prison and kept sheep,
I should be as merry as the day is long.
And so I would be here, but that I doubt
My uncle practises more harm to me.   20
He is afraid of me, and I of him.
Is it my fault that I was Geoffrey's son?
No, indeed is't not. And I would to God
I were your son, so you would love me, Hubert.
HUBERT (*aside*)
If I talk to him, with his innocent prate
He will awake my mercy, which lies dead.
Therefore I will be sudden and dispatch.
ARTHUR
Are you sick, Hubert? You look pale today;
In sooth, I would you were a little sick,
That I might sit all night and watch with you.   30
I warrant I love you more than you do me.

12 me!] THEOBALD; ~ : F   18 I should] F; 'Should FLEAY   be as] F; be POPE   23 God]
OXFORD; heauen F

12 **'Mercy** F's apostrophe marks the absence
of 'God's'; see 'God's mercy, maiden!
Does it curd thy blood' (*All's Well*
1.3.145).

15 **as sad as night** The analogy arises from
sad = dark-coloured   and = mournful
(*a.* II.8 notes this mixture of meanings).

16 **wantonness** caprice, whim (so 1g, citing
this line, although 'disappointed or unfulfilled lasciviousness' seems possible)
By my christendom i.e., 'As I am a
Christian' (1b)

17 **and kept sheep** As Henry VI also wishes;
see *3 Henry VI* 2.5.21 ff.

18 **as merry as the day is long** Tilley D57
(Wilson, *ODEP*, has an example from
1566); the line has been emended to
regularize the metre, but the actor's slurring might be sufficient.

19 **doubt** fear

20 **practises** contrives, plots (Schmidt). See
1.1.214 and 4.3.63.

24 **son, so** F's punctuation indicates that
so = as a consequence, although *so*
might introduce a conditional clause: 'if
you loved me, I would then wish that I
were your son'.

29 **In sooth** truly

30 **watch** i.e., remain awake with a sick
person or at his bedside, for the purpose
of rendering help or comfort (I.1e: earliest
citation from 1691)

31 **warrant** declare, assert. Arthur unconsciously echoes another use of *warrant*
(l. 6), and Hubert immediately hands
the document to the prince. Although a
disyllable elsewhere in *K. John*, *warrant*
(pronounced 'warn') is here monosyllabic (see C. T. Onions, *A Shakespeare
Glossary* (1911) and *As You Like It* TLN
1989, 'God warne vs').

HUBERT *(aside)*

   His words do take possession of my bosom.

   (To Arthur) Read here, young Arthur. *(Aside)* How now,
      foolish rheum?

   Turning dispiteous torture out of door?

   I must be brief, lest resolution drop

   Out at mine eyes in tender womanish tears.

   (To Arthur) Can you not read it? Is it not fair writ?

ARTHUR

   Too fairly, Hubert, for so foul effect.

   Must you with hot irons burn out both mine eyes?

HUBERT

   Young boy, I must.

ARTHUR   And will you?

HUBERT   An I will.   40

ARTHUR

   Have you the heart? When your head did but ache,

   I knit my handkerchief about your brows—

   The best I had, a princess wrought it me—

   And I did never ask it you again;

   And with my hand at midnight held your head,

   And like the watchful minutes to the hour,

---

40 An] F (And) 42 handkerchief] F (hand-kercher) 46 watchful minutes, to] THEOBALD;
watchfull minutes, to F; minutes watchful to DELIUS *conj.*

34 **dispiteous** pitiless, merciless. *OED* does
not regard 'despiteous' (where it cites
this line) as archaic, although all but one
of its nineteenth-century citations use
the form adopted here.

35 **brief** quick, short
resolution Determination, but *resolution*
and *dissolution*, *resolve* and *dissolve* were
thoroughly mixed in their Elizabethan
meanings, so a pun on 'melting into
liquid' (see *resolution*, I.4, 'conversion to
a fluid state', first cited from 1644) is
probable.

37 **Can you not read it?** The question intensifies the moment's pathos, since fulfilment of the *writ* will prevent Arthur from
reading anything.
fair writ clearly written, but ironically
alluding to the moral sense of *fair*

40 **must . . . will** A common expression joins
must and *will*: Dent M1330.1 'I (etc.)
must and will'; see next n.

An if. Many editors retain F's *And* (the
copulative), and Dent M1330.1 supports
that reading. *An*, however, continues
Hubert's wavering at ll. 33 ff.

42–3 **I knit . . . wrought it me** For the
Elizabethan audience, this anecdote
would succinctly convey Arthur's
generosity; handkerchiefs were expensive and fashionable, articles of adornment more than use, as their prominence
in contemporary aristocratic portraiture
suggests. See Linthicum, p. 270; Max U.
von Boehn, *Modes and Manners*, trans. J.
Joshua, 4 vols. (1932–5), ii. 191 and
iii. 162; Norbert Elias, *The History of
Manners: The Civilizing Process*, vol. 1,
trans. E. Jephcott (New York, 1978),
Chap. 6; for illustrations, see Roy Strong,
Tudor and Jacobean Portraits, 2 vols.
(1969), plates 111, 379, 618.

46 **watchful minutes** The phrase blends the
meaning of *watch* in l. 30 with *watch* =

Still and anon cheered up the heavy time,
Saying, 'What lack you?' and 'Where lies your grief?'
Or 'What good love may I perform for you?'
Many a poor man's son would have lain still   50
And ne'er have spoke a loving word to you;
But you at your sick service had a prince.
Nay, you may think my love was crafty love,
And call it cunning. Do, an if you will.
If heaven be pleased that you must use me ill,
Why then you must. Will you put out mine eyes—
These eyes that never did, nor never shall,
So much as frown on you?
HUBERT   I have sworn to do it.
And with hot irons must I burn them out.
ARTHUR
Ah, none but in this iron age would do it!   60
The iron of itself, though heat red-hot,
Approaching near these eyes, would drink my tears
And quench this fiery indignation
Even in the matter of mine innocence;

50 lain] F4; lyen F1. *See note.*   52 sick service] F; *hyphenated by* DELIUS   54 an] F (and)
60 it!] CAPELL; ~ : F   63 this] F; his CAPELL   64 matter] F; water DYCE 1864 (*conj.*
Williams)

timepiece and *watchful* = on guard, as
the minutes await the approaching
hour; Smallwood plausibly supposes that
Arthur's 'solicitous inquiries' divide 'the
heavy time' (l. 47) as minutes do an
hour, making it pass more quickly.
47 **heavy** slow-moving, sluggish
49 **love** act of kindness, a favour. See *Pericles*
8.44–6, when Helicanus asks a delay in
being named Pericles' substitute: 'But if
I cannot win you to this love, | A
twelvemonth longer then let me entreat
you | Further to bear the absence of your
king', and perhaps *Measure* 2.3.42–3:
'O injurious love [F: many editors read
'law'], | That respites me a life'.
50 **Many a poor . . . lain still** The line may
imply that Arthur and Hubert, prisoner
and jailor, shared a room or, as Elizabethan custom had it, a bed.
50 **lain** F's *lyen* had become archaic by the
nineteenth century, and F prints *laine*
(*Hamlet* 5.1.168) where Q2 reads *lyen*
(M3ᵛ).

53 **crafty** hypocritically self-serving
54 **an if** if
55–6 **must . . . must** See Tilley M1331,
'What must (shall, will) be must (shall,
will) be'; Wilson has an example from
1519, and there are numerous Shakespearian uses.
57 **never did, nor never shall** Delius pointed
out that the same phrase occurs at
5.7.112.
60 **iron age** The last, gloomiest, most degenerate of the four classical ages of the
world: Gold, Silver, Bronze, Iron; Arthur
finds the instrument of torture appropriately made of iron.
61 **heat** heated. For the grammatical form,
see 3.1.173, 4.1.105–7n, and Abbott
§342. Malone cites Daniel 3: 19: 'He
charged and commanded that they
should heat the furnace one seven times
more than it was wont to be heat'.
64 **matter** Substance. A misreading of manuscript *wat(t)er* is unlikely.

Nay, after that, consume away in rust,
But for containing fire to harm mine eye.
Are you more stubborn-hard than hammered iron?
An if an angel should have come to me
And told me Hubert should put out mine eyes,
I would not have believed him. No tongue   70
But Hubert's.

> *Hubert stamps*

HUBERT (*to Executioners*) Come forth!

> *Enter Executioners with heated iron*

                                    Do as I bid you do.

ARTHUR

O save me, Hubert, save me! My eyes are out
Even with the fierce looks of these bloody men.

HUBERT (*to Executioners*)

Give me the iron, I say, and bind him here.

> *He takes the iron*

ARTHUR

Alas, what need you be so boist'rous-rough?
I will not struggle; I will stand stone-still.
For God's sake, Hubert, let me not be bound.
Nay, hear me, Hubert! Drive these men away,
And I will sit as quiet as a lamb.
I will not stir, nor wince, nor speak a word,   80
Nor look upon the iron angrily.

---

67 stubborn-hard] THEOBALD 1740; *not hyphenated in* F   68 An] F (And)   70–1 No tongue | But Hubert's] HONIGMANN; *as one line* F   71 *Hubert stamps*] *not in* F   71 forth!] HONIGMANN; ~ : F   *Enter . . . iron*] *not in* F   72 me!] THEOBALD; ~ : F   74.1 *He . . . iron*] OXFORD; *not in* F   75 boist'rous-rough] THEOBALD; boistrous rough F   76 stone-still] ROWE; *not hyphenated in* F   77 God's] MATCHETT; heauen F   78 Hubert!] CAPELL; *Hubert,* F   80 wince] F (winch)   81 angrily] F (angerly)

68 **An if** if
70–1 **I would . . . Hubert's** These lines occur in the very crowded first column of a page set late in the gathering; Compositor B could not now rectify any errors in casting off and would therefore be likely to compress his text as much as possible, especially when he foresaw the number of short lines each needing a speech-prefix at 4.1.89–90. Casting off may not have taken sufficient account of the numerous scene headings in this quire; note also the absence of directions for the executioners' second entry and exit.

71 **with heated iron** See 4.1.1n and 4.1.74.
72–3 **My eyes . . . bloody men** i.e., the executioners' terrible appearance is sufficient to blind me (*out* = 'dislocated, extracted')
76 **stone-still** A conventional analogy: Dent S879.1 (Whiting has numerous examples from *c.*1200 onward).
79 **quiet as a lamb** Tilley L34, 'As gentle (quiet, meek, mild, etc.) as a lamb' (from 1520 and several uses in Shakespeare)
80 **wince** recoil in pain or fear
81 **angrily** with resentment. F's *angerly* is archaic.

Thrust but these men away, and I'll forgive you,
Whatever torment you do put me to.
HUBERT (*to Executioners*)
Go stand within. Let me alone with him.
AN EXECUTIONER
I am best pleased to be from such a deed.

Exeunt Executioners

ARTHUR
Alas, I then have chid away my friend!
He hath a stern look, but a gentle heart.
Let him come back, that his compassion may
Give life to yours.
HUBERT   Come, boy, prepare yourself.
ARTHUR
Is there no remedy?
HUBERT   None, but to lose your eyes.   90
ARTHUR
O heaven, that there were but a mote in yours,
A grain, a dust, a gnat, a wandering hair,
Any annoyance in that precious sense!
Then, feeling what small things are boisterous there,
Your vile intent must needs seem horrible.
HUBERT
Is this your promise? Go to! Hold your tongue!
ARTHUR
Hubert, the utterance of a brace of tongues
Must needs want pleading for a pair of eyes.
Let me not hold my tongue. Let me not, Hubert,
Or Hubert, if you will, cut out my tongue,   100
So I may keep mine eyes. O, spare mine eyes,
Though to no use but still to look on you.

85.1 *Exeunt Executioners*] CAMBRIDGE; *not in* F   86 friend!] CAMBRIDGE; ∼, F   91 mote] F (moth)   93 sense!] CAPELL; ∼ : F   96 to!] This edition; too, F   tongue!] SMALLWOOD; toong. F   100 will,] F4; will∧ F1

84 **Let** leave
85 **from** away from, absent from
86 **chid away** driven off through complaints
90 **no remedy . . . but** a common verbal formula (Dent RR2)
94 **boisterous** painfully rough (so *a.* I.4, quoting this line and *Romeo* 1.4.26 as earliest instances)
96 **Go to!** exclamation expressing protest or

remonstrance (*v.* VII.91)
97–8 **utterance . . . eyes** i.e., two (= *a brace of*) tongues must lack (= *want*) sufficient power to beg for two (= *a pair of*) eyes
98 **want** lack
100 **cut out my tongue** See Edward Coke's comment quoted in the Introduction, p. 45 n. 1.
102 **still** always

Lo, by my troth, the instrument is cold
And would not harm me.

HUBERT　　　　　　　　　　I can heat it, boy.

ARTHUR

No, in good sooth. The fire is dead with grief,
Being create for comfort, to be used
In undeserved extremes. See else yourself:
There is no malice in this burning coal;
The breath of heaven hath blown his spirit out,
And strewed repentant ashes on his head.　　　　　　110

HUBERT

But with my breath I can revive it, boy.

ARTHUR

An if you do, you will but make it blush
And glow with shame of your proceedings, Hubert.
Nay, it perchance will sparkle in your eyes,
And, like a dog that is compelled to fight,
Snatch at his master that doth tar him on.
All things that you should use to do me wrong
Deny their office. Only you do lack
That mercy, which fierce fire and iron extends,
Creatures of note for mercy, lacking uses.　　　　　　120

112 An] F (And)　116 tar] F (tarre)　120 mercy, lacking] F; mercy-lacking POPE

105–7 **The fire . . . undeserved extremes**
i.e., since fire was created (= *create*; see
Abbott §342) to give comfort, it feels grief
and dies when used as an instrument of
unjust (= *undeserved*) severity (= *extremes*). Honigmann aptly cites *in ex-
tremis*, the last moments of life (so also
C.2).

109 **breath of heaven** divine grace, divine
intervention
spirit Since the fire is personified, *spirit*
probably means 'anger, hostility' but
may also mean 'essence'; see 5.1.71n
and 5.2.74.

110 **strewed repentant ashes on his head**
As a religious penitent might do in
humility. The imagery, if not the sentiment, strongly recalls Sonnet 73, and
the entire passage parallels *Richard II*
5.1.46–9: 'the senseless brands will
sympathize | The heavy accent of thy
moving tongue, | And in compassion
weep the fire out; | And some will mourn
in ashes, some coal black'.

111 **my breath . . . can revive it** Hubert
can reverse the effects of 'The breath of
heaven' (l. 109).

112 **An if** if

114 **sparkle** Throw off sparks or embers (*v.*[1]
I.2), thereby harming Hubert's eyes (see
ll. 91–2), but since *sparkle* also frequently
describes bright or lively *eyes*, there may
be word-play on the fire's reflection in
Hubert's eyes and a transferred sense,
'dazzle'.

115–16 **like a dog . . . him on** These lines
encapsulate the principal–agent relation
analysed in John's attack on Hubert at
4.2.208 ff.

116 **tar** incite, urge. *OED* regards *tarre*
(printed by many editors) as archaic.

118 **office** function, duty

119 **fire . . . uses** Tilley F254, 'Fire and
water have no mercy' (from 1585; close
analogue in Whiting from 1515 and see
his F188 and F209).

120 **Creatures . . . lacking uses** i.e., (fire and
iron may be considered) merciful when

HUBERT

Well, see to live. I will not touch thine eye
For all the treasure that thine uncle owns.
Yet am I sworn, and I did purpose, boy,
With this same very iron to burn them out.

ARTHUR

O, now you look like Hubert. All this while
You were disguisèd.

HUBERT   Peace, no more. Adieu.
Your uncle must not know but you are dead.
I'll fill these doggèd spies with false reports,
And, pretty child, sleep doubtless and secure
That Hubert for the wealth of all the world   130
Will not offend thee.

ARTHUR   O heaven! I thank you, Hubert.

HUBERT

Silence, no more. Go closely in with me.
Much danger do I undergo for thee.   *Exeunt*

4.2   ⌐*Flourish.*⌐ *Enter King John, the Earls of Pembroke*
and Salisbury, and other lords. King John ascends the
throne

122 owns] F (owes)   131 heaven] F (heauen); God OXFORD
   4.2] F (*Scena Secunda*)   0.1 Flourish] OXFORD; *not in* F   0.1–2 *Enter . . . lords*] F (*Enter
Iohn, Pembroke, Salisbury, and other Lordes.*)   0.2–3 *King . . . throne*] OXFORD; *not in* F

they are not put to the merciless use you,
Hubert, intend. Pope's popular emendation makes the line mean, 'fire and
iron are notable for their merciless uses'.
121 **see to live** literally, attend to the needs
of living (*see*, *v*. B.II.25b), but mixed with
'retain your sight in order to live'
122 **owns** Honigmann finds a pun: the treasure John *owns*, and the reward he *owes*
Hubert and promised in 3.3; 'all the
treasure', however, makes the first reading dominant, perhaps exclusive, since
Hubert wishes to intensify the magnitude
and the danger of sparing Arthur, not to
complain about unfulfilled promises.
125–6 **now you look . . . disguisèd** Hubert's
appearance and others' interpretation of
it are central issues in 4.2; see Introduction, pp. 46–8.
128 **doggèd** Dog-like (*a.* 1a, citing 4.3.149),
but presumably with some pejorative

canine associations (e.g., surly), but
hardly 'cruel' (as many editors claim)
since the executioners have shown themselves quite otherwise.
false reports Hubert 'caused it to be
bruited abroad through the country that
the King's commandment was fulfilled,
and that Arthur through sorrow and
grief was departed out of this life. For
the space of fifteen days, this rumour
incessantly ran through both the realms
of England and France' (Holinshed,
165b; P3); see 4.2.69 ff.
129 **doubtless** free of fear. See 4.1.19.
132 **closely** secretly, covertly
133 **undergo** suffer, bear
4.2 Location: the royal court, somewhere in
England. This scene and the next bridge
the two historical periods Shakespeare
dramatizes, the early part of the reign
(from John's accession to Arthur's death

KING JOHN

Here once again we sit, once again crowned,
And looked upon, I hope, with cheerful eyes.

PEMBROKE

This 'once again', but that your highness pleased,
Was once superfluous. You were crowned before,
And that high royalty was ne'er plucked off,
The faiths of men ne'er stainèd with revolt;
Fresh expectation troubled not the land
With any longed-for change or better state.

SALISBURY

Therefore, to be possessed with double pomp,
To guard a title that was rich before,   10
To gild refinèd gold, to paint the lily,
To throw a perfume on the violet,

---

1 again crowned] F3; against crown'd F1   8 longed-for change] F4; long'd-for-change F1

in 1203) and the late (Peter's prophecy in 1212 and execution in 1213 to Louis's invasion and John's death in 1216).

0.2 *other lords* For the staging, see Introduction, pp. 22–3.

0.2–3 *King . . . throne* In the Elizabethan theatre, John's recent recoronation might have been emphasized visually through giving the actor a more formal costume than he wore earlier or by representing a more ceremonious entry (with orb, sceptre, or mace, for instance) than accompanied his earlier appearances. Many modern productions (e.g., Old Vic, 1953) have John enthroned for this scene, as line 1 implies.

1 **again** F3's emendation has been widely accepted, although *OED, against, adv.,* C cites 'against' = 'again' once (from *c.*1480).

2 **cheerful eyes** Synecdoche: *eyes* = noblemen; see Introduction, pp. 46–8.

4 **superfluous** Multiple coronations were common into the thirteenth century (Henry II, Richard I, and Henry III were all crowned twice), but they would have seemed strange and perhaps suspicious to Elizabethans; see Fig. 2 and, for John's coronations, P. E. Schramm, *A History of the English Coronation*, trans. L. G. Wickham Legg (Oxford, 1937), pp. 58–9.

6 **stainèd** dyed, (dis)coloured; figuratively, tainted with guilt

7 **Fresh expectation** new, or renewed, anticipation

9 **be possessed with double pomp** be made owner (or ruler) of England in a second (= *double*) ceremony (= *pomp*); be owned by excessive ceremony. In this construction, 'with' is both a prepositional complement to the verb and part of an adverbial prepositional phrase: 'be possessed with' and 'with double pomp'. Shakespeare omits direct mention of what John possesses (crown, state, England) to permit the double meaning and to initiate the nobles' *sotto voce* claim that John is not the legitimate, but only the stronger, monarch. For related uses of 'to possess', see 4.2.145n, 4.2.203n, 4.3.23n, and Introduction pp. 49–51.

10–15 **To guard . . . garnish** Honigmann (4.2.11–12n) sees a version of rhetorical 'climax' or *gradatio*: 'from part-perfect to wholly perfect' instances and 'motion upwards' from beneath the earth's surface to the heavens.

10 **guard** word-play: decorate with 'guards', the ornamental border or trimming of a garment; defend, protect

11 **gild refinèd gold** *Gild* = to cover a less precious material with gold or other precious metal; gilding gold is therefore an example of supererogation. Like much else in the speech, the image may be conventional; see Introduction, p. 81.

To smooth the ice, or add another hue
Unto the rainbow, or with taper-light
To seek the beauteous eye of heaven to garnish,
Is wasteful and ridiculous excess.

PEMBROKE

But that your royal pleasure must be done,
This act is as an ancient tale new told,
And in the last repeating, troublesome,
Being urged at a time unseasonable.   20

SALISBURY

In this the antique and well-noted face
Of plain old form is much disfigurèd,
And like a shifted wind unto a sail,
It makes the course of thoughts to fetch about,
Startles and frights consideration,
Makes sound opinion sick and truth suspected,
For putting on so new a fashioned robe.

PEMBROKE

When workmen strive to do better than well,

20 urged] F (vrged); urgèd DYCE   21 well-noted] POPE; *not hyphenated in* F

13–14 **add . . . rainbow** Salisbury presumably regards this as a difficult or impossible task: see Tilley C519, 'As many colors
as there are in the rainbow' (Wilson,
ODEP, has examples from 1562; Shakespeare uses the analogy on two other
occasions to express multitude).
14–15 **taper-light . . . garnish** See Tilley
S988, 'To set forth the sun with a candle
(lantern, taper)'.
15 **eye of heaven** the sun (a conventional
Elizabethan periphrasis)
18–19 **ancient tale . . . troublesome** See
3.4.108n.
20 **Being . . . unseasonable** The line does not
scan easily, although *urged* may be given
full syllabic value and *unseasonable*
slightly slurred.
21 **antique** ancient
well-noted widely known, and properly
so, but mixed with 'distinguished, celebrated, famous' (*ppl. a.* 1)
23 **shifted** changed in direction. This line is
OED's earliest citation for the *ppl. a.*,
which also antedates uses of the finite
verb (*v.* 14).
24 **It** i.e., the second coronation

fetch about change tack or direction.
The verb completes a series of nautical
metaphors.
25 **consideration** attentive thought, reflection, but perhaps also in this context
'regard among men, esteem' (8)
26 **sound** healthy
27 **so new a fashioned robe** garment recently
made; garment in up-to-date style. This
'robe' serves treble metaphoric duty: it
disfigures old form (ll. 21–2); it changes
the appearance of truth and puts it in
doubt (ll. 26–7); it clothes the newly-
crowned John. Clothing imagery has
already appeared in 'plucked off' (l. 5)
and 'stainèd' (l. 6).
28–9 **do better . . . covetousness** See Tilley
W260, 'Let well alone' (Wilson, *ODEP*,
has an instance from Chaucer); for other
versions of the idea, see 'Were it not
sinful then, striving to mend, | To mar
the subject that before was well?' (Sonnet
103.9–10); 'Striving to better, oft we
mar what's well' (*Lear* 1.4.325); Dent
M875.1, 'To mend and to mar'; Introduction, pp. 79–80.

They do confound their skill in covetousness,
And oftentimes excusing of a fault   30
Doth make the fault the worse by th'excuse,
As patches set upon a little breach
Discredit more in hiding of the fault
Than did the fault before it was so patched.

SALISBURY

To this effect, before you were new crowned,
We breathed our counsel; but it pleased your highness
To overbear it, and we are all well pleased,
Since all and every part of what we would
Doth make a stand at what your highness will.

KING JOHN

Some reasons of this double coronation   40
I have possessed you with, and think them strong.
And more, more strong, than lesser is my fear
I shall endue you with. Meantime, but ask
What you would have reformed that is not well,
And well shall you perceive how willingly
I will both hear and grant you your requests.

PEMBROKE

Then I, as one that am the tongue of these

---

31 worse] F; worser SMALLWOOD (*conj.* Maxwell²). *See note.*   th'] F; the CAMBRIDGE   35
new crowned] F; *hyphenated by* POPE   42 than] F (then); when TYRWHITT (*conj.* Thirlby);
the THEOBALD   lesser] F; less F2 (*subs.*)   is] F; in KEIGHTLEY

29 **confound** foil
   covetousness 'eager emulation' (Theobald); the desire 'to do better than well'
30–4 **And oftentimes . . . so patched** i.e.,
   excuses, like repairs of insignificant blemishes (e.g., in a wall, or on a face), often
   draw attention to what they would hide
   or extenuate. See Tilley E215, 'To excuse
   is to accuse'.
31 **Doth make . . . th'excuse** F's line is
   metrically suspect (elision in *th'excuse*,
   for example, was not forced on the compositor); since the two words most important to Pembroke's point are *worse*
   and *by*, an emphatic pause between them
   may have stretched the line into near-
   regularity, but Maxwell's conjecture is
   plausible and attractive.
35 **new crowned** i.e., crowned anew,
   crowned once more
38 **all and every** A legal formula; see, e.g.,
   Hughes and Larkin, 714 (1589).

39 **stand** stop, halt (Schmidt). 'If *stand* means
   withdrawal or cessation, this is a most
   dutiful speech, but it may equally well
   mean a defensive stance, and this is what
   Salisbury would like it to mean' (Mahood,
   p. 34).
42 **more strong, than lesser is my fear** 'i.e.,
   reasons stronger than my fear is less, or
   as strong as my fear is little' (White)
43 **endue** 'supply with' (so *endue, v.* 8c,
   quoting this line). F's *indue* existed side-
   by-side with *endue*, now the accepted
   form for 'all the living senses' (*OED*).
47–66 **Then I . . . his liberty** On this complex
   speech, see Introduction, pp. 41–3. Acting texts often cut the speech heavily: the
   Kemble prompt-book cuts 4.2.48–
   51, 54–60, 64–7, and even as late as
   1925, a Stratford production cut from
   the end of l. 52 to the beginning of l. 62
   and ll. 64–7.

To sound the purposes of all their hearts,
Both for myself and them, but chief of all
Your safety, for the which myself and them   50
Bend their best studies, heartily request
Th'enfranchisement of Arthur, whose restraint
Doth move the murmuring lips of discontent
To break into this dangerous argument.
If what in rest you have in right you hold,

---

55 rest] F; wrest STEEVENS *conj.*

---

48 **To sound** a pun: to measure the depth;
to utter, to give voice to
52 **enfranchisement** liberation from imprisonment (so 1, quoting this line as its
earliest example)
52–3 **whose restraint | Doth move** Part of
the speech's repeated contrasts between
immobility or imprisonment and action
or liberty; see *rest, hold, steps, move, mew
up, choke, exercise, ask* (ll. 55, 57, 58, 60,
63).
54 **this dangerous argument** A compressed
phrase: 'this summary of danger to
come'; 'this seditious subject matter'.
Pembroke described the restive populace
at ll. 6–7, but the phrase also introduces
the next six lines and emphasizes their
status as a report; the couplet closes
one phase of the speech and marks the
beginning of another.
55 **If . . . hold** The alliterating verbs appear
in two common Elizabethan contexts: (1)
vernacular deeds of conveyance, where
they translate *habendum et tenendum* in
Law French (see *OED, habendum,* and
Paul S. Clarkson and Clyde T. Warren,
*The Law of Property in Shakespeare and
the Elizabethan Drama* (1942; repr. New
York, 1968), pp. 124–5), and (2) the
marriage service in all the major pre-
Reformation service books and post-
Reformation books of common prayer
(see J. H. Blunt, *The Annotated Book of
Common Prayer* (1903), p. 453). Clarkson
and Warren find only one matrimonial
and two legal uses of 'to have and to
hold' in the drama, to which the matrimonial use in Marston's *Antonio and
Mellida* (Q1602), H4ᵛ, may be added, but
OED, have, v. B.I.1c traces the phrase
from *Beowulf* forward. See also Dent,
PLED, HH10.1. If the ritual echo
predominates here, an Elizabethan
audience might have continued the

allusion with the phrase 'till death us
depart' (see Sonnet 11.2 and Booth,
p. 150). Alliteration may also have
dictated an aphetic form (*rest* from
arrest; see *v.*¹ 2 and *sb.*¹ 1b). As part of
Shakespeare's attempt to put John's
authority in doubt, Pembroke may
simply repeat Eleanor's early contrast
between 'strong possession' (= [ar]rest)
and 'right' (1.1.40). The distinction is a
legal one between 'naked possession'
and 'justifiable claim' (see, respectively,
W. L. Rushton, *Shakespeare's Legal Maxims*
(1859; repr. 1907), pp. 19–20 and *right,
sb.*¹ II.7, also illustrating the phrase 'in
right'). Two other meanings have been
offered for *rest*: 'wrest' (Steevens) and
'quiet possession' (Wright; the meaning
of *rest, sb.*¹ I.4c). Even when reporting
what 'they say', Pembroke is unlikely to
use 'wrest', which implies coercion or
violence (neither of which has been
shown except for Arthur's imprisonment
and John's victory in France); *OED* provides neither a suitable definition nor
evidence for the phrase 'in wrest', but
see 'wrested pomp' (4.3.154), the punning on 'ill-wresting world' (Sonnet
140.11), and 'love's ill rest', l. 8, in the
version of Sonnet 138 printed in *The
Passionate Pilgrim* (see Booth, pp. 476,
479–80). The second gloss seems possible
and is supported by *rest, sb.*¹ I.4c, but
that meaning minimizes or obliterates
the antithesis implied by syntax and
alliteration. Finally, 'in rest' may derive
from primero, a card game in which
'rest' had two related meanings: 'the
name given to the stakes kept in reserve;
when these were lost the game termin-
ated. One's rest, therefore, became anything that one stood to win or lose'
(*Shakespeare's England,* ii. 473; see Nares,
rest, for illustrative quotations) and 'the

Why then your fears, which—as they say—attend
The steps of wrong, should move you to mew up
Your tender kinsman and to choke his days
With barbarous ignorance, and deny his youth
The rich advantage of good exercise.   60
That the time's enemies may not have this
To grace occasions, let it be our suit
That you have bid us ask his liberty,
Which for our goods we do no further ask,
Than, whereupon our weal on you depending
Counts it your weal, he have his liberty.

KING JOHN

Let it be so. I do commit his youth
To your direction—

56 then] F; should POPE   57 should] F; then POPE   60 exercise.] ROWE 1714; ~, F   65
Than,] F (Then,); ~ ∧ CAMBRIDGE

cards on which one stands to win' (Moore
Smith, 4.2.55n). Thus, the entire phrase
may mean: 'if your total committed stake
(in legitimacy) wins the game'.

56–7 **Why then . . . mew up** Pope's unlikely
emendation clarifies Pembroke's deliberate obscurity. The Earl must make his
plea for Arthur while attributing 'this
dangerous argument' to anonymous
others; hence *should* (l. 57) blends the
usage 'in the oblique report of another's
statement in order to imply that the
speaker does not commit himself to the
truth of the alleged fact' (*shall*, B.II.15)
with the usage 'In the apodosis of a
hypothetical proposition . . . indicating
that the supposition, and therefore its
consequence, is unreal' (B.II.19).

56 **as they say** Either a reminder that these
are reported attitudes, or a tag indicating
that 'fears . . . attend | The steps of
wrong' is proverbial. See: 'The wicked
flee when no man pursueth' (Proverbs
28 : 1), Tilley C606, 'A guilty conscience
feels continual fear' (Wilson, *ODEP*, has
an example from 1545), and F139, 'He
that lives ill, fear follows him' (earliest
example 1640). Giovanni Torriano, *Piazza universale di proverbi italiani* (1666),
lists several apposite phrases, including
'Who liveth an ill life, fear attends him'
(p. 196; see also pp. 48, 50).

58 **tender** youthful, immature. Armado justifies *tender* to Moth 'as a congruent
epitheton appertaining to thy young

days, which we may nominate "tender"'
(*LLL* 1.2.13–15).

60 **exercise** Since Arthur has been imprisoned, *exercise* may simply mean
'physical exertion or activity', but the
mention of 'barbarous ignorance' indicates a more general sense, 'practice for
the sake of training or improvement,
either bodily, mental, or spiritual' (*sb*. 6).
Orlando uses the word this way when he
demands a 'good education . . . such
exercises as may become a gentleman'
(*As You Like It* 1.1.63–4, 67–8).

62 **grace occasions** dignify or embellish pre-
texts or excuses

64–6 **Which . . . liberty** i.e., our welfare
depends upon yours and we seek what
is best for you; to gain our happiness we
ask only that Arthur be freed. Pembroke
tries to identify the nobles' aims with
John's while iterating (from ll. 62–3)
their submission; *whereupon* refers to
'goods' or to its clause (*adv*. II.3b), and
moving 'whereupon . . . your weal' to
follow 'our goods' clarifies the syntax
slightly.

64 **goods** happiness

65 **whereupon** about, as to, concerning
which (5)
weal happiness, prosperity

67–8 **commit his youth | To your direction**
i.e., give you charge over his education
and training

68–82 **To your direction . . . child's death**
Editors have added stage directions (e.g.,

Enter Hubert

Hubert, what news with you?

John takes Hubert aside

PEMBROKE (*to Salisbury*)

This is the man should do the bloody deed;
He showed his warrant to a friend of mine.   70
The image of a wicked heinous fault
Lives in his eye. That close aspect of his
Does show the mood of a much troubled breast,
And I do fearfully believe 'tis done,
What we so feared he had a charge to do.

SALISBURY (*to Pembroke*)

The colour of the King doth come and go
Between his purpose and his conscience,
Like heralds 'twixt two dreadful battles set.
His passion is so ripe it needs must break.

68 *Enter Hubert*] DYCE; *after l. 66* F   68.1 *John . . . aside*] CAPELL (*subs.*); *not in* F   73 Does]
F4; Do F1

Capell's *Taking him apart* at l. 68 and
Turning to the lords at l. 82) to indicate
that John and Hubert converse inaudibly
while Salisbury and Pembroke speculate
about what they see but do not hear;
the directions added here seem slightly
less arbitrary and restrictive than the
traditional ones.

68 *Enter Hubert* F places this entrance before
John's speech at l. 66, and many editors
believe that John agrees to his nobles'
request only after seeing Hubert and
assuming that he has arrived to report
Arthur's death. It may be so, but: (1) F's
placement of directions does not always
inspire confidence, (2) John might hypocritically agree without the added assurance of Hubert's silent presence, and (3)
if Hubert's appearance is supposed to be
sufficient warrant for John's confidence,
then John presumably has had few
doubts that his orders will have been
carried out. Leaving the direction in F's
position gives the audience a visible
reason for doubting John's sincerity, but
that doubt will in any case rest upon
earlier acting and staging decisions; F's
implied staging risks, moreover, being
rather crude and obvious. Repositioning
the direction has the merit of consistency
and hardly constrains theatrical freedom.

71–2 **image . . . eye** perhaps referring to the
belief, based on contemporary optical

theory, that the eye retained an impression (= *image*) of what it perceived

72 **close aspect** secretive expression, reticent
face; accent on second syllable of *aspect*.
Pembroke's assumption that appearance
signifies morality anticipates John's accu-
sations against Hubert (ll. 220 ff.).

73 **Does** F1's *Do* might represent a slurring
(*Does show* becoming *Do' show*) in spoken
dialogue or in the compositor's memory
of the line.
mood Both 'disposition' and 'the external
expression of a feeling'; Schmidt cites 'In
many's looks the false heart's history | Is
writ in moods and frowns and wrinkles
strange' (Sonnet 93.7–8).

76–8 **The colour . . . battles set** i.e., the
normal colour of John's complexion
waxes and wanes as if his blood attended,
as heralds do, first one army (*his purpose*)
and then an opposing army (*his conscience*). For a similar association of an
alternately red and white complexion
with 'heraldry' and 'silent war', see
Lucrece 52–7, partly quoted at 3.1.85–
6n. The expression 'come and go' (= appear and disappear) was common: see
Dent CC16.

78 **battles set** troops drawn up in formation
(before a battle). See 'The French are
bravely in their battles set' (*Henry V*
4.3.69).

79 **passion . . . break** i.e., John's passion is

PEMBROKE (*to Salisbury*)

And when it breaks, I fear will issue thence   80
The foul corruption of a sweet child's death.

KING JOHN

We cannot hold mortality's strong hand—
Good lords, although my will to give is living,
The suit which you demand is gone and dead.
He tells us Arthur is deceased tonight.

SALISBURY

Indeed, we feared his sickness was past cure.

PEMBROKE

Indeed, we heard how near his death he was
Before the child himself felt he was sick.
This must be answered either here, or hence.

KING JOHN

Why do you bend such solemn brows on me?   90
Think you I bear the shears of destiny?
Have I commandment on the pulse of life?

SALISBURY

It is apparent foul play, and 'tis shame
That greatness should so grossly offer it.
So thrive it in your game, and so farewell.

PEMBROKE

Stay yet, Lord Salisbury. I'll go with thee
And find th'inheritance of this poor child,
His little kingdom of a forcèd grave.

82 hand —] CAPELL (*subs.*); ~. F   93 foul play] CAPELL; *hyphenated in* F

an abscess near to rupture. See 'break out', l. 101.

82 **We . . . hand** This line seems to be the last John addresses to Hubert before speaking to the noblemen (l. 83: 'Good lords . . .'), but it may also be a line that 'covers' the actor's movement from his private interview with Hubert to his more public, theatrically more central debate with the nobles.

84 **gone and dead** The expression (Dent DD9, 'Dead and gone') is common from at least 1482 (*dead, a.* VI.32a).

89 **answered** accounted for, justified **here, or hence** both 'in this place, or elsewhere' and 'now, or later'

90 **bend** turn, incline

91 **shears of destiny** i.e., John is not Atropos, the Fate who cuts the thread of life spun by Clotho according to a lot assigned by Lachesis

93 **apparent** manifest, obvious, palpable

94 **greatness should so grossly offer it** i.e., 'a person of high rank should present it for (our) acceptance so palpably', but the assonance indicates word-play on *greatness* = large size and *grossly* = densely, thickly; see the antithesis on *foul* and *sweet* (l. 81).

95 **So** i.e., shamefully **game** deception, intrigue (*sb.* 5, without citations between *c.*1500 and 1614)

98 **forcèd** violently enforced, compelled

218

That blood which owned the breadth of all this isle,
Three foot of it doth hold. Bad world the while!   100
This must not be thus borne; this will break out
To all our sorrows, and ere long, I doubt.

> *Exeunt Pembroke, Salisbury, ⌐and other lords⌐*

KING JOHN

They burn in indignation. I repent.
There is no sure foundation set on blood,
No certain life achieved by others' death—

> *Enter Messenger*

A fearful eye thou hast. Where is that blood
That I have seen inhabit in those cheeks?
So foul a sky clears not without a storm;
Pour down thy weather: how goes all in France?

MESSENGER

From France to England. Never such a power   110
For any foreign preparation
Was levied in the body of a land.

---

99 owned] F (ow'd)   breadth] F (bredth); breath ROWE   100 while!] POPE; ~ : F   102.1
Pembroke . . . lords] OXFORD; *Exeunt* F; *Exeunt Lords* CAPELL   105.1 *Enter Messenger*] *as here*,
JOHNSON; *after* 'repent', *l.* 103 F (*Enter Mes.*)   110 MESSENGER] F (*Mes⟨senger⟩.; and thus
throughout*)

99–100 **blood which owned . . . Three foot
of it doth hold** See Tilley F582 'Six feet
of earth make all men equal' (Whiting
has examples—with 'seven feet'—from
about 1325); the idea also appears in
Richard II 3.3.152, 158, and Moore
Smith compares Hal's farewell to Hotspur
(*1 Henry IV* 5.4.88–91).

100 **Bad world the while!** it is a bad world
so long as (= *the while*) such things
happen. See 'God help the while. A bad
world, I say' (*1 Henry IV* 2.5.131–2).

102 **doubt** 'anticipate with apprehension' (*v.*
II.6a)

102.1 *Pembroke . . . lords* Hubert presumably remains in the background where
John left him at l. 82 and from which
John summons him at l. 155; this staging
is not especially clear or effective, and
it may even diminish the powerful exchange between John and the Messenger.
TR arranges these events very differently
(see Introduction, pp. 6–9).

104 **no sure foundation set on blood** A
similar phrase appears in Thomas Heywood's *The Iron Age, Part 2* (*c.*1612;
published 1632), Act 5: 'no building

long hath stood | Whose slight foundation
hath been laid in blood' (*Dramatic Works*,
ed. John Pearson, 4 vols. (1874), iii.
421). See 3.4.147–8n.

105.1 *Enter Messenger* F's positioning of
this stage direction may be 'anticipatory'
(either warning the actor to enter or
indicating the moment he physically step-
ped on stage), but Compositor B had even
less room in his measure at l. 105 than
at l. 103.

106 **fearful** Perhaps 'frightened' (because
the Messenger fears John's reaction), but
more likely 'fearsome, frightening', the
usual Shakespearian use of passive for
active (Abbott §3).

109 **weather** tempest, storm

110 **From France to England** The Messenger
turns John's general question, 'How goes
all in France', into a specific reply: all of
France *goes* (= travels) into England.
For the Messenger's word-play, see
Appendix B.

a power an armed force

111 **foreign preparation** military formation
(army, fleet) gathered to fight abroad;
preparation has five syllables

The copy of your speed is learned by them,
For when you should be told they do prepare,
The tidings comes that they are all arrived.

KING JOHN

O, where hath our intelligence been drunk?
Where hath it slept? Where is my mother's care,
That such an army could be drawn in France,
And she not hear of it?

MESSENGER   My liege, her ear
Is stopped with dust. The first of April died   120
Your noble mother; and as I hear, my lord,
The Lady Constance in a frenzy died
Three days before, but this from rumour's tongue
I idly heard. If true, or false, I know not.

KING JOHN *(aside)*

Withhold thy speed, dreadful Occasion!
O, make a league with me till I have pleased
My discontented peers. What? Mother dead?
How wildly then walks my estate in France!—
Under whose conduct came those powers of France,
That thou for truth giv'st out are landed here?   130

MESSENGER

Under the Dauphin.

KING JOHN   Thou hast made me giddy
With these ill tidings—

120, 122 died] F (di'de)   125 Occasion!] THEOBALD; ~ : F   128 France!] F (France?)

113 **copy** example
115 **tidings comes** singular verb with plural
   subject (Abbott §33)
116 **intelligence** 'secret service' (Wilson,
   Glossary)
117 **care** The initial letter is damaged in F;
   see Appendix B.
120 **The first of April** Eleanor died 1 April
   1204 (see Introduction, p. 15 n. 4);
   while retaining the historical day and
   month, Shakespeare has placed Eleanor's
   death (1204) before Arthur's (1203) and
   almost simultaneously with Constance's
   (1201).
122–3 **Constance . . . three days before**
   Historically, Constance died 31 August
   1201, almost three years (not days) before Eleanor.

125–8 *(aside)* . . . **France!—** The added
   direction at l. 125 and punctuation at
   l. 128 suggest that John is not (yet?) so
   frantic as to reveal his distress to the
   Messenger at ll. 129–30.
125 **Occasion** coincidence, eventuality. 'Occasion' was often personified as a fleeing
   woman whose progress could be controlled only through grasping a forelock
   on her otherwise bald head (see Tilley
   T311, quoted at 3.1.324n).
126 **make a league** form an alliance
128 **wildly** randomly, in disorder
   walks progresses, moves
   my estate my interests, my affairs
130 **thou for truth giv'st out** you report as
   accurate

Enter Bastard and Peter of Pomfret

                                          Now? What says the world
To your proceedings? Do not seek to stuff
My head with more ill news, for it is full.

BASTARD

But if you be afeared to hear the worst,
Then let the worst, unheard, fall on your head.

KING JOHN

Bear with me, cousin, for I was amazed
Under the tide, but now I breathe again
Aloft the flood and can give audience
To any tongue, speak it of what it will.   140

BASTARD

How I have sped among the clergymen,
The sums I have collected shall express.
But as I travelled hither through the land,
I find the people strangely fantasied,
Possessed with rumours, full of idle dreams,
Not knowing what they fear, but full of fear.
And here's a prophet that I brought with me
From forth the streets of Pomfret, whom I found
With many hundreds treading on his heels;
To whom he sung in rude harsh-sounding rhymes,   150

---

132 *Enter . . . Pomfret*] *as here,* JOHNSON; *after* 'Dauphin', *l.* 131 F   Now? What] F; ~, ~
ROWE   138 breathe] F (breath)   143 travelled] F (trauail'd)   150 harsh-sounding] POPE;
not hyphenated in F

---

132 *Peter of Pomfret* Holinshed (180a–b;
N4ᵛ) describes this 'prophet' and his
execution; Pomfret = Pontefract (now
in West Yorkshire).

135 **afeard to hear the worst** Proverbially,
'It is good to fear the worst' (Tilley W912)
because one may then take precautions,
as the Bastard implies (l. 136).

137 **amazed** Elizabethans understood a possible etymology in this word: John has
been in a 'maze'; see 4.3.140 and 'like
a labyrinth to amaze his foes' (*Venus*
684).

138 **tide** figuratively, the violent assault of
bad news, 'flooding' in upon John

139 **aloft** above, over. *OED* has only three
citations, the latest 1613, for *aloft* as a
preposition, and this is Shakespeare's
only such use.

141 **sped** succeeded, fared. Honigmann also
sees a pun: hastened.

143 **travelled hither** Two meanings: jour-
neyed to this place; laboured (= F's
trauail'd) to this purpose (i.e., collecting
money; see *hither, adv.* and *adj.* 4). The
quibble is common.

144 **strangely fantasied** unexpectedly or
abnormally (= *strangely*) filled with
imaginary ideas or visions. The Bastard
finds not the ideas but the condition and
its universality strange.

145 **Possessed with rumours** controlled by
or subjected to rumours; see 4.2.9n and
4.2.203n.

150 **rude harsh-sounding** For this sequence
of words, see 'How dares thy harsh
rude tongue sound this unpleasing news'
(*Richard II* 3.4.75).

That ere the next Ascension Day at noon,
Your highness should deliver up your crown.
KING JOHN
Thou idle dreamer, wherefore didst thou so?
PETER OF POMFRET
Foreknowing that the truth will fall out so.
KING JOHN
Hubert, away with him. Imprison him,
And on that day at noon whereon he says
I shall yield up my crown, let him be hanged.
Deliver him to safety and return,
For I must use thee.   *Exeunt Hubert and Peter*
         O my gentle cousin,
Hear'st thou the news abroad, who are arrived?   160
BASTARD
The French, my lord, men's mouths are full of it.
Besides, I met Lord Bigot and Lord Salisbury,
With eyes as red as new-enkindled fire,
And others more, going to seek the grave
Of Arthur, whom they say is killed tonight
On your suggestion.

159 *Exeunt . . . Peter*] THEOBALD (*subs.*); *not in* F   163 new-enkindled] POPE; *not hyphenated
in* F   165–6 Of . . . suggestion] ROWE 1714; *as one line* F

151 **Ascension Day** 'Holy Thursday', forty
days after Easter, commemorating
Christ's ascent to heaven, and the day
from which John's regnal year is reckoned; this line and 5.1.22, 25, 26 are
Shakespeare's only references to the feast.
151–2 **noon | . . . crown** The Bastard appar-
ently distorts the usual pronunciation of
crown to produce an exemplary 'harsh-
sounding' rhyme (see Cercignani, pp.
197–8).
152 **deliver up** surrender, hand over
154 **fall out** prove to, turn out
    so not a harsh rhyme, but an unimagin-
ative one
158 **safety** custody, confinement. John's
Deliver mocks Peter's reported prophecy
(l. 152).
159 **gentle** courteous, generous. Ingrati-
ation conveys John's anxiety and fear.
161 **men's mouths are full of it** A common
phrase (Dent MM19), cited by *OED*,
mouth, sb. 3g from after 1300; see
4.2.187.
163 **as red as new-enkindled fire** A conven-

tional image: Tilley F248, 'As red (bright)
as fire'.
165–6 **Of Arthur . . . your suggestion** F
prints as a single line with a turnover;
Compositor B was very close to the end
of the second column of b2^r here and
seems to have been crowding text; relineation also restores regular iambic
pentameter (see 4.1.70–1n). Since
tonight = last night, there are two grammatical confusions in l. 165, *whom* for
'who' and *is* for 'was'; the former may
simply be the common accusative-
through-attraction to the nearby verb
(here *say*), but both could have arisen if
the Bastard hovers between direct discourse (quoting the lords) and indirect
(reporting what 'they say') and thus both
accuses and does not accuse John of
inciting Arthur's death. In the latter
case, the Bastard here repeats the lords'
experience (and some of their verbal
antics) earlier in the scene.
166 **suggestion** prompting or incitement to
evil (1)

KING JOHN   Gentle kinsman, go
And thrust thyself into their companies.
I have a way to win their loves again;
Bring them before me.

BASTARD   I will seek them out.

KING JOHN

Nay, but make haste! The better foot before!   170
O, let me have no subject enemies,
When adverse foreigners affright my towns
With dreadful pomp of stout invasion.
Be Mercury, set feathers to thy heels,
And fly like thought from them to me again.

BASTARD

The spirit of the time shall teach me speed.

Exit Bastard

KING JOHN

Spoke like a sprightful noble gentleman—
Go after him; for he perhaps shall need
Some messenger betwixt me and the peers,
And be thou he.

170 haste!] SMALLWOOD; ~ : F   before!] HONIGMANN; ~ . F   171 subject] F1 (subiect);
subjects F2   176.1 *Exit Bastard*] F (*Exit*)

168 **a way to win their loves again** This
way is never specified, although an
audience might imagine that John intends to sacrifice Hubert to the nobles'
wrath.

170 **The better foot before** i.e., quickly, at
once. The same proverbial phrase (Tilley
F570) occurs at *Titus* 2.3.192.

171 **subject enemies** i.e., subjects (English
citizens) who are enemies. Almost an
oxymoron with the connotation of 'subjected, defeated, thrown down'.

173 **dreadful** i.e., inspiring dread, fear, or
awe (the passive for the active form; see
Abbott §3). See 'This to me | In dreadful
secrecy   impart   they   did'   (*Hamlet*
1.2.206–7).
pomp 'splendid show or display along a
line of march' (*sb.* 2)

174 **set feathers to thy heels** Like the goddess Fortune, Mercury is often represented with winged feet or sandals.

175 **fly like thought** A conventional (Tilley
T240) and ancient (Whiting has examples from *c.*1200 onward) simile that

Shakespeare used very frequently (see
Schmidt, *thought*, 2).

176 **spirit . . . speed** In a general sense,
the Bastard means that circumstances
require immediate response, but al-
chemical literature used 'spirit' as a central term, sometimes referring specifically
to mercury among the three or four
fundamental substances: '*Mercury* is a
sharp liquor . . . penetrable . . . a
most pure & *Æthereal* substantial body: a
substance airy, most subtle, quickening,
and full of spirit . . . . These three
beginnings, were by *Hermes* the most
ancient Philosopher, called *Spirit*, *Soul*,
and *Body*. *Mercury* the *Spirit*, *Sulphur* the
Soul, *Salt* the *Body*' (Joseph Du Chesne,
*The Practise of Chymicall and Hermeticall
Physicke*, trans. Thomas Timme (1605),
D1ᵛ; see also K3ᵛ and P4ᵛ). The Bastard's
'spirit of the time' may therefore respond
directly to John's request that he 'Be
Mercury'.

177 **sprightful** animated, lively (first citation
for *a.* 1). John plays on 'spirit' (l. 176).

4.2 		*The Life and Death of King John*

MESSENGER 		With all my heart, my liege. 			180

KING JOHN My mother dead!
    Enter Hubert
HUBERT
  My lord, they say five moons were seen tonight:
  Four fixèd, and the fifth did whirl about
  The other four in wondrous motion.
KING JOHN
  Five moons?
HUBERT 			Old men and beldams in the streets
  Do prophesy upon it dangerously.
  Young Arthur's death is common in their mouths,
  And when they talk of him, they shake their heads
  And whisper one another in the ear.
  And he that speaks doth grip the hearer's wrist 			190
  Whilst he that hears makes fearful action
  With wrinkled brows, with nods, with rolling eyes.
  I saw a smith stand with his hammer, thus,
  The whilst his iron did on the anvil cool,
  With open mouth swallowing a tailor's news,
  Who, with his shears and measure in his hand,
  Standing on slippers which his nimble haste
  Had falsely thrust upon contrary feet,
  Told of a many thousand warlike French
  That were embattailèd and ranked in Kent. 			200

180.1 *Exit Messenger*] ROWE (*subs.*); *not in* F 		181 dead!] ROWE; ~? F 		200 embattailèd]
F; embattled DELIUS

182 **five moons** These 'moons' appear as a
  special stage-effect in *TR*. In *The True*
  Tragedy of Richard Duke of York (1595) a
  direction reads, 'Three suns appear in
  the air' (B3ᵛ), and they are referred to in
  the dialogue of F's analogous passage, 3
  Henry VI, TLN 677 ff.
  tonight in Elizabethan usage often = 'last
  night'; see 4.2.165–6n
184 **wondrous** causing wonder or conster-
  nation
  motion trisyllabic
186 **dangerously** Three meanings: 'riskily'
  (as Peter of Pomfret's case demonstrates);
  'boldly' (*adv.* 3); 'of dangerous matters'
  (i.e., a grammatically transferred sense
  —from manner to subject-matter—not in

  OED). See 4.2.54n and Pandulph's prediction at 3.4.153 ff.
189 **whisper one another** whisper to one
  another
190 **grip** seize, clutch with the hand
191 **fearful action** 'Gestures or looks expressing fear', and, perhaps, 'gestures arous-
  ing fear in the auditor or spectator';
  action is trisyllabic.
193 **thus** The actor is directed to imitate the
  smith's pose.
196 **measure** graduated rod or tape for meas-
  uring cloth
198 **contrary** (accent on second syllable)
199 **a many thousand** many thousands of
200 **embattailèd** Either 'drawn up in battle
  array' or 'filled or covered with troops in

Another lean, unwashed artificer
Cuts off his tale and talks of Arthur's death.

KING JOHN

Why seek'st thou to possess me with these fears?
Why urgest thou so oft young Arthur's death?
Thy hand hath murdered him; I had a mighty cause
To wish him dead, but thou hadst none to kill him.

HUBERT

No had, my lord! Why, did you not provoke me?

KING JOHN

It is the curse of kings to be attended
By slaves that take their humours for a warrant
To break within the bloody house of life,   210
And on the winking of authority
To understand a law, to know the meaning
Of dangerous majesty, when perchance it frowns
More upon humour than advised respect.

HUBERT

Here is your hand and seal for what I did.
     He shows a paper

205 murdered] F (murdred)   207 HUBERT] F (H⟨ubert⟩.)   lord!] F (Lord?)   215 HUBERT] F
(Hub⟨ert⟩.; *and thus subs.* (Hu.) *for remainder of play*)   215.1 He . . . paper] OXFORD; *not in* F

battle array' (*ppl. a.*[1], 1 and 2); F's form
is needed for the metre and to distinguish
the word from the modern 'embattled'
meaning 'engaged in battle', 'under attack'.
   ranked drawn up in ranks (*ppl. a.*; earliest
citation 1786)
201 **artificer** artisan, workman. The sole use
in Shakespeare.
202 **Cuts off his tale** interrupts his speech
203 **possess me with these fears** communicate these fears to me; make these fears
own me (with a hint of diabolical 'possession'). See 4.2.9n, 4.2.145n, 4.3.23n.
205 **Thy hand . . . mighty cause** Metrically
powerful: a spondee begins the line,
another follows the caesura.
207 **No had** had I not, had I none. Though
well-attested, the usage is un-Shakespearian and may have been forced on
the compositor since the line is a very
full one, with the speech-prefix in F
reduced to H.
   provoke incite, urge, spur on
209–10 **a warrant . . . of life** i.e., the king's

transient whim becomes a legal document (= *warrant*) permitting entrance
into private property, the body itself,
filled with life-sustaining blood and *bloody*
when wounded
209 **their humours** i.e., temporary states of
kings' dispositions
210 **house of life** body. Cleopatra threatens,
'This mortal house I'll ruin' (*Antony*
5.2.50).
211–12 **winking . . . law** i.e., a small gesture
of connivance or inveiglement becomes
a mandate
213 **dangerous** threatening
   frowns Third in a series of less and less
overt signs of encouragement (*warrant*,
winking, *frowns*).
214 **advised respect** judicious or considered
attention or deliberation. *Respect*, *sb.*,
does not satisfactorily define this usage.
215 **hand and seal** i.e., autograph signature
and the wax impression of the royal
signet. Halliwell added a direction, 'The
King snatches the warrant out of Hubert's hand', and some such action would

KING JOHN

O, when the last account 'twixt heaven and earth
Is to be made, then shall this hand and seal
Witness against us to damnation.
How oft the sight of means to do ill deeds
Makes deeds ill done! Hadst not thou been by,   220
A fellow by the hand of Nature marked,
Quoted, and signed to do a deed of shame,
This murder had not come into my mind.
But taking note of thy abhorred aspect,
Finding thee fit for bloody villainy,
Apt, liable to be employed in danger,
I faintly broke with thee of Arthur's death.
And thou, to be endearèd to a king,
Made it no conscience to destroy a prince.
HUBERT My lord—   230

KING JOHN

Hadst thou but shook thy head, or made a pause
When I spake darkly what I purposèd,
Or turned an eye of doubt upon my face,

216 account] F (accompt)   220 Makes] THEOBALD; Make F   deeds ill done] F; ill deeds
done KNIGHT (*conj.* Thirlby); deeds ill-done FLEAY   done!] F (~ ?)   230 lord—] ROWE 1714;
Lord. F

make l. 217 literal (with John gesturing
at the paper), and give the metaphors of
ll. 221–2 a physical basis (John reads
Hubert's face as one may read the warrant).
216 **last account** last judgement
219–20 **ill deeds . . . deeds ill done** Immoral
acts . . . poorly or unskilfully accomplished acts. John continues the
scene's intermittent reference of symbolic
actions to physical ones; see the early
comparison of 'double pomp' with
'workmen . . . excusing of a fault' (ll. 9,
28–30).
221–2 **marked, | Quoted, and signed** All
three verbs can mean 'noted' or 'identified', but the phrase suggests a sequence: noted; written down or enrolled
(*quote, v.* II.5 cites 4.2.222 for this figurative meaning); ratified by signature. The
overriding metaphor remains that of
facial characteristics as expressive of
moral or psychological states (see 3.1.45 ff.
on Arthur's 'blots'). Some productions

literalize John's words through Hubert's
make-up: Michael Benthall's staging
(Stratford, 1948) gave Hubert (William
Monk) a Cyrano-grotesque nose and a
large wen on the left cheek.
224 **abhorred aspect** hateful appearance,
ugly face; accent on second syllable of
'aspect'. Again, John's present attitude
(revulsion) is treated as a quality of
Hubert. See 4.2.72 and n.
226 **liable** suitable, apt
227 **faintly** tentatively, hesitantly
    broke with thee mentioned to you, dis-
    cussed with you
228–9 **endearèd . . . destroy** The phonic
echo helps establish a slightly false antithesis that then carries into *king* and
prince.
229 **conscience** matter of conscience (III.8b,
with one citation from 1557)
232 **darkly** mysteriously, inexplicitly
233–4 **an eye . . . | As bid** i.e., such an
eye . . . as bid. *As* = such . . . as (see
Schmidt and Abbott §280), a correlative

As bid me tell my tale in express words,
Deep shame had struck me dumb, made me break off,
And those thy fears might have wrought fears in me.
But thou didst understand me by my signs
And didst in signs again parley with sin;
Yea, without stop, didst let thy heart consent,
And consequently thy rude hand to act   240
The deed which both our tongues held vile to name.
Out of my sight and never see me more!
My nobles leave me, and my state is braved,
Even at my gates, with ranks of foreign powers;
Nay, in the body of this fleshly land,
This kingdom, this confine of blood and breath,
Hostility and civil tumult reigns
Between my conscience and my cousin's death.
HUBERT
Arm you against your other enemies;
I'll make a peace between your soul and you.   250
Young Arthur is alive. This hand of mine
Is yet a maiden and an innocent hand,

234 As] F; Or POPE; And KEMBLE   242 more!] POPE; ∼ : F   246 breath] F (breathe)   252–
3 hand, . . . blood.] POPE; hand. . . . blood, F

construction with a missing element similar to Elizabethan 'Or . . . or' (4.3.42) for
modern 'either . . . or'.
  express plain or clear, leading to the
antithetical *dumb* (l. 235)
237–8 **my signs . . . sin** *Sin* could be spelled
  signe (Honigmann, 4.2.238n), and the
  words may have sounded sufficiently
  similar for word-play, but they did not
  rhyme (Cercignani, p. 349). John's metaphor suggests either *sin* is external to
  both Hubert and himself, an entity to
  which Hubert acts as emissary, or
  Hubert's external *signs* (appearance, expression) communicate with an internal
  sin.
238 **parley** treat, discuss terms (*v.*¹ 2; see
  parle, v. 2)
239–41 **heart consent . . . to name** The
  division of motive and act into heart
  (or head) and hand is characteristically
  Shakespearian; varied combinations of
  head, hand, heart, and tongue often
  serve as images of (in)sincerity: see *Hamlet* 1.2.47–8, *Two Gentlemen* 1.3.46
  (where *hand* = handwriting, as at *Richard*

II 5.3.51), *1 Henry VI* 5.5.17, *Errors*
4.2.18 and 4.2.28, *Shrew* 4.3.77, *Richard
II* 1.4.11. Sonnets 24, 46, 47, 93, 132,
and 133 are all what Booth (p. 489) calls
'eye and heart' poems and sometimes
address topics similar to John's here.
242 **never see me more** The phrase intensifies John's command; for its figurative
  significance, see Introduction, p. 48.
243 **braved** challenged tauntingly
245–8 **the body . . . cousin's death** The lines
  rest on a metaphor of England-as-body,
  a body of flesh, blood, and breath, but
  civil (= domestic, not foreign; civilian,
  not military) begins the transition to
  an inward rebellion within the king-as-
  England, the monarch as microcosm;
  Brutus claims that 'the state of man, |
  Like to a little kingdom, suffers then |
  The nature of an insurrection' (*Caesar*
  2.1.67–9) when he contemplates civil
  war.
252–3 **maiden . . . blood** Hubert analogizes
  the spilling of Arthur's blood with the
  blood of a virgin's ruptured maiden-
  head.

Not painted with the crimson spots of blood.
Within this bosom never entered yet
The dreadful motion of a murderous thought,
And you have slandered nature in my form,
Which howsoever rude exteriorly,
Is yet the cover of a fairer mind
Than to be butcher of an innocent child.
KING JOHN
Doth Arthur live? O, haste thee to the peers!   260
Throw this report on their incensèd rage
And make them tame to their obedience.
Forgive the comment that my passion made
Upon thy feature, for my rage was blind,
And foul imaginary eyes of blood
Presented thee more hideous than thou art.
O, answer not, but to my closet bring
The angry lords with all expedient haste.
I conjure thee but slowly. Run more fast!

Exeunt

260 peers!] SMALLWOOD; ~ , F   265 foul imaginary] F; foul-imaginary DYCE 1864 (*conj.* Walker)   269 fast!] HONIGMANN; ~ . F

255 **motion** 'Proposal, suggestion, instigation' (*sb.* 7) rather than 'inward prompting . . . instigation . . . from within' (*sb.* 9) which Hubert rejects; he thereby emphasizes John's responsibility.

257 **exteriorly** outwardly. Shakespeare's sole use of the word.

261 **Throw** cast, pour. The submerged metaphor is either that of water upon a fire (hot *rage*) or, more likely, the casting of incense, inspired by a pun on *incensèd* (see *All's Well* 5.3.24–5: 'deeper than oblivion we do bury | Th'incensing relics of it' [Bertram's offence]).

262 **make them tame to their obedience** i.e., 'make them tractable and submissive to authority' (*obedience*, 2, where there is no parallel for this construction until 1827); *tame*, *v.*[1] does not satisfactorily define the use here. See, however, Schmidt and *Troilus* 3.3.8–10, 'all | That time . . . Made tame and most familiar to my nature' and *Tragedy of Lear* 4.5.220, 'made tame to fortune's blows'). See 4.3.64 and n.

263 **comment** exposition, commentary

264 **feature** lineaments of the face (a collective noun; see 3)

265 **imaginary** 'Imaginative' (*a.* 2, citing this line as its earliest example), creating (false) images (the passive for the active adjective), but perhaps a play upon 'having no real existence' (1) since John has just declared that his 'rage was blind'.

266 **Presented . . . art** Faulty vision has distorted what it sees, another way of expressing the revulsion and guilt of l. 242.

267 **closet** private chamber

268–9 **The angry . . . more fast** A couplet (see Cercignani, p. 176) as F's spelling *hast* here and in rhymes elsewhere (*Romeo* 2.2.93–4; *Richard III* 2.4.14–15) makes clearer; the compositor may have been saving space when he set *hast* in l. 260; *hast* also appears in Qq of *Lucrece* and *Venus*.

268 **expedient** See 1.1.49n.

4.3   *Enter Arthur, disguised as a ship-boy, on the walls*

ARTHUR

The wall is high, and yet will I leap down.

Good ground, be pitiful and hurt me not!

There's few or none do know me; if they did,

This ship-boy's semblance hath disguised me quite.

I am afraid, and yet I'll venture it.

If I get down and do not break my limbs,

I'll find a thousand shifts to get away.

As good to die and go as die and stay.

  He jumps

O me, my uncle's spirit is in these stones!

Heaven take my soul, and England keep my bones! 10

            He dies

  Enter the Earls of Pembroke and Salisbury and Lord
  Bigot

SALISBURY

Lords, I will meet him at Saint Edmundsbury.

It is our safety, and we must embrace

This gentle offer of the perilous time.

PEMBROKE

Who brought that letter from the Cardinal?

SALISBURY

The Count Melun, a noble lord of France,

Whose private with me of the Dauphin's love

4.3] F (*Scoena Tertia*)   0.1 *Enter Arthur, disguised as a shipboy, on the walls*] F (*Enter Arthur on the walles*)   2 not!] POPE; ∼ : F   8.1 *He jumps*] *not in* F   9 stones!] CAPELL; ∼ , F   10 bones!] THEOBALD; ∼ . F   10.1 *He dies*] F (*Dies*)   10.2–3 *Enter . . . Bigot*] F (*Enter Pembroke, Salisbury, & Bigot.*)   11 Saint] F2; S. F1   15 Melun] ROWE; Meloone F (*and thus throughout except* Melloone *at* 5.2.1)   16 Whose] F (Whose); Who's OXFORD   Dauphin's] F (Dolphines)   love₍ₐ₎] This edition; loue, F; ∼ ; OXFORD

4.3 Location: outside the prison of 4.1.

7 **shifts** devices, plans. Honigmann finds a pun on *shifts* = changes of clothing.

8 **As good . . . stay** i.e., it is better to risk death by trying to escape than remain and suffer certain death. On a similar passage in Marlowe, N. W. Bawcutt suggests an 'inversion' of Tilley S491, 'Better sit still than rise and fall' (see *The Jew of Malta*, The Revels Plays (1978), 2.1.40n).

9 **spirit** (pronounced as a monosyllable)

10.2–3 **Lord Bigot** Historically, Roger Bigot,

Earl of Norfolk, and one of John's enemies.

11 **him** Louis. Historically, the nobles travelled to St. Edmundsbury in 1214 and Louis landed in 1216.

13 **perilous** The metre requires the syncopated form, 'parlous'.

16 **private** confidential communication (sole citation for *a.* (*sb.*) II.5, but see II.4; *privacy*, *sb.* 4a and 5; Abbott §5). Staunton (vol. 1, 'Addenda and Corrigenda') quoted Jonson, *Every Man in his Humour* 4.7.58: 'I will tell you, sir, by the way

Is much more general than these lines import.

BIGOT

Tomorrow morning let us meet him then.

SALISBURY

Or rather then set forward, for 'twill be

Two long days' journey, lords, or ere we meet.   20

    Enter Bastard

BASTARD

Once more today well met, distempered lords!

The King by me requests your presence straight.

SALISBURY

The King hath dispossessed himself of us;

We will not line his thin bestainèd cloak

With our pure honours, nor attend the foot

That leaves the print of blood where'er it walks.

Return and tell him so. We know the worst.

BASTARD

Whate'er you think, good words I think were best.

SALISBURY

Our griefs and not our manners reason now.

BASTARD

But there is little reason in your grief.   30

Therefore 'twere reason you had manners now.

PEMBROKE

Sir, sir, impatience hath his privilege.

17 Is] F; 'Tis OXFORD   24 thin bestainèd] ROWE; *hyphenated in* F

of private, and under seal'. The Oxford
editor's emendations in this and the following line replace the unusual use of
'private' with a more common one. In
Thomas Moffett's *The Silkworms and their
Flies* (1599), manuscript 'Priuie' was
mis-set as 'priuate', according to the
errata list.

17 **more general** 'larger, more comprehensive', but an antithetical play upon *private*
(l. 16)

19 **set forward** march on, get moving

20 **we** i.e., the English lords and Louis

21 **distempered** Vexed, troubled; earliest citation for *ppl. a.*, 2. For the latent image,
see 5.1.12–13n.

22 **straight** at once

23 **dispossessed** deprived (*v.* 1b). *OED v.* 2
has numerous examples of the verb used
to describe exorcism, freeing from dia-
bolic possession, etc. See Introduction,
pp. 49–53.

25–6 **foot . . . print of blood** The compressed
image recalls Pandulph's expansive
claims at 3.4.147–52.

27–8 **We know . . . best** Salisbury and the
Bastard share the proverb alluded to
earlier (see 4.2.135n).

28 **good words** i.e., 'do not speak so fiercely'
(*adj.* 7b). The phrase is common (and see
Tilley W803–11).

29 **reason** speak, talk

30 **reason in your grief** fact or circumstance
supporting your unhappiness. A play
upon *grief* as emotional and *reason* as
unemotional.

31 **'twere reason** i.e., it would be logical,
rational, or based on fact (*sb.*[1] II.8a)

32 **impatience hath his privilege** i.e., anger
or hot emotion commands a freedom
from customary restraint or mannerly
behaviour. See 'anger hath a privilege'
(*Tragedy of Lear* 2.2.70).
his its
privilege licence, right, immunity

BASTARD

'Tis true, to hurt his master, no man's else.

SALISBURY

This is the prison.

He sees Arthur's body

                    What is he lies here?

PEMBROKE

O death, made proud with pure and princely beauty!

The earth had not a hole to hide this deed.

SALISBURY

Murder, as hating what himself hath done,

Doth lay it open to urge on revenge.

BIGOT

Or, when he doomed this beauty to a grave,

Found it too precious-princely for a grave.   40

SALISBURY (*to Bastard*)

Sir Richard, what think you? You have beheld.

Or have you read, or heard, or could you think,

Or do you almost think, although you see,

That you do see? Could thought, without this object,

Form such another? This is the very top,

---

33 man's] F1 (mans); man F2; manners HONIGMANN   34 *He . . . body*] SMALLWOOD; *not in*
F   35 PEMBROKE] F (P⟨embroke⟩.)   beauty!] THEOBALD; beuty, F   40 precious-princely]
CAPELL; *not hyphenated in* F   41 you? You have beheld.] FLEAY; you? you haue beheld, F1;
you? have you beheld F3   44 That] F; What POPE

33 **'Tis true . . . else** F's line makes good
sense if Pembroke's 'impatience hath his
privilege' is understood as preceding 'to
hurt his master, no man's else': an
impatient man will give his emotion
rein, even if he harms himself (= 'his
[Impatience's] master'), but no other
person will grant him or his emotion the
same licence (= 'no man's [privilege]
else'). F2 as usual simplifies its way out
of difficulty, and editors have acquiesced.
Honigmann, plausibly hypothesizing an
overlooked manuscript *er*-suspension,
emends to continue the word-play, but
thereby makes the Bastard less forceful
and adamant than he appears in the
ensuing argument or even here, if we
accept the reading 'man's'. Dent suggests
some link with Tilley A247, 'Anger pun-
ishes itself' (versions of the idea appear
in Erasmus, *De Parabolis sive Similibus*
(1513), 588C, and in Lyly, *Euphues and*

his England (1580), ii. 66: 'it fell out with
him as it doth commonly with all those
that are choleric, that he hurt no man
but himself').

36 **had not a hole** i.e., Prince Arthur lies
unburied because no grave could be
found that would conceal his murder

41 **You have beheld.** Salisbury's subsequent
rhetorical questions work best if they
intensify the pain of fact, simply declared:
Arthur is dead. You have seen the body.

42–3 **Or . . . or . . . or . . . Or** successive uses
of the Elizabethan 'or . . . or' construction
(= modern 'either . . . or'): have you
either read or heard; could you either
think or (even) almost think, etc.

44 **That** The word serves double grammatical duty as pronoun (= Arthur's body;
that which you see) and conjunction;
Pope's emendation produces only a pronoun.

45 **very top** apex, pinnacle, extreme

The height, the crest, or crest unto the crest,
Of murder's arms. This is the bloodiest shame,
The wildest savagery, the vilest stroke,
That ever wall-eyed wrath or staring rage
Presented to the tears of soft remorse.   50

PEMBROKE

All murders past do stand excused in this.
And this, so sole and so unmatchable,
Shall give a holiness, a purity,
To the yet unbegotten sin of times
And prove a deadly bloodshed but a jest,
Exampled by this heinous spectacle.

BASTARD

It is a damnèd and a bloody work,
The graceless action of a heavy hand,
If that it be the work of any hand.

SALISBURY

If that it be the work of any hand!   60
We had a kind of light what would ensue.
It is the shameful work of Hubert's hand,
The practice and the purpose of the King—
From whose obedience I forbid my soul,
Kneeling before this ruin of sweet life,

---

54 yet unbegotten] F; *hyphenated by* POPE   60 hand!] F (∼ ?)

---

46 **crest, or crest unto the crest** The top-most portion (= *crest*) of a coat of arms is here itself figuratively 'crested' or overgone by yet another portion; see 4.3.149–50.

47 **arms** coat of arms, heraldic insignia

48 **savagery** cruelty, fierceness. This line is *OED*'s first citation.

49 **wall-eyed** with glaring eyes (*OED*'s earliest citation for a dubious definition) **staring** looking fixedly, with wide-open eyes

50 **remorse** pity, compassion

51 **murders past** previous homicides **excused** justified, held faultless or guiltless

54 **times** the future, eras to come (*OED* so defines only the phrase 'time(s) to come')

55–6 **prove . . . spectacle** i.e., demonstrate judicially (= *prove*) that this terrible sight is the legal precedent (= *example*) for regarding any other murder as (comparatively) a joke

56 **Exampled** furnished with a precedent (*sb.* I.3c, quoting this line). See 3.4.13n.

58 **graceless . . . heavy** i.e., damned and inelegant . . . wicked and clumsy. The quibble mixes morality and dexterity.

60 **any hand?** F's mark of interrogation might represent an exclamation, but the play is filled with statements ironically repeated as questions (many of which could, of course, be spoken as angry exclamations).

61 **light** intimation (not quite the definition of *sb.* 6b where this line is cited)

63 **practice** deceitful or underhanded scheme. See 1.1.214 and 4.1.20. **purpose** aim, goal

64 **obedience** Both the 'practice of obeying' and 'command or authority'; see 4.2.262 and n.

And breathing to his breathless excellence
The incense of a vow, a holy vow,
Never to taste the pleasures of the world,
Never to be infected with delight,
Nor conversant with ease and idleness,   70
Till I have set a glory to this hand
By giving it the worship of revenge.

PEMBROKE *and* BIGOT

Our souls religiously confirm thy words.
        Enter Hubert

HUBERT

Lords, I am hot with haste in seeking you.
Arthur doth live; the King hath sent for you.

SALISBURY

O, he is bold, and blushes not at death!
Avaunt, thou hateful villain! Get thee gone!

HUBERT

I am no villain.

SALISBURY   Must I rob the law?
        He draws his sword

BASTARD

Your sword is bright, sir; put it up again.

71 hand] F (∼,); head SINGER (*conj.* Farmer)   73 PEMBROKE *and* BIGOT] F (*Pem.Big.*)   76
death!] This edition; ∼, F   77 villain!] COLLIER; ∼, F   78.1 *He draws his sword*]
SMALLWOOD; *not in* F

66 **breathless** 'Dead'; but since *breath* and
breathe were not yet clearly distinguished
orthographically (Ff1–2 print *breathe* and
F3 *breath* at 4.2.246, for example), there
may be verbal play on the meaning
'breathe-less' or 'unbreathable', where
breath(e) means 'to utter or declare' (as
at 4.2.36), hence 'beyond saying' or
'unspeakable' in the usual Shakespearian
sense.
67 **incense** perfume or smoke of the aromatic
materials burned as an oblation (*sb.* 2
and above, 4.2.261n). Salisbury substitutes the vapour of incense and the
breath of his vow for Arthur's lost breath.
69 **infected** affected with, influenced by (so *v.*
8, citing this line as the earliest example).
The usage could (and can still) be neutral
or positive, so Salisbury need not regard
delight as an infectious disease.
71 **set** applied, given
glory special distinction (*sb.* 3)

hand i.e., Salisbury's own hand, a common oath. Honigmann's suggestion that
the actor might place his hand on his
sword hilt is supported by Edward's oath,
'By this right hand, and by my father's
sword' (*Edward II* 3.1.130). Against the
emendation 'head' (i.e., Arthur's),
Vaughan (p. 75) aptly cites 'let Aeneas
live— | If to my sword his fate be not the
glory' (*Troilus* 4.1.26–7, where Diome-
des' sword is analogous to Salisbury's
hand).
72 **worship** respect, honour
74 **hot with haste** See 2.1.449n and
5.7.50n.
77 **Avaunt** be gone
78 **rob the law** i.e., deny justice its due (by
killing you myself)
79 **bright** untarnished by rust or blood,
unused. The Bastard contemptuously
suggests that Salisbury wears the sword
as an ornament (hence *bright* is an ironic

233

SALISBURY

Not till I sheathe it in a murderer's skin.   80

HUBERT

Stand back, Lord Salisbury, stand back, I say.

By heaven, I think my sword's as sharp as yours.

I would not have you, lord, forget yourself,

Nor tempt the danger of my true defence,

Lest I, by marking of your rage, forget

Your worth, your greatness, and nobility.

BIGOT

Out, dunghill! Dar'st thou brave a nobleman?

HUBERT

Not for my life, but yet I dare defend

My innocent life against an emperor.

SALISBURY

Thou art a murderer.

HUBERT   Do not prove me so;   90

Yet I am none. Whose tongue soe'er speaks false,

Not truly speaks. Who speaks not truly, lies.

PEMBROKE

Cut him to pieces!

BASTARD   Keep the peace, I say.

SALISBURY

Stand by, or I shall gall you, Faulconbridge.

---

87 dunghill!] THEOBALD; ~ : F   89 life] F; self DYCE 1864   93 pieces!] HONIGMANN; peeces. F

compliment) and will not wish to mar its attractiveness; see 'Keep up your bright swords, for the dew will rust 'em' (*Othello* 1.2.60).
put it up sheathe it

80 **sheathe . . . skin** Since scabbards (in John's day and Shakespeare's) were ordinarily made of leather or leather- or vellum-covered wood, Salisbury may be making a gruesome joke: the murderer's skin will substitute for the animal's; see Beaumont and Fletcher, *Philaster* 5.4.79: 'let me have his skin to make false scabbards'.

84 **tempt the danger** risk the peril
defence both the legal term for the 'accused's spoken or written response to a complaint' and the 'act of protecting'

85 **marking of** noting, heeding, paying

attention to

87 **dunghill** The insult commonly implied the victim's low social status (a peasant); see *Tragedy of Lear* 4.5.242: 'Out, dung-hill!'
brave challenge, threaten

90 **prove me so** i.e., make me a murderer (here and now, by forcing me to defend my honour)

91 **Yet** until now

91–2 **Whose tongue . . . lies** The circumlocutions (*false, Not truly, lies*) avoid direct, challengeable accusation; Touchstone analyses similar 'escape clauses' comically (*As You Like It* 5.4.67 ff.).

93 **pieces . . . peace** (feeble word-play)

94 **Stand by** remain a spectator; keep out of it
gall wound

BASTARD

    Thou wert better gall the devil, Salisbury.

    If thou but frown on me, or stir thy foot,

    Or teach thy hasty spleen to do me shame,

    I'll strike thee dead. Put up thy sword betime,

    Or I'll so maul you and your toasting-iron

    That you shall think the devil is come from hell.   100

BIGOT

    What wilt thou do, renownèd Faulconbridge?

    Second a villain and a murderer?

HUBERT

    Lord Bigot, I am none.

BIGOT   Who killed this prince?

HUBERT

    'Tis not an hour since I left him well.

    I honoured him, I loved him, and will weep

    My date of life out for his sweet life's loss.

SALISBURY

    Trust not those cunning waters of his eyes,

    For villainy is not without such rheum,

    And he, long traded in it, makes it seem

    Like rivers of remorse and innocency.   110

    Away with me, all you whose souls abhor

    Th'uncleanly savours of a slaughterhouse,

    For I am stifled with this smell of sin.

BIGOT

    Away, toward Bury, to the Dauphin there!

PEMBROKE

    There tell the King he may enquire us out.

                             Exeunt Lords

---

106 life's] F (liues)   115.1 Exeunt Lords] F (Ex. Lords.)

97 **hasty spleen** quick anger, reckless irascibility. See 2.1.68n, 2.1.449n, and 5.7.50n.

98 **betime** at once, in good time

99 **toasting-iron** The Bastard contemptuously suggests that Salisbury's sword is useful (or used) only for toasting cheese over the fire; see 'It will toast cheese, and it will endure cold, as another man's sword will' (*Henry V* 2.1.7–9).

102 **Second** 'support' or 'back', as a 'second' does a principal in a duel

106 **date** term or limit, a sense common in the Sonnets (e.g., 14.14), as is the sentiment and the language of ll. 105-6 (e.g., Sonnet 30)

109 **traded** professional (Schmidt); having practised villainy as an occupation

112 **slaughterhouse** shambles, abbatoir. Shakespeare uses the word elsewhere only in *Lucrece* and the first tetralogy; see especially England described as 'this slaughterhouse' (*Richard III* 4.1.43).

BASTARD

  Here's a good world! Knew you of this fair work?
  Beyond the infinite and boundless reach
  Of mercy, if thou didst this deed of death,
  Art thou damned, Hubert.

HUBERT

  Do but hear me, sir—

BASTARD   Ha? I'll tell thee what.   120

  Thou'rt damned as black—nay, nothing is so black—
  Thou art more deep damned than Prince Lucifer.
  There is not yet so ugly a fiend of hell
  As thou shalt be, if thou didst kill this child.

HUBERT

  Upon my soul—

BASTARD   If thou didst but consent
  To this most cruel act, do but despair,
  And if thou want'st a cord, the smallest thread
  That ever spider twisted from her womb
  Will serve to strangle thee. A rush will be a beam
  To hang thee on. Or wouldst thou drown thyself,   130
  Put but a little water in a spoon,
  And it shall be as all the ocean,
  Enough to stifle such a villain up.
  I do suspect thee very grievously.

HUBERT

  If I in act, consent, or sin of thought

---

116 BASTARD] F (*Ba⟨stard⟩.*)   world!] CAPELL; ~ : F   117–19] *as here*, POPE; *as two lines, breaking after* 'mercy', 'Hubert' F   120 sir—] HONIGMANN; ~. F   BASTARD] F (*Bast⟨ard⟩.; and thus for remainder of play*)   125 soul—] THEOBALD; soule. F

116 **Here's a good world** *World* = state of affairs; the phrase also appears in *Richard III* 3.6.10.

117–19 **Beyond . . . Hubert** Compositor B was crowding text here, setting *P.* for *Pem.* and *Ex. Lords* for *Exeunt Lords* (l. 115) and using *y̆* for *thou* (l. 119); the unemphatic pentameter rhythm and the creation of an incomplete pentameter (as in Pope's relineation) may have helped the move to prose.

122 **Thou art . . . Lucifer** The line has ten syllables, but the scansion is difficult.

123–4 **not yet . . . shalt be** Since Hubert's damnation exceeds Lucifer's (ll. 121–2),

when Hubert reaches hell he will become the ugliest denizen there; once again, morality and appearance are co-ordinate.

126 **but despair** only despair; do nothing but abandon all hope of salvation

127 **want'st a cord** lack a rope (for hanging)

133 **stifle . . . up** drown or suffocate with water

135 **act, consent, . . . thought** Hubert replies to the charges of murder (ll. 121–4), of being an accomplice to it (ll. 125 f.), of having contemplated it (ll. 116 f.), and his abjuration echoes the general confession before communion (Book of Common Prayer); see 4.2.239–40.

Be guilty of the stealing that sweet breath
Which was embounded in this beauteous clay,
Let hell want pains enough to torture me.
I left him well.
BASTARD   Go, bear him in thine arms.
   Hubert takes up Arthur's body
I am amazed, methinks, and lose my way   140
Among the thorns and dangers of this world.
How easy dost thou take all England up!
From forth this morsel of dead royalty,
The life, the right, and truth of all this realm
Is fled to heaven, and England now is left
To tug and scramble, and to part by th' teeth
The unowed interest of proud-swelling state.

139.1 *Hubert . . . body*] COLLIER 1858 (*subs.*); *not in* F   142–3 up! | . . . royalty,] THEOBALD;
vp, | . . . Royaltie? F; up | . . . royalty! HONIGMANN   146 scramble] F (scamble)   147
proud-swelling] POPE; *not hyphenated in* F

137 **embounded** confined, contained. This
line is *OED*'s earliest citation for the *ppl.
a.*; there are no citations for the finite
verb.
   clay flesh. The commonplace metaphor
emphasizes transience.
140 **amazed** See 4.2.137n.
142 **take all England up** The Bastard refers
to (1) Hubert's action (lifting the body of
Arthur, of 'England' in the same sense
that Philip is 'France', for example, at
1.1.1 or John is 'England' at 2.1.56) and
(2) the likely consequences of Arthur's
death (the taking up, the raising in arms,
of the nation). The phrase in the first
meaning may have been conventional
(see, e.g., Kyd, *The Spanish Tragedy*
2.5.64, 4.4.210 and the direction at the
former); on the second meaning (= 'to
levy') Schmidt cites *2 Henry IV* 2.1.188
and 4.1.252. Superstitious members
of the audience would have expected
Arthur's wounds to bleed in the presence
of his murderer; Hubert's action further
testifies to his innocence.
142–3 **up! . . . royalty,** Theobald's punctuation does not destroy the quibble of
l. 142 as Honigmann asserts, and it
obviates the strained syntax of 'take . . .
up . . . from forth'; some editors understand F's '?' as '!'
143 **morsel** fragment, referring to Arthur's
size and youth. The Elizabethan actor
taking this part was 'Probably a *very*

small boy, since . . . his body has to be
picked up, without effort, by a single
actor, while another stands by and comments on the ease with which he does
it' (Holmes, pp. 140–1).
145 **fled to heaven** 'Vanished from the world
of men', just as Arthur's soul has flown
to heaven; the image may be based upon
the classical myth of the virgin Astraea,
or Justice, who takes refuge in heaven
and whose return to earth will usher in
the second Golden Age (see 4.1.60n). See
Titus 4.3.4 ff., where Ovid's description
of Astraea's flight is partly quoted.
146 **scramble** This form has 'superseded'
(*OED*) F's *scamble*; the word connotes
an indecorous, demeaning struggle for
something lying on the ground (*v.* 1,
quoting this line).
147 **unowed interest** Probably a pun on
owe and *own*: (1) because there is no
recognized, legitimate authority, there is
no hierarchy and therefore no social
order; consequently, no individual(s)
own(s) a rightful share (*interest*, *sb.* 1) in
pomp and social status (*OED*, *state*, *sb.*
II.15, 17); (2) were there a legitimate
authority, persons of high station would
owe it their allegiance, but that allegiance
is now accruing like monetary interest
without a beneficiary, without an owner
to whom it is properly owed. See 'lineal
state' (5.7.102). This line is *OED*'s only
citation of *unowed* as a *ppl. a.*

Now for the bare-picked bone of majesty
Doth doggèd war bristle his angry crest
And snarleth in the gentle eyes of peace.   150
Now powers from home and discontents at home
Meet in one line; and vast confusion waits,
As doth a raven on a sick-fall'n beast,
The imminent decay of wrested pomp.
Now happy he whose cloak and ceinture can
Hold out this tempest. Bear away that child
And follow me with speed. I'll to the King.
A thousand businesses are brief in hand,
And heaven itself doth frown upon the land.
          Exeunt, Hubert carrying Arthur's body

153 sick-fall'n] F (sicke-falne)   155 ceinture] F (center)   159.1 *Exeunt . . . body*] COLLIER 1858 (*subs.*); *Exit*. F

148 **bare-picked bone of majesty** Struggle for power has stripped that power of its attractiveness, its majestic quality; *majesty* does not = *state* in the preceding line.

149 **doggèd** 'persistent, tenacious', but also (in view of the line's imagery) dog-like, canine
bristle his angry crest raise its (a dog's) hackles in rage; flaunt its (war's) personal heraldic device (*crest, sb.*[1] 3) so as to foster violence. 'Angry' is a transferred epithet; for 'crest' as 'the ridge or surface line of the neck of a horse, dog, or other animal; sometimes applied to the mane which this part bears', see *sb.*[1] 8.

151 **powers from home** troops or armies away from their native land: the French who are 'abroad' in England
discontents discontented persons. See 5.2.151n and 5.4.7n.

152 **Meet in one line** are unanimous (*line, sb.*[2] II.13, quoting this line). As the usage in *Hamlet* Add. Pass. H.9 ('in one line two crafts directly meet') suggests, Shakespeare uses the phrase paradoxically: hostile forces meet to fight, are unanimous in disagreement.

152–3 **waits | As doth . . . beast** i.e., like a carrion-eater awaiting the death of a sick animal, social chaos will follow upon the monarchy's final collapse

152 **waits** awaits, expects

154 **imminent** impending (Schmidt)
wrested acquired by force (so *ppl. a.* 3, quoting this line)

155 **ceinture** A spelling of 'cincture' (girdle or belt) attested by a single quotation (from 1856) in *OED*, but regarded as current by major U.S. dictionaries; this line is *OED's* first citation (of two, the second from 1624) for the spelling 'cen-ture' or 'center'. At *1 Henry VI* 2.2.5–6 ('the market place | The middle centre of this cursèd town'), F prints *centure*, although elsewhere *center* predominates (ten times in all, as against *centre* and *centry* once each); thus *center* here permits a pun on 'ceinture' (easily spelt *centure* in manuscript) and 'centre' meaning 'soul, as opposed to the body' (so Schmidt, citing this line).

156 **Hold out** 'bear or sustain to the end' (*v.* B.41g)
Bear carry

158 **businesses** tasks, jobs, things to do
are brief in hand The grammar is unclear; the common Shakespearian idiom is 'to have in hand' and means either 'to be occupied with' (*Merchant* 3.4.57–8: 'I have work in hand | That you yet know not of') or 'to take place' (*Merry Wives* 2.1.187 ff.: 'We have sport in hand . . . there is a fray to be fought'). The idiom appears only one other time with 'to be' and there refers to current preparations for a future event: 'a solemn hunting is in hand' (*Titus* 2.1.113). Thus, 'businesses are in hand' means 'jobs are being done' or 'jobs are to be done'. The addition of *brief*, however, makes for some difficulty since the *OED* rightly doubts that this

5.1 ⌈*Flourish.*⌉ *Enter King John, Cardinal Pandulph, and their attendants*

KING JOHN

Thus have I yielded up into your hand
The circle of my glory.

CARDINAL PANDULPH (*handing the crown to John*) Take again
From this my hand, as holding of the Pope,
Your sovereign greatness and authority.

KING JOHN

Now keep your holy word. Go meet the French,
And from his holiness use all your power
To stop their marches 'fore we are inflamed.
Our discontented counties do revolt;
Our people quarrel with obedience,
Swearing allegiance and the love of soul   10

5.1] ROWE; *Actus Quartus, Scaena prima* F   0.1 *Flourish.*] OXFORD; *not in* F   0.1–2 *Enter . . . attendants*] F (*Enter King Iohn and Pandolph, attendants.*)   2 *handing . . . John*] THEOBALD (*subs.*); *not in* F   7 inflamed] F (enflam'd)

line should be cited for the meaning 'rife, common'; prevalent' (*adj.* A.5; Nares offers this definition). This context seems to require that 'brief' serve as an adverb meaning 'within a short time . . . soon' (the obsolete meaning of 'briefly' at 2), the word's apparent sense in 'how brief the life of man | Runs his erring pilgrimage' (*As You Like it* 3.2.126–7). Thus, the Bastard's line might be paraphrased: 'a thousand tasks will soon occupy or demand our attention'.

5.1 Location: the English court. John's act of homage made the Pope both temporal and spiritual lord of England, as sixteenth-century Roman Catholic controversialists emphasized. Although this opening is linked with that of 4.2 through John's being newly 're-crowned' in both scenes, their differences measure his diminished power and independence.

1–2 Thus . . . Take again F gives no stage directions here, but Pandulph's imperative *Take* indicates a concurrent action; whether he has entered with the crown or John has handed it to him (while speaking l. 1) is uncertain: *thus* followed by the past tense sometimes means 'in the manner recently described or exemplified' (e.g., at *Two Gentlemen* 1.3.78) or 'in the manner you have recently perceived off-stage' (e.g., at

1 Henry VI 1.8.3); very frequently, however, *thus* accompanies an action (as it does at 4.2.193).

2 circle of my glory i.e., the crown that represents my special distinction (as king); see 4.3.71n and *Antony* 3.12.18. *OED* quotes this line, *circle*, *sb.* II.10; the presence of Pandulph, however, may evoke a more subtle series of associations in which *circle* = 'a luminous ring in the sky, a halo' (*sb.* I.6) or *glory* = 'an aureole or nimbus' (*glory*, *sb.* 9, earliest citation 1646) as in pictorial representations of holy beings. These associations, if present, appropriately bring together John's secular authority and his renewed religious obedience to Rome (made explicit in ll. 3–4).

2–4 Take . . . authority The elliptical syntax attaches both a concrete and an abstract meaning to l. 4: John is to 'Take again' his crown (= 'Your sovereign greatness and authority'), but he also regains sovereignty over England (= 'Your sovereign greatness and authority') through submission to Rome (= 'as holding of the Pope').

7 inflamed i.e., set on fire, engulfed in flames

8 counties either 'shires' or 'counts, noblemen'

To stranger blood, to foreign royalty;
This inundation of mistempered humour
Rests by you only to be qualified.
Then pause not, for the present time's so sick
That present medicine must be ministered,
Or overthrow incurable ensues.

CARDINAL PANDULPH

It was my breath that blew this tempest up
Upon your stubborn usage of the Pope.
But since you are a gentle convertite,
My tongue shall hush again this storm of war   20
And make fair weather in your blust'ring land.
On this Ascension Day, remember well,
Upon your oath of service to the Pope,
Go I to make the French lay down their arms.

⌈*Exeunt all but John*⌉

---

11 stranger blood] THEOBALD; *hyphenated in* F
Exeunt . . . John] CAPELL (*subs.*); *Exit* F. *See note.*

16 incurable] F1; incurably F4   24.1

11 **stranger** foreign, alien. *OED* dates the
adjectival use from 1593, citing *Lucrece*
99 and *Richard II* 1.3.137; the metaphor
of *mistempered humour* (l. 12), however,
may retrospectively add a sense of 'tem-
peramentally unbalanced, not healthy'
to *stranger*.

12 **inundation** As at 4.2.138, John imagines
his troubles as a flood.

12–13 **mistempered humour . . . qualified** A
compact phrase mixing the quibble of
mistempered = 'ill-tempered' or 'angry'
with a more specific medical sense in
which the unbalanced humours consti-
tuting an individual's (or here a nation's)
nature require mitigation or moderation
through the addition of compensatory
humours (see *temper*, *sb.* II.4 and *v.* II.2
and *qualify*, *v.* II.8 and especially 10);
see 2.1.66n. Since the humours were
liquid, John speaks of an *inundation*. Medical terminology continues through the
speech. Perhaps through association
with the 'hot' humour, choler, or with
'temper' = 'to bring' a metal 'to a proper
degree of hardness and elasticity' (*v.*
III.14), Shakespeare often joins 'qualify'
or 'temper' with 'flame' or 'fire'; hence,
perhaps, 'inflamed' (l. 7) and such lines
as 'absence seemed my flame to qualify'
(Sonnet 109.2) or 'is your blood | So
madly hot that no discourse of reason

| . . . | Can qualify the same?' (*Troilus*
2.2.114–17).

15 **present** 'immediate, instant', but probably with the more restricted sense 'Of
a remedy or poison: Taking immediate
effect, acting speedily' (*a.* II.9b)
medicine disyllabic ('med'cine')

18 **usage of** treatment of, or conduct toward

19 **convertite** 'a person converted to a religious life, or to an approved course of
action' (2, quoting this line as the earliest
citation)

21 **make fair weather** A common expression
(Tilley W221) meaning, in Honigmann's
words, 'be conciliatory' and 'pretend that
something is better than it is'.
blust'ring tempestuous, an epithet transferred from *this tempest* (l. 17) and *this
storm of war* (l. 20)

22–4 **remember . . . their arms** Pandulph
stresses that he goes to make peace as a
result of (= *upon*) John's sworn 'service
to the Pope'.

24.1 *Exeunt . . . John* Jowett (in Oxford)
explains the theatrical force of leaving
King John alone on stage and adds, 'The
conversation with the Bastard [ll. 30 ff.]
is most effective as a private dialogue'
(*Textual Companion*, p. 321). It is not
clear, however, what duty or protocol
might motivate the exit of all John's
attendants along with Pandulph's.

KING JOHN

Is this Ascension Day? Did not the prophet
Say that before Ascension Day at noon,
My crown I should give off? Even so I have;
I did suppose it should be on constraint,
But, heaven be thanked, it is but voluntary.
   Enter Bastard

BASTARD

All Kent hath yielded; nothing there holds out   30
But Dover Castle. London hath received
Like a kind host the Dauphin and his powers.
Your nobles will not hear you, but are gone
To offer service to your enemy,
And wild amazement hurries up and down
The little number of your doubtful friends.

KING JOHN

Would not my lords return to me again
After they heard young Arthur was alive?

BASTARD

They found him dead and cast into the streets,
An empty casket, where the jewel of life   40
By some damned hand was robbed and ta'en away.

KING JOHN

That villain Hubert told me he did live.

BASTARD

So on my soul he did, for aught he knew.
But wherefore do you droop? Why look you sad?
Be great in act, as you have been in thought:

28–9 **constraint | . . . but voluntary** An ironic comment, since John has been constrained by the French invasion and earlier (3.1.155–8) regarded his relation with *heaven* as requiring no mediation; F's *heav'n* indicates an appropriate monosyllabic pronunciation.

32 **kind host** A quibble: like an innkeeper (= *host*), the city politely welcomes the Dauphin; the French force seems a friendly army (= *host*) to the rebellious citizens; the former (and dominant) meaning would be especially bitter since London was known as *camera regis*: 'Welcome, sweet Prince, to London, to your chamber' (*Richard III* 3.1.1).

35 **hurries** A transitive use, 'drive confusedly' (Schmidt), but until we hear 'your doubtful friends', the word evokes a personification, Amazement, that itself *hurries*.

36 **doubtful** 'fearful', but perhaps also 'unreliable' or 'worthy of being doubted' (the latter meaning is not fully supported by 4, 'giving cause for apprehension')

40 **jewel of life** A periphrasis for 'soul, spiritual essence'; see 'mine eternal jewel' (*Macbeth* 3.1.69).

44 **droop** i.e., gaze downward, with eyelids lowered

45 **Be great . . . thought** See 'King, be thy thoughts imperious like thy name' and

Let not the world see fear and sad distrust
Govern the motion of a kingly eye;
Be stirring as the time, be fire with fire,
Threaten the threat'ner, and outface the brow
Of bragging horror. So shall inferior eyes,   50
That borrow their behaviours from the great,
Grow great by your example and put on
The dauntless spirit of resolution.
Away, and glisten like the god of war
When he intendeth to become the field;
Show boldness and aspiring confidence.
What, shall they seek the lion in his den
And fright him there? And make him tremble there?
O, let it be not said! Forage, and run
To meet displeasure farther from the doors   60
And grapple with him ere he come so nigh.
KING JOHN
The legate of the Pope hath been with me,
And I have made a happy peace with him,
And he hath promised to dismiss the powers
Led by the Dauphin.

54 glisten] F (glister)   59 said!] POPE; ∼ : F

'great lords, be as your titles witness, |
Imperious' (*Titus* 4.4.81, 5.1.5–6).
    act deeds, action
46 **sad distrust** solemn or downcast fear or
anxiety
47 **motion** movement, action
48 **Be stirring as the time** i.e., be as active,
energetic (= *stirring*) as events (= *the
time*) are
    be fire with fire proverbial; see 3.1.277n
49 **outface the brow** defy the face or counten-
ance
50 **bragging** swaggering, boastful
    inferior eyes Periphrasis for 'subordinate
persons' (as distinct from 'kingly eye',
l. 47); see Introduction, pp. 46–8.
54 **god of war** Mars
55 **become** Both 'to come to a place, to
arrive' (I. 1) and 'grace or adorn' (III.9c);
see 'Did ever Dian so become a grove |
As Kate this chamber' (*Shrew* 2.1.253–
4).
57–9 **shall they seek . . . Forage** See *Edward*

III 2.1.395–6, describing the King and
using *become* as in l. 55: 'The lion doth
become his bloody jaws, | And grace his
foragement by being mild'; I. John also
cites *Edward III* 4.3.81: 'And forage their
country as they have done ours'. Three
of Shakespeare's four uses of 'forage' in
canonical texts apply the word to lions,
and in *Henry V* 1.2.110 the word refers to
Edward the Black Prince. The association
may have been (or become) a commonplace: 'th'innative fire of spirit and great-
ness | That lions free breathe, foraging
for prey' (Chapman, *The Revenge of Bussy*
2.1.159–60).
57 **lion** Presumably an allusion to the
heraldic symbol of England.
59 **Forage** raid, here synonymous with
'foray' (see *sb.* 2 and *v.* 2b and Cotgrave,
fourragement and *fourrager*)
60 **displeasure**   A   near-personification
(= the enemy).
64 **powers** forces, army

BASTARD   O inglorious league!
　　Shall we upon the footing of our land
　　Send fair-play orders and make compromise,
　　Insinuation, parley, and base truce
　　To arms invasive? Shall a beardless boy,
　　A cockered silken wanton, brave our fields   70
　　And flesh his spirit in a warlike soil,
　　Mocking the air with colours idly spread,
　　And find no check? Let us, my liege, to arms!
　　Perchance the Cardinal cannot make your peace,
　　Or, if he do, let it at least be said
　　They saw we had a purpose of defence.
KING JOHN
　　Have thou the ordering of this present time.

65 league!] POPE; ~ : F   67 fair-play orders] F (fayre-play-orders); fair-play offers SINGER
1856 (*conj.* Collier, *Notes*)   70 cockered silken] FLEAY (cock'red silken); cockred-silken F;
cockred, silken POPE

65 **inglorious league** The Bastard described
the earlier Anglo-French alliance as 'mad
composition' (2.1.561).
66 **footing of** walking or pacing upon (by
foreign troops)
67 **fair-play orders** Literally, orders to
conduct a game honourably or with
equitable conditions and opportunities
afforded to each side (*fair*, *a*. and *sb.*²
III.10c, giving this line as the earliest
citation). Since no orders fair or foul have
yet been sent, the Bastard may here
continue his campaign to encourage the
wavering king: the French invasion so
heinously violates the rules of inter-
national relations that the English ought
to retaliate with unfair conduct, not
compromise. Invoking the language of
game (and implicitly the image of Pandulph as umpire) intensifies the sarcasm.
68 **base** cowardly
69 **invasive** invading. Shakespeare's only
use of the adjective.
　　beardless See 5.2.133 and n.
70 **cockered** pampered
　　silken 'Delicate' in a pejorative sense,
'effeminate', but perhaps also 'clad in
silk', inappropriate garb for war; banners
(= *colours*, l. 72) were made of taffeta, a
silk fabric, and the words may have been
linked associatively in Shakespeare's
mind (see *LLL* 5.2.407: 'taffeta phrases,
silken terms precise').
　　wanton spoiled child (so *OED*, quoting

this line)
　　brave challenge tauntingly
71 **flesh his spirit in a warlike soil** i.e.,
express his angry courage (= *spirit*; see
sb. III.12 and 13) for the first time by
attacking this martial nation (= *soil*; see
*sb.*¹ I.3 and 4a). *Flesh* means to plunge
a weapon into some object (*2 Henry IV*
4.3.260–1: 'the wild dog | Shall flesh his
tooth on every innocent') and particularly applies to the first occasion on which
a warrior experiences battle (*flesh, v.* 3a).
Honigmann understands *flesh* as 'initiate
or inure to bloodshed' (*v.* 2a). The Bastard
has frequently mocked the Dauphin's
youth and inexperience, and he does so
here and earlier in this speech. Latent
imagery of boars and boar-hunting may
appear in *soil* which also means 'a muddy
place used by a wild boar for wallowing
in' (*sb.*³ I.1). Finally, if *fields* and *check*
represent imagery from hunting or hawk-
ing, *soil* may be an error for *spoil*; see
All's Well 4.3.17: 'he fleshes his will in
the spoil of her honour'.
72 **idly** carelessly; pointlessly
73 **check** rebuke, restraint. See 2.1.123n.
74–6 **Perchance . . . defence** Kemble cut
these lines and inserted five jingoistic
ones in their place; see Introduction,
p. 84.
76 **purpose of defence** intention or aim to
defend
77 **ordering** 'returning to order, organizing',

BASTARD

Away, then, with good courage! (*Aside*) Yet I know
Our party may well meet a prouder foe.   *Exeunt*

5.2 *Enter* (*in arms*) *Louis the Dauphin, the Earl of*
Salisbury, Count Melun, the Earl of Pembroke, Lord
Bigot, and French and English Soldiers

LOUIS THE DAUPHIN

My Lord Melun, let this be copied out
And keep it safe for our remembrance;
⌈*He hands a paper to Melun*⌉
Return the precedent to these lords again,
That having our fair order written down,
Both they and we, perusing o'er these notes,
May know wherefore we took the sacrament,
And keep our faiths firm and inviolable.

SALISBURY

Upon our sides it never shall be broken.
And, noble Dauphin, albeit we swear
A voluntary zeal and unurged faith   10
To your proceedings, yet believe me, Prince,

5.2] F (*Scoena Secunda*)   0.1–3 *Enter . . . Soldiers*] F (*Enter* (*in Armes*) *Dolphin, Salisbury,*
Melooue, Pembroke, Bigot, Souldiers.)   2.1 *He . . . Melun*] *not in* F   3 precedent] F (president)
10 and] POPE; and an F; an CAPELL. *See note.*

but with perhaps a more specifically military sense (drawing an army into orderly
ranks, or designing strategy as at *Richard*
III 5.6.22)
    present immediate, current
79 **prouder** braver, mightier (II.7a and see
French *preux*)
5.2 Location: the French encampment, perhaps near St. Edmundsbury (modern
Bury St. Edmunds), an important provincial centre in Suffolk (see 4.3.11 and
114 and 5.4.16–20); on Shakespeare's
historical conflation here, see 4.3.11n.
0.1–3 *Louis . . . Bigot* If the order of names
reflects stage practice, the mingling of
French and English leaders would indicate their alliance. F's phrase '(in Armes)'
is likely to derive from the theatre as a
reminder of props needed rather than
from any literary purpose; the manuscript of *Woodstock* (MSR) has been
marked as a prompt-book and has the

direction, '. . . (4.) other knights (In
Greene) . . .'. For Melun's title, see 4.3.15.
3 **precedent** original, perhaps 'original
draft'. In *Tamburlaine, Part 2* 1.1.137 ff.,
written oaths are exchanged as confirma-
tion of spoken vows. Elision (e.g., *pre-*
cedent as a disyllable) makes the line
metrically regular.
4 **fair** If *fair* modifies *order*, then it = just,
good; if it modifies *written*, then it =
neatly, clearly.
10 **A voluntary . . . faith** F's line is hypermetric. Substituting 'unurgèd' for F's *vn-*
urg'd produces a regular alexandrine,
but loses the appropriate dramatic stress
on 'unurged'. Compositor C, who set this
line, was prone to interpolate articles and
modals, especially to regularize metre or
grammar (O'Connor, pp. 64, 74), and he
may have inserted *an* or duplicated it
from *and*. Omitting *an* restores a regular
pentameter and stresses *un*urged.

I am not glad that such a sore of time
Should seek a plaster by contemned revolt
And heal the inveterate canker of one wound
By making many. O, it grieves my soul
That I must draw this metal from my side
To be a widow-maker. O, and there
Where honourable rescue and defence
Cries out upon the name of Salisbury.
But such is the infection of the time   20
That for the health and physic of our right
We cannot deal but with the very hand
Of stern injustice and confusèd wrong.
And is't not pity, O my grievèd friends,
That we, the sons and children of this isle,
Was born to see so sad an hour as this
Wherein we step after a stranger, march
Upon her gentle bosom, and fill up
Her enemy's ranks? I must withdraw and weep
Upon the spot of this enforcèd cause,   30
To grace the gentry of a land remote
And follow unacquainted colours here.
What here? O nation, that thou couldst remove,
That Neptune's arms who clippeth thee about
Would bear thee from the knowledge of thy self

26 Was] F1 ; Were F2   29 enemy's] F (Enemies)

12 **sore of time** wound or abscess of the
   present
13 **plaster** medicinal dressing
   contemned despised
14 **canker** ulcer
   one wound i.e., Arthur's death
16 **metal** sword
17 **widow-maker** Shakespeare's only use of
   the phrase.
18–19 **honourable rescue and defence | Cries
   out upon** The double subject produces
   two antithetical meanings: *honourable
   rescue* (of England, from John) appeals for
   (= *cries out upon*) Salisbury's assistance;
   defence (what the English loyal to John
   are doing) condemns or exclaims against
   (= *cries out upon*) Salisbury's actions.
   The confusion of right and wrong, self-
   interest and public interest, reappears

here; see 4.2, esp. 47–66.
21 **physic** cure
26 **Was** According to *OED*, F1's *Was* existed
   as an available plural form.
29 **enemy's** See 3.1.102n.
30 **spot** blot, moral stain, dishonour. Salisbury uses the same word when he vows
   renewed faith to Henry III (5.7.107).
32 **unacquainted** unfamiliar, strange
33–4 **nation . . . Neptune's arms** The image
   of England sailing the ocean is treated as
   a hyperbolic impossibility in Marlowe's
   Edward II 1.4.49.
33 **remove** move to some other place (*v. intr.*
   II.9)
34 **clippeth** embraces, hugs. Citations at *v.*[1]
   2 suggest that the word's figurative application to the sea was common.
35 **Would . . . self** See 3.4.49n.

And grapple thee unto a pagan shore,
Where these two Christian armies might combine
The blood of malice in a vein of league,
And not to spend it so unneighbourly.

LOUIS THE DAUPHIN

A noble temper dost thou show in this,   40
And great affections wrestling in thy bosom
Doth make an earthquake of nobility.
O, what a noble combat hast thou fought
Between compulsion and a brave respect.
Let me wipe off this honourable dew
That silverly doth progress on thy cheeks.
My heart hath melted at a lady's tears,
Being an ordinary inundation,
But this effusion of such manly drops,
This shower blown up by tempest of the soul,   50
Startles mine eyes, and makes me more amazed
Than had I seen the vaulty top of heaven

---

36 grapple] POPE; cripple F; gripple OXFORD (*conj.* Steevens)   41 wrestling] F (wrastling)
43 thou] F4; *not in* F1

36 **grapple** bind or fasten; particularly used
of grappling hooks that join two ships
for hand-to-hand combat. The nautical
metaphor is appropriate for a context
in which England sails the ocean. A
misreading or mis-correction of *gripple* (a
current form of *grapple* but not, apparently, a Shakespearian spelling) might
produce F's *cripple*; Honigmann's defence
of F is complex and unconvincing.
pagan shore foreign country, perhaps
particularly the Holy Land, where
Christian armies (l. 37) might fight on
crusade

37–9 **two Christian armies . . . unneighbourly** See the Bastard's advice at
2.1.377 ff. and his mention of 'the
mutines of Jerusalem'.

42 **make an earthquake of nobility** i.e., blow
up, explode your dignity, your code of
conduct. Earthquakes were believed to
be the result of tumultuous winds within
the earth; the image of conflicting pas-
sions as an earthquake appears memor-
ably in Chapman's *Bussy D'Ambois*
2.2.34–41; see S. K. Heninger, *Handbook
of Renaissance Meteorology* (Durham, NC,
1960), pp. 128–34, for further literary

examples.

44 **compulsion** obligation (to resist John);
but the word neatly recalls John's use of
'constraint' (5.1.28)
brave respect worthy regard (for England)

45 **Let me wipe** The actor might here gesture
to or even touch Salisbury.

46 **silverly** The only Shakespearian use and
OED's earliest citation.
doth progress There may be a latent
image of a royal 'progress', or official
visit to the countryside; see 2.1.339–40.

47–59 **My heart . . . gossiping** The grandi-
loquent imagery may signal Louis's
hypocrisy and recalls the language of
5.1.12–21 and 5.2.12–15.

48 **ordinary** usual, common

51 **Startles** Frightens, shocks (as at 4.2.25),
but *OED* records a single intransitive use
with 'eyes' meaning 'start from their
sockets'; this latter meaning might introduce *amazed* and the idea of meteors in
heaven.

52–3 **Than had I seen . . . meteors** Louis's
analogy may arise from the correlation
of the human head and face with the
'heaven' of reason, the faculty mankind

Figured quite o'er with burning meteors.
Lift up thy brow, renownèd Salisbury,
And with a great heart heave away this storm;
Commend these waters to those baby eyes
That never saw the giant world enraged,
Nor met with fortune other than at feasts,
Full warm of blood, of mirth, of gossiping.
Come, come, for thou shalt thrust thy hand as deep   60
Into the purse of rich prosperity
As Louis himself—so, nobles, shall you all
That knit your sinews to the strength of mine.
And even there, methinks an angel spake.
    Enter Pandulph
Look where the holy legate comes apace
To give us warrant from the hand of heaven
And on our actions set the name of right
With holy breath.
CARDINAL PANDULPH Hail, noble Prince of France!
The next is this: King John hath reconciled
Himself to Rome; his spirit is come in   70
That so stood out against the holy church,
The great metropolis and see of Rome.
Therefore, thy threat'ning colours now wind up
And tame the savage spirit of wild war,
That like a lion fostered up at hand
It may lie gently at the foot of peace
And be no further harmful than in show.
LOUIS THE DAUPHIN
    Your grace shall pardon me, I will not back.

56 baby eyes] CAPELL; *hyphenated in* F   57 giant world] THEOBALD; *hyphenated in* F   59
Full warm of] F; Full-warm of THEOBALD; Full of warm CAMBRIDGE (*conj.* Thirlby)   64.1
Enter Pandulph] *as here*, HALLIWELL; *after l.* 63 F (*Pandulpho*)   66 heaven] F (heauen); God
MATCHETT   73 threat'ning] F (threatning)

shares with the angels; a tearful face, a
face distorted by human emotion, appears like a zenith disfigured by ominous
meteors (see 5.7.74 and n). The analogy
between microcosm ('cheeks', 'manly',
'baby') and macrocosm ('heaven', 'meteors') continues in Louis's next
lines.
59 **Full warm of blood** 'The substantive to
warm is *feasts*, and the line's sense—

feasts in which the blood ran full high,
and mirth and gossiping kept pace with
the blood' (Capell, *Notes*).
64 **an angel spake** See Appendix C.
70 **come in** submitted, yielded
73 **threat'ning** F's *threatning* indicates disyllabic pronunciation.
   wind up furl, fold up and put away
75 **fostered up at hand** raised by hand
77 **show** appearance (as opposed to fact)

I am too high-born to be propertied,
To be a secondary at control,   80
Or useful servingman and instrument
To any sovereign state throughout the world.
Your breath first kindled the dead coal of wars
Between this chastised kingdom and myself,
And brought in matter that should feed this fire,
And now 'tis far too huge to be blown out
With that same weak wind which enkindled it.
You taught me how to know the face of right,
Acquainted me with interest to this land,
Yea, thrust this enterprise into my heart.   90
And come ye now to tell me John hath made
His peace with Rome? What is that peace to me?
I—by the honour of my marriage-bed—
After young Arthur claim this land for mine.
And now it is half-conquered, must I back
Because that John hath made his peace with Rome?
Am I Rome's slave? What penny hath Rome borne?
What men provided? What munition sent
To underprop this action? Is't not I
That undergo this charge? Who else but I,   100
And such as to my claim are liable,
Sweat in this business and maintain this war?
Have I not heard these islanders shout out
'*Vive le roi*', as I have banked their towns?

---

83 coal of wars] F; coal of war POPE; coals of war HUDSON 1881 (*conj.* Capell, *Notes*)   93
marriage-bed] F4; *not hyphenated in* F1   95 half-conquered] CAMBRIDGE; *not hyphenated in* F

79 **propertied** made a tool of, used as someone else's 'property' (this line is *OED*'s earliest citation)
80 **secondary at control** deputy at the command of another. This line is the first citation for *secondary*, *a.* and *sb.* B.1.
83–7 **Your breath . . . enkindled it** Perhaps these lines allude to the idea of Tilley W424, 'A little wind kindles, much puts out the fire' (certainly present in *Shrew* 2.1.134–5).
83 **coal of wars** The collective *coal* of 4.1.108 makes the singular plausible here, although shifting the *s* from one noun to the other would also be a likely compositorial error (see Collation).

89 **Acquainted me with** made me aware of, informed me of
   interest to specifically, 'a legal right or title to'; more generally, 'advantageous concern with'
98 **munition** The singular usually refers specifically to powder, bullets, etc. (modern 'ammunition').
99 **underprop** support, maintain
100 **undergo** sustain, endure. The word may appear as a feeble echo of *underprop* (l. 99), but it has a wide range of meanings including 'undermine' and 'deceive'; see 4.1.133.
101 **liable** See 2.1.491n.
104 *Vive le roi* i.e., long live the king. The

Have I not here the best cards for the game
To win this easy match played for a crown?
And shall I now give o'er the yielded set?
No, no! On my soul, it never shall be said!

CARDINAL PANDULPH

You look but on the outside of this work.

LOUIS THE DAUPHIN

Outside or inside, I will not return   110
Till my attempt so much be glorified
As to my ample hope was promisèd
Before I drew this gallant head of war,
And culled these fiery spirits from the world
To outlook conquest and to win renown
Even in the jaws of danger and of death.

    A trumpet sounds

What lusty trumpet thus doth summon us?

    Enter Bastard

108 No, no!] This edition; No, no, F; No POPE; No! No, SMALLWOOD   said!] SMALLWOOD;
said. F   116.1 *A . . . sounds] not in* F

terminal *e* of '*Vive*' is sounded. The phrase
appeared on early playing cards (see
Honigmann's edn., p. 170, citing the
work of F. M. H. Bone); for other card-
playing terms, see ll. 106n and 107n.

banked A puzzling word, which Staunton
claimed was 'an allusion to card-playing'
where *banked* = 'won their towns, put
them in bank'. This sense of 'bank' (a
verb) is not recorded in *OED* in Shakespeare's time, nor is the sense of 'bank' =
'a card dealer's stake', but Bone found
closely apposite meanings in most European languages and allusions in English
(Honigmann, p. 170 and n.2). In *N. &*
Q., 200 (1955), 474–5, Ernest Schanzer
supports this interpretation, but shows
that there is no connection between this
passage and a similarly-phrased one in
TR 2.517–22, as Honigmann claimed
(pp. 170–1). Vaughan (pp. 85–6) supported Steevens's tentative gloss—'thrown
up entrenchments before them [the
towns]'—by citing 2 Samuel 20: 15,
'And they came and besieged him . . . and
they cast up a bank against the city, and
the people thereof stood on the ramper'.
It is also possible that *banked* = 'confined
within banks', i.e., is captured; see *v.* 3,
trans. (earliest citation 1622).

106 **match** 'game' or 'contest', but perhaps

recalling his marriage (= *match*) to
Blanche, the basis for his claim on the
English throne

crown a coin worth five shillings, but
punning on the royal regalia and, perhaps, on a bet at cards

107 **set** game or match, a card-playing term.
See the proverbial 'As sure a card as ever
won the set' (*Titus* 5.1.100).

109 **You look but on the outside** Pandulph
schools Louis more confidently and ver-
bosely at 3.4.112 ff.

112 **As . . . promisèd** The phrase modifies
both the preceding line ('so much . . .
As . . . was promisèd') and the following
line ('As . . . was promisèd | Before I
drew').

   ample great, extensive, but almost a
transferred sense (i.e., 'amply promised')

113 **head** force, group of people (here,
soldiers), 'esp. in insurrection' (so *sb.*
III.30)

114 **culled** picked, selected

115 **outlook** outstare, overawe (*OED*'s
earliest citation for this meaning)

116 **jaws of danger and of death** Louis
now adopts the Bastard's imagery
(2.1.352 ff.): language and rhetoric have
followed the shift of military and political
advantage.

BASTARD

According to the fair play of the world,
Let me have audience. I am sent to speak.
My holy lord of Milan, from the King   120
I come to learn how you have dealt for him,
And, as you answer, I do know the scope
And warrant limited unto my tongue.

CARDINAL PANDULPH

The Dauphin is too wilful-opposite,
And will not temporize with my entreaties;
He flatly says he'll not lay down his arms.

BASTARD

By all the blood that ever fury breathed,
The youth says well! Now hear our English King,
For thus his royalty doth speak in me:
He is prepared—and reason too he should—   130

---

118 fair play] POPE; *hyphenated in* F   124 wilful-opposite] THEOBALD; *not hyphenated in* F
128 well!] SMALLWOOD; ~. F   130 He is prepared—and reason too he should—] F (He is
prepar'd, and reason to he should,); He is prepared, and reason too he should. WILSON

---

118 **fair play of the world** Although the
Bastard had earlier scorned 'fair-play
orders' and 'compromise' (5.1.67) when
encouraging John, he is now an official
emissary considering diplomatic as well
as military choices.

121 **dealt for him** Negotiated on his behalf,
but in view of the gaming language at
ll. 104 ff., there may be a hint of 'played
cards for him'.

122–3 **I do know . . . my tongue** i.e., I will
be able to judge the latitude (= *scope*)
and authority (= *warrant*) of what I
may say, acting under the restrictions
(= *limited unto*) of my duties. Claudius
gives his ambassadors to Norway 'no
further personal power . . . than the scope
| Of these dilated [= expressed at length]
articles allow' (*Hamlet* 1.2.36–8).

125 **temporize with my entreaties** negotiate
or compromise with my requests or pleas.
OED, *temporize*, *v.* 4, represents this usage
as occurring only in negotiations with
persons (rather than with the abstract
entreaties); Pandulph may here attempt
to make his requests appear objective
and to separate those requests from the
hostility Louis (or the Bastard) might feel
toward him personally.

126 **flatly** bluntly, without qualification

127 **all the blood . . . breathed** Perhaps a
reference to the Eumenides, the Furies,
associated classically and in Elizabethan
times with blood and poison (as they
were in the dumbshows of Peele's *The
Battle of Alcazar*, and see Kyd, *The Spanish
Tragedy* 1.1.65); Smallwood, however,
paraphrases: 'all those brave spirits who
ever breathed the fury of battle'.

130 **He . . . should** Neither F's punctuation
nor any editorial repunctuation produces
good grammar and good sense. It may
be that the Bastard interrupts himself to
comment on John's behaviour and then
changes the sentence's construction, but
the formality of his introduction (l. 129)
and the rhetorical regularity of the
anaphora in ll. 131–3 and 138–42 make
this more casual comment seem out of
place and ineffective. It is possible that
Shakespeare changed his mind *currente
calamo* or that a copyist or the compositor
failed to note a mark of deletion. The
speech reads very well if l. 130 is omitted,
but many acting texts (e.g., Kemble,
Macready, Kean, and some twentieth-
century versions) have instead cut
ll. 131–4.

This apish and unmannerly approach,
This harnessed masque and unadvisèd revel,
This unheard sauciness and boyish troops,
The King doth smile at and is well prepared
To whip this dwarfish war, these pigmy arms,
From out the circle of his territories.
That hand which had the strength, even at your door,
To cudgel you and make you take the hatch,
To dive like buckets in concealèd wells,

---

133 unheard] F (vn-heard); unhair'd THEOBALD (*conj.* Thirlby)   troops] F; troop DYCE 1864 (*conj.* Capell, *Notes*)   135 these] F (this)

131 **apish and unmannerly** Ape-like and impolite, but the first adjective also means 'fantastically foolish, affected, silly' (2) and the second puns on 'unmanlike, not human' (see 1.1.37n) and 'unmanly, cowardly'. Shakespeare and his contemporaries often used *ape* and its derived forms to criticize fashionable imitation; see 'with French nods and apish courtesy' (*Richard III* 1.3.49); Biron, of Boyet, 'This is the ape of form, Monsieur the Nice' (*LLL* 5.2.326); a French noble, of the English, 'we shall see them imitate | . . . the fashions of our Courts, | As they have ever ap'd us in attire' (Chapman, *Bussy D'Ambois* 1.2.39–41)

132 **harnessed** armoured. Since the Bastard contemptuously regards the French as masquers or revellers rather than serious military opponents, *harnessed* may further connote richly (and excessively) decorated armour better fit for courtly entertainment than battle (see *harnessed, ppl. a.*, 'mounted with silver or other metal', without citations after 1538).
unadvisèd rash, ill-considered

133 **unheard** This group of letters appears four times in F: twice as *vnheard* and twice as *vn-heard*, the latter two both in *K. John* (in this line, set by Compositor C, and at 4.2.136, set by Compositor B). Three meanings are syntactically and orthographically possible: unheard of, strange; unnoticed, unattended to; unhaired, unbearded, hence puerile. The last meaning and modernization (not emendation) have appealed to many editors since Theobald's day, although *OED* cites only Theobald's reading for 'hairless, beardless' and there is only one close semantic parallel in Shakespeare, 'his

hairless face' (*Venus* 487). The transitive verb, 'unhair' ('to deprive (the head, etc.) of hair') dates from 1382 and is used by Shakespeare once (*Antony* 2.5.64), but intransitive usages are cited only from the nineteenth century, as is the *ppl. a.* 'Unhaired' pairs well with 'boyish' later in the line, matching the near-redundancies of l. 131, 'apish and unmannerly', and l. 135, 'dwarfish . . . pigmy'; if the Bastard says *unheard* (= 'unheard of'), he may seem to accord the French too much respect since the usage often occurs in serious contexts with weighty nouns (e.g., 'wickedness', 'wonder', 'malady', all cited at *ppl. a.* 2); finally, if the Bastard says *unheard* (= 'unattended to', hence, perhaps, 'negligible'), he both diminishes the French and neatly escalates the insult of *unadvisèd*.
boyish troops An insult to the young Dauphin, to his unseasoned army, and to his puerile ambitions in England; see 5.1.69.

135 **these** F's *this* was an obsolescent form even in Shakespeare's time (see *these*, A.γ).

136 **circle** circuit, compass, but echoing 'The circle of my glory' (5.1.2)

138 **take the hatch** i.e., leave by leaping over the half-gate or lower half of a divided door. 'Dogs leapt the hatch, and all are fled' (*Tragedy of Lear* 3.6.31) may imply Shakespeare's associations with the phrase (see l. 140: 'crouch in litter of your stable planks').

139 **dive . . . wells** i.e., seek the concealment of wells, do anything to save yourselves. Honigmann compares Tilley B695, 'Like two buckets of a well, if one go up the other must go down'.

To crouch in litter of your stable planks,   140
To lie like pawns locked up in chests and trunks,
To hug with swine, to seek sweet safety out
In vaults and prisons, and to thrill and shake
Even at the crying of your nation's crow,
Thinking this voice an armèd Englishman—
Shall that victorious hand be feebled here,
That in your chambers gave you chastisement?
No! Know the gallant monarch is in arms
And like an eagle o'er his eyrie towers
To souse annoyance that comes near his nest.   150
And you degenerate, you ingrate revolts,
You bloody Neroes, ripping up the womb
Of your dear mother, England: blush for shame,
For your own ladies and pale-visaged maids
Like Amazons come tripping after drums,
Their thimbles into armèd gauntlets change,

145 this] F; his ROWE   Englishman—] This edition; ~. F; ~; CAMBRIDGE   148 No!]
COLLIER; ~ : F   153 mother, England:] This edition; Mother-England: F; mother England,
THEOBALD

140 **To crouch . . . planks** i.e., lie down in
the animals' bedding on the floors of your
stables. Tamburlaine uses similar words
when promising punishment for his
enemies: 'I'll have you learn to feed on
provender | And in a stable lie upon the
planks' (*Tamburlaine, Part 2* 3.5.106–7).
141 **pawns** objects left as security for a loan,
hence 'inactive, useless'
142 **hug** embrace
143 **vaults** underground chambers, perhaps
specifically cellars or burial chambers,
crypts (hence the antithetical play between 'vaults and prisons' and 'seek
sweet safety out' in places one would not
expect to find either comfort or safety)
143–5 **to thrill . . . Englishman** See Introduction, pp. 12–13.
143 **thrill** Shiver (Honigmann), but *v.*¹ II.5c
cites this line in support of 'to be moved
by a thrill of emotion'.
144 **Even . . . crow** '[T]he reverend Mr.
Smith of Harleston, Norfolk', cited in
Zachary Grey, *Critical, Historical, and Ex-
planatory Notes on Shakespeare* (1754),
saw a parallel between this line and
1 Henry VI 1.6.20–2, where Talbot is
called 'the terror of the French | The
scarecrow that affrights our children
so'.

149 **o'er his eyrie towers** soars above his
nest or brood (i.e., above England and
John's subjects, his 'children'). For the
imagery of parent and child and of
England as a body here and in the next
few lines, see 4.2.245–8 and Salisbury's
lament (5.2.25 ff).
150 **souse** swoop or pounce upon (this line
is *OED*'s earliest citation for the figurative
use drawn from the hawk's attack on its
prey). 'Strike, smite' is another contemporary meaning (supported by *cudgel*, l.
138).
151 **revolts** revolters, rebels; an obsolete
noun (so *sb.*², not citing this line). See
2.1.358n and 5.4.7.
152–3 **ripping . . . mother** So the Emperor
Nero was held to have done.
154–8 **For your own ladies . . . bloody
inclination** Noble (p. 117) thought Joel
3: 10 ('Break your ploughshares into
swords and your scythes into spears,
let the weak say, I am strong') had
influenced this passage, and Honigmann
adds Micah 4: 3 (a reciprocal passage:
'. . . of their swords they shall make
ploughshares, and scythes of their
spears . . .') and numerous parallels from
the literature of the 1580s.
154 **ladies** wives

Their needles to lances, and their gentle hearts
To fierce and bloody inclination.

LOUIS THE DAUPHIN

There end thy brave and turn thy face in peace.
We grant thou canst outscold us. Fare thee well,   160
We hold our time too precious to be spent
With such a brabbler.

CARDINAL PANDULPH   Give me leave to speak.

BASTARD

No, I will speak.

LOUIS THE DAUPHIN We will attend to neither.
Strike up the drums, and let the tongue of war
Plead for our interest and our being here.

BASTARD

Indeed, your drums, being beaten, will cry out,
And so shall you, being beaten. Do but start
An echo with the clamour of thy drum,
And even at hand a drum is ready braced
That shall reverberate all as loud as thine.   170

170 all∧] THEOBALD; ~, F

157 **needles** F's *Needls* may indicate monosyllabic pronunciation and is possibly a
Shakespearian spelling.

158 **inclination** disposition; pronounced as
having five syllables

159 **brave** taunt, challenge

160 **outscold** outdo in scolding; *OED*'s
earliest citation

162 **brabbler** quarreller, brawler

164–5 **Strike . . . here** Richard III similarly
threatens to use the music of war to
drown an unwelcome 'accent of reproof'
(*Richard III* 4.4.149–59).

166 **your drums, being beaten** Francis
Gentleman complained of this passage,
'he poorly and indelicately puns upon
the beating of drums' (ii. 165), and
Branam writes that 'Cibber refused Faulconbridge the privilege of playing with
the idea of drums in a passage that
undoubtedly violated Cibber's sense of
propriety' (p. 87). The indelicacy's precise
nature is hard to recover, but it evidently involves fornication, a growling
stomach, and beaten buttocks. Face, for
example, advises Doll on how to handle
Surly: 'he shall be brought here . . . and

thrown | In a down-bed, as dark as any
dungeon; | Where thou shalt keep him
waking, with thy drum; | Thy drum, my
Doll' (Jonson, *The Alchemist* 3.3.41–5).
Cotgrave defines: 'tabourer' as 'To
drum. . . . also to strike, or bump on
the posteriorums'; 'tabourin' as '. . . a
Drum . . . also, a Timpany in the belly';
'taboureur' as 'A Drummer . . . also, a
thumper, bumper, knocker; whoremon-
ger'. *OED*'s most apposite citations also
appear under *tabor, v.* 3; for example, 'I
would tabor her, | Till all the legions that
are crept into her, | Flew out with fire
i'the tails' (Fletcher, *The Woman's Prize*,
2.4.21–3) and Charles Sorel, *The Comical
History of Francion* (1655): 'a score of
handsome lasses . . . came all frisking
towards me, beating the Switzers march
upon their buttocks; and after some
pretty freaks . . . they fell to tabor mine
to the same tune' (H4; lib. 3, p. 55).

169 **ready** prepared for instant use
braced i.e., with the skin stretched tight
(= *braced*)

170 **reverberate all as loud as thine** F's

Sound but another, and another shall
As loud as thine rattle the welkin's ear
And mock the deep-mouthed thunder. For at hand—
Not trusting to this halting legate here,
Whom he hath used rather for sport than need—
Is warlike John, and in his forehead sits
A bare-ribbed death, whose office is this day
To feast upon whole thousands of the French.

LOUIS THE DAUPHIN
Strike up our drums to find this danger out.

BASTARD
And thou shalt find it, Dauphin, do not doubt.   180

Exeunt severally

5.3   *Alarums. Enter King John and Hubert, ⌐severally⌐*
KING JOHN
How goes the day with us? O, tell me, Hubert.
HUBERT
Badly, I fear. How fares your majesty?

---

173 deep-mouthed] THEOBALD; *not hyphenated in* F   180 *severally*] *not in* F
    5.3] F (*Scaena Tertia*)   0.1 *severally*] *not in* F. *See note.*

punctuation may indicate two meanings
for the phrase: the English drum will
equal in amount (*all*) the French drum-
ming; the English drum will be entirely
as loud as the French drum (where
all intensifies the *as . . . as* construction).
172 **welkin's** sky's, heavens'. Honigmann
    notes that 'Shakespeare usually used *wel-
    kin* in "extravagant" poetry'.
173 **mock the deep-mouthed thunder** In
    honour of Hamlet's decision to remain
    in Denmark, Claudius orders cannon to
    be fired 'Re-speaking earthly thunder'
    each time he drinks (*Hamlet* 1.2.125–8).
174 **halting** hesitating, wavering, shifting
    (so *ppl. a.* 3, without citations between
    1585 and 1875)
175 **for sport** for pleasure, as a jest (the
    Bastard's own view of Pandulph, not
    John's)
176–8 **warlike . . . feast** Proverbial imagery;
    see 2.1.352–4n.
177 **A bare-ribbed death**, F's punctuation
    emphasizes the Bastard's personification;
    he imagines numerous 'deaths', a specific

one of which has the duty (= *office*) of
taking French lives. Steevens cited 'a
bare-boned death' (*Lucrece* 1761).
179 **find this danger out** search for or un-
    cover this peril
180 **find** A pun: discover; suffer. See
    3.1.28n.
5.3 Location: a field of battle. James Hirsh
    describes this and the following two
    scenes as 'a series of episodes in parallel
    scenic structure' because 'in each the
    direction of the scene is changed by a
    character who enters mid-way to deliver
    a message'; see *The Structure of Shake-
    spearean Scenes* (New Haven, Conn.,
    1981), pp. 123–4.
0.1 *Alarums* The word directs the sounds of
    battle off-stage; see 3.2.0.1n and head-
    note to 3.3.
    severally from different (and in the
    Elizabethan public theatre perhaps op-
    posite) entrances to the stage. As the
    characters' immediate questions suggest,
    they are ignorant of each other's suc-
    cess and hence should enter as if from
    different parts of the field.

KING JOHN

This fever that hath troubled me so long
Lies heavy on me. O, my heart is sick!
    Enter a Messenger

MESSENGER

My lord, your valiant kinsman Faulconbridge
Desires your majesty to leave the field
And send him word by me which way you go.

KING JOHN

Tell him, toward Swinstead, to the abbey there.

MESSENGER

Be of good comfort, for the great supply
That was expected by the Dauphin here   10
Are wrecked three nights ago on Goodwin Sands.
This news was brought to Richard but even now.
The French fight coldly and retire themselves.

KING JOHN

Ay me, this tyrant fever burns me up
And will not let me welcome this good news.
Set on toward Swinstead. To my litter straight;
Weakness possesseth me, and I am faint.   *Exeunt*

4 sick!] POPE; sicke. F   12 now.] JOHNSON; ~, F. *See note.*   14 Ay me] F (Aye me)   16
Swinstead] F; Swineshead HALLIWELL. *See note to 5.3.8.*

3 **This fever** John's illness has not been
mentioned before.

8 **Swinstead** An error for another Lin-
colnshire town, Swineshead, to which
John travelled shortly before his death
and where there was a Cistercian abbey;
on the error's possible source, see Introduction, p. 17 n.1. Historically, John died
in Newark Castle.

9 **supply** reinforcements of troops. On the
similarity of ll. 9–11 to 5.5.12–13, see
Introduction, p. 37.

11 **Are** As a collective noun, *supply* could
take either the singular or the plural
(see *was* at l. 10 and *Are* at 5.5.13);
Honigmann regards *was* (l. 10) and *Are*
as confusions of tense and number, but
the Messenger's tenses reflect Louis's present ignorance and the past fact of the
lost supply.
Goodwin Sands '[A] shoal off the coast
of Kent between the Isle of Thanet and
the S. Foreland' (Sugden); Salerio calls
the Goodwins 'a very dangerous flat and
fatal' (*Merchant* 3.1.4–5).

12–13 **This news . . . themselves** Jowett
(in Oxford) repunctuates to change F's
apparent meaning: 'This news was
brought to Richard, but even now | The
French fight coldly and retire themselves.' The punctuation adopted here
assumes that the Messenger first conveys
the Bastard's urgent military advice
(John should depart immediately); only
then, perhaps in response to John's appearance, does the Messenger explain the
Bastard's reasoning: the enemy has lost
troops and heart.

12 **Richard** the Bastard (see 1.1.162 and
Appendix A2)

13 **retire themselves** retreat, withdraw.
OED's entry for the reflexive does not
include a specifically military sense.

14 **Ay me** See 3.1.305n; *OED*'s earliest
citation is from 1591.

16 **my litter** In *TR*, this 'litter' may appear
on stage: *Enter King John carried between
2 Lords* (2.785.1).
straight at once

5.4 ⌈*Alarum.*⌉ *Enter the Earls of Salisbury and Pembroke,*
        and Lord Bigot

SALISBURY

I did not think the King so stored with friends.

PEMBROKE

Up once again! Put spirit in the French;

If they miscarry, we miscarry too.

SALISBURY

That misbegotten devil Faulconbridge,

In spite of spite, alone upholds the day.

PEMBROKE

They say King John, sore sick, hath left the field.
        Enter Melun, wounded, ⌈*led by a soldier*⌉

MELUN

Lead me to the revolts of England here.

SALISBURY

When we were happy, we had other names.

PEMBROKE

It is the Count Melun.

SALISBURY   Wounded to death.

MELUN

Fly, noble English; you are bought and sold.   10

Unthread the rude eye of rebellion

And welcome home again discarded faith.

5.4] F (*Scena Quarta*)   0.1 *Alarum*] OXFORD; *not in* F   0.1–2 *Enter . . . Bigot*] F (*Enter Salisbury, Pembroke, and Bigot.*)   6.1 *led by a soldier*] OXFORD; *not in* F

5.4 Location: a field of battle, late in the day (ll. 33 ff.).

1 **stored** stocked, supplied, provided

2 **Up once again!** back to the battle! to arms!

5 **In spite of spite** i.e., defying defiance (*sb.* 5c, from 1592, but earlier in Sidney's *Astrophil and Stella* 59.10; see also Dent SS18)

6.1 *Melun* Mentioned at 4.3.15 ('Count Melun') as bearing a letter from Pandulph to the rebel lords and a silent presence in 5.2, Melun's appearance here comes as a shock, intensified by his urging the English lords to return to John. Holinshed describes a 'Viscount of Melune' who 'at the point of death' did indeed warn the English rebels (193b; R5).

7 **revolts of England** English revolters, rebels

10 **bought and sold** A common expression (Tilley B787; Whiting has many instances from *c.*1325 onward).

11 **Unthread . . . rebellion** This line is *OED*'s earliest citation for *unthread*. The metaphor is from sewing: like the needle joined with thread, rebellion is effective only when combined with the lords' service. 'Our author is not always careful that the epithet which he applies to a figurative term should answer on both sides. *Rude* is applicable to *rebellion*, but not to *eye*. He means, in fact,—the eye of rude rebellion' (Malone). On the image, see *More*, Addition III, ll. 19–21: 'to be great | Is, when the thread of hazard is once spun, | A bottom great wound up, greatly undone'.

12 **discarded** Literally, cast off, rejected (*OED*'s earliest citation for this meaning,

Seek out King John and fall before his feet,
For if the French be lords of this loud day,
He means to recompense the pains you take
By cutting off your heads. Thus hath he sworn,
And I with him, and many more with me,
Upon the altar at Saint Edmundsbury,
Even on that altar where we swore to you
Dear amity and everlasting love.   20

SALISBURY

May this be possible? May this be true?

MELUN

Have I not hideous death within my view,
Retaining but a quantity of life,
Which bleeds away, even as a form of wax
Resolveth from his figure 'gainst the fire?
What in the world should make me now deceive,
Since I must lose the use of all deceit?
Why should I then be false, since it is true
That I must die here and live hence by truth?
I say again, if Louis do win the day,   30
He is forsworn if e'er those eyes of yours
Behold another daybreak in the east.
But even this night, whose black contagious breath

14 French] F; Prince KEIGHTLEY lords] F; lord CAMBRIDGE *conj.*   15 He] F; Lewis HONIGMANN
17 more] F (moe)   18 Saint] F2; S. F

now antedated by Schäfer to Nashe's *Unfortunate Traveller*, ii. 216, l. 9; the next citation is from 1718). It is more likely that the sewing metaphor of l. 11 has developed into one from the preparation of wool for spinning into yarn or cloth; 'card' = a tined instrument used to comb raw wool.

14 **loud** noisy, clamorous

15 **He** i.e., Louis, whom Melun does not name in the rest of his speech. The English lords immediately understand and thereby suggest how dependent they are on the French and how wavering their determination is. Shakespeare uses 'he' after a collective 'The French' at *Henry V* 4.4.72, as does Marlowe after 'The Turks' at *The Jew of Malta* 1.1.182, 185.

23 **quantity** small piece, fragment (II.8), probably of time (I.3), which the meta-

phor of the next line transforms into a small amount of liquid (wax, blood)

24–5 **wax . . . fire** A common image: Dent W137.1, 'To melt (etc.) like wax against the fire' (examples from *c.*1300; for additions to Dent, see *3 Henry VI* 3.2.51 and *Two Gentlemen* 2.4.198–200).

25 **Resolveth** melts, dissolves. See 4.1.35n.
   his figure its shape

26–9 **What in the world . . . hence by truth** See Tilley M514, 'Dying men speak true'.

29 **die here and live hence** Melun's contrast is probably spatial: *here* = in this world; *hence* = in the next world, although *hence* could also mean 'henceforth'.

31 **forsworn** i.e., he will break his oath (to execute you) if he allows you to live

33 **night** For the moral connotations of night, see 3.3.37 ff. and 5.6.19–20, for example.

Already smokes about the burning crest
Of the old, feeble, and day-wearied sun,
Even this ill night, your breathing shall expire,
Paying the fine of rated treachery
Even with a treacherous fine of all your lives,
If Louis by your assistance win the day.
Commend me to one Hubert with your King.   40
The love of him and this respect besides,
For that my grandsire was an Englishman,
Awakes my conscience to confess all this.
In lieu whereof, I pray you bear me hence
From forth the noise and rumour of the field,
Where I may think the remnant of my thoughts
In peace, and part this body and my soul
With contemplation and devout desires.

SALISBURY

We do believe thee, and beshrew my soul,
But I do love the favour and the form   50
Of this most fair occasion, by the which
We will untread the steps of damnèd flight,
And like a bated and retirèd flood,
Leaving our rankness and irregular course,
Stoop low within those bounds we have o'erlooked
And calmly run on in obedience

---

34 crest] F (Crest); cresset OXFORD (*conj.* Cambridge)

34 **smokes** rises, spreads, or moves like
smoke (so *v.* 2b, citing this line as its first
example and the next from 1726–46)
crest i.e., the arc of the setting sun
and, proleptically, the defiled plumes or
heraldic arms of the treasonous English
lords. 'Cresset' (= torch, fire-basket) is a
plausible emendation, but it flattens the
image.

36 **your breathing** i.e., your lives

37–8 **Paying the fine . . . fine of all your
lives** In both lines, *fine* may = 'penalty',
but the antimetabole (fine, treachery/
treacherous fine) suggests word-play on
two further meanings of *fine*, 'result,
consequence' and 'conclusion, death':
the consequence of treachery is death as
a traitor; a traitor's death is a treacherous
result of his actions.

37 **rated** reckoned, assessed (so *ppl. a.*¹, citing
this line as its earliest example). There

may be a hint of the other principal
meaning of *rated*: chastised or reproved.

44 **In lieu whereof** in return for (the only
Shakespearian sense)

45 **rumour** confused din (Honigmann)

47 **part** Sever, sunder; but Melun may also
be speaking subjunctively, 'allow my
body and soul to depart' (see *may* in
l. 46).

50 **favour** appearance, aspect (so *sb.* 9,
citing this line), but probably also
'charm, attractive aspect' and even,
with sycophantic hyperbole, 'exceptional
kindness, boon'
form external appearance, manner

52 **untread** retrace, but perhaps recalling
unthread (l. 11)

53–7 **a bated . . . ocean** The imagery recalls
that of 2.1.442–5.

54 **rankness** condition of overflowing, swelling above banks

Even to our ocean, to our great King John.
My arm shall give thee help to bear thee hence,
For I do see the cruel pangs of death
Right in thine eye. Away, my friends! New flight,   60
And happy newness, that intends old right!   *Exeunt*

5.5   ⌜*Alarum; retreat.*⌝ *Enter Louis the Dauphin, and
his train*

LOUIS THE DAUPHIN
The sun of heaven, methought, was loath to set,
But stayed and made the western welkin blush,
When English measured backward their own ground
In faint retire. O, bravely came we off,
When with a volley of our needless shot,
After such bloody toil, we bid good night
And wound our tott'ring colours clearly up,
Last in the field, and almost lords of it.
     Enter a Messenger

61 right!] THEOBALD; ∼. F

5.5] F (*Scena Quinta*)   0.1 *Alarum; retreat*] OXFORD; *not in* F   0.1–2 *Enter . . . train*] F
(*Enter Dolphin, and his Traine.*)   3 measured] POPE; measure F   7 wound] F (woon'd)
clearly] F; chearly CAPELL, *Notes, conj.*; cleanly CAMBRIDGE *conj.*

60–1 **Right . . . old right** The couplet gets its
energy from the superficial contradiction
between the rhyme words.

60 **Right** 'unmistakably' (Wilson), plainly.
OED offers no support for this gloss,
although it defines the adjective in reference to the eyes as 'directed straight
forward' (as Melun's may be literally—
he is near death, his eyes almost 'set'—
or figuratively—he has his eyes properly,
another meaning of *right*, directed toward
heaven rather than earth). Editors have
proposed many emendations.
New flight 'New' as opposed to the 'old'
flight (= *damnèd flight* of l. 52) *from* their
allegiance to John (= *old right* of l. 61).

61 *Exeunt* Line 58 suggests Salisbury should
help the dying Melun to leave the stage.

5.5 Location: a field of battle. This scene is
often cut from acting texts (e.g., those
of Kean, Macready, Irving, and several
twentieth-century productions).

0.2 **train** customary attendants, here probably nobles and staff officers in sufficient
number to make the Messenger's question (l. 9) plausible

1 **loath** reluctant, unwilling

3 **measured backward** marked or paced off
in retreat. The past tense seems logically
required by the preceding verbs; the
compositor may have made the common
e/d error, setting F's *measure* for manuscript 'measurd'.

4 **faint** weak, cowardly
retire retreat
bravely splendidly, proudly as well as
courageously

5 **needless** Both 'unnecessary' (because the
English have left the field) and 'superfluous' (because the salute, the 'good
night', is directed at no object); Louis
echoes his father (2.1.251–2).

7 **wound** furled
tott'ring colours i.e., banners (= *colours*)
that are waving (= *tott'ring*) or shaking
in the wind and banners that are or
have been shredded or made ragged (=
tattering, a spelling variant of *tott'ring*)
through the effects of the enemy's shot
clearly without (English) encumbrance
or interference. The popular conjectural
emendation, 'cleanly', amounts to the

259

MESSENGER

Where is my prince, the Dauphin?

LOUIS THE DAUPHIN   Here. What news?

MESSENGER

The Count Melun is slain; the English lords   10
By his persuasion are again fall'n off,
And your supply, which you have wished so long,
Are cast away and sunk on Goodwin Sands.

LOUIS THE DAUPHIN

Ah foul, shrewd news! Beshrew thy very heart!
I did not think to be so sad tonight
As this hath made me. Who was he that said
King John did fly an hour or two before
The stumbling night did part our weary powers?

MESSENGER

Whoever spoke it, it is true, my lord.

LOUIS THE DAUPHIN

Well, keep good quarter and good care tonight;   20
The day shall not be up so soon as I
To try the fair adventure of tomorrow.   *Exeunt*

5.6   *Enter Bastard and Hubert, severally*

HUBERT

Who's there? Speak, ho! Speak quickly, or I shoot.

14 shrewd] F (shrew'd)   news!] THEOBALD;   ∼. F   heart!] CAPELL;   ∼: F
   5.6] F (*Scena Sexta*)   1–6] *See Appendix D.*   1 ho!] THEOBALD; hoa, F

same thing (see *clean, a.* 1d, without
citations after 1300); note the antithesis
with *tott'ring.*

13 **Are** See 5.3.11n.
14 **shrewd** troubling, attended by misfor-
tune. As F's *shrew'd* (= 'shrewed') suggests, the adjective is historically related
to *shrew* and *beshrew* as verbs.
   Beshrew curse (a play upon *shrewd*)
18 **stumbling** A transferred adjective: the
night causes men to stumble.
20 **keep good quarter** keep good watch,
preserve good order (so *quarter, sb.*
III.14d, citing this line as its earliest
example), but a soldier in *Antony* urges
his comrades to 'Follow the noise so far
as we have quarter' (4.3.19), i.e., to
the limits of our assigned positions or
stations; thus 'keep good quarter' may

mean something like 'remain at your
duty posts'.
22 **try the fair adventure** test the promising
hazard or peril. Etymologically, *adventure*
is related to French *avenir* (Cotgrave:
advenir), the future, that which is to
come.
5.6 Location: a place not far from John's
fictional refuge at Swinstead Abbey (see
5.3.8n and 5.6.43–4); the scene occurs
at night (see l. 12), and the Oxford edn.
underscores the fact by equipping the
Bastard *with a light* (and Hubert *with a
pistol*).
0.1 *severally* See 5.3.0.1n.
1–6 **Who's there . . . perfect thought** For
the reassignment of speeches here, see
Appendix D.

BASTARD

A friend. What art thou?

HUBERT   Of the part of England.

BASTARD

Whither dost thou go?

HUBERT   What's that to thee?

BASTARD

Why may not I demand of thine affairs

As well as thou of mine? Hubert, I think.

HUBERT Thou hast a perfect thought.

I will upon all hazards well believe

Thou art my friend, that know'st my tongue so well.

Who art thou?

BASTARD   Who thou wilt. An if thou please,

Thou mayst befriend me so much as to think   10

I come one way of the Plantagenets.

HUBERT

Unkind remembrance! Thou and endless night

Have done me shame. Brave soldier, pardon me

That any accent breaking from thy tongue

Should scape the true acquaintance of mine ear.

BASTARD

Come, come, sans compliment. What news abroad?

9 An] F (And)   12 remembrance!] THEOBALD; ~ : F

2 **part** side, allegiance

3 **What's that to thee?** A common question, perhaps a challenging catch-phrase: Dent W280.4, 'What is that to you (thee)', citing examples from *c.*1593–1614 and four other Shakespearian uses.

6 **perfect** accurate, true

7 **upon all hazards** See 1.1.119, 2.1.71, and notes.

9 **An if** if

10 **befriend** act as a friend toward; but since the passage has twice stressed *friend* (ll. 2, 8), the Bastard may be joking about the word's over-use. In that case, it means 'to call . . . to dub with the title' (i.e., the title of 'friend'); see *be-*, *prefix* 5b, giving no examples with 'friend'. The orthography here, *be-friend*, is unique in F.

11 **come one way** i.e., trace my descent via one parent

12 **Unkind remembrance!** unnatural or thoughtless memory. Hubert upbraids his

(personified) memory.

endless night total darkness. As Honigmann shows, the adjective is a common intensive and this phrase almost cliché. Hubert's news and despair (ll. 19–20) make the moment a little less melodramatic in retrospect.

14 **accent** word, speech (Honigmann)

breaking bursting into utterance

15 **scape** An aphetic form (= 'escape'); *OED* regards as poetical diction.

16 **sans compliment** without (= *sans*, a French loan word) undue politeness or formality. The Bastard is brusque, but not angry: Hubert's words (ll. 12–15) are inopportune rather than excessive or ridiculous (compare the 'dialogue of compliment' at 1.1.201 and see Bevington, p. 154: 'Often the disruption in the form of greeting is caused by some crisis and consequent need for haste that abort accustomed ceremony').

HUBERT

  Why, here walk I in the black brow of night
  To find you out.

BASTARD   Brief, then, and what's the news?

HUBERT

  O my sweet sir, news fitting to the night,
  Black, fearful, comfortless, and horrible.   20

BASTARD

  Show me the very wound of this ill news;
  I am no woman, I'll not swoon at it.

HUBERT

  The King, I fear, is poisoned by a monk;
  I left him almost speechless and broke out
  To acquaint you with this evil, that you might
  The better arm you to the sudden time
  Than if you had at leisure known of this.

BASTARD

  How did he take it? Who did taste to him?

HUBERT

  A monk, I tell you, a resolvèd villain,
  Whose bowels suddenly burst out. The King   30
  Yet speaks and peradventure may recover.

BASTARD

  Who didst thou leave to tend his majesty?

HUBERT

  Why, know you not? The lords are all come back

22 swoon] F (swound)   33 Why,] THEOBALD; ~∧ F

17 **black brow** dark forehead. Probably a
neutral metaphor as 'loving, black-
browed night' in Juliet's invocation
(*Romeo* 3.2.20) and Puck's description
of spirits 'exiled from light' that 'must
for aye consort with black-browed night'
(*Dream* 3.2.388) suggest. F's reading
echoes the ten other uses of *brow*(s) in
the play (the highest number of any
Shakespeare text; the next highest are
LLL, nine, and *Romeo*, seven).
18 **Brief** i.e., be brief
21 **very wound** precise injury
22 **swoon** faint, lose consciousness. F's
swound represents a contemporary pronunciation and creates an internal, if
unwitty, rhyme with *wound* (l. 21; see
Cercignani, p. 318), but it is hard to

imagine a modern production retaining
the pronunciation and rhyme.
23 **The King . . . monk** An intolerably
clumsy piece of exposition, if the audience
does not know its history, or *TR*.
26 **sudden time** i.e., these events that come
without warning and all at once (see
sudden, adj. A.1, quoting this line)
27 **at leisure** without haste or 'when you
were less occupied'
28 **How did he take it?** i.e., how did he come
to eat (the poisoned food)?
    taste to him i.e., serve as his 'taster',
an individual who sampled food before
another ate it
31 **Yet** still
33 **know you not?** As in l. 23, the exposition is crude, and the Bastard comically

And brought Prince Henry in their company,
At whose request the King hath pardoned them,
And they are all about his majesty.

BASTARD

Withhold thine indignation, mighty heaven,
And tempt us not to bear above our power!
I'll tell thee, Hubert, half my power this night,
Passing these flats, are taken by the tide—   40
These Lincoln Washes have devourèd them;
Myself, well mounted, hardly have escaped.
Away before! Conduct me to the King;
I doubt he will be dead or ere I come.   *Exeunt*

5.7   *Enter Prince Henry, the Earl of Salisbury, and Lord
        Bigot*

PRINCE HENRY

It is too late. The life of all his blood
Is touched corruptibly, and his pure brain,
Which some suppose the soul's frail dwelling-house,
Doth by the idle comments that it makes
Foretell the ending of mortality.
        Enter Pembroke

---

37 heaven] F (heauen); God MATCHETT   38 power!] CAPELL; ~. F   41 Lincoln Washes]
THEOBALD; Lincolne-Washes F   43 before!] CAPELL; ~ : F
    5.7] F (*Scena Septima*)   0.1–2 *Enter . . . Bigot*] F (*Enter Prince Henry, Salisburie, and Bigot.*)

ignorant, unless the audience is aware
of the legend.

38 **tempt us not to bear above our power**
i.e., do not induce or call upon us to
suffer or exert ourselves beyond our capacity. See 'There hath no temptation
taken you, but such as followeth the
nature of man: but God is faithful, which
shall not suffer you to be tempted above
that you are able: but shall with the
temptation make a way to escape, that
ye may be able to bear it' (1 Corinthians
10: 13, cited by Carter, p. 216 and
Noble, p. 118).

40 **Passing these flats** i.e., crossing these
sandbanks or shoals (some of which
are uncovered at low tide). Shakespeare has transferred to the Bastard
a disaster that historically (and in *TR*)
befell John.

41 **Lincoln Washes** 'The Wash is the bay

S.E. of Lincoln. It is full of dangerous
sandbanks' (Sugden).

42 **well mounted** seated on a good horse (so
ppl. a. 1, citing this line as its earliest
example)
    hardly 'Barely' and/or 'with difficulty'
are the primary senses, but 'violently'
and 'boldly, hardily' may also be present.

44 **doubt** fear, expect apprehensively

5.7 Location: the fruit and herb garden (see
l. 10) of Swinstead Abbey.

0.1 *Prince Henry* John's eldest son (born
1206; reigned 1216–72); at least as
recently as a Ben Iden Payne production
(Stratford, 1940), the part has been
taken by an actress (and see Sprague,
pp. 22–3).

2 **touched** infected, tainted (this line is
OED's earliest citation at *v*. I.7)

4 **idle comments** incoherent or nonsensical
remarks

263

PEMBROKE

His highness yet doth speak and holds belief
That being brought into the open air,
It would allay the burning quality
Of that fell poison which assaileth him.

PRINCE HENRY

Let him be brought into the orchard here.   10

                                        Exit Bigot

Doth he still rage?

PEMBROKE   He is more patient
Than when you left him; even now he sung.

PRINCE HENRY

O vanity of sickness! Fierce extremes
In their continuance will not feel themselves.
Death, having preyed upon the outward parts,
Leaves them invisible, and his siege is now
Against the mind, the which he pricks and wounds
With many legions of strange fantasies,
Which, in their throng and press to that last hold,
Confound themselves. 'Tis strange that death should
    sing.   20
I am the cygnet to this pale faint swan

10.1 *Exit Bigot*] CAPELL; *not in* F   13 sickness!] ROWE; sicknesse: F   15 preyed] F (praide)
16 invisible] F (inuisible); invincible SMALLWOOD (*conj.* Steevens); invasible WILSON *conj.*   17
mind] ROWE 1714; winde F   21 cygnet] ROWE 1714; Symet F

9 **fell** deadly

10 **orchard** garden

11 **rage** rave

13 **vanity** futile activity

14 **will not feel themselves** See 3.4.49n.

15–20 **Death, having preyed . . . themselves**
The imagery of possession so common in
4.2 now becomes more literal as death
captures and conquers John.

16 **invisible** invisibly. The same metaphors in
'Death with armies of Cimmerian spirits |
Gives battle 'gainst the heart of Tamburlaine . . . These cowards invisibly assail
his soul | And threaten conquest on our
sovereign' (*Tamburlaine, Part 2* 5.3.8 ff.)
appear to have caused semantic or
graphic difficulty: the 1590 octavo reads
inuisiblie, the 1592/3 octavo, *inuincible*.
Similarly, F1 prints *incureable* at 5.1.16
where F4 reads *incurably*; adjectives ending in *-ble* and adverbs ending in *-blie*
would have been easy to confuse in
manuscript and their grammatical dis-

tinction was not yet fixed (see Abbott
§1, without examples of the *-able/-ably*
interchange).

18 **legions** Both 'hosts' or 'multitudes' and
'groups of armed men'; see *siege* and *hold*
in ll. 16, 19 and *legions* in Matthew 26:
53.
strange fantasies Earlier, the people were
'strangely fantasied' (see 4.2.144 and
n.).

19 **throng and press** The image is of a crowd,
perhaps at court, perhaps at a doorway,
as in 'Much like a press of people at a
door | Throng her inventions, which shall
go before' (*Lucrece* 1301–2).
hold stronghold, last refuge. The metaphor refers to the most defensible and
best defended portion of a castle.

20 **Confound** defeat, encumber

21–2 **swan . . . death** Tilley S1028 (examples
from *c.*1489 and four other uses in
Shakespeare).

Who chants a doleful hymn to his own death
And from the organ-pipe of frailty sings
His soul and body to their lasting rest.

SALISBURY

Be of good comfort, Prince, for you are born
To set a form upon that indigest
Which he hath left so shapeless and so rude.

　　John brought in

KING JOHN

Ay, marry, now my soul hath elbow-room;
It would not out at windows nor at doors.
There is so hot a summer in my bosom   30
That all my bowels crumble up to dust;
I am a scribbled form, drawn with a pen
Upon a parchment, and against this fire
Do I shrink up.

PRINCE HENRY　　How fares your majesty?

KING JOHN

Poisoned, ill fare; dead, forsook, cast off,

27.1 *John brought in*] F (*Iohn brought in*); *Enter Attendants, and Bigot, carrying King John in a chair* CAPELL　　28 Ay, marry,] F (I marrie,)

26 **form** See 5.4.50.
　　indigest shapeless mass (*sb.* B, citing this line only). Shakespeare would have known the Ovidian tag, *Quem dixere chaos, rudis indigestaque moles* (*Metamorphoses*, i. 7: 'What [men] call chaos, a rough, unordered mass'). Shakespeare uses 'indigest' (as an adjective) in only one other place, Sonnet 114.5, and 'indigested' twice (*2 Henry VI* 5.1.155 and *3 Henry VI* 5.6.51).
27 **rude** immature, undeveloped, unfinished
27.1 *brought in* i.e., carried in a chair, presumably; an unusual staging in F. See *1 Henry VI* 2.5.0.1 and TLN 1469–70, *2 Henry VI* 2.1.67.2–3, *3 Henry VI* 4.4.0.3–4, *Lear* TLN 2771, and, for similar staging in *TR*, see 5.3.16n.
28–48 **now my soul . . . condemnèd blood** Ernest Schanzer (*N. & Q.*, 201 (1956), 509–10) shows John's speeches here to be analogous to, perhaps based on, the cries of the poisoned Hercules in Seneca's *Hercules Oetaeus* 1359–71.
28 **Ay** yes. John affirms to himself or the company that being out of doors has eased his distress (see ll. 6–9).

marry a weakened form of an oath ('by the Virgin Mary') intensifying John's statement
elbow-room *OED* and Tilley (E104, 'Now he has elbow-room enough to turn him in') date this compound from *c*.1540.
32 **scribbled form** carelessly written or sketched shape
34 **shrink up** As parchment does when brought near heat; the shrivelling of the parchment imitates the 'scribble' of the lines on it. John's body now becomes as *shapeless* and *rude* (l. 27) as his kingdom's; he soon wishes (ll. 38–9) he could merge one body with the other.
35 **Poisoned, ill fare** John's subsequent joke on 'cold comfort' (l. 42) activates the common Shakespearian quibble on *fare* = do and = food; John answers Prince Henry's question (I am poisoned; I fare ill) and alludes to the fatal meal (I have eaten poisoned fare). For other examples, see Schmidt, *vb.* 3, and *Edward III* 4.8.1–2. A Shakespearian tradition held that dying men jest: 'How oft, when men are at the point of death, | Have they been merry, which their keepers call |

And none of you will bid the winter come
To thrust his icy fingers in my maw,
Nor let my kingdom's rivers take their course
Through my burned bosom, nor entreat the north
To make his bleak winds kiss my parchèd lips   40
And comfort me with cold. I do not ask you much;
I beg cold comfort. And you are so strait
And so ungrateful, you deny me that.

PRINCE HENRY

O that there were some virtue in my tears
That might relieve you!

KING JOHN   The salt in them is hot.
Within me is a hell, and there the poison
Is, as a fiend, confined to tyrannize
On unreprievable, condemnèd blood.

    Enter Bastard

BASTARD

O, I am scalded with my violent motion
And spleen of speed to see your majesty!   50

KING JOHN

O cousin, thou art come to set mine eye!

---

42 strait] F (straight)   43 ungrateful] F (ingratefull)   45 you!] THEOBALD; ~. F   48 unreprievable, condemnèd] POPE; *not punctuated in* F   50 majesty!] HALLIWELL; Maiesty. F   51 eye!] SMALLWOOD; ~: F

A lightning before death' (*Romeo* 5.3.88–90).

36–7 **winter . . . icy fingers** In *Lust's Dominion* (*c.*1599; printed 1657), attributed to Dekker and others, a character who is apparently dying claims 'the cold hand of sleep | Hath thrust his icy fingers in my breast' (3.2.65–6); 'Death's frozen hand' appears at 1.1.167); Hoy (iv. 88) records three other phrases in Dekker analogous to 'icy fingers' here.

37 **maw** stomach (usually used of animals)

39 **north** north wind

42 **cold comfort** Tilley C542 (examples from 1571 onward); John wishes to be cooled, but *cold comfort* is no comfort at all (hence the irony of being refused even it).
strait stingy, illiberal

44 **virtue** strength, power, capacity

47 **as a fiend, confined** i.e., like Satan confined by God to Hell, so the poison is confined to John's inner hell, where it

torments his blood as Satan torments damned souls

48 **unreprievable** John takes Henry's *virtue* (l. 44) to mean 'morally positive quality' and claims that his soul is condemned beyond reprieve.

49 **scalded** Figuratively, 'inflamed' or 'burned' (with my desire to see you; so *scald, v.* II.7 *trans.*, citing this line); literally, the Bastard is sweaty with haste. See next n.

50 **spleen** eagerness (see 2.1.449n). The Bastard's heated imagery echoes John's.

51–3 **to set . . . sail** Mahood sees unconscious word-play here: 'In a sixteenth-century sailing ship, the dead man's eyes (now the deadeyes) were part of the tackle, consisting of paired wooden discs, which joined the shrouds to the channels. One kind of deadeye is called a heart' (p. 21).

51 **set mine eye** close my eye(s) after death. *Eye* is an archaic plural.

The tackle of my heart is cracked and burnt,
And all the shrouds wherewith my life should sail
Are turnèd to one thread, one little hair.
My heart hath one poor string to stay it by,
Which holds but till thy news be utterèd,
And then all this thou seest is but a clod
And module of confounded royalty.

BASTARD

The Dauphin is preparing hitherward,
Where God he knows how we shall answer him!   60
For in a night the best part of my power,
As I upon advantage did remove,
Were in the Washes all unwarily
Devourèd by the unexpected flood.   *John dies*

SALISBURY

You breathe these dead news in as dead an ear—
My liege! My lord!—But now a king, now thus.

PRINCE HENRY

Even so must I run on, and even so stop.
What surety of the world, what hope, what stay,
When this was now a king, and now is clay?

60 God] HONIGMANN (*conj.* Walker); heauen F   him!] SMALLWOOD; ~. F   64 *John dies*] ROWE (*subs.*); *not in* F   65–6 ear— | My liege! My lord!—But] THEOBALD (*subs.*); eare | My Liege, my Lord: but F

52 **tackle** Literally, the rope rigging of a ship and hence the nautical imagery of *shrouds* (= sails) and *sail* (= navigate) in l. 53 and *stay* in l. 55; figuratively, John refers to his 'heartstrings', the tendons or nerves surrounding the heart and believed to break in death.

53–4 **shrouds . . . hair** See Tilley T250, 'It hangs (To hang) by a thread (hair)'; 'hair' appears in the expression from 1581, 'thread' occurs after 1396 in Whiting.

55 **to stay** to support, but also to hold a ship's mast in position through using a 'stay', a large rope

57 **clod** lump (specifically, of earth or clay)

58 **module** 'Mere image' or 'counterfeit' (*sb.* 2c, citing this line as the earliest of three examples, the last from 1608), but since John has insisted on his sense of becoming smaller in death (l. 34), another meaning, 'model, small replica' is probably present also.

confounded defeated, thwarted

59 **preparing hitherward** getting ready to come this way (or perhaps, already on the way: see *adv.* 3)

60 **answer** meet in battle, encounter (see *v.* 26, where the latest citation is from 1586)

61 **best part** majority

62 **advantage** See 2.1.297n; the last of the word's numerous appearances in the play.

63 **unwarily** unexpectedly, unawarely. Shakespeare's only use of this form of the adverb.

65 **dead** deadly (but also, perhaps, 'past, superseded')

65–6 **You breathe . . . now thus** This punctuation assumes that Salisbury interrupts himself to address the dead king, perhaps in sorrow, perhaps to demonstrate the truth of his statement.

68–9 **What surety . . . clay** Henry's couplet picks up a word, *stay*, and several images from John's last speech.

BASTARD

Art thou gone so? I do but stay behind   70
To do the office for thee of revenge,
And then my soul shall wait on thee to heaven,
As it on earth hath been thy servant still.
Now, now, you stars that move in your right spheres,
Where be your powers? Show now your mended faiths
And instantly return with me again
To push destruction and perpetual shame
Out of the weak door of our fainting land.
Straight let us seek, or straight we shall be sought;
The Dauphin rages at our very heels.   80

SALISBURY

It seems you know not, then, so much as we.
The Cardinal Pandulph is within at rest,
Who half an hour since came from the Dauphin,
And brings from him such offers of our peace
As we with honour and respect may take,
With purpose presently to leave this war.

BASTARD

He will the rather do it when he sees
Ourselves well sinewèd to our defence.

SALISBURY

Nay, 'tis in a manner done already,
For many carriages he hath dispatched   90

88 well sinewèd] F; *hyphenated by* CAPELL

70–3 **I do . . . still** See Kent's farewell to
Lear, 'I have a journey, sir, shortly to
go: | My master calls me; I must not say
no' (*Tragedy of Lear* 5.3.297–8).

70 **stay** remain (a neat antithesis to the *stay*
or support John has lacked and the
Bastard has provided for England in
the past and perhaps will provide in the
future)

73 **still** always. The Bastard stresses that his
worldly devotion to John will continue
briefly, to be replaced by an eternal
service.

74 **right spheres** Proper (heavenly) locations; the nobles have wandered (like
portentous meteors, not planets) from
their correct, loyal places; Henry IV uses
the same imagery to describe the rebellious nobles of his reign (*1 Henry IV*

5.1.15–21).

75 **mended** (earliest citation for the *ppl. a.*)

79 **Straight** immediately, at once

81–6 **It seems . . . this war** This information
oddly undercuts the Bastard's preceding
and following speeches.

85 **respect** 'self-respect' (Wilson, without
direct support in *OED*, but see *sb.*
IV.16a and c)

86 **With purpose . . . war** i.e., in addition
to the peace offer, Pandulph has also
conveyed Louis's *purpose* to end the war
presently (= immediately)

87 **the rather** the more quickly, the sooner

88 **sinewèd** strengthened with sinews,
powerful (earliest citation at *ppl. a.* is from
1604). The last appearance of images
drawn from ligaments and supports of
the body and its organs.

To the seaside and put his cause and quarrel
To the disposing of the Cardinal,
With whom yourself, myself, and other lords,
If you think meet, this afternoon will post
To consummate this business happily.

BASTARD

Let it be so. And you, my noble Prince,
With other princes that may best be spared,
Shall wait upon your father's funeral.

PRINCE HENRY

At Worcester must his body be interred,
For so he willed it.

BASTARD   Thither shall it then.   100
And happily may your sweet self put on
The lineal state and glory of the land.
To whom, with all submission, on my knee
I do bequeath my faithful services
And true subjection everlastingly.
          He kneels

SALISBURY

And the like tender of our love we make,
To rest without a spot for evermore.
          The lords kneel

PRINCE HENRY

I have a kind soul that would give thanks
And knows not how to do it but with tears.

---

96 so.] COLLIER; ~ , F   102 land.] This edition; Land, F; land! SINGER   103 submission,
on my knee] CAMBRIDGE; submission on my knee, F   105.1 *He kneels*] OXFORD; *not in* F
107.1 *The lords kneel*] CAPELL (*subs.*); *not in* F   108 give thanks] F; give you thanks ROWE

94 **If you think meet** The English lords have
   accepted the Bastard as *de facto* leader of
   the nation (*meet* = proper, suitable).
97 **princes** nobles. Shakespeare does not restrict the term to royal males (see, e.g.,
   Henry V 5.2.11 and 5.2.22, where
   assemblies of noblemen are described as
   'princes English, every one' and 'you
   English princes all'). *OED* II.7b first cites
   this generalized usage from 1707.
98 **wait upon** attend, serve as retinue for
99 **Worcester** Where John's tomb (Fig. 3) is
   still to be seen, the earliest royal funerary
   monument in England.

102 **lineal state** hereditary royal station. See
   2.1.85.
   glory See 4.3.71 and 5.1.2.
104 **bequeath** deliver, hand over; see
   1.1.149. The word need not suggest that
   the Bastard expects to die soon, although
   it may do so.
107.1 *The lords kneel* Salisbury's 'the like
   tender . . . we make' (l. 106) virtually
   stipulates this direction; the lords may
   remain kneeling through the Bastard's
   final speech, or they may rise (for the
   ceremonial *Exeunt*) at ll. 110–11.

269

BASTARD ⌐*rising*⌐

    O, let us pay the time but needful woe,   110
    Since it hath been beforehand with our griefs.
    This England never did, nor never shall,
    Lie at the proud foot of a conqueror
    But when it first did help to wound itself.
    Now these her princes are come home again,
    Come the three corners of the world in arms
    And we shall shock them! Naught shall make us rue,
    If England to itself do rest but true.   *Exeunt*

110 time‸] ROWE; time: F   117 them!] THEOBALD; ~ : F

110 **O . . . woe** F's colon is a strong stop suggesting a meaning that the repunctuation obscures in favour of another. In F, the Bastard may mean, 'Let us give this present time its full due of sorrow; such sorrow is only proper (*but needful* = precisely necessary) because our earlier times have produced griefs that went unsorrowed'; the repunctuated line makes the Bastard less concerned with mourning John: 'since so many griefs have preceded this one, let it receive only (= *but*) the minimum of sorrow that decorum requires'.

112–18 **This England . . . but true** This sort of patriotic effusion, often a prayer for Elizabeth in ostensible form, was a common feature of Tudor plays, including Bale's *King Johan*, from at least 1560 through the 1590s and occasionally later; see E. C. Wilson, *England's Eliza* (Cambridge, Mass., 1939), pp. 96–125.

113–14 **Lie . . . wound itself** Homer Nearing, Jr. suggested in *N. & Q.* 192 (1947), 256–7, that these lines refer to Julius Caesar's invasion of England through the aid of a native traitor, Androgeus.

115 **Now** now that

116 **three corners** The Bible often treats the world or earth as having four corners or regions (Ezekiel 7: 12, Isaiah 11: 12, Revelations 7: 1); Shakespeare's phrase may refer to such a four-cornered world, with England ('that utmost corner of the west' at 2.1.29) the fourth arrayed against the other three. Antony speaks of 'The three-fold world' (*Caesar* 4.2.14) and Octavius regards the 'world' as 'three-nooked' (*Antony* 4.6.5); these latter examples may recall Ovid's *triplex mundus* (*Metamorphoses* xii. 40: 'threefold world')—sky, land, water—or refer to an outmoded (for the Elizabethan audience) three-continent world (as at *Tamburlaine, Part 1* 4.4.78). In any case, the line represents England as embattled by all the rest of creation.

117–18 **Naught . . . but true** Hastings similarly assures Montague 'that of itself | England is safe, if true within itself' (*3 Henry VI* 4.1.38–9). For the popularity of this idea, see Appendix E.

118 *Exeunt* On the Elizabethan stage, John's body would have been ceremoniously carried off, probably to the accompaniment of a *Flourish* or other music, with the other characters forming a rank-ordered cortège.

SPEECH-PREFIXES IN ACT 2

1. 2.1.149 ff.

THIS page (a2ᵛ) and its forme-mate (a5) were the first to be set by Compositor C (Hinman, ii. 515). Only once in the two pages is the King of France given a proper name (at 3.1.191, the very end of a5); in these two pages, King Philip usually appears in speech-prefixes, stage directions, and dialogue as variants of 'King' or 'France'. Thus, if Compositor C were to read some version of '*Kin. Lewis*, determine . . .', he might include the line in Austria's speech because he believed the play's French king to be 'Lewis', when in fact he had run together a speech-prefix and the first word of a new speaker's dialogue. The next line of text, '*Lew.* Women & fooles . . .', would not tell him he had made an error. It is true that F (and presumably compositors' copy) uses '*King.*' or '*Kin.*' for Philip when he is the only royal figure on stage (here, 2.1.1–83) and generally distinguishes the French and English kings when they are on the stage together, but one slip (e.g., '*Kin.*' for '*Fra.*') at line 149 is quite plausible.[1] It is also possible, of course, that Shakespeare himself was confused over the French king's personal name or considered changing it at some point to prevent confusion with 'Philip' Faulconbridge and that the 'error' consequently stood in copy (see, e.g., Greg, *Ed. Prob.*, p. xi n. 2). Finally, if this speech-prefix does contain an error, it may be related to a controversial speech-prefix at 2.1.1 (F: *Lewis*; here emended to *King Philip*) in the next two pages (a2 and a5ᵛ) Compositor C set (see 2.1.1n). Again, author, scribe, or compositor may have identified the French monarch with the wrong proper name, abetted, perhaps, by the scene's opening stage direction, where F seems to identify three French characters ('. . . *Philip King of France, Lewis, Daulphin* . . .') and the all-important royal title might have been read as preceding 'Lewis' rather than following 'Philip'.

[1] A curiously similar situation seems to exist in the early quartos of Marlowe's *Edward II*, where modern editions divide 2.2.81–2 (part of the physical struggle to capture Gaveston) between Pembroke, a noble hostile to the King, and King Edward, but the early texts read, '*Penbrooke*. Heere, here King: convey hence Gaveston, thaile murder him.' Many students of the problem, including Bowers and Greg (in MSR), understand the first two words as Pembroke's ironic answer to Edward's question, 'whers the traitor?' and believe 'King:' an errant speech-prefix meant to assign the following words to Edward. Since the quarto speech headings always use '*Edward*' (or a variant) for the King and use a full stop rather than a colon, a natural inference would be that the King's speech 'was a marginal addition written in by a different hand or at least on a different occasion' (Greg).

Justifying the reassignment of line 149 from Austria to Philip, Edward Capell, in *Notes*, explains the dramatic value of Philip's requesting Louis to speak: 'The father, indeed, may very reasonably make his son the declarer of a thing praeconcerted . . . it shews the son's consequence, and weight with the father; and . . . rescues him from the state of a cypher in a scene of great length'. Capell's point is well taken. According to F, the Dauphin speaks TLN 294–304 (the opening lines of the scene), 311, 450–4, and then not until 812–19, when his father (again?) invites him to speak. Reassigning all, or all-but-one, of TLN 450–4 to another character creates even more problems for the actor and director than does F's (and this edition's) assignment. (Reassigning TLN 294–304, as I do, diminishes the Dauphin's stature at the scene's very start, but does not silence him completely.) Ernst Honigmann accepts Capell's description of the dramatic value of reassigning line 149 and then, inconsistently I think, rejects it for lines 151–4 (his edition, pp. xxxiv–xxxv). Instead, Honigmann believes that another speech-prefix (e.g., '*King*') has been dropped before line 151 and supports his argument by noting that 'the *I* claiming *In right of Arthur* (l. 153) can only be Philip' (p. xxxv n. 1). This complaint seems over-ingenious: Louis could hardly use the royal pronoun *we*, and therefore must use *I*; any more elaborate explanation of the French claim to Angers might make too plain the real doubt over that claim's legitimacy (see, for example, Robert Smallwood's comment quoted at 2.1.105n) and would demolish the very attempt to give Louis's role some substance, as Capell described it. In other words, giving one line ('Women and fools, break off your conference') to Louis makes him more, not less, of a cipher; giving him the entire speech (lines 150–4) accomplishes some at least of what Capell claimed for the reassignment. As Robert Smallwood notes (pp. 353–4), the arrangement justified here produces a nine-syllable line, because 'Lewis' seems generally to be monosyllabic in *K. John*.

2. 2.1.200 ff.

After almost two hundred lines of argument about who has sovereignty over Angers, the Kings of France and England decide to ask the citizens 'Whose title they admit' (2.1.200). The Folio directs:

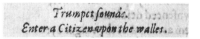

This actor speaks, and his four brief but intransigent speeches in the next ninety-odd lines are all headed *Cit*. After an inconclusive battle, first a French Herald enters '*to the gates*' and then an English one, each demanding some pledge of loyalty. The reply begins:

> *Hubert.* Heralds, from off our towres we might behold

(2.1.325/TLN 636)

This speaker, like *Cit.*, resists the heralds' and, soon, their kings' demands for a decision; with the exception of a single error (*Fra.* at 2.1.368), this speaker's prefix is *Hub.* for the remainder of the scene, and *Cit.* never reappears. Since Dover Wilson's edition (pp. xlv ff.), editors have suggested that *Cit.* and *Hubert* might be the same character, and three recent editors (Honigmann, Matchett, and Smallwood, respectively) have merged the characters into a single 'Hubert' who, of course, (re)appears in 3.3, in all three scenes of Act 4, in 5.3, 5.6, and possibly in 5.7 (at the end of 5.6, the Bastard says to Hubert, 'Conduct me to the King', but Faulconbridge enters alone in 5.7 and Hubert has no lines in that scene).

Before we consider the explanations proposed for F's evidence, we should note the following:

1. The line in which *Hubert* appears as a speech heading is full and justified: it is indented less than usual and no space was set between the stop following the speech heading and the first word of text.

2. In F *King John*, speech headings do not customarily give a full name upon a character's first speaking (with the usual exception of the play's very first speaker and these further exceptions: *Essex* at 1.1.44, *Lewis*—erroneously—at 2.1.1, and perhaps *Philip* at 1.1.50 and *Robert* at 1.1.56), and very rarely do so for a character's subsequent speeches (*Philip* at 1.1.59 and 1.1.92, *Elinor* at 1.1.148 and 155, *Lewis*—another error—at 2.1.18, *Arthur* at 2.1.163, *France* at 2.1.235, *Blanch* at 3.1.300). A spot check of three plays set before *K. John* suggests that no convention governed the setting of full names in speech headings and that full names are very rare.

3. *Hubert.* appears in the first page of the first forme of *King John* to be composed; Compositor B was working 'outward' in the gathering and would therefore not have had the reader's sense that *Cit.* had changed to *Hubert* and *Hub.* Rather, the compositor would find speeches assigned to *Hub.* in text following the point where he set the name for the first time and (if he thought about it) no assignments in text that preceded that first setting.

4. The Folio contains several apparent confusions of names in speech headings in Act 2 (or 'Scaena Secunda' as F calls this division), and I discuss the most troublesome in Appendices A1 and 3. To them, we may add the following: John's mother is called *Queene* in the entry

direction at 2.1.83.1 and *Queen*, *Qu. Mo.*, *Qu.*, and *Que.* in the speech headings for all of Act 2, but some variant of 'Eleanor' or 'Elinor' for all her other speeches in the play (that is, in Acts 1 and 3). The only anomalous speech headings outside 'Scaena Secunda' are two for Philip Faulconbridge; the heading for his speeches changes to *Bast.* at 1.1.151, but reverts to *Phil.* at 3.1.131 and 133, and then changes back to *Bast.* at 3.1.199 where it remains (with one *Ba.*) for the rest of the play.

5. 'Hubert' does not occur in the dialogue until 3.3, when King John repeats the name eight times in 53 lines; Arthur also uses the name frequently two scenes later (4.1).

6. Professional actors and directors might be expected to cope with discrepancies, but the audience is much less flexible and much more ignorant. It is therefore not surprising that the dialogue contains few confusions of names. Nor is it surprising that they all involve Philip Faulconbridge, knighted as 'Sir Richard and Plantagenet' (1.1.162). John addresses him as 'Richard' (1.1.178), and he immediately calls himself 'Sir Richard' (1.1.185); he soon rejects Gurney's 'good Philip' (1.1.231), only later to call himself 'Philip' (3.2.4), by which name King John immediately addresses him (3.2.5). A Messenger calls him 'Faulconbridge' (5.3.5, and then 'Richard' at l. 12) as does Salisbury, 'devil Faulconbridge' (5.4.4). In 4.3, where the names appear as part of an increasingly angry conversation and are probably used as social obloquy, the Bastard is first addressed as 'Sir, sir' (32), then 'Sir Richard' (41), and then 'Faulconbridge' (94, 101). Otherwise the dialogue emphasizes his bastardy (1.1.246 ff., 2.1.65, 2.1.276, 3.4.171), his new familial relation to the royal characters (John and Eleanor use 'cousin', 'kinsman', and 'gentleman' when they require his assistance: 3.3.6, 3.3.17 (twice), 4.2.137, 159, 166, 177), or his anonymity ('One', 'cracker', 'villain', 'ruffian', 'Brave soldier', 'sweet sir' at 2.1.135 and 147, 3.1.132, 3.1.200, 5.6.13, and 5.6.19, respectively).

7. Shakespeare seems to have had trouble keeping his characters and their historical names straight. 'Cardinal Pandulph', for instance, combines two, perhaps three, historical figures, and the historical model for most of Pandulph's fictional acts was never a cardinal. This confusion is not bothersome, and it is theatrically apt: a cardinal's red robes would have burned the brighter on a Protestant stage. Similarly, the merging of Richard I's captor, the Duke of Austria, with the man, Viscount of Limoges, who commanded the castle where Richard received his mortal wound, causes no difficulty because the two historical events are themselves merged. The way the speech headings and/or dialogue waver over who is King of France—Philip or Louis—early in Act 2 and the suggestion that 'Lewis' and 'Daulphin' are two different characters (in the entry direction of Act 2) are not encouraging, nor is the dialogue's

uncertainty over the precise familial relation among Geoffrey, Richard, John, and Arthur (2.1.6 and 13).

8. F's stage directions here, as elsewhere, do not provide all the information the contemplative reader might wish: after the entry for *a Citizen upon the walls*, there are no explicit exit directions for the subsequent actions, but instead only entries for the two heralds (*Here, after excursions, enter* . . .) and the two Kings. The editorial addition of an exit when the Kings depart to do battle is easy and obvious, but what about Citizen? The usual assumption (partly supported by the text: 'from off our towers we might behold . . . the onset and retire | Of both your armies') seems to be that he remains *upon the walls*, although only Smallwood makes this assumption explicit in additional stage directions.

9. Before the battle, Citizen speaks in the plural, and the Kings address a plural audience (my italics):

> Who is it that hath warned *us* to the walls
>
> You *men* of Angers, and my loving *subjects*
>
> You loving *men* of Angers, Arthur's *subjects*
>
> In brief, *we* are the king of England's *subjects*,
> For him . . . *we* hold this town
>
> That can *we* not . . .
> To him will *we* prove loyal . . .
>
> *We* for the worthiest hold the right from both.

After the battle, the heralds and kings again address a plural audience, and Hubert uses plural pronouns (*we, our*) twelve consecutive times until he uses *I* when proposing the marriage between Blanche and Louis: 'Vouchsafe a while to stay, | And I shall show you peace and fair-faced league' (2.1.417–18).

Analyses of the Citizen/Hubert problem have been confused through editors' arguing *from* their theories of F's copy *to* this evidence and *from* this evidence *to* conclusions about copy. Inference should instead flow in one direction only: either unequivocal evidence of F's copy establishes a plausible assumption which controls argument here *or* this evidence is logically prior to conclusions about F's copy. The argument probably cannot escape the hermeneutic circle, but we should try to run around that circle in one direction only. Since evidence for F's copy is inconclusive, we are left asking how the problem in 2.1 might have evolved, and I would like to suggest some inferences from the observations just listed.

First, the compositor probably did not create the difficulty. It is nearly certain that Compositor B read *Hubert* as a speech heading at *K. John*

2.1.325, and it is probable that he perceived this prefix more emphatically than most other speech headings: economy of space in the line (paragraph 1, above) and his practice elsewhere in *K. John* and earlier in F (paragraph 2) strongly suggest that his inclination would have been to abbreviate the name. (But, as in paragraph 3, we must remember that Compositor B was now only getting started on a new play and new copy, and we may want to speculate on how *Hubert* came to be or was made emphatic.) Second, anomalous speech headings are concentrated in this unit of *K. John*, but the Citizen/Hubert problem, like all but two of the other confusions, would not necessarily trouble theatre professionals the way they do a reader (paragraph 4). Third, the moment when a character is 'named'—either by identifying props or a proper noun—is an important moment for an audience and the dramatist; 'Hubert' is not identified until 3.3, but he is then very deliberately and frequently named (paragraphs 5 and 6). That is, if Hubert speaks from the walls of Angers, the theatre audience could not identify him as 'Hubert' until 641 lines after F first assigns him a speech heading.[1] Fourth, if Shakespeare was confused about and/or running short of more-or-less historical names, he may first have wanted a named citizen of Angers and then might have decided to make him anonymous, in order to 'save' a vaguely historical name for Arthur's jailor and near-murderer. Fifth, F's evidence for the staging of the scene is slightly inconclusive, but it seems most likely that at least one actor might remain *on the walls* during the *excursions* of battle, since *excursions* usually, if not invariably, refers to sound effects (paragraph 8, and see 3.2. headnote). If we take F's direction literally, only one actor (*a Citizen*) has been directed to enter, only he remains, and only he addresses the heralds when they appear. We have, however, to take account of the dialogue's consistent evidence that more than one actor has entered *on the walls* (paragraph 9).

Two principal explanations have been offered for F's evidence. J. P. Collier and Aldis Wright suggested that the same actor played the distinct roles of Citizen and of Hubert, and in the middle of the second act someone consequently chose to call Citizen first *Hubert* and then *Hub.* (or something the compositor could plausibly print thus). It is certainly possible to double Citizen and Hubert; indeed, a minimum casting for the play would assign one actor the roles of James Gurney, Citizen, and Hubert. If the roles were doubled, however, they none the less could, and probably would, have remained distinct for the audience. Doubling Citizen and Hubert while keeping them distinct characters

[1] In 'Character Identification in the Theatre: Some Principles and Some Examples', *Renaissance Papers 1967* (1968), pp. 55–67, Charles B. Lower describes some ways dialogue identifies a character by function rather than name, even if a name exists in those parts of the text (stage directions, speech headings) not spoken in the theatre.

assumes, of course, that the actor performs 'Citizen' through 2.1 and then appears as 'Hubert' in 3.3. (Otherwise, we must imagine a single actor who exits after his first four speeches and then re-enters, having changed costume or other features of his visual and vocal presence to indicate a new identity!) Moreover, a mixture of speech headings as a consequence of doubling 'has no comparable parallel in the canon' (Honigmann, p. xxxvii; Smallwood, p. 354, concurs); Honigmann continues, 'In those plays where doubling is thought to have caused confusion of names only *isolated* instances of confusion are known . . . in *John* Hubert takes over the Citizen's part *systematically* from II.i.325' (p. xxxvii n. 2).[1] This latter comment of course assumes that the parts are the same, or were eventually conceived of as the same (otherwise 'takes over' would be illogical).

Dover Wilson and, with more conviction, Ernst Honigmann argued that Shakespeare changed his mind, seeking to make 'Citizen' less anonymous and to link the important, named character (Hubert) of the play's second half with an unimportant one in the first half; unfortunately, Shakespeare did not finish (or someone else did not finish for him) rewriting the speech headings of Citizen's first four speeches. The mechanical (or manual) element in this argument is attractive, but reversible. In principle, the 'Hubert' of Act 2 could be in the process of metamorphosing into 'Citizen' as plausibly as the reverse.

The further arguments for conflating Citizen and Hubert turn upon assumptions about Shakespeare's techniques of dramatic organization and characterization. It is difficult to find a theatrical or critical justification for merging the two characters.[2] Honigmann offers the best argument (p. xxxvii). He emphasizes three points: the implausibility of the alternative explanation based on doubling (see above); the play's fluctuation between impersonal and individualizing speeches; John's reference to Hubert's 'voluntary oath' (3.3.23).

Like Matchett (see his p. xxix) and Smallwood (see especially his pp. 36–7), who accept the argument, Honigmann regards Hubert as a fence-

[1] Honigmann and Smallwood may be correct for the Shakespeare canon, but the early texts of Marlowe's *Edward II* (especially in Act 2, Scene 5, less extensively elsewhere) thoroughly mix the speech headings for two characters, Arundel and Matrevis, apparently as a consequence of the roles having been doubled; see Bowers's introduction, ii. 8–9.

[2] Jones, *Origins*, pp. 283–5, also argues against merging the characters, although he believes Citizen alone speaks from the walls of Angers. Critics have debated whether Shakespeare modelled his 'Hubert' on Hubert de Burgh, mentioned in Holinshed and historically a very important personage whose name editors have often given to this character, as does *TR*. Jones claims that the play's 'Hubert' is meant to be recognized as the historical Hubert de Burgh, but from 'Bigot's contemptuous question at 4.3.87', Wilson (p. xlvii) deduced 'that Hubert is of very mean birth', and I doubt the historical identification.

sitter compelled to choose sides; the fearful but politically disinterested 'Citizen' (now to be conflated with Hubert) throws in with John and agrees to kill, not keep, his prisoner. Deciding to join John in 3.3, however, 'Hubert still [presumably this *still* refers to the speeches assigned to a named Hubert in 2.1] speaks impersonally', and Honigmann guesses that 'Shakespeare may have decided to heighten the impersonal impression through identification with the Citizen, so that Hubert's thawing out in IV.i . . . would give edge to that central scene'. Some critics might find Hubert's 'thawing out' finely managed within 4.1 itself and his deferential monosyllables in 3.3 a sufficient contrast. Although Smallwood merges Citizen and Hubert, for instance, he explicitly locates the 'impersonal' Hubert not in 2.1 but in the 'taciturnity with which he accepted John's terrible commission in Act III, scene 3' (p. 36). Even granting Honigmann's premiss of impersonal/personal alternations, one should not fit Hubert into the pattern quite so quickly. While his threats from the walls of Angers may be magniloquence or rant, they do not seem impersonal to the Bastard:

> . . . Here's a large mouth indeed
> That spits forth death and mountains, rocks and seas;
> Talks as familiarly of roaring lions
> As maids of thirteen do of puppy-dogs.
> What cannoneer begot this lusty blood?
> He speaks plain cannon—fire, and smoke, and bounce;
> He gives the bastinado with his tongue.
> Our ears are cudgelled; not a word of his
> But buffets better than a fist of France.
> Zounds, I was never so bethumped with words
> Since I first called my brother's father Dad.
>
> (2.1.458–68)

Nor should we forget that for a theatre audience, Honigmann's version of this change from impersonal to individual requires that we retrospectively integrate the character given a name at 3.3.19 with the anonymous speaker we last heard 493 lines ago (at 2.1.482).

When he first addresses a character explicitly named 'Hubert', John says,

> Come hither, Hubert. O my gentle Hubert,
> We owe thee much. Within this wall of flesh
> There is a soul counts thee her creditor,
> And with advantage means to pay thy love.
> And, my good friend, thy voluntary oath
> Lives in this bosom, dearly cherishèd.
> Give me thy hand. I had a thing to say,

> But I will fit it with some better tune.
> By heaven, Hubert, I am almost ashamed
> To say what good respect I have of thee.
>
> (3.3.19–28)

Honigmann comments, 'As the two other voluntary oaths (V.i.29, V.ii.10) show, a vassal's oath of allegiance is meant. John's thanks are not altogether too extravagant if *Hubert* swore on behalf of Angiers. The *Citizen* had repeatedly refused to pay allegiance on behalf of Angiers till one king should prove the greatest: as John did prove greatest, and Angiers did submit to him (III.iii.6), continuity of character seems to be urged by the action quite apart from the essential corroboration of the text' (p. xxxvii). At once, we may recall Greg's dry comment: 'it is surely not unlike Shakespeare to give solidity to a character by casual allusions to supposed happenings beyond the scope of the action as known to the spectator' (*First Folio*, p. 249 n. 7). (John's 'way to win' the nobles' 'loves again' (4.2.168) and his 'fever' (5.3.3) are similarly unexplained.)

Just as the claims about Hubert's impersonality may be the result of unwarranted assumptions, Honigmann's argument here may scant certain evidence. The representative of Angers in Act 2 (whether 'Citizen' or 'Hubert') never swears allegiance. 'Hubert', it is true, produces an ingenious proposal—the marriage of Blanche and Louis—that spares Angers from the united enmity of France and England, but King John fulfils neither *Cit.*'s demand that the winning contestant be 'he that proves the King' (2.1.270) nor *Hubert*'s demand that 'One must prove greatest' (2.1.332) in the sense that he demonstrates his superior claim to Angers by right or might. John explicitly exempts Angers from the political settlement and the marriage dowry (2.1.489–91: 'all that we upon this side the sea— | Except this city now by us besieged— | Find liable to our crown and dignity'), and it is King Philip who, much later, calls Angers 'lost' in the line Honigmann cites ('III.iii.6', or 3.4.6 in most editions) after a battle quite separate from the original argument over Angers.

It is also stretching a point to treat 'the two other voluntary oaths' as evidence for regarding 'thy voluntary oath' as 'a vassal's oath of allegiance'. The two other oaths are, respectively, John's allegiance to Rome and the rebellious English nobles' allegiance to the invading Louis. The only verbal connection is *voluntary* (i.e., unforced, willing). The two later instances may be *oaths* of vassalage and *voluntary*, but that does not mean that 'voluntary oath' necessarily means 'a vassal's oath of allegiance'. The words may mean nothing other than *voluntaries* does at 2.1.67, i.e., that Hubert is a willing, not a compelled, soldier in the English cause (compare *Troilus* 2.1.98–9: 'Ajax was here the voluntary, and you as under an impress'). Furthermore, *voluntary* is patently ironic in one of Honigmann's examples: it describes John's desperate search for some support against the French. The Bastard's surprise (5.1.65 ff.: 'O inglorious league!' etc.) ensures we understand that irony. And *voluntary* certainly could be ironic when it describes the nobles' search, perhaps equally desperate, for some ally to counter John. Thus, for Honigmann and Wilson, whom he follows here, as for all the editors and critics who never boggled at the phrase 'thy voluntary oath', the phrase must refer to an unstaged event. Honigmann simply makes a hypothetical interpretation of a hypothetical event.

The dialogue virtually stipulates that more than one actor enters on the walls of Angers; I conclude that both Citizen and the character (and actor) the dialogue later names as 'Hubert' both enter at 2.1.200.2 and that Citizen speaks the pre-battle speeches and the character eventually identified (in Act 3, Scene 3) as 'Hubert' speaks the post-battle speeches. (I would further speculate that for some reason one of these originally anonymous citizens was subsequently designated 'Hubert', leading to the speech-prefixes for that character in F's Scaena Secunda, although I can think of no good literary or critical justification for making one citizen less anonymous than another.) That is, F's speech headings are accurate and one stage direction is not.

This invented direction might appear to create a technical anomaly: except for the pronouns, the text does not acknowledge plural presences on the walls of Angers and provides neither distinction nor dialogue among these hypothetical citizens. Other Shakespearian and quasi-Shakespearian texts do, however, dramatize episodes very like this one in *King John*. In *3 Henry VI*, Act 4, Scene 8, a stage direction reads '*Enter on the Walls, the Maior of Yorke, and his Brethren*' (TLN 2511–12), but only the Mayor appears in speech-prefixes, and he employs the first person plural throughout until he concedes to Hastings's demand, 'Open the Gates, we are King *Henries* friends', with 'I [Ay], say you so? the Gates shall then be opened', and the actor is directed, '*He descends*' (TLN 2525–7). *The True Tragedy of Richard Duke of York* (anonymous octavo, 1595) bears some close affinity to *3 Henry VI*; in the scene corresponding with Shakespeare's Act 4, Scene 8 there appears only 'Enter the Lord Maire of *Yorke* vpon the wals' (D7),[1] although here too the Mayor uses the first person plural exclusively before speaking in the first person and acting as he does in the Folio. A later scene in the octavo, analogous to Shakespeare's Act 5, Scene 1, directs, 'Enter *Warwicke on the walles*', and he proceeds to inquire for and then question two messengers and Summerfield. All three interlocutors may be in a

---

[1] All quotations are from the facsimile prepared by W. W. Greg (Oxford, 1958), with long s modernized and signatures cited parenthetically.

different acting space from Warwick (they on the main stage, he 'above'), but that leaves little room for the other actors who immediately follow: 'Enter *Edward* and his power.' The Folio version clears the doubt by directing '*Enter Warwicke, the Maior of Couentry, two Messengers, and others vpon the Walls*' (TLN 2672–3), but only Warwick and the two Messengers have any dialogue. While the octavo and Folio possibly, even probably, reflect different stagings of the respective scenes, the texts variously testify to the following: directions may mention a single actor when more than one has entered; directions may mention more actors than subsequently speak; groups of actors (especially groups designated as a category) may be directed to enter without the text providing them with distinctive actions, different points of view, and so forth; one actor from an otherwise silent group may speak for all until the action requires a specific, personal action or reaction.

If we wish, we may accept Honigmann's critical argument concerning Hubert's move from impersonality to individuality (only four short 'impersonal' speeches are given to 'Citizen') and locate the first shift when he drops *we* for *I* at 2.1.418, but Honigmann's case is—in the theatre—more probable based on dialogue from 3.3 up to and including 4.1 and need not be extended back to 2.1. We do not have to attach the phrase 'voluntary oath' to any of the events dramatized in the play.

We may speculate that '*Hubert.*' was a late(r) thought, so emphatically marked in the printer's copy that Compositor B set the full name, but the thought may or may not have been Shakespeare's, may or may not have been prompted by the play's casting-pattern, may or may not have been partially or completely realized in the manuscript the compositors set. Certain features to be expected in an author's earliest draft have survived, it seems, into copy for Act 2 (or 'Scaena Secunda'): the apparent uncertainty about the personal name of the French king, the genealogical confusion, and the functional rather than personal designations for Queen Eleanor suggest as much. It is therefore possible that the (re)designation of *a* citizen as 'Hubert' was part of an uncompleted tidying process. Finally, since theatre professionals would not have much trouble performing F, there is no reason to suppose that F would have been 'corrected' to remove the Citizen/Hubert 'confusion' or the other problems I have mentioned even if F's copy originated in the theatre or had been partially marked up for production: the dialogue pretty certainly straightens out the confusion over the French King's name; the audience might not notice the genealogical muddle; Eleanor's speech headings are perfectly lucid since she is the only 'queen' on stage. My hypothetical stage direction postulates only that professionals might freely vary, might even expect to vary, the number of characters in a stage direction, without leaving any trace in the script.[1] The numerous unspecific directions in *King John*, elsewhere in F, and in manuscript prompt-books make this assumption plausible in general, although they do not weigh on either side in any specific instance.

3. 2.1.368

The emendation of *Fra<nce>.* either to *Hubert* or to a heading for the anonymous citizen of Angers is an easy and plausible one. How the compositor came to make the mistake (if it is compositorial and not Shakespeare's lapse) can be explained in several ways. In F's 'Scaena Secunda' (Act 2 in modern editions), speeches certainly belonging to King Philip are headed *King.* (or an abbreviation of it) until John's entrance after l. 83; thereafter, speeches certainly belonging to King Philip are headed *Fran.*, *Fra.*, or *France.*, and speeches certainly belonging to King John are headed *K. Iohn.*, or *Iohn.* An obvious inference is that *King.*, etc. is satisfactory only so long as a single king is on stage; when there are two kings on stage, they must be distinguished. Given the play's title, the choice for the English monarch is easy. *France.* (rather than, e.g., *King Philip.*, *K. Phil.*, etc.) is an economical choice, conveying both nationality and royal status.

Explaining how the confusion in *King John* arose depends in part upon an unknowable feature of the compositor's copy-text (or, hypothetically, of some manuscript earlier in the sequence of transmission): were the speech-prefixes in the compositor's copy text written uniformly in italic, uniformly in secretary hand, or (perhaps most likely) in a mixture of the two? Ernst Honigmann argues that King Philip's speeches were headed *King* (or some abbreviation of it) throughout the manuscript of Act 2 (see his edition, pp. xxxv–xxxvi); he claims, 'Our contention . . . gains strength from [this] crux . . . *Hu[bert]* misread as *Fra.* looks improbable: *Hu* misread as *Ki[n.]*, or Hu. as Ki[n.] (Secretary hand)— normalized to *Fra.*—would be a simple error' (p. xxxvi). Other hypotheses might, however, be offered in support of a compositor's misreading of an abbreviation for *Hubert* as *France.* In secretary hand F was represented by doubled lower-case *f*; consequently, 'Hu' (for *Hu<bert>*) in either secretary or italic hands could resemble the secretary ff- (for upper-case *F*) followed by the common u-shaped *r*, and thus could be misread as *Fr* (= *France*). Moreover, this page (a3ᵛ, mis-signed Aa3) and its forme-mate (a4) were the very first in *K. John* to be set (see Hinman, ii. 515).

---

[1] Most productions place several actors on the walls of Angers, but Arthur Colby Sprague notes a Birmingham production of 1823 which was criticized for using a single citizen, and he defends 'stylized treatment of this scene' (Sprague, pp. 24–5). It may be over-literal to demand plural citizens, but the dialogue certainly seems to stipulate them.

Compositor B, who set this page, would therefore have had little experience in setting the characters' names, although he and Compositor C may of course have glanced through their manuscript copy from start to finish before beginning work. Compositor B had set only *Hubert.* (2.1.325) and *Hub.* (2.1.363) for this character and may well have assimilated a puzzling or unclear heading to a more familiar and 'appropriate' prefix (*Fra.* or some variant).

'CARE' (4.2.117)

> *Ioh.* Oh where hath our Intelligence bin drunke?
> Where hath it slept? Where is my Mothers care?
> That such an Army could be drawne in France,

AT 4.2.117, F reads *care*. The first letter is damaged, and Hinman has traced its uses through the Folio (it is his 'c24'). This type's immediately preceding appearance is on page b4, where it was correctly set by Compositor C in 'saw*c*inesse' (*K. John* 5.2.133). When Compositor B distributed b4, he put this type into his *e* box. Compositor B set and distributed the pages containing this type's next three appearances; in the order of printing they are: '*c*are' (b2); 'Thre*c*' (b6ᵛ: 'Threc parts of that receipt I had for Callice', *Richard II* 1.1.126); 'm*c*e' (Y4ᵛ: 'If you will not murther me for my loue, let mce be your seruant', *Twelfth Night* 2.1.31–2); 'touch' (c3ᵛ: 'And shortly meane to touch our Northerne shore', *Richard II* 2.1.290). That is, Compositor B twice used this *c* as if it were an *e* before he correctly distributed it into the *c* box. With 'touch' and thereafter in F, the type represents only the letter *c*, including many later occasions on which B set and/or distributed the type. For a time, however, he regarded it as representing an *e*; only in *King John*, however, did his actions produce a semantically plausible word. The *e/c* error came easily to Compositor B, who is responsible for all obvious examples in *K. John*: 'Towne' (2.1.402); 'Lcgate' (5.2.174); 'Brcefe' (5.6.18, in the forme preceding the one containing 'care').

If Compositor B meant to set *care*, what led him to distribute the type into the *e* box; if *eare*, what caused him to set *c* for *e*? The answer to the first question would seem to be that the damaged *c* looked like an *e* when read upside down and backwards as Compositor B distributed type from the bottom toward the top of the column; since he had just distributed *eare* in line 119, he might have been unconsciously predisposed to see *eare* in line 117. The answer to the second question might be that the case had become foul between Compositor C's setting of *sawcinesse* and the moment B set *care*: that is, the damaged type was already in the *e* box; alternatively or additionally, Compositor B seems habitually to have erred in setting *c* for *e* and this may be a further instance. In sum, the bibliographical facts and hypotheses will support reading either *care* or *eare*, and the editorial decision becomes a critical one.

Like so many other characters in *K. John*, the Messenger seems given to word-play, specifically a kind of 'tagging' or 'capping' of the King's speeches. The Messenger's very first line picks up and puns on John's use of 'goes' ('how goes all in France?' | 'From France to England'), and his second speech similarly plays on John's use of 'hear' by moving antithetically between what the dead Eleanor can no longer 'hear' and what he himself has 'heard' ('And she not hear of it?' | 'as I hear . . . I idly heard'). In both cases, the Messenger seizes a word in John's final line, and in neither case does John respond to the 'wit'. Instead, John's speech containing the disputed *care* begins with two metaphorical questions and concludes with a practical demand for information. It seems to me that *care* rather than *eare* fits the pattern of John's speech (it mediates between the metaphorical and the pragmatic) and the pattern of the Messenger's word-play, which turns on the concluding line of the King's two speeches, not some word used earlier. I admit that relying on a 'pattern' in such a brief passage is feeble argument at best, and if the compositor's copy read 'eare', one could argue (contrary to my view) that John momentarily indulges the Messenger's humour.

'AN ANGEL SPAKE' (5.2.64)

As *K. John* 5.2 opens, the rebellious English lords have just religiously confirmed their alliance with the Dauphin Louis. Mingling sincerity and hypocrisy, Salisbury laments that circumstances have forced the English into this treasonous union—'I am not glad that such a sore of time | Should seek a plaster by contemned revolt' (5.2.12–13). Louis first compliments Salisbury upon his 'noble temper', his 'noble combat . . . Between compulsion and a brave respect' (5.2.40, 43–4; the latter lines themselves are rather slippery), and then reasserts the alliance and the benefits the English may expect. F reads:

> Come, come; for thou shalt thrust thy hand as deepe
> Into the purse of rich prosperity
> As *Lewis* himselfe: so (Nobles) shall you all,
> That knit your sinewes to the strength of mine.
> > *Enter Pandulpho.*
> And euen there, methinkes an Angell spake,
> Looke where the holy Legate comes apace,
> To giue vs warrant from the hand of heauen,
> And on our actions set the name of right
> With holy breath.

What, the editors have wondered, does 'methinkes an Angell spake' (5.2.64) mean? There's no difficulty showing that the phrase was a popular one from about 1590 (see Wilson, *ODEP*, and Tilley A242, 'There spoke an angel') nor in noting that the phrase quibbles on *angel* = a gold coin, bearing the image of the archangel Michael (see Fig. 7) and worth about 10 shillings (half a pound sterling). The problem lies in understanding (*a*) the meaning of the phrase itself and (*b*) to what Louis refers when he speaks the line. If we assume that the quibble on coins is primary, we note that the *angel* was also known as a 'noble', and then suppose that Louis continues (perhaps aside, as the Cambridge editors speculate) the word-play of *purse* (l. 61) and *nobles* (l. 62), thereby attempting a witty commentary on the financial benefits the English may expect. That is: avarice will triumph over loyalty; an *angel* will silence a *noble*; money talks. Alternatively, Louis may be complimenting himself on his inspired reassurance of the wavering English lords: 'There spake an angel' quite clearly means 'That was an inspired suggestion' in *Eastward Ho* (ed. R. W. Van Fossen, The Revels Plays (Manchester, 1979), 2.2.301). In this interpretation, Louis says (again, perhaps, *sotto*

7. An Elizabethan 'angel', bearing the image of the archangel Michael; see *King John* 2.1.590 and 5.2.64.

voce): 'How clever I am to remind them of their financial stake in joining me against John'.[1]

Unaware of these possibilities or unsatisfied with them, however, some editors have adopted a rather desperate expedient. They invent a flourish or trumpet-call preceding Pandulph's entry and claim that Louis's line refers to that angelic sound.[2] Louis's next line—'Look, where the holy legate comes apace'—suggests, however, that he did not immediately recognize the sound (if sound there was) as Pandulph's personal signature. In support of adding a stage direction, editors have pointed to the absence of a sound-cue when the Bastard next enters, but there the cue is indisputably present in the verse: 'What lusty trumpet thus doth summon us?' (l. 117).

One obvious way to test the likelihood of this added sound cue is to examine other occasions in F where there are such cues, or where there are not and might plausibly be in an Elizabethan or modern production.[3] On seven occasions, F provides a sound-cue: *Drum beats* (2.1.75.1/TLN 372; alluded to in dialogue); *Trumpet sounds* (2.1.200.1/TLN 504; also alluded to); *with Trumpets* (2.1.299.2–3/TLN 609; i.e., trumpeters, accompanying a herald); *with Trumpet* (2.1.311.1/TLN 622; ditto);

[1] One proposed meaning for the phrase is surely wrong. Tilley's confusing entry has misled E. A. J. Honigmann into believing that Giovanni Torriano's gloss 'Ironically spoken oft times, as if one would say, There spake Wisdom it self' refers to 'There spoke an angel'; it refers instead to another proverbial phrase 'There spake a sybill' (see *Piazza universale di proverbi italiani*, 1666, pp. 259 and 276, n. 136).

[2] The addition of a sound cue was first suggested by the Cowden Clarkes in the Cassell's Illustrated edition and supported by Furness. Dover Wilson adds the direction, and Smallwood follows him.

[3] The 1984 BBC television production preceded each of Pandulph's entries with monkish chant; I caught only the phrase *'Salvator mundi'*.

Allarum[s] (3.2.0.1/ TLN 1282, 3.3.0.1/TLN 1297, 5.3.0.1/TLN 2439;
none mentioned in dialogue). There are numerous occasions when one
might expect a sound cue and finds none: the ceremonial entrances of
one or more royal figures at 1.1.0.1 (John), 2.1.83.1 (John), 2.1.333.1
(John and Philip and *their powers*), 3.1.74.3 (John and Philip), 3.4.0.1
(Philip, Louis in defeat), 4.2.0.1 (John, after recoronation), 5.1.0.1
(John, after reconciliation with Pandulph and Rome). Similarly, since F
provides sound cues for some battle scenes, we might expect them at
5.2.0.1/TLN 2250 (*Enter* (*in Armes*) . . .), 5.4.0.1/TLN 2459 (a glimpse
of the English lords during the final conflict), 5.5.0.1/TLN 2524 (a
parallel glimpse of the French side), but they do not appear. These seem
to be the indisputable examples. The tally is seven cued sounds and ten
uncued sounds, if we total cues for royal entrances, for heralds and
warlike approaches, and for battle.[1]

Consider the more problematic cases. As I have already mentioned,
the dialogue alludes to the trumpet call preceding the Bastard's entrance
at 5.2.117/TLN 2370, although there is no stage direction for it. The
Bastard serves as John's messenger one other time (4.3.20.1/TLN 2018),
and he arrives in haste to witness John's death at 5.7.48.1/TLN 2658.
On neither occasion (both scenes set out of doors, one may note) is there
a directed sound cue or any mention of sound in the dialogue. At
5.7.0.1/TLN 2603, Prince Henry makes his first appearance, and there
is neither cue for nor mention of sound. Chatillon enters at 2.1.49.1/TLN
343, bringing John's retort to the French demand for territory, and
again there is no sound cue, although Philip greets his arrival verbally:
'Lo, upon thy wish | Our messenger Chatillon is arrived' (2.1.50–1).
There remain only two further examples, both occasions when
Pandulph enters a scene already in progress. The first lacks a sound cue
(3.1.134.1/TLN 1061: *Enter Pandulph*), but Philip says, 'Here comes the
holy legate of the Pope' (3.1.135); the second example is the disputed
one in 5.2 for which editors have deemed a direction necessary to
rationalize 'methinks an angel spake'.

We may conclude that F provides sound cues rather haphazardly.
Since F establishes no pattern, one may hypothesize (or 'restore') as one
will,[2] but equally, the *presence* of a sound cue (e.g., at 5.2.117) in a

---

[1] Compositors B and C set *K. John*, and there appear to be no obvious variations
between them in setting or failing to set sound cues: B set four sound cues,
Compositor C set three; Compositor B did not set sound cues where they might
be expected on six occasions, Compositor C did not on eight (excluding TLN 2370,
where the cue is in the verse).

[2] It does seem probable that anyone writing for the theatre (or preparing an
authorial manuscript for performance) could assume that certain typical occasions
(e.g., royal entrances and battles) would receive appropriate aural accompaniment
without specific instructions in the manuscript.

direction or in the verse cannot be regarded as reason to insert a new cue at another point where there is no incontrovertible evidence for one. If we restrict our attention to Pandulph's two mid-scene entries, we find perfectly conventional signals that do not demand a sound cue: Pandulph's first entrance is greeted with a formula ('Here comes') that implies nothing about sound (cf., for example, Philip's response to Constance's arrival, 'Look who comes here', 3.4.17), and his second entrance has a similar verbal formula: 'Look where the holy legate comes apace' (5.2.65), again with no suggestion of a formal sonic prelude.

F's habitual treatment of certain cues cannot justify editorial intervention here because there is no such 'habit'; instead, the editor may logically defend an addition only through justifying a perceived semantic meaning for 'methinks an angel spake'. The phrase has sufficient contextual meaning within Louis's own speech (and, indeed, within the wider contexts of his 'character' and the play's incessant verbal play) to allow an editor to forgo—this once—intervention.

LINEATION AND SPEECH ASSIGNMENTS AT 5.6.1–6

CONJECTURAL and actual rearrangements of the speeches at 5.6.1–6 have been many, and the major choices are reproduced in the Table below.[1] The questions involved and the reasons for my own choices may best be introduced by considering the scene's opening direction, '*Enter Bastard and Hubert, severally*'.

Compositor C set ten directions of the form *Enter* + two or more named or identifiable characters, including mutes and groups. In eight of these ten, the character listed first also speaks first; in all eight, this first-listed, first-to-speak character is also the highest ranking character (postulating the English aristocratic hierarchy and assuming that John outranks Philip, the Dauphin outranks the English lords, and men outrank women). The two remaining examples are:

1. *Enter before Angiers, Philip King of France, Lewis, Daulphin, Austria, Constance, Arthur.* (TLN 292/2.1.0.1–4)

2. *Enter King Iohn, France, Dolphin, Blanch, Elianor, Philip, Austria, Constance.* (TLN 998/3.1.74.3–4)

After (1), the opening speech is assigned to *Lewis.* and many editors have found reasons to emend to *Philip* (DYCE 1864; *conj.* Theobald), particularly since the stage direction incorrectly regards 'Lewis' and 'Daulphin' as different characters. So emended, of course, the speech-prefix now fits the pattern of stage directions in which the character listed first also speaks first, although no editor has emended specifically to co-ordinate stage direction and first speaker. Example (2) may patriotically (?) list John first although Philip, listed second, speaks first, and Constance, Austria, and 'Philip' (i.e., Faulconbridge, the Bastard) all speak before John speaks one line at 3.1.134 (TLN 1060) and enters the dialogue fully at line 147 (TLN 1074) when he begins to argue with the newly arrived Pandulph. The second stage direction is, therefore, anomalous; it is, moreover, the only stage direction including both Kings to be set by Compositor C.

Compositor B set eleven relevant entry directions of which nine list

---

[1] The version headed 'Folio' is lightly modernized; that headed 'Watkiss-Lloyd' represents William Watkiss-Lloyd's manuscript conjectures recorded in the Cambridge edition, and other cited editions refer to the 'Editions of Shakespeare' and 'Abbreviations and References' (above).

first the character who speaks first, although it might be more accurate to exclude from both counts two stage directions, one for imprecision ('*Enter the two Kings*' at 2.1.333.1/TLN 646) and one because it identifies a single character accompanied by mute characters (5.5.0.1–2/TLN 2523: '*Enter Dolphin, and his Traine*'). Thus, on seven of the nine possible occasions, Compositor B ranges with C's usual practice in setting stage directions. And again, the seven examples of first-listed, first-to-speak accord that honour to the highest-ranking character on stage. The remaining two instances among Compositor B's work are:

3. *Enter Pembroke, Salisbury, & Bigot.* (4.3.10.1–2/TLN 2007)

4. *Enter Bastard and Hubert, seuerally.* (5.6.0.1/TLN 2550)

After (3), Salisbury speaks first; after (4), Hubert. If the scribe or the compositor regarded the three rebel English lords with the indifference Shakespeare lavished on their creation, it may not be very significant that one lord is substituted for another—in a stage direction or a dialogue. The final anomalous stage direction (4) differs in type from the others; they are 'processional', while this one directs entrances from two different locations. The processional pattern of first-mentioned, first-to-speak might none the less hold in an 'Enter . . . severally' direction, in which case, the dialogue should be initiated by the Bastard rather than by Hubert. John Dover Wilson thought so, not from an analysis of the play's stage directions, but because 'the impetuosity of the opening speech is clearly more appropriate to the B.[astard] than to Hubert' (see his edition, 5.6.1–6n; according to Honigmann, Karl Elze first suggested the emendation in 1880). The frequency with which the first character to speak coincides with the first character listed in an entry direction (for Compositor B, 78%; for C, 80%) offers a different kind of evidence for Dover Wilson's choice, although it is perhaps equally possible that these percentages identify a trick of Shakespeare's earlier dramaturgy (rank enters and speaks first) and/or a similar sensitivity to rank in the compositors or in whoever wrote (or copied) the stage directions in manuscript.

The Folio's lineation and assignment of speeches following stage direction (4) may be acted or read with few problems, and all editors agree that the Bastard says, 'Hubert, I think' and that Hubert replies, 'Thou hast a perfect thought'. Some editors, however, have been troubled by the Folio's assignment of the following questions to a single speaker:

> What's that to thee?
> Why may not I demand of thine affairs
> As well as thou of mine?

The first question evidently responds to an earlier question ('Whither dost thou go?'), but the second question suits a speaker who has just sought information better than one who has tried to avoid replying. On this theory of conversational exchange (by no means, of course, the only one), editors have reassigned or conjectured reassigning one or the other question. Assigning 'What's that to thee' to Hubert requires no further intervention, although editors have in fact gone on to propose all the likeliest permutations, including Dover Wilson's summary decision to have the Bastard open the scene. Solutions that do not require redistributing the speeches involve imagining some stage action (a gesture of threat or surprise, for example) between the two sentences, or imagining, as Honigmann does, some brief pause between them (he inserts a stage direction to that effect and further argues that F's 'Why' is best represented as the modern 'Why,'—an exclamation, not an interrogative).[1]

A mechanical explanation for F's possibly mislining this dialogue is easy to hypothesize. Scribes typically wrote speech headings in a separate column to the left of the text-block (with stage directions in an answering column to the right) and often, it appears, copied an entire page of text before returning to 'fill in' the prefixes (which were often written in a different hand, italic, from the secretary hand used for the main text). In more or less stichomythic dialogue between two characters (as in *King John* 5.6), the scribe would probably notice that he had omitted a speech heading because the error requires his writing the same prefix in succession; misaligning a prefix, however, is an error to which the practice of adding the speech headings separately to the text was always and naturally prone. If the manuscript copy for F compressed the text from 'What's that . . . ' to '. . . thou of mine?' into two lines, the scribe need misalign the speech heading for the Bastard by only one line space to transfer text from one speaker to the other. Moreover, if the scribe *were* adding the speech headings after copying a page of text and in a separate column, the name 'Hubert' (or as F prints it, '*Hubert*')

[1] Audrey Stanley, an experienced director of Shakespeare, has suggested to me that this second question ('Why may not I . . .') *could* belong to the speaker who asked the first question if we suppose that some non-verbal gesture (e.g., a 'fig', or a dismissive wave of the hand) or sound not represented in the text (e.g., a negative grunt) has occurred. That is, F may be retained on approximately the same grounds that it is changed in 5.2 (see Appendix C): something happens for which there is no unequivocal verbal evidence. A gesture certainly *may* have occurred, but because there is no check, no logical restraint, upon such hypothesizing (and therefore no way to distinguish likely from unlikely invented gestures—or likely or unlikely additional sound cues, at least in the case of *K. John*), I would prefer to edit the words and whatever action they stipulate rather than to imagine action and then to edit *that*. For enlightening remarks on the way dramatic texts do or do not stipulate stage action, see Raymond Williams, *Drama in Performance* (Harmondsworth, 1968), Chap. 8.

at the start of a manuscript line might have momentarily or subliminally appeared a speech heading and might, therefore, have caused the slightest irresolution in where to place the true speech headings for Hubert and Bastard, respectively.

Whether articulated or not, a variety of critical assumptions also guides editorial treatment here, and those assumptions covertly— because silently—guide the actors and the reader. The dramatic situation is simple enough; on to the large and bare stage of the Globe enter two actors, 'severally' (presumably they enter from opposite sides of the stage, perhaps through two entry-doors in the wall of the tiring-house). The audience may recognize by costume, gait, or voice that the actors represent Hubert and the Bastard. They speak. Following F's lineation, the first eight lines include five questions, two statements that may be answers, and one imperative. The actors, of course, arrive to 'make their presence real by claiming position in th[e] field of force that the open stage represents', as G. K. Hunter puts it,[1] but the editor's decisions here determine the actors' presences—or, rather, the quality and nature of those presences. Reciprocally, the editor's assumptions about those presences will dictate the editorial decisions.[2] If one supposes the Bastard impetuous (still?) and the first speech a rude or reckless threat, then the two seem made for one another. The scene is evidently set at night (as line 17 later confirms: 'here walk I in the black brow of night'), but are we to imagine two individuals each moving cautiously through the night or is one (Hubert) more scout- or sentry-like and hence more proprietary, more likely to challenge an intruder? This latter conjectural context for the scene makes the first question not 'impetuosity', but loyal vigilance. Or should we imagine that Hubert, seeking the Bastard, has left John, the English court, and Swinstead Abbey far enough behind to justify our imagining that the stage represents an undifferentiated piece of ground, a place where either Hubert or the Bastard might plausibly challenge a moving shadow? Recent scenes, especially 5.3 and Melun's assumption that Hubert will be found 'with your King' (5.4.40), would suggest to the audience that Hubert's attitudes and 'location' coincide with John's while the Bastard, they might assume, has arrived from another place, the location of the battle itself. The scene eventually confirms this set of assumptions, but only *after* the opening interrogative barrage. Finally, these exchanges might be staged to produce the eerie effects of *Hamlet*'s initial lines, where Barnardo—coming to relieve the sentinel on duty—actually challenges him first, so that Francisco must reassert his duty and advantage: 'Nay, answer me. Stand and unfold yourself'.

[1] G. K. Hunter, 'Flatcaps and Bluecoats: Visual Signals on the Elizabethan Stage', *Essays and Studies*, NS 33 (1980), 21–2.

[2] This situation is circular, but I see no way out of it.

Deciding to change or retain F, the editor (again, perhaps unconsciously) will answer at least two further questions: (1) does Hubert's 'I will . . . believe | Thou art my friend' echo the Bastard's 'A friend' or does Hubert himself speak both lines? and (2) how much must the Bastard hear before identifying the speaker as Hubert? While these questions, like some of the earlier ones, may appear over-literal, or over-scrupulous, the answers to them manifestly affect editorial treatment of the passage and, presumptively, its staging. In passing, we may note that metrical analysis will not provide an unambiguous pattern for the dialogue: the opening speech is a pentameter, as are (together) the third and fourth questions: 'Whither dost thou go? What's that to thee?' The next Folio line ('Why . . . thine affairs') is a pentameter, but 'Hubert, I think' might link with either 'As well . . . mine' or 'Thou . . . thought'. Yet the Folio's lineation gives 'Hubert, I think' a visual, perhaps rhetorical, emphasis befitting the drama of recognition and released tension.

My choices for this passage follow those made by Dyce in his edition of 1864 and conjectured by Ingleby and Watkiss-Lloyd. That is, Dover Wilson's claim of 'impetuosity' seems, to me, unfounded, but I agree with many editors that F has combined two speakers' separate questions into a single speech. The arrangement adopted here has the following advantages: it implies that Hubert has some *locus standi*, some right to challenge *any* unknown individual, even one who proves his social and military superior; it follows the play's insistent device of echo and repetition by giving 'A friend' to one speaker and 'I will . . . believe | Thou art my friend' and 'Thou mayst befriend me' (cf. 5.6.10n) to another; it supports the characterization (seen as recently as 5.2) of the Bastard as both maturely self-confident and humorous by giving him 'Why may not I demand of thine affairs | As well as thou of mine?' as a preparation for 'Who thou wilt . . .'. The disadvantages of this arrangement are: it may improperly stipulate a staging (Hubert more static, in command; the Bastard initially uncertain, at a disadvantage); it may undervalue 'Hubert, I think' rhythmically and even syntactically; it may strike some audiences as requiring clairvoyance for the Bastard to recognize Hubert at first hearing.

Table: *King John* 5.6.1–6 in the Folio and some modern editions and conjectured assignments

FOLIO

HUBERT
  Who's there? Speak ho, speak quickly, or I shoot.
BASTARD
  A friend. What art thou?
HUBERT
  Of the part of England.
BASTARD
  Whither dost thou go?
HUBERT
  What's that to thee?

  Why may not I demand of thine affairs
  As well as thou of mine?
BASTARD
  Hubert, I think.
HUBERT
  Thou hast a perfect thought.

VAUGHAN

HUBERT
  Who's there? speak, ho! speak quickly, or I shoot.
BASTARD
  A friend. What art thou?
HUBERT
  Of the part of England. Whither dost thou go?

WATKISS-LLOYD

HUBERT
  Who's there? speak, ho! speak quickly, or I shoot.
BASTARD
  A friend.
HUBERT
  What art thou?
BASTARD
  Of the part of England. Whither dost thou go?
HUBERT
  What is that to thee?
BASTARD
  Why may not I demand of thine affairs
  As well as thou of mine? Hubert, I think.

HUBERT
  Thou hast a perfect thought.

DYCE 1864

HUBERT
  Who's there? speak, ho! speak quickly, or I shoot.
BASTARD
  A friend. What art thou?
HUBERT
  Of the part of England.

BASTARD
   What is that to thee?
HUBERT
   'What's that to thee?' Why may not I demand
   Of thine affairs as well as thou of mine?
BASTARD
   Hubert, I think.
HUBERT
   Thou hast a perfect thought.

DOVER WILSON

BASTARD
   Who's there? speak, ho! speak quickly, or I shoot.
HUBERT
   A friend. What art thou?
BASTARD
   Of the part of England.
HUBERT
   Whither dost thou go?
BASTARD
   What's that to thee?
HUBERT
   Why may not I demand
   Of thine affairs, as well as thou of mine?
BASTARD
   Hubert, I think.
HUBERT
   Thou hast a perfect thought.

BASTARD
   Whither dost thou go?
HUBERT
   What is that to thee?
BASTARD
   Why may not I demand of thine affairs,
   As well as thou of mine? Hubert, I think.
HUBERT
   Thou hast a perfect thought.

THIS EDITION

HUBERT
   Who's there? Speak, ho! Speak quickly, or I shoot.
BASTARD
   A friend. What art thou?
HUBERT
   Of the part of England.
BASTARD
   Whither dost thou go?
HUBERT
   What's that to thee?
BASTARD
   Why may not I demand of thine affairs
   As well as thou of mine? Hubert, I think.
HUBERT
   Thou hast a perfect thought.

5.7.117–18

HONIGMANN observes that 'Armada pamphleteers . . . popularized this watch-word' (his edition, 5.7.117–18n, citing *TR* and other texts of 1588, 1591, and 1595, respectively), but the claim is classical (see L. A. Post in *MLN* 41 (1926), 535), and language very like Shakespeare's appears quite regularly at critical moments through the later sixteenth century. Isaac Reed found the sentiment of these lines as far back as the period of Henry VIII's diplomatic and domestic difficulties; see Andrew Borde, *The First Book of the Introduction of Knowledge* (1548): 'if they [Englishmen] were true within themselves they need not fear although all the nations were set against them' (A4ᵛ) and 'if all the world were set against England it might never be conquered they [Englishmen] being true within themself' (G2ᵛ). Steevens cited Thomas Churchyard, *A Discourse of Rebellion* (1570):

> Britain blood, mark this at my desire,
> If that you stick together as you ought,
> This little isle may set the world at nought.
> If no, then look for plague at prince's hand.
> (A3ᵛ)

G. B. Harrison (in *TLS*, 13 November 1930) found a marginal note 'England can not perish but by English men' in William Covell's *Polimanteia* (Cambridge, 1595), V2 and 'This is the common saying: if we be true within ourselves, we need not care or fear the enemy' in C[harles] G[ibbon], *A Watchword for War* (Cambridge, 1596), A3; Dent L54.1 quotes W. Seres, *Answer to the Proclamation of the Rebels* (1569): 'A proverb old, no land there is | that can this land subdue, | If we agree within our selves, | and to our realm be true' (A8ᵛ) and cites (p. 19 n. 4) similar language in W. Burton, *The Rousing of the Sluggard* (1595; in *Works*, 1602, p. 467).

It is at first astonishing that Shakespeare would think to end this rousing speech and the play with proverbial words, but the very platitudinous quality (if Seres and Gibbon are accurate in calling the sentiment 'a proverb old' and a 'common saying') underscores the unifying purpose of the speech and the sense of a return to the good old ways of loyalty and community.

INDEX

THIS index lists points of more than routine interest, but does not duplicate the headings in the Introduction and Appendices nor does it list editorial decisions in Editorial Procedures. Biblical and proverbial phrases and allusions, respectively, are grouped, as are discussions of acting texts, rhyme and verse forms, staging and casting, and the law. Citations from Shakespeare's works are not indicated. References to the commentary are not limited to lemmata and include significant discussions of other words and phrases in the notes. Asterisks identify entries which supplement the *Oxford English Dictionary*.

Index

A SELECTION OF   **OXFORD WORLD'S CLASSICS**

The Anglo-Saxon World

Lancelot of the Lake

The Paston Letters

The Romance of Reynard the Fox

The Romance of Tristan

GEOFFREY CHAUCER   **The Canterbury Tales**
                    Troilus and Criseyde

JOCELIN OF BRAKELOND   **Chronicle of the Abbey of Bury**
                       St Edmunds

GUILLAUME DE LORRIS   **The Romance of the Rose**
and JEAN DE MEUN

WILLIAM LANGLAND   **Piers Plowman**

	Oriental Tales
WILLIAM BECKFORD	**Vathek**
JAMES BOSWELL	**Boswell's Life of Johnson**
FRANCES BURNEY	**Camilla**
	Cecilia
	Evelina
	The Wanderer
LORD CHESTERFIELD	**Lord Chesterfield's Letters**
JOHN CLELAND	**Memoirs of a Woman of Pleasure**
DANIEL DEFOE	**Captain Singleton**
	A Journal of the Plague Year
	Memoirs of a Cavalier
	Moll Flanders
	Robinson Crusoe
	Roxana
HENRY FIELDING	**Joseph Andrews** and **Shamela**
	A Journey from This World to the Next and **The Journal of a Voyage to Lisbon**
	Tom Jones
	The Adventures of David Simple
WILLIAM GODWIN	**Caleb Williams**
	St Leon
OLIVER GOLDSMITH	**The Vicar of Wakefield**
MARY HAYS	**Memoirs of Emma Courtney**
ELIZABETH HAYWOOD	**The History of Miss Betsy Thoughtless**
ELIZABETH INCHBALD	**A Simple Story**
SAMUEL JOHNSON	**The History of Rasselas**
CHARLOTTE LENNOX	**The Female Quixote**
MATTHEW LEWIS	**The Monk**

American Literature

British and Irish Literature

Children's Literature

Classics and Ancient Literature

Colonial Literature

Eastern Literature

European Literature

History

Medieval Literature

Oxford English Drama

Poetry

Philosophy

Politics

Religion

The Oxford Shakespeare

A complete list of Oxford Paperbacks, including Oxford World's Classics, OPUS, Past Masters, Oxford Authors, Oxford Shakespeare, Oxford Drama, and Oxford Paperback Reference, is available in the UK from the Academic Division Publicity Department, Oxford University Press, Great Clarendon Street, Oxford OX2 6DP.

In the USA, complete lists are available from the Paperbacks Marketing Manager, Oxford University Press, 198 Madison Avenue, New York, NY 10016.

Oxford Paperbacks are available from all good bookshops. In case of difficulty, customers in the UK can order direct from Oxford University Press Bookshop, Freepost, 116 High Street, Oxford OX1 4BR, enclosing full payment. Please add 10 per cent of published price for postage and packing.

American Literature

British and Irish Literature

Children's Literature

Classics and Ancient Literature

Colonial Literature

Eastern Literature

European Literature

History

Medieval Literature

Oxford English Drama

Poetry

Philosophy

Politics

Religion

The Oxford Shakespeare

A complete list of Oxford Paperbacks, including Oxford World's Classics, OPUS, Past Masters, Oxford Authors, Oxford Shakespeare, Oxford Drama, and Oxford Paperback Reference, is available in the UK from the Academic Division Publicity Department, Oxford University Press, Great Clarendon Street, Oxford OX2 6DP.

In the USA, complete lists are available from the Paperbacks Marketing Manager, Oxford University Press, 198 Madison Avenue, New York, NY 10016.

Oxford Paperbacks are available from all good bookshops. In case of difficulty, customers in the UK can order direct from Oxford University Press Bookshop, Freepost, 116 High Street, Oxford OX1 4BR, enclosing full payment. Please add 10 per cent of published price for postage and packing.